TEACHING IN AMERICAN CULTURE

KALIL I. GEZI

Associate Professor of Education
Division of Education

JAMES E. MYERS

Associate Professor of Anthropology
and Head, Department of Anthropology

Chico State College

HOLT, RINEHART AND WINSTON, INC.

New York · Chicago · San Francisco · Atlanta
Dallas · Montreal · Toronto · London

Dedicated to Our Wives and Children

PREFACE

"The true test of a civilization," Emerson said, "is not the census, nor the size of the cities, nor the crops, but the kind of man the country turns out." The kind of man a country turns out is patterned by the type of education he receives both in the school and from other institutions in society. The realization of this fact has resulted in a mounting concern for education which is exemplified by its receiving more attention and support from community members, state legislatures, and the federal government. More than ever before, teacher training has become the shared responsibility of the entire college and university. In higher education, educationists are being joined by an increasing number of social scientists who are devoting more of their time to research in the exploration of teaching and learning in American culture. With this increasing interdisciplinary effort, teachers and prospective teachers are being provided with an invaluable source for the understanding of the educational process.

It is this recognition that has prompted us to base this book on an interdisciplinary approach to the study of education. Reinforcement of the value of such an approach has come through feedback from college professors representing various fields, students, professional meetings and literature, and public and private school personnel. Our enthusiasm for this approach stemmed also from our educational background and cross-cultural experience: We have both taught social studies in public and private secondary schools, and our college teaching has included courses in the departments of education, anthropology, and sociology.

Our experiences in Europe and the Middle East have confirmed our belief in the value of studying education in a cultural perspective.

The selection of the content of this book was guided largely by student responses to informal surveys conducted by us over the past four years. The criteria used in choosing each article were: Is it informative, readable, and important? Is the author competent to write on a particular subject? Does the article raise important questions for the student and motivate him to think further about an issue? All articles were chosen because they contributed to an understanding of teaching in American culture.

In order to satisfy the various needs of students, and to stimulate their learning through offering a variety of articles, the range of selections includes descriptive articles, research articles, and anecdotal articles.

This book is organized into two parts. The first contains three chapters which deal with the historical, socio-anthropological, and cross-cultural perspectives on teaching. Chapter 1 focuses on the evolution of education in the United States, presenting past and present contrasts in teaching. Chapter 2 centers upon the social forces which influence the child, the teacher, and the school in American culture. This chapter helps the teacher to better understand his role as a transmitter of culture, the school as an agency of society, and the child as an object of enculturation. Chapter 3, examines education in several cultures in various stages of development. Learning about education in other cultures can not only aid the teacher in achieving a greater insight into American education but also lead to the development of international understanding.

The second part, containing the three remaining chapters of the book, serves as a general introduction to education for prospective teachers. Chapter 4 brings to the attention of the student some of the most important controversies in American education today. A prospective teacher will be better equipped to meet educational problems if he is made aware of them early in his career. Chapter 5 familiarizes the student with important innovations in American education today and attempts to stimulate him to become an innovator in his own classroom. Chapter 6 focuses on the controversial issue of progressive education—its meaning, its philosophical bases, its contributions, its alleged failures, and its present status in American education.

This book would be of particular value to students in introductory and social foundations courses in education; it would serve as well as a source book for advanced students in education, experienced teachers, and lay citizens. This book will have achieved its purpose if it contributes in some way to the student's understanding of teaching in American culture, for education has never been so important in our culture as it is today. "No people," Commanger has written, "ever demanded so much of education as the Americans. None ever have been served so well by its schools and its educators."

Finally, acknowledgments are due many persons who have aided us in the development of this book. We would like to thank Dr. R. Freeman Butts, Associate Dean for International Studies, Teachers College, Columbia University, and Dr. George D. Spindler, Professor of Education and Anthropology and Chairman of the Department of Anthropology, Stanford University, for their constructive criticism and helpful advice; the editorial staff of Holt, Rinehart and Winston for their continued support; our students and colleagues who offered relevant ideas and suggestions; and the authors and publishers who allowed us the use of their materials.

K. I. G.
J. E. M.

Chico, California
January 1968

CONTENTS

PART ONE

PERSPECTIVES ON TEACHING

1

HISTORICAL PERSPECTIVES

INTRODUCTION

Why should teachers study the history of education? Since one of the roles of education is the transmission of culture, a study of the history of education will help the teacher understand the changes that have taken place in the process and content of that which is being transmitted. The history of education provides the teacher also with a broader perspective on what he is doing today—history is a continuing process, and in order to fully assess present educational ideas and practices, teachers must understand the reasons, the people, and the circumstances associated with the development of the educational heritage. The study of the history of education can, in addition, be inspirational to the teacher, for he can pride himself in the great part that education has played in developing and maintaining our free society.

Specifically, the "History of Education can make its greatest contribution by helping in the determination of broad educational policy in deciding the directions in which education should move and the aims or objectives it should seek to achieve." [1]

In order to give the student an adequate historical background of the development of education in the United States, the articles by Butts and Elsbree were selected. In the readings by Mann and Conant the student can see examples of the writings of two highly esteemed American educators, one in the nineteenth century and the other in our time. In the selections by Woody and Priwer anecdotal accounts are made by teachers

---

[1] Committee on Historical Foundations of the National Society of College Teachers of Education, *The Role of the History of Education in the Professional Preparation of Teachers* (National Society of College Teachers of Education, 1957), p. 95.

3

in the past and the present of their classroom practices and their relationships with students. The chapter ends with a discussion by Gezi and Myers of the important factors which have exerted considerable influence on the course of American education.

The value of this chapter is best summed up in the statement of the nineteenth century American philosopher Santayana, who cautioned: "Those who cannot remember the past are condemned to repeat it."

SEARCH FOR FREEDOM: *The Story of American Education*

In the following selection noted historian and educator R. Freeman Butts traces the attempts of education over the years to meet the changing needs of a growing American society. He believes that without the proper kind of education available to everyone a free man and a free society can no longer endure. He asks, "What kind of education will best develop the free citizen and the free person?" He also asks other questions that have persisted in American education, devoting the rest of his discussion to some of the answers that have been put forth to these questions from colonial days to the present, providing an excellent outline of the story of American education.

R. *Freeman Butts*

"Search for Freedom—the story of American education," The NEA Journal (*March 1960*), 33–48. *Reprinted by permission of the publisher and the author.*

The story of American education needs constant retelling. It is a story that few of us know well enough. Yet, education directly involves more than one-half of all Americans and indirectly affects the lives, welfare, security, and freedom of everyone. Students, teachers, and other citizens cannot afford to ignore it.

Fortunately, most Americans have faith in education and believe that educated young people are better equipped to "get ahead" in the world than uneducated ones are. However, the really important reason for believing in the value of education is that it can be the foundation of freedom. In the first place, a truly democratic society must rest upon the knowledge, intelligence, and wisdom of all the people. Without the proper kind of education available to everyone, a free society cannot long endure. Therefore, all people must have the kind of education that will fit them for freedom as responsible citizens.

In the second place, without the proper kind of education, the individual will not be able to develop his own powers as a person. He will not be able to give direction to his own action and thought as he may wish. He will not be able to decide wisely for himself what he should do or think.

Freedom from arbitrary restraint, from compulsion, or from tyranny is essential for the free man, but that alone is not enough. If each person is to achieve the genuine freedom of self-direction and self-fulfillment, he must have an education befitting a free man.

Now, what kind of education will best develop the free citizen and the free person? This is the persistent question that runs through the story of American education. It has been answered in different ways at different times in our history. It is still being debated vigorously, and sometimes angrily, today.

This question is so important that every American—and above all, every student and teacher—should make it his business to learn all he can about it. The first requirement is a knowledge of the history of American education. Here are some of the fundamental questions that mark the high lights of the story:

1. What kind of schools and colleges will promote maximum freedom in society?
   a. To what extent should a free society encourage public schools in contrast to private schools?
   b. Is freedom better served by religious schools or by secular schools?
   c. Is a free society better served by local control or by central control of schools?
   d. Should a free society maintain common schools and colleges open equally to all, or should it divide students into separate schools and colleges according to their race, religion, social class, prospective vocation, or intellectual ability?
2. What kind of educational program will promote maximum freedom for all individuals?
   a. Should schools and colleges stress practical training or purely intellectual studies?
   b. Should schools and colleges offer students preparation for many vocations or for just a few?
   c. Should educational methods stress learning by direct experience or by reading books?
   d. Should a liberal education be designed for a few or for the many?

If we can understand some of the major answers given to these questions during our history, we shall be on the way to understanding the central idea of American education.

I. EDUCATION UNDER COLONIAL RULE (1600 TO 1770's)

For nearly 175 years the source of governmental authority for the American colonies was the crown and parliament of England. The colonists were, however, ruled locally by legislative assemblies or by individual proprietors, or by royal governors who received their authority from the English government in London.

This authority included jurisdiction over education. From the very beginning of American history, education was a function of government. It continued to be so after the states were independent.

The various colonies, however, handled educational matters differently. In the New England colonies, the governing bodies not only exerted general authority over education but also established, supported, and directly administered their own schools.

For example, the colonial legislature of Massachusetts passed a law founding Harvard College in 1636; in the following years it took hundreds of actions concerning the college. In the 1630's, the governments of several towns in New England established schools under their direct jurisdiction and supervision.

In 1642 the colonial legislature of Massachusetts passed a general educational law applying to all parts of the colony. It required all parents to see that their children were taught to read, learn the major laws, know the catechism, and learn a trade. It authorized and required the town officials to see that parents obeyed the law and to levy fines upon those parents who disobeyed.

In 1647 the Massachusetts legislature passed a second law, this time requiring all towns of fifty or more families to appoint a teacher and permitting the towns to pay him out of public taxes if the people so voted. Such a teacher was to teach reading and writing. (We would call him an elementary-school teacher.) Furthermore, the law of 1647 required towns of one hundred or more families to appoint a teacher of Latin grammar. (We would call him a secondary-school teacher.)

The New England version of state authority in education came to this: The colonial government could require parents to have their children educated; the central government of the colony could require local towns to appoint teachers (establish schools); public funds could be raised by taxation to pay the teachers; and public teachers were subject to direct supervision and control by governmental authorities (either the town meeting as a whole or the selectmen or the education committee).

In the Southern colonies the colonial governments had the same legal authority to legislate on educational matters, but they did not pass laws requiring *all* children to be educated. They rather assumed, as in England, that any parent who could afford to educate his own children should do so by making individual arrangements with a private tutor or by sending them to a private school.

The Southern legislatures, however, did pass laws requiring that poor children and orphaned children be apprenticed to a trade and taught the rudiments of reading and religion by their masters.

The governmental attention in the South was directed mainly at lower-class underprivileged children who had no parents or whose parents could not care for them. Even so, the parish or county governments sometimes legislated on educational matters through their boards of vestrymen or magistrates.

Some efforts were even made in the colonial legislatures of Maryland, South Carolina, and Virginia to establish colony-wide systems of public schools. These were unsuccessful, not because there was no governmental authority for education, but because the people at that time did not believe they were necessary.

In the Middle Colonies the same governmental authority was used by the Dutch to establish public schools in New Netherland and by the Quakers in Pennsylvania. But a more tolerant policy toward religion had attracted several different religious denominations to these colonies.

Each group wanted its own religious principles taught in its own school. It was consequently more difficult to teach a single religious outlook in a public school open to children of different faiths than it had been in New England, where most people were Congregationalists or in the South, where most people were Anglicans.

In the eighteenth century the colonial governments began to permit the different religious groups to establish their own schools in which they could teach their own religious doctrines and their own languages (whether German, Dutch, French, or Swedish). In this way the state gave to religious and charitable bodies the right to conduct schools.

In like manner the colonial governments began to grant charters to small groups of businessmen or landowners. An educational charter gave these groups the right to incorporate as a board of trustees. They could then buy land, build buildings, appoint teachers, and generally manage a school.

Some of these corporate schools came to be known as "academies." One of the most famous was the Philadelphia Academy founded in 1751 by Benjamin Franklin. Others were the Newark Academy in Delaware, the Washington Academy in New Jersey, and the Dummer Academy and Phillips Academy in Massachusetts.

These incorporated academies made education attractive and available to children of middle-class merchants who could afford the tuition. At first it was unclear whether these denominational schools and incorporated academies were public or private schools, but eventually they came to be known as "private" schools in American terminology.

Other private schools were run by individual teachers as profit-making, business enterprises. In the seacoast cities of the eighteenth century these private teachers began to give young people direct preparation for jobs in commerce and trade. In general, the private-school teacher accepted or rejected students as he pleased. He charged what fees he could get, and he managed his affairs as he saw fit—so long as he had enough students to stay in business.

By contrast, the "public" school in the eighteenth century was a nonprofit school under the supervision of a governmental agency or a corporate board of control. The parents had the right to send their children to it; the governing body set the fees and employed the teacher. Hence a "public" school was not run for the teacher's private profit.

The standards of curriculum were established and the achievement of pupils evaluated by the board of control, whether governmental or corporate. Later on, the corporate school came to be known as a "private" school because it was not operated directly by a governmental board.

In the seventeenth century the "public" or town schools of Massachusetts, Connecticut, and New Hampshire taught the doctrines of a specific religion, that is, Congregational Calvinism. This was so because the Congregational church was established by the law of the legislature in those colonies.

This practice, known as "an establishment of religion," was common throughout Europe in the sixteenth and seventeenth centuries. The laws of the state required all people to accept the doctrines and rituals of the established church and authorized punishment for those who objected. The law levied taxes on everyone to support the ministers of the established church or churches. The Church of England, for example, was the established church in several of the Southern colonies; therefore, orthodox Anglicanism was taught in their schools.

But in the course of the eighteenth century, the idea of religious freedom gained great headway in the American colonies. This meant that such minority religious groups as Quakers, Presbyterians, Baptists, Dutch Reformed, Lutherans, Methodists, Mennonites, and others gained freedom to worship as they pleased. As a result, such groups did not wish to send their children to town schools where their children would be obliged to accept a religion in which they did not believe. The established churches would not at first consent to the removal of their religion from the public schools.

The solution in the eighteenth century was to permit the minority religious groups to establish their own schools. This meant that private religious schools could operate alongside the public schools. Although the public schools were weakened, this arrangement contributed to freedom at a time when the majority religious groups insisted that the public schools teach *their* religion and *only* their religion.

A few voices began to argue that if public schools did *not* teach a sectarian religion then all children could attend them freely. This was argued by William Smith in Pennsylvania, by William Livingston in New York, and by Thomas Jefferson in Virginia.

But the time was not yet ripe for such a solution. Although it was a gain for freedom to permit people to pursue their own way in religion and education, most people were not yet convinced that *others* should have the same freedoms *they* had. Nor were they convinced that an education separated from specific religious doctrines was desirable. The search for freedom continued.

Meanwhile, as people moved out of the New England towns and cities into the unsettled lands of the country, they could no longer send their children long distances back to the town schools. They therefore began to set up their own local schools. This was the origin of the "district" school.

Representing the ultimate in local control, the district system reflected a decline in central state control of schools as the eighteenth century came to a close. This system had the advantage that it kept the schools close to the people, but it had the disadvantage that some districts ran low-quality schools or none at all. Local control was no guarantee that the quality of schools would be uniformly high.

At the end of colonial rule, common schools in which children of different religions or races learned together were still the exception. It was generally felt that schools should perpetuate the religious or cultural beliefs of the sponsoring agency. Some groups did go so far as to try to set up schools for Indians. Few but Quakers tried to do so for Negroes.

Seldom was it argued in colonial times that the aim of education was to empower every individual to make the most of himself as a person. The first system of education set up in America served to maintain the class distinctions imported from Europe.

Children of poor, lower-class parents had no education at all or were bound out as apprentices to learn a trade. Children of upper-class parents (public officials, clergymen, wealthy landowners) were expected to have an education appropriate to their station in life. The New England colonies broke this pattern somewhat when they required the towns to provide a minimum amount of education for *all* children.

Not all children actually received an education, but the principle was established that a commonwealth must rest upon an educated citizenry even if the education amounted only to bare literacy. Added to this was the Protestant belief that all adherents to the true faith should be able to read the Bible for themselves so that they could know the grounds and reasons for their faith. In any case, the New England town schools went a long way in seeing that a large number of their children received some education. This was the first step toward an education for freedom.

Learning to read, write, recite the catechism, and possibly do some arithmetic was the essence of a beginning or elementary education. In the earliest days, school books were rare and materials were scarce. A common device for teaching reading was a hornbook, a piece of wood with the alphabet and Lord's Prayer on it. The child could carry this around with him until he had learned everything on it.

Somewhat later in the seventeenth century books began to be used; the most famous was *The New England Primer*. This consisted of the alphabet, simple syllables, words, sentences, and stories, all of a religious and moral character. A child may have spent two or three years obtaining this kind of elementary education. Taking the thirteen colonies as a whole, probably only one child in ten went to school at all.

What we would call secondary education was offered in Latin grammar schools. The immediate reason for stress on Latin was that Harvard College required it for admission because the main bodies of knowledge throughout Europe since the days of the Roman Republic and the Roman Empire had been written in Latin.

Even though the common languages of the people (vernaculars) were being used more widely by the sixteenth and seventeenth centuries, it was still the custom for an educated person to know Latin—and some Greek, if possible.

So the Latin grammar school was designed to prepare sons of the privileged classes for college in order that they might eventually enter one of the "higher" professions, such as the ministry, law, medicine, teaching, or simply that of "gentleman." Relatively few in the total population were expected to attain these callings in life. Most were expected to be tradesmen, farmers, workers, mechanics, or servants. For these an elementary education was considered sufficient—or even more than necessary.

In the course of the eighteenth century, however, cities and towns grew rapidly in size, trade and commerce increased, immigration rose, and goods and services were much more in demand than in the seventeenth century.

The cry was heard that the old classical Latin education was no longer appropriate for preparing young people to engage in these new important occupations of making goods, distributing them, and selling them. Education, some said, should become more practical, not solely intellectual or literary.

Two types of intermediate or secondary schools tried to meet this need. Some were "English" schools, so called because they were taught in English rather than in Latin. The instructors tried to offer whatever studies the young people desired, for example, English language; French, German, Spanish, Italian (languages useful for trade); mathematics (useful for navigation and surveying); commercial arithmetic and bookkeeping (useful in business); geography, history, and drawing (useful for leisure).

In the early decades of the eighteenth century these private-venture schools responded to the needs of the growing middle classes (merchants and tradesmen). They gave an education directly aimed at occupations other than the learned professions, and they catered to girls as well as to boys.

A second type of practical school was the academy. which was usually residential and often under the auspices of a religious denomination or a nonsectarian board of control. The curriculum of these schools, at least as proposed by Benjamin Franklin, was likely to be much broader than that of the Latin grammar school. It might include geography, history, science, modern languages, and the arts and music, as well as the classical languages and mathematics.

Both of these types of schools contributed to freedom by increasing the range of occupations for which they gave preparation. In this way an increasing number of young people from all social classes could gain a larger measure of self-direction and improve their position in society. Both types of schools were frowned upon by the classicists, but the academy survived the opposition because it met the needs of the middle classes. It eventually drove the Latin grammar school out of existence.

Meanwhile, the opportunities for college education were expanding. Eight colleges besides Harvard were founded prior to the Revolutionary War. Most of them reflected specific denominational outlooks, and their courses of study were largely linguistic, mathematical, and bookish.

Some outstanding leaders tried to change the character of college studies by stressing the new sciences and social sciences. Among these were William Smith at the College of Philadelphia, William Livingston and Samuel Johnson at the founding of Kings College (Columbia), and Thomas Jefferson at the College of William and Mary.

But the tradition of classical studies supported by religious discipline was too strong for these reformers. Harvard (1636), Yale (1701), and Dartmouth (1769) remained Congregational in outlook; William and Mary (1693) and Columbia (1754), Anglican; Princeton (1746), Presbyterian; Brown (1764), Baptist; and Rutgers (1766), Dutch Reformed.

The College at Philadelphia, the only college to be nondenominational at the outset (1755), was a forecast of the future, but it soon came under Anglican domination.

In general, then, the colonial period saw gains for freedom in the growth of representative government, the spread of religious freedom, and the rise of energetic middle classes of free men in town and country alike. Education tried to respond to these social movements as well as to a growing liberalism in thought and belief.

At the beginning of the colonial period, orthodoxies in theology, philosophy, and politics dominated the schools. Children were looked upon as sinful creatures who could be ruled only by harsh discipline, fear, and unrelenting obedience. By the end of the period, a growing liberalism meant that, here and there, children and adults alike were treated more humanely and less brutally. Human dignity and respect for persons were safer than they had been.

During most of the colonial period, education for developing a free person moved slowly and haltingly. For the most part, education at all levels was concerned as much with moral training as with intellectual training. If anything, the moral was considered more important and closely bound up with orthodox religion. Teachers were expected to conform in their beliefs to the dictates of whatever group controlled the schools. It was seldom argued that the teacher had a claim to freedom of teaching as an essential characteristic of a free society, a claim to deal freely with ideas even though they might be distasteful to the immediate managers of the school.

The founding of nine colleges of liberal arts in the thirteen colonies was a remarkable achievement by men who would be free, but the dominant view was definitely that a liberal education (and thus the educational basis for freedom) was for the few, not for the many. There was reluctance to expand the range of liberal studies beyond the traditional classics, mathematics, and philosophy, even though the explosion of knowledge was already beginning to crackle and pop in the seventeenth and eighteenth centuries.

The notion that education had a clear responsibility for enabling each individual to develop himself to the utmost was beginning to be stated but was not yet widely accepted. Building schools for a colonial society prior to the Revolutionary War was a dress rehearsal for freedom, not the main performance.

II.   A CENTURY OF REPUBLICAN EDUCATION [1]
(1770's TO 1870's)

From the 1770's to the 1870's Americans planned, built, changed, argued, and fought over the kinds of free institutions that should replace colonial rule. One of these institutions was education. As they set up and operated a republican form of government dedicated to equality, democracy, and freedom, they found that they needed an educational system appropriate to such a government.

In many different ways they said that if a republican government —or society—were to prosper and endure, then the people who elected the government, held office, made laws, enforced laws, and consented to be ruled must be educated as responsible citizens.

James Madison, father of the Constitution and author of the Bill of Rights, put it this way:

> A popular Government, without popular information, or the means of acquiring it, is but a Prologue to a Farce or Tragedy; or, perhaps both. Knowledge will forever govern ignorance; and a people who mean to be their own Governors must arm themselves with the power which knowledge gives.

But this was not easy to do. The people who had won the Revolutionary War—these so-called Americans—were not really Americans, at least *not yet*. They were English, Scottish, French, German, Dutch, Swedish, and a good many more. And they were soon to be Irish, Italian, Hungarian, Polish, and Russian as well. They spoke different languages and they had different customs. Some had no tradition of self-government and others were fiercely proud or jealous of rule by others.

When it was finally decided that they should all learn the same language and the same principles of republican government, how was this to be done?

The answer was that it could best be done by a common school, taught in English, to which all the children of all the people could go together and learn how to live together and govern themselves.

But some people were poorer and some richer; some had good manners and others were coarse and rude. Should *all* these people really be educated?

Yes, they must be—if free government is to endure.

Well, but who is to pay for the poor ones?

Everyone must pay for all. If there are weak spots anywhere, the

[1] *The terms* republican *and* democratic *are used in their general sense in this feature and do not refer to political parties.*—The Editors

whole community of freedom is weakened. So the common schools must be supported by taxes paid by all.

All right, but who is to control these schools?

The only institution of a free society which serves everyone equally and is controlled by everyone is the government. So the government should control the common schools. And to keep the schools close to the people, the state and local governments, rather than the national government, should control the schools.

But won't the schools be subject to political and partisan prejudice?

Well, they might be, so we must create something genuinely new, something that will give all the people their say but keep the schools free of narrow, partisan politics. This can be done by a series of local boards of education subject to but separate from the executive, legislative, and judicial branches of government.

These school boards, often elected directly by the people, could constitute a kind of "fourth branch of government." They would exert direct control over local education under the general authority set up by the state governments and subject to the guarantees of equality and freedom laid down in the United States Constitution and applying to all Americans.

So far so good, but what about religious education? Don't all these Americans with different religions have freedom to run their own schools under the First Amendment of the Constitution and under their state constitutions?

Yes, indeed, they do. But each American will have to decide for himself whether the education that supports a free society should be conducted in separate schools in which religion provides the fundamental framework for all studies or in common schools devoted primarily to the whole range of free institutions in America. If they decide the first way, the children will be divided into separate schools for their entire education and this division will be along religious lines. If the second way, the children will attend the same public school together for their common education and only be separated for their religious education, which can be conducted as may be desired by the home or by the church or by the synagogue.

In the century of republican education most Americans chose the common school, controlled and supported in common, and embracing a nonsectarian religious outlook.

Their primary concern was to design a universal, free, public school that would promote free institutions and free citizenship. For the first one hundred years of the Republic, the need for creating the common bonds and loyalties of a free community was paramount.

Less attention was given to the claims of diversity and difference as the essence of freedom for individuals. This came later when the Union had been established, made secure against internal opposition, defended against outside invaders, and preserved despite a war between the states themselves.

The republican ideal of the first century of nationhood gave the following answers regarding the control of education:

A free society required public elementary schools to provide the basic information, literacy, and moral teachings required by every free man. For most Americans the term "free man" was limited to white men, until the Civil War legally introduced Negroes to citizenship. Private elementary schools continued to exist but they were declining in numbers and in importance by the 1870's.

Under the effective and determined leadership of an extraordinary galaxy of "public-school men," the idea of universal common schooling was widely accepted in the new United States during the first half of the nineteenth century. Outstanding among these were Horace Mann and James G. Carter in Massachusetts, Henry Barnard in Connecticut, Calvin Stowe in Ohio, Caleb Mills in Indiana, John D. Pierce in Michigan, Ninian Edwards in Illinois, Calvin Wiley in North Carolina, and Charles F. Mercer in Virginia. These men and others made speeches before thousands of people; wrote hundreds of pamphlets, articles, and reports; organized scores of groups and societies to agitate for common schools; and held dozens of positions in state governments or school systems.

They argued that the payment of tuition for schooling was unfair to children of poor parents, who could not pay for an education. They argued that the older forms of public support, like land grants from the federal Land Ordinances of 1785 and 1787, would not support schools on the vast scale now necessary.

They argued that the term "free school" should no longer mean a school in which only the poor children were given free education and all others paid tuition.

They argued that class distinctions could be lessened only when a "free school" meant that *all* children were given a free education together and when the entire school system was supported by taxes levied upon everyone.

Aiding their efforts were the newly formed labor unions, which demanded that the public schools provide universal education.

The states gradually accepted this idea of a free public school. The state legislatures passed laws *permitting* local school districts to tax themselves for such schools; they sometimes gave state funds to *encourage* local districts to tax themselves; and they finally *required* all local districts to tax themselves and establish public schools.

By these means, the local freedom of districts to ignore schooling for their children gave way to the larger freedom to be gained by a total population enlightened by education of all. Local control by districts was gradually limited by requirements set by state constitutions, state legislatures, state boards of education, and state superintendents of schools. It was decided that a free society would be better served if education were planned by the central authority of the states rather than left wholly to the completely decentralized control of local school boards. This was not done without bitter conflict, for many believed that state, as opposed to local, control would be undemocratic and destroy freedom.

But in the 1820's, 1830's, and 1840's it was decided that a state government, responsive to public control, could serve freedom as well as, if not better than, the hundreds of local school districts could do. If a local district were left free to provide a poor education or no education at all for its children, those children would be deprived of their birthright to an education that would prepare them for free citizenship. Thereby, the state's own freedom would be endangered.

A smaller freedom must be limited in the interests of a greater freedom. And to guarantee the larger freedom, the state must exert its authority to see to it not only that schools were available to all but that all children actually attended school. Massachusetts led the way by passing its compulsory attendance law in 1852.

The solution was a genuinely creative one. Authority for providing education was defined in state constitutions and in state laws. State authority for education was carried out by state superintendents of schools responsible to a state board of education, elected by the people or appointed by the governor. New York State created the office of state superintendent of schools in 1812. Massachusetts established a state board of education in 1837 with Horace Mann as secretary, and Connecticut did likewise in 1839 with Henry Barnard as secretary. Other states followed.

These state agencies could then set minimum standards for all the schools of the state. Meanwhile, the direct management of schools would be left in the hands of locally elected school boards, local superintendents, and locally appointed teachers. Local management served the cause of flexibility, diversity, and freedom.

This arrangement was designed to assure that schools would serve the whole *public* and would be controlled by the *public* through special boards of education, not through the regular agencies of the state or local governments. This is why in America we use the term "public schools," not simply "state schools" or "government schools," as they are often called in those countries that have centralized systems of education.

Since the United States Constitution had not mentioned education as a function of the federal government, the free states after the Revolution reclaimed the authority over education that had been the prerogative of the colonial legislatures.

But the United States Constitution and the state constitutions *did* proclaim freedom of religion and separation of church and state as one of the essentials of republican government. That is, neither the federal government nor state governments could interfere in the affairs of churches or use public funds to support them. Therefore, the states could not give public money to schools under the control of churches.

But what about religious instruction in the common public schools? It was soon evident that if common schools taught the doctrines of a particular church they would violate the freedom of conscience of all those who did not agree.

Could the common schools find a common religious outlook and teach that? Many Protestants thought so. They tried to find the common religious doctrines of Christianity and they found them in the Bible. If the schools would teach only the nonsectarian principles of Christianity as contained in the Bible, they argued, all sects would be satisfied. This might have been the case if America had remained exclusively Protestant.

But immigration had brought increased numbers of Roman Catholics and Jews. Besides, many Americans had never officially belonged to any church. Catholics charged that the so-called "nonsectarian" schools were really Protestant in character and that they were therefore sectarian. So Catholics established their own schools and many demanded a share in the public tax funds to support them. Most Protestants and Jews opposed the giving of public money to parochial schools.

Most states finally decided to prohibit any sectarian control over common schools and to prohibit use of public money for private schools under sectarian control. Especially bitter struggles between Protestants and Catholics were decided for the time being by legislation in New York in 1842 and by constitutional amendment in Massachusetts in 1855. Nearly every state had a similar struggle and enacted similar laws.

By the end of the first century of republican education the general decision was that a free society was better served if the majority of children went to common, nonsectarian schools than if they went to separate, sectarian religious schools. This made it possible for the United States to build a universal system of free elementary schools sooner than any other country in the world.

The line of argument went like this: Nonsectarianism would provide a greater measure of national unity than could be achieved when each sectarian group shepherded its own children into its own schools. The range of communication among children would be restricted if each group continued to run its own schools differently in religion and language from others. Separate schools would create and perpetuate divisions among the people—thus narrowing their outlooks and reducing free interchange of ideas. Free common schools would more certainly serve the cause of free institutions.

At the end of the first century of the Republic secondary schools, however, were still largely in private and religious hands. This fact did not seem undesirable to most Americans of that particular period.

The private academies provided considerable opportunity to those who could afford some education beyond the essentials. Likewise, most of the 200 colleges were under private and religious control. This, too, seemed reasonable to the majority of Americans at that time: Elementary education for all at public expense would be sufficient to guarantee the basic security of a republican government; advanced education for *leadership* in the state and in the professions could then be obtained privately by those who could afford it.

A few spokesmen, however, began to argue that a free society needed "free" secondary and higher institutions as well as free elementary schools. The public high school, for example, appeared as early as 1821 in Boston. The idea spread rapidly, but the public high schools did not dominate the secondary-school field till the late nineteenth century.

Advocates of free higher education tried to transform some of the private colleges into state institutions. This happened at the College of William and Mary in Virginia, at Columbia in New York, and at the College of Philadelphia.

The most notable attempt, however, occurred when the New Hampshire legislature tried to transform Dartmouth College into a state university. But the United States Supreme Court in 1819 (*Trustees of Dartmouth College v. Woodward*) decided that the college was a private corporation and that its charter was a contract which the state could not change unless "the funds of the college be public property."

Following the Dartmouth College decision, private colleges increased in numbers, most of them sponsored by religious denominations. Especially active were Presbyterians, Congregationalists, Episcopalians, Methodists, and Roman Catholics. But the advocates of public higher education also redoubled their efforts. State universities were established in twenty states before the Civil War. The earliest universities to be set up under state control (but not free of tuition) were in Georgia, North Carolina, and Vermont.

The ideal of freedom as a basis for a state university was most eloquently proclaimed by Thomas Jefferson at the University of Virginia, which opened in 1825. In Virginia, as elsewhere, religious groups were bitterly opposed to the state university and tried to prevent its establishment or to divert public funds to their own institutions.

Federal land grants authorized by the Morrill Act in 1862 gave a significant boost to the state-university movement. Funds from these grants were used by the states to establish agricultural and engineering colleges or to strengthen their state universities.

Despite the advocates of free and equal education for all, the era of republican education tried to get along with common schools at the elementary level, but with secondary and higher institutions divided along denominational lines. In general, while the elementary schools served everyone, the academies and colleges and universities catered to the wealthier and upper social classes rather than to the ordinary people.

The major failure to achieve the reformers' goal of a common universal school was the system of segregated schools for Negroes, which appeared occasionally in the North as well as generally in the South. In fact, it was the Roberts case in the Massachusetts Supreme Court in 1849 which set forth the principle that separate schools for Negroes were permissible so long as their facilities were equal to those of the white schools. Charles Sumner's argument that separate schools violated the equal rights of Negroes was rejected by the court, but, even so, Massachusetts and other Northern states moved soon thereafter to abolish their segregated schools by law.

Turning now to the kind and quality of education achieved in the first century of the Republic, we find the main elements of the common-school curriculum continued to be reading, writing, and arithmetic. These three R's were supposed to give the elements of literacy and the intellectual tools necessary for acquiring the knowledge and "popular information" of which Madison spoke.

But, said the school reformers, the citizen of the new Republic needed more than this—much more. He needed a knowledge of history and geography to instill feelings of patriotism, loyalty, and national pride. He needed moral teachings to instill habits of "republican" character. And he needed some practical studies, like bookkeeping or manual training, so that he could get and keep a job.

The common school was designed to do more than give intellectual training. It was to provide citizenship training, character education, and a means by which every child might advance up the economic and social scale as far as his talents would carry him.

By providing such equal opportunity, the common school would protect free institutions. It would promote progress and prosperity; it would reduce poverty and prevent crime. This was a big order to hand to the schools, but the optimism, energy, and faith of the times all prodded the schools to try to do their share—sometimes more than their share—in making the American dream come true.

The "new" school had to have new methods as well as new subjects. Such school reformers as Joseph Neef and Horace Mann argued that the customary strict discipline, corporal punishment, and slavish memorizing of textbooks were not good enough to carry the burden the school must carry. They therefore argued for the enthusiasm, excitement, interest, and eager learning that could come with a more humane and sympathetic attitude toward children.

Of course, the conservatives charged that the reformers would spoil the children if they spared the rod, but the reformers persisted despite the opposition.

The main trouble was that the teachers were not trained to deal with small children constructively. Would the liberal-arts colleges provide this training? Some proposals were made—at Amherst, at Brown, at Michigan, and elsewhere—that they should do so, but the colleges were not interested. So, entirely new institutions called normal schools were created to give their whole attention to the training of elementary-school teachers.

The first of these were founded as private normal schools in the 1820's by Samuel R. Hall at Concord, Vermont, and by James G. Carter at Lexington, Massachusetts. The first state normal school was opened in 1839 at Lexington, and the idea eventually spread throughout the country.

The normal schools taught young people of high-school age how to teach the elementary-school subjects. Compared with the better colleges of the day, their quality was low, but they made possible the rapid building of the common school systems in the several states. They raised school teaching above the level of incidental apprenticeship and began the process of making it a profession, narrow though the training was in the beginning. If the colleges of liberal arts had been as much interested in school teaching as they were in law, medicine, or other professions, the quality and status of the elementary-school teacher might have been higher much sooner than they were.

The curriculum of the secondary schools also began to respond to the political and economic progress of the times. The academies, replacing the Latin grammar schools, taught a wider range of subjects. Thus, students began to have some freedom of choice of studies. And some academies opened their doors to girls, a notable victory for freedom. By the 1870's some 6000 academies dotted the educational landscape.

But the common-school reformers felt that the private academies could never do the job that needed to be done. They therefore argued that free public high schools should be created to provide a practical education for those boys and girls who would not or could not go on to college.

Offering a practical nonclassical curriculum to youth who could live at home while attending secondary school, the public high school was destined to become ever more popular after the Civil War. It added to the range of vocations for which the schools prepared and in this way opened up possibilities of self-improvement through careers that had never before been within reach of the majority of youth.

Reformers such as George Ticknor at Harvard and Henry Tappan at Michigan also tried to broaden the curriculum of the colleges to make them serve the commercial, business, and political needs of the rapidly growing nation. They wanted to make real universities out of the small colleges.

Classicists put up great resistance against such reforms. Especially powerful was the report of the Yale faculty in 1828, which condemned practical courses and argued that the colleges should continue to stress the mental discipline to be acquired by strict study of Greek, Latin, mathematics, and philosophy.

Colleges should give a *liberal* education, said the Yale faculty, not a vocational education. Colleges should lay the *foundation* for later professional study; they should not give the professional study itself.

By the 1870's the dominant view of higher education came down to this: Liberal education was the only proper education for a free man, but relatively few young men (and no young women) could profit from such a training. Universal education may be all right for the common man, but college education should be reserved for the uncommon man.

The republican ideal of free universal education had not yet been applied to secondary schools or to colleges. The second century of the Republic, the century of democracy in education, did just this.

III.   NEARLY A CENTURY OF DEMOCRATIC EDUCATION
(1870's TO 1960's)

Whereas the republican ideal had been to provide *some* education for all and *much* education for a few, the democratic goal was to provide *as much education as possible for all*. The keynote of the century of democratic education was "more education for more people." It had its drawbacks, its setbacks, and its ups and downs, but nothing seemed able to stop for long the surge to education as the essence of the search for freedom.

The march to the schools came faster, the lines stretched longer, and the students grew older as the second century of the Republic moved from the 1870's to the 1960's. By 1900 the great majority of children aged six to thirteen were in elementary schools; by 1960 over ninety-nine per cent were in attendance. Universal elementary schooling for all children had been won.

More remarkable, however, was the march to the secondary schools. By 1900 about ten per cent of children aged fourteen to seventeen were actually in school; in 1930 more than fifty per cent attended; and by 1960 nearly ninety per cent were attending. This comes close to universal secondary education, something not dreamed of by the republican leaders of the first century of nationhood.

In 1760 the average colonist may have had two to three years of schooling; by 1960 the average American had ten to eleven years of schooling. And the end has not been reached. The average years of schooling will probably go to twelve or even to fourteen within a decade or two.

Still more remarkable was the stepped-up tempo of the march to college. In 1910 about five per cent of all youth aged eighteen to twenty-one were attending college; by 1960 nearly forty per cent of all such youth were attending institutions beyond high school. Millions more were attending adult-education classes and courses of instruction being offered by business, industry, labor, the armed services, churches, and voluntary agencies. And education by television and other automatic devices had scarcely begun. The potentials were staggering.

How did all this happen and why? The story is complicated, but a few elements are clear. Republican education may have been sufficient for a society marked by a relatively small population scattered over large areas of rich land and relying mainly upon farming and trading for subsistence. But in a society that relied on science and technology, the situation was radically different.

Not only did the leaders, scholars, experts, and professional men need more and better education, but also the kind of education that *everyone* needed grew steadily greater in quantity and higher in quality. For *this* kind of industrial society, a democratic education would be necessary if freedom were to be maintained.

A society based on steam power, electric power, or nuclear power can be managed and controlled by relatively few people. Technical power leads to political and economic power. To prevent autocratic, dictatorial use of political and economic power by a few, everyone must have an education devoted to freedom. There is no other satisfactory way to limit political or economic power.

So it became increasingly clear that the opportunity to acquire an expanded and extended education must be made available to *all*, to the poor as well as to the rich, to the slow student as well as to the bright, to the South and West as well as to the North and East, to girls as well as to boys, to Negroes as well as to whites, to immigrants as well as to native-born, to Catholic and Jew as well as to Protestant and non-churchgoer.

The century of democratic education took the doctrines of the common school and applied them almost completely to the secondary school and in part to the college. Equality of opportunity stood alongside freedom as the prime goals of education.

Let us see what happened to the organization and control of education in the age of democratic education:

The nineteenth-century solution to the problem of public and private schools came to this: A system of public institutions ranging from primary school to university, open for everyone as long as his abilities justify, is the best guarantor of a free society based upon equality of opportunity. Private institutions are free to operate alongside the public institutions, but these should be supported voluntarily and should not be given public funds.

In the 1870's a series of court cases (especially the Kalamazoo case in Michigan) agreed that the people of the states could establish and support public high schools with tax funds if they so desired. Thereupon the public high-school movement spread rapidly, and the private academy shrank in importance. Furthermore, all states passed compulsory attendance laws requiring attendance to at least age sixteen. Provision of public secondary schools thereupon became an *obligation* of the states, not just a voluntary matter for the local districts to decide.

Children were permitted to attend properly approved nonpublic schools as a way of meeting state attendance laws. This principle was affirmed by the United States Supreme Court in the Oregon case of 1925 (*Pierce v. Society of Sisters*).

States had the right to supervise, inspect, and set minimum standards for *all* schools and to require children to attend *some* school, but the state could not compel students to attend public schools if their parents preferred private schools. Freedom to have a say in the education of their children was a constitutional right of parents under the Fourteenth Amendment. Besides, private schools were valuable property which could not be destroyed by action of the state without due process of law.

By 1930 the preference of most Americans for public schools was clear; only about nine per cent of children attended nonpublic schools. The public policy hammered out in the nineteenth century was also clear: Public funds should not be used to support private schools. Beginning in the 1930's, however, the clamor began to rise again that the private schools should be given some public aid. Campaigns to get parents to send their children to private schools began to show results.

Today more than sixteen per cent of children are in nonpublic schools, a gain so spectacular that the American people have to face up to certain questions more directly than at any time since the 1830's: Shall we encourage private schools as well as public schools with public money? Is the present balance among public and private schools about right? If not, should we favor private or public schools?

Through the years, much of the controversy over public and private schools has been basically sectarian. Today more than ninety per cent of children attending nonpublic schools are enrolled in parochial schools conducted by the Roman Catholic Church. A whole series of laws and court cases in the nineteenth century decided that religious freedom and separation of church and state meant that the states could not give tax money to support private education. But from 1930 onward, exceptions began to be made.

The Cochran case in 1930 permitted Louisiana to spend tax funds to give free textbooks to children in private as well as public schools; the Everson case in 1947 permitted New Jersey to provide bus transportation for parochial-school pupils; in 1948 the School Lunch Act gave federal money to parochial schools even though state funds could not be so used. Advocates of parochial schools were now arguing that public funds should be used to pay for auxiliary services that benefited the child but were not direct aid to the school as such.

In recent decades, the arguments for diverting public funds to private schools have changed. It is now argued that the states should aid all parents to send their children to the kind of school they wish. This would not aid *schools*; it would aid parents to exercise their freedom of educational choice. So if parents want their children to go to religious schools, they should receive their fair share of tax funds. If they want their children to go to all-white schools, they should receive tax funds to help them do this. Obviously, the whole idea of a common school is now under severe attack.

What the American people will decide in the years to come is in doubt. In fact, the whole idea inherited from republican days that a free society rests upon a common school system maintained and controlled by the free government is in peril.

"Freedom" may come to mean that parents can divide up among themselves the public funds which had originally been designed to support a free educational system which in turn was designed to perpetuate the free society itself. Does freedom of choice for parents mean that the state is obligated to support and pay for that choice?

Such questions as these came to focus sharply in the problem of central and local control. If some towns or regions in a state could not or would not provide good schools for their children, should the children suffer, or should the state try to equalize the burden by giving financial aid to those towns? The answer turned out to be clear: Equalize the burden in fairness to the children.

Most states use tax money, raised all over the state, to support schools in all parts of the state wherever and whenever local property taxes did not provide enough money to operate good schools. Central control in state hands seemed desirable for the purpose.

But what about the federal government? Will the same answer be given? If some *states* cannot or will not provide good schools for their children, should the federal government try to equalize the burden by giving financial aid to the states? If all states try hard, and still some states cannot provide acceptable educational opportunity for all children, should the federal government step in and help out? By and large, the answer thus far has been no; a qualified no, but still no.

To be sure, the Land Ordinances of 1785 and 1787 and other grants gave millions of acres of land to the states for education; the Morrill Act of 1862 helped establish land-grant colleges; the Smith-Lever Act of 1914 supported agricultural and home-economics instruction; the Smith-Hughes Act of 1917 aided vocational education in high schools.

Emergency aid was given in the 1930's and the National Youth Administration and Civilian Conservation Corps helped youth in the depression; a bill was passed to provide aid for federally impacted school districts; the G. I. Bill of Rights helped millions of veterans of World War II and the war in Korea to get an education; and the National Defense Education Act of 1958 gave loans to students and supported specific programs in foreign-language training, science, guidance, and audiovisual methods.

But up to the present, the idea of federal-state partnership in public-school support has not been squarely faced by the federal government. For nearly a hundred years a whole series of bills had been introduced in Congress to achieve this purpose. Beginning with the Hoar bill, Perce bill, and Burnside bill of the 1870's and the several Blair bills in the 1880's, Republicans were the chief advocates of federal aid, but Democrats of the South were afraid that the federal government was trying to punish them and impose Northern ideas upon them.

In the decade between 1950 and 1960 it was the liberal Democrats from the North and West who tried to achieve federal aid, but were thwarted by economy-minded Republicans and by some Southern Democrats who feared federal imposition of integrated schools upon the South. Throughout the century many Roman Catholic leaders opposed federal aid unless it would help parochial as well as public schools.

The race issue, the religious issue, and the economy issue successfully blocked federal aid for decades. After the close of the Civil War, it was touch and go for a while whether federal action would result in equal educational opportunity for Negroes in the South.

The Fourteenth Amendment (1866) guaranteed "equal protection of the laws" to all citizens, but the federal education bills failed and the Civil Rights Act of 1875 was declared unconstitutional. The Southern states proceeded to set up segregated school systems, one system for Negroes and one for whites. The United States Supreme Court decision in *Plessy v. Ferguson* (1896) was taken to mean that separate school systems were permissible provided they had equal facilities.

In the 1940's a whole series of court cases began the process of gaining access for Negroes to the public institutions of the South—first to the universities and then to the schools. The historic decisions headed by the Brown case of May 17, 1954, reversed the "separate but equal" doctrine of Plessy and declared that segregated schools were inherently unequal even if each had "equal" amounts of money spent on it.

In the following years, case after case was taken to court to require boards of education to admit Negroes to the public schools on an unsegregated basis.

Violence, often instigated by outside agitators, broke out in Clinton, Tennessee, and a number of other places; and federal troops were called to Little Rock, Arkansas, when the governor interfered with a federal court order to integrate the schools. Gradually, however, desegregation spread through the border states and by 1960 was being faced in the "Deep South."

Some Southern governors and legislatures tried to prevent integration by legal devices. Laws were passed to close the public schools, to give public money to parents so they could send their children to segregated private schools, and even to abolish the public-school system itself.

These actions posed the most serious threat to the ideals of both republican and democratic education it was possible to pose. Does a state have the right to abolish its "fourth branch of government"? What *is* essential to a "republican form of government" (as guaranteed in the United States Constitution) if public education is not? Could the principles of a free society withstand this onslaught safely?

If the demands for private religious education and the demands for private segregated education were joined by economy demands for reducing public-school budgets, the result could be a repudiation of the public-school idea itself and a return to the "voluntary" principle of the sixteenth and seventeenth centuries in Europe: Let those have an education who can pay for it; let education be fully private. Or, alternatively: Let us divide up the public moneys among competing racial and religious groups so they can set up their own private schools; let us have many free *private* educational systems.

In either of these cases, the central idea of American education would disappear. An unlimited role for free private enterprise in education would take the place of a limited role for free public enterprise. The freedom of segmented voluntary groups to work at cross purposes would replace the freedom of the people as a whole to work through a system of public schools. The 1960's will doubtless see the struggles heightened. How will the search for freedom come out?

Just as the keynote to *quantity* in education for the century of democratic education has been "more education for more people," so the keynote to *quality* in education has been "better education for all." Each decade had its reformers who demanded better education than the schools were then offering, but there has been little agreement concerning what is "better."

Different reformers have demanded different measures at different times. As the times changed, the schools were behind the times for different reasons. Nowhere else in the world have so many people been so much concerned about education so much of the time—and almost never has everyone been satisfied.

No sooner had the elementary schools been established to start six-year-olds on the road to formal schooling than reformers began to argue that we ought to have a pre-school school called the kindergarten. So, borrowing ideas from Friedrich Froebel in Europe, we began to attach kindergartens to the public schools, beginning in the 1870's. The idea was to help children of four to six years learn by directed play activities.

By 1960 most American cities had kindergartens, and some of them had even established nursery schools for two-to-four-year-olds.

The elementary school itself was subject to recurring reforms. No sooner did it make headway in teaching the three R's to every child than someone, outside the schools or in, would urge it to broaden its curriculum: Add drawing and the arts; add geography and history; add nature study; hygiene and physical training; manual training; domestic science. And these all seemed reasonable.

The famous Swiss educator, Pestalozzi, had said so; Edward A. Sheldon, founder of the Oswego (New York) Normal School, said so; Francis W. Parker, superintendent of schools in Quincy, Massachusetts, said so. And so said a host of others, including such diverse characters as the presidents of Harvard (Charles W. Eliot) and of Columbia (Nicholas Murray Butler), publicists like Joseph Mayer Rice, social workers like Jane Addams and Lilian Wald, reformers like Jacob Riis and Walter Hines Page.

Social reformers, humanitarians, and philanthropists, especially in the cities of the 1890's, were indignant about the endless memory work that marked most schools. Schools, they said, were far too intellectualistic—they dealt almost exclusively with words and numbers that did not mean very much to the children. They felt that schools should be alive, interesting, exciting, practical, and useful.

This seemed fair enough. John Dewey took up the ideas in his experimental school at the University of Chicago, and Teachers College at Columbia University applied them in its experimental Lincoln School. Eventually, "progressive" schools mushroomed on the landscape, and "progressive" ideas became popular in the 1920's and 1930's. Chief among the spokesmen after John Dewey was William H. Kilpatrick at Teachers College, Columbia University.

All sorts of plans were devised to loosen up the formal curriculum and give it life and vitality—units, projects, activities, excursions and visits, handicrafts, gardens, laboratories, audio-visual aids, and much else—anything to overcome the slavish drill on the textbook or notebook. There was little doubt that the general quality of learning for most children was raised as the school added vitality and zest to the learning process.

But in the 1940's and 1950's a new set of "reformers" began to charge that the schools were too soft. Schools, they said, were just letting children play and not teaching them anything. Elementary schools were exhorted to return to the three R's and stiffen up discipline and concentrate on intellectual studies.

Many of the criticisms were overdrawn and unfair, but many had some truth in them. Progressive methods *had* been carried to an extreme by a few spokesmen and by a few teachers who assumed that all children learned better by "direct" experiences, by visits, or by physical activities than they did by reading or writing. A general tightening of school methods was evident by 1960.

Sputnik and Russian education strengthened the critics' hands. But how long would it be before "loosening" and flexibility in the curriculum would again be necessary and a new wave of progressive reform to overcome excessive academic formalism be desirable?

Meanwhile, the controversy over religion in the public schools continued. By the beginning of the twentieth century, most public schools had not only dropped sectarian religious teaching but also much of the nonsectarian religious instruction they had attempted in the early nineteenth century. In other words, although the public schools dealt with moral and spiritual values, they no longer tried to deal with religion at all; they were secular. But after World War II the demand arose again that the public schools restore some kind of religious instruction.

Some Protestants proposed that the Bible be read without comment by the teacher, but Catholics and Jews opposed this as really sectarian. It was proposed that students be given time off from regular classes to receive sectarian instruction from their own religious teachers (released time).

In 1948 the United States Supreme Court in the McCollum decision said that released-time religious instruction could not be given inside public-school buildings, but in 1952 (Zorach decision) the Supreme Court said it could be done outside schools if the public teachers did not coerce or persuade students to go to the religious classes. Neither of these decisions has satisfied many people. Some educators have proposed that public schools avoid religious instruction as such but undertake factual study about religion right along with the study of other regular school subjects, but most religious groups have been cool to this proposal. The formula for honoring religious diversity while still promoting social unity through common schools had not been satisfactorily found.

Reform movements stirred through secondary as well as elementary schools. Most revolutionary reform was the very idea of a secondary school which would accept students of the whole range of ability and try to give all a course of study suited to their abilities and their possible vocations in life.

Most other countries divide children at age eleven or twelve, send a few to academic (college preparatory) schools, others to vocational schools, and the majority directly to work. The American high school, however, has tried to be a comprehensive school, one in which students from all walks of life would study and work and play together. This meant that many new subjects and courses have been added periodically to the high-school curriculum.

The resulting number of elective studies has worried the colleges. As early as 1893 the National Education Association tried to encourage a standardized high-school curriculum. Noteworthy were the efforts of the Committee of Ten (1893) and the Committee on College Entrance Requirements (1899).

These "reforms" stressed those academic studies which should be required for college entrance; namely, four units in foreign language, two in mathematics, two in English, one in history, and one in science. (The relative inattention to science is at least sixty years old.) It was assumed that such studies would be good for all students whether they were headed for college or not. This was fair enough at a time when seventy-five per cent of high-school graduates were going on to college.

But after 1900 the pressures of enrollment on the high schools grew stronger. By 1918 an NEA Committee formulated *The Seven Cardinal Principles of Secondary Education,* in which preparations for college was definitely less important than it had been twenty years before. Now, the high school's aims were to give attention to health, command of the fundamental processes, worthy home membership, vocational preparation, citizenship, leisure-time activities, and ethical character.

This note continued to be emphasized in the 1930's and 1940's. By 1950 about thirty per cent of high-school graduates were going to college. Preparation for college had actually become a minor function of the high schools.

However, a new wave of reaction (or was it reform?) began to criticize secondary schools for permitting low academic standards, for not stimulating youth to rigorous study, for letting youth take so-called "easy" courses instead of working hard at the regular academic subjects. The success of Russian space flights and the threat of falling behind in the armament race raised fears that American high schools were not doing their jobs.

Many of the critics did not know what they were talking about, but some did. There was little doubt that many high schools could do a better job for college-bound youth than they were doing. Some high-school educators were still assuming that only a small minority of high-school graduates were headed for college. They had not noticed that by 1960 many more high-school students were expecting to go to college.

It might not be long until we would be back where we were in 1900 with seventy-five per cent of high-school graduates bound for college, but with this vast difference: In 1900 only ten per cent of youth were in high school; today ninety per cent are there.

The potential enrollments called for a drastic new look at the secondary school, at both the junior-high and senior-high levels. The first thing the schools did was to give more attention to the academic subjects, especially to the foreign languages, science, and mathematics. The time was ripe, however, for a complete overhauling of the junior-high school, which was just about fifty years old and born in a very different age from that of the 1960's.

Undoubtedly the pressure of high-school graduates upon college doors would lead to even further drastic expansion of junior colleges and other two-year institutions. They too were just about half a century old and, in some ways, the epitome of the democratic movement in American education.

It was being estimated that by the decades following 1970 all students with an IQ of one hundred or over would be finishing at least a two-year college. If this proved to be true, standards of admission to some colleges would go up and in others they were bound to go down.

Finally, the upward push of the educational surge left its unmistakable mark on the four-year colleges and universities. In the 1870's most institutions of higher education were relatively small undergraduate colleges. Their curriculums were still largely devoted to the liberal arts of Greek and Latin, mathematics, and philosophy; and these courses were all required of all students.

In a relatively short time, however, new studies, like the modern languages, English, modern history and the social sciences, modern science, and the fine arts found a place in the curriculum. Students had to be given a choice because they could not possibly study all these subjects in four years. So the elective system was instituted.

Meanwhile, graduate study began to change the whole character of higher education. When Johns Hopkins University opened its doors in 1876, it helped to set the pattern for graduate schools devoted to the advancement of knowledge and research in the entire range of the arts and sciences. Professional schools of medicine, law, education, engineering, agriculture, business administration, and the like began to flourish.

This meant that universities were now devoted to direct professional preparation for an ever larger number of vocations rather than for just a few. Some liberal-arts colleges tried to maintain their nonvocational and nonprofessional character, but most were not able or did not care to do so. The democratic surge was too strong.

In the 1920's and 1930's a number of experimental colleges tried to grapple with the overcrowded curriculum and to design new patterns of liberal education. Bennington, University of Wisconsin, Sarah Lawrence, Bard, University of Minnesota were among them.

Critics arose, such as Robert Hutchins and Alexander Meiklejohn, to call for preservation of the liberal-arts college free from professionalism and vocationalism. They were struggling against the tide. Nevertheless, undergraduate colleges did institute a wide variety of programs which, in one way or another, tried to assure that all students would have some acquaintance with the humanities, the social sciences, the sciences and mathematics, and the fine arts. Whatever a liberal education or a general education was supposed to be, it was to deal with these fields of knowledge.

Much criticism was directed at the professional schools for not giving enough attention to the liberal arts. They began to give heed. As the 1960's opened, considerable ferment was evident in medical schools, business schools, engineering schools, and schools of education.

It seemed likely that the teachers college, as a separate institution devoted exclusively to the training of teachers, would disappear. Normal schools had become teachers colleges, and now teachers colleges were becoming state colleges and even state universities. These changes were signs on the road of the march of democratic education.

Higher education was no longer confined to the few nor to the upper classes of wealth or privilege. It was on the way to becoming financially free, as secondary and elementary education had become before it. The opportunity was great.

The question was whether all this educational activity could measure up to the intellectual and moral demands of a free society in the modern world. If individuals used the vast resources of American higher education simply to further their own interests, this was one kind of small freedom all right, but in the long run would it serve the cause of the free society? How to enable American education to serve the cause of the larger freedoms was the paramount question. The answer to this question cannot be rigged. The fate of the nation rides upon it.

At the heart of the answer to the fateful question is the scholarship, the wisdom, the vitality and the freedom of American teachers. If teachers are weak, timorous, or poorly trained, the American idea of education has little chance of success. If powerful or selfish groups demand that teachers conform to *their* ways of thinking or to *their* beliefs, education will be a narrow little thing. And our history here is not too reassuring.

Orthodoxy of belief in colonial days was a prime requirement for teaching. Oaths of loyalty to the crown and to the doctrines of the church were familiar trappings of colonial rule. The American Revolution in its turn demanded that teachers be faithful to the Revolution rather than to the crown; and, similarly, Congress exacted loyalty oaths to the Union in the Reconstruction Period after the Civil War.

Conformity of economic belief, faith in private business enterprise, and opposition to any radical movements were expected of teachers in the nineteenth century. State laws required special loyalty oaths from teachers as early as the 1920's, and as late as 1958 the National Defense Education Act required such oaths from students applying for federal loans.

After World Wars I and II, thirty states passed laws requiring teachers to sign special loyalty oaths. Other laws (notably the Feinberg law of 1949 in New York State) were passed to hunt down and dismiss teachers suspected of belonging to subversive organizations. Many patriotic organizations served as self-appointed censors of school textbooks and complained about outspoken teachers.

The frantic search for communist teachers and others suspected vaguely of "leftist" leaning was fired up by McCarthyism and the wave of legislative investigations that swept the country in the early 1950's.

As a result, a cloud of timidity, suspicion, and fear settled down upon the schools and colleges in what the *New York Times* called "a subtle, creeping paralysis of freedom of thought." Classroom teachers and school administrators tended to avoid acts or ideas that might "cause any trouble" or arouse any criticism.

This general atmosphere of caution and anxiety affecting millions of students did infinitely more damage to the cause of freedom in education than the handful of communist teachers could possibly do. Fortunately, the most active "Red hunts" have now passed, but their revival is an ever-present danger, especially if teachers and students are fearful or are indifferent to the importance of freedom in education.

The first defenses of freedom in education are strong professional organizations of teachers like the American Association of University Professors and the National Education Association. If they do their jobs, they will insist upon high-quality training for teachers, upon fearless and competent scholarship in the classroom, and upon freedom to seek the truth in research and in the publication of findings. They will defend those qualified teachers who came under attack.

The ultimate defenses of freedom in education, however, are the people themselves who will realize that education's main function is to free the minds of the younger generation and to equip them as free citizens and free persons.

The schools and colleges must therefore generate a spirit of intellectual, political, and personal freedom throughout the land. To do this, they must in turn have a genuine measure of self-government resting upon the competent scholarship of the teachers.

The most distinctive mark of a free society is that it specifically delegates to its educational institutions the task of constant study and criticism of the free society itself. No other kind of society dares to permit such a thing. No other kind of society prevents its government from endangering the liberties of the people and at the same time entrusts the government with the obligation to guarantee the rights of the people against attack by powerful groups or individuals in the community.

Just as a free government guarantees the freedom of the press, of association, of religion, and of trial by jury, so must a free government guarantee the freedom of teaching and learning.

A free society knows that its surest foundation rests upon the liberal education of the people—a liberal education available freely and equally to all, beginning with the earliest stages of the elementary school, extending to the highest reaches of the university, and limited only by considerations of talent.

As the fourth century of American history reaches its mid-point and as the second century of the American Republic draws to a close, the search for freedom in American education has just well begun. That is why the story of American education must continue to be, in the future even more than in the past, the unflagging search for freedom.

HISTORY OF TEACHER EDUCATION
IN THE UNITED STATES

The previous article dealt with the history of education in general. In the following selection educator Willard S. Elsbree describes the evolution of teacher education in the United States and the significant changes that have occurred in professional education, such as the changes in standards of admission, types of programs, and other phases of teacher education. He traces the development of teacher certification and the accreditation of professional programs in the different teacher-training institutions from 1800 to the 1960s, describing the problems which have confronted teacher education and citing the progress that has been made. The student will find it valuable to ponder these problems and to think about some of the possible solutions to them.

Willard S. Elsbree

"*Teacher Education in the United States,*" The Education and Training of Teachers (*in The Year Book of Education, ed. G. Bereday and J. Lauwerys [New York: Harcourt, Brace & World, Inc., 1963], pp. 177–191. Reprinted by permission of the copyright owners, Evans Brothers Limited.*

To appreciate fully the significance of the achievements in teacher education in this country, as is unquestionably true of similar developments elsewhere in the world, it is essential to be well informed with respect to the country's history. Social, economic, and political forces have influenced both the nature and the extent of teacher education in the United States. Unfortunately, it is quite impractical to deal adequately with the impact of these influences in this article. For an analysis of those conditions which undoubtedly have had an important influence on teacher education, the curious-minded student will do well to draw on such scholarly volumes as *The American Republic* by Hofstadter, Miller, and Aaron, *The Growth of the American Republic* by Morison and Commager, and *History of the American People* by Carman, Syret, and Wishy, three basic texts in American history.

TEACHER EDUCATION, 1800–1836

Prior to 1800 there were no systematic efforts to prepare teachers for their responsibilities. This is not to suggest that anyone was considered qualified to teach or that education in the broad or liberal sense of the term was not deemed an important requisite. But the earliest date when anything like a planned effort appears to have been made was 1806, when the Lancastrian method of teaching with its model schools for demonstration purposes was brought to New York and applied in the schools operated by the Free School Society. Lancastrian schools were also established in Massachusetts and Pennsylvania. Many individuals aspiring to teach attended the model schools and thereby acquired a knowledge of the instructional plan, which they in turn used when employed as teachers. Whatever limitations this instructional method had, it appears to have stimulated great interest in teacher preparation and is often referred to as the forerunner of the normal school.

During this same period ideas regarding teacher education were stirring in Vermont, and in 1823 the Reverend Samuel R. Hall established a seminary for the preparation of teachers in Concord; and in 1830 he established a similar seminary at Phillips Academy at Andover, Massachusetts. While private in nature, Hall's seminaries possessed many of the characteristics of the public normal school of a later date. In fact, it was at Phillips Academy that Horace Mann gleaned some of his ideas about teacher training which were soon to bear fruit in Massachusetts. However, the period from 1800–1836 was not marked by any widespread establishment of teacher seminaries. Rather it was a period of agitation. Travellers to European countries came home with interesting reports of experiments in Germany and helped to set the stage for the educational awakening in America which marked the period between 1836 and the close of the Civil War.

Some mention should be made of the role which academies played in the preparation of elementary teachers during the period under discussion. For the most part, despite the hopes of many educators, the academy, the secondary school of this period, contributed little to the solution of the training problem. A few departments such as the one at Taunton, Massachusetts, attempted to give "instruction in the art of teaching and the use of apparatus"; but for the most part, the academy program for teacher preparation did not vary significantly from the general program available to regular students.

To summarize, there was little special preparation of teachers with emphasis upon methodology and pedagogical principles provided prior to 1836, and one would have to be something of an optimist to conclude on the basis of teacher preparation that the public school pupils of Andrew Jackson's day were markedly better equipped to face the world upon graduation than those whose schooling antedated the Revolutionary War.

RISE OF THE PUBLIC NORMAL SCHOOL, 1837–1865

Students of education have frequently debated the origin of the American normal school, some contending that it was European, especially German, in origin, and others that it was the logical outgrowth of the academy and of such experiments as Hall had carried on in the teachers' seminary at Concord, New Hampshire, and the school operated by Carter a few years later in Lancaster, Massachusetts.

Certainly, in the minds of the American public the early normal schools were adaptations or extensions of the academy. However, it is certain that Americans learned much from the experience of German educators and from men like Charles Brooks, Henry Barnard, Calvin E. Stowe, and Professor Alexander Bache, who spoke and wrote extensively of their observations of European schools and teacher training. To assert, therefore, that the American normal school was wholly indigenous is to overlook the early literature bearing on the subject, and its almost certain impact on the nature of the teacher education program.

Publicly supported institutions for the preparation of teachers in America developed slowly. The first step was not infrequently state aid to academies ear-marked for teacher preparation. Following this came separate schools for teachers. The first public normal school in the United States was established in Lexington, Massachusetts, on July 3, 1839. Cyrus Peirce, the principal of this school, described his task in an early journal.[1] It seems almost unbelievable, but he taught ten subjects in a single term and seventeen different subjects in the course of a year, supervised a model school of thirty pupils, acted as demonstration teacher, developed the professional materials to be taught, and served as janitor of the building. The one-year program of studies included the following:

(1) A review of the common branches—spelling, reading, writing, grammar, and arithmetic; (2) advanced studies (except ancient languages) as time permitted (e.g. geometry, algebra, natural, intellectual, and moral philosophy, political economy, and natural history); (3) the physical, mental, and moral development of children; (4) the science and art of teaching each of the common branches; (5) the art of school

[1] Cyrus Peirce and Mary Swift, "The First Normal School in America; The Journals of Cyrus Peirce and Mary Swift," *Harvard Documents in the History of Education*, Vol. I (Cambridge, Harvard Press, 1926).

government; and (6) practice in teaching and governing a "model" school.

The growth of state-supported normal schools was slow and by 1861, just prior to the Civil War, there were only eleven state schools, four of which were located in Massachusetts. A few municipal normal schools and teacher training schools to satisfy local demands were established during this period. Among these were schools in Boston, New York City, Philadelphia, San Francisco, Baltimore, St. Louis, and Trenton. For the most part these schools offered no formal instruction in methods, beyond the opportunity to do practice teaching under the direction of instructors. The emphasis was placed on mastering subject-matter, and while the latter admittedly contributed much to the quality of teaching, it fell far short of ideal preparation.

The characteristics of the ideal teacher as envisioned by educators of the period under discussion included many of the traits and qualities which are commonly advocated today. Judging by the reports of examiners and those of state and county superintendents, moral character ranked high. Competency in the three R's, together with some knowledge of orthography, English grammar, and geography and capacity to govern a school, were also mentioned frequently by early educators as essential for success in teaching.

Any discussion of teacher training in America which omitted the role played by teachers' institutes would be incomplete. During the decades just prior to the Civil War, when the demand for qualified teachers greatly exceeded the supply, something short of a normal school diploma had to suffice as a standard for most school systems in selecting teachers. To meet this pressing need, institutes ranging in duration from a few days to several weeks were planned and held throughout many states. Instruction in methodology and the general principles of school government was offered, although most institutes laid the greater stress on subject-matter. Arithmetic, grammar, geography, and reading constituted the core subjects, and it was not uncommon to give students in attendance an examination at the end of the institute session on the subject-matter learned.

Most observers agree that the institutes provided an opportunity for thousands of young persons to acquire at least an elementary knowledge of the task of teaching and hence enabled them to enter the classroom better equipped to serve their pupils than would otherwise have been possible. In short, they constituted one step in the evolution of teacher preparation, primitive though it was, which should not be dismissed as unimportant.

It may not be amiss to point out that self-instruction was a common method of preparing for the vocation of teaching during these middle years of the century. Teacher certification often called for an examination of the candidate, especially of his knowledge of academic subjects. Written examinations were rather generally adopted, and gradually were extended to cover a wide range of subject-matter. While no single sample can be assumed to represent the examinations given throughout the various states, a list of printed questions used in teachers' examinations in Columbus, Ohio, in 1859 throws some light on the scope of some of the examinations given. The nature of this particular examination is indicated by the questions asked. They were distributed as follows: five general, five government, five grammar, five reading, five orthography, five penmanship, five arithmetic, five geography, five definitions, and five theory of teaching.

When measured against today's standards the provisions for the preparation of teachers in 1865 were pitifully inadequate. But viewed in historical perspective, the progress made between 1836 and the close of the Civil War was substantial. While only eight states had actually established normal schools during this period, the idea was now generally accepted as sound in principle and it was only a matter of time before every state was destined to make similar provision for teacher preparation.

TEACHER EDUCATION, 1865–1910

The years immediately following the Civil War saw an expansion of the normal school movement and a continued emphasis in the curriculum on teaching the subject-matter commonly required of elementary school pupils. Late in the century, instruction in pedagogy was extended and educators were in rather general agreement that a body of professional knowledge existed and could be communicated to future teachers. One can understand the thinking about the role of the normal school which was current during these days by examining the committee reports setting forth objectives. The function of the normal school as expressed in a report of a National Education Association Committee in 1899 was "the teaching of subjects that they in turn may be taught . . . the development of character that it in turn may be transfigured into character . . . a preparation for life that it in turn may prepare others to enter fully, readily, and righteously into their environment." [2]

To give meaning to the above, the committee recommended one year each of psychology, pedagogy, observation, and practice teaching. Under pedagogy was included philosophy of education, science and art of teaching, history of education, and social economics.

[2] "Report of the Committee on Normal Schools," *Addresses and Proceedings* (National Education Association, 1899), p. 838.

While the recommendations of a committee such as the one just referred to cannot safely be interpreted to mean that all or even a majority of normal schools adopted the program outlined, the committee's proposals did influence practice significantly, and soon after the turn of the century the subject areas just listed were fairly standard in the better normal schools.

PREPARATION OF SECONDARY SCHOOL TEACHERS

Until about 1900 little thought was given to the preparation of secondary school teachers. The Committee of Ten on Secondary School Studies in their deliberations in 1894 gave attention to pedagogical training, placing emphasis, as in the past, on command of subject-matter. "Methods of teaching" was subordinated to academic training. It is interesting to note that in 1895 a sub-committee of a committee on the training of teachers suggested that philosophy of education and school economy, the latter to include a study of the school systems of England, France, and Germany, should be included in the curriculum. However, the prevailing point of view at the turn of the century was that, while secondary teachers needed to be trained, college graduation insured adequate general education and competent special knowledge of the subjects to be taught. A few educators, of whom James E. Russell, Dean of Teachers College, Columbia University, was the most articulate spokesman, argued for professional training. Specifically, Russell in 1899 in an address on "The Training of Teachers for Secondary Schools" recommended that teachers should possess the following qualifications; namely, general knowledge, professional knowledge, special knowledge, and skill in teaching. He stressed the importance of a knowledge of the psychology of the adolescent period. But admittedly the educators at that time could not point to any well-organized and developed materials in methodology or courses of instruction that were available to students interested in meeting Russell's standards. Proposals were made by special committees appointed to study the problem, and in 1907 the following joint recommendation of the Committee of Seventeen of the Department of Secondary Education of the NEA appeared and was widely discussed:

> II. That definite study be given to each of the following subjects, either in separate courses or in such combinations as convenience or necessity demands:
>   (a) History of Education:
>   (1) History of general education.
>   (2) History of secondary education.
>   (b) Educational Psychology with emphasis on adolescence.

(c) The principles of education, including the study of educational aims, values, and processes. Courses in general method are included under this heading.

(d) Special methods in the secondary school subjects that the students expect to teach.

(e) Organization and management of schools and school systems.

(f) School hygiene.

III. That opportunity for observation and practice teaching with secondary pupils be given.[3]

This proposal called for not less than fifteen semester hours of time to be devoted to professional subjects distributed through the last two years of the college course. It seems quite clear from various articles and reports that history of education and educational psychology were emphasized to a greater degree than the other subjects mentioned.

The gains made in teacher education during the forty years following the Civil War were not outstanding. The stage had been set earlier in the century for the type of curriculum deemed appropriate and essential for the preparation of elementary school teachers. But one might logically claim that there was an observable trend in the direction of a standard pedagogical program.

However, as late as the school year 1896–7 the total number of students graduating from normal schools was only 8,188, which was less than one-sixth of the total number of school teachers needed to fill the annual vacancies. One of the most favourable situations existed in Massachusetts, where one-third of all elementary teachers was reported to be normal school graduates.

Two years of high school education were all that were commonly required for admission to normal school, and hence the total number of years of teacher preparation in 1900 was substantially less than would be deemed necessary to meet the minimum requirements today.

It was in the institutions where secondary school teachers were prepared, however, that the most significant advance was registered. Educators at the turn of the century were pointing out the desirability of combining instruction in methods with instruction in subject-matter and emphasizing the need for integration of the two. It was urged that while a student was learning his mathematics he should also be learning how to teach it to others. This was also the period during which recognition was given to the value of general education for secondary as well as for

[3] "Joint Recommendations of the Committee of Seventeen on the Professional Preparation of High School Teachers," *Addresses and Proceedings* (National Education Association, 1907), p. 537.

elementary school teachers. While the achievements of this period should not be underestimated, the major task of persuading colleges and universities that there were techniques of instruction that could systematically be communicated to aspiring secondary teachers to the latter's advantage was far from completed.

DEVELOPMENTS DURING THE LAST FIFTY YEARS

The developments in teacher education during the past fifty years do not point clearly towards any single pattern of preparation. Some of the trends have been of fairly short duration, and the differences in point of view among both educators and lay leaders with respect to the type of education which promises to produce the best teachers at times seem almost irreconcilable. The reasons for the apparent confusion and uncertainty as to what the future holds for teacher education are manifold. To a much greater degree than is the case with medicine and law, teaching is a vocation about which every adult is likely to have strong opinions. After spending twelve or thirteen years under the tutelage of fifteen to twenty different classroom teachers, it is understandable that pedagogues are rather well typed. This familiarity with the teacher's *modus operandi* has not in many instances added to the teachers' professional prestige. Since teachers live in a glass bowl, their idiosyncrasies are more visible than those of most other professional workers and it is their apparent weaknesses rather than their strengths which seem to leave the deepest impression on the minds of those taught. Since some teachers have not always measured up to their professional responsibilities, the image of the teacher in America has not been consistently favourable. Unfortunately, this has not led the public to encourage marked changes in teacher preparation either with respect to type or amount.

A second factor which further impeded progress relates to the need for an extended period of preparation comparable to that required for admission to other professions. It is quite generally agreed that one important characteristic of a profession is the long period of preparation required of members for entrance coupled with the possession of unique skills and knowledge. Because teachers are by far the largest among the groups laying claim to professional status, the small proportion of their members which has fully met the criterion of training has created serious doubts in the minds of many as to the place of public school teaching among the professions. If, as some contend, it is not really a profession and doesn't need to be to fulfil its function in society, why the cry for so much preparation? Throughout the last half century this question has been continuously debated. The tax-conscious public needs much assur-

ance as to the importance of a long extended training period for classroom teachers before it will be willing to provide the money to support
it.

The third, and perhaps the greatest obstacle in the way of advancing the educational background of teachers, has been the population explosion which followed World War II and is still with us. Apparently
this trend defied most predictions. Since 1945 the pupil population has
increased by 70 per cent, causing a demand for school teachers beyond
the capacity of most states to produce. The economic implications of this
have been most distressing. The budget for teachers' salaries during the
last thirty years has risen steadily except for brief intervals marked by
depressions. While the American people appear willing to support many
services that bring them either physical comfort or security, they have
been less enthusiastic about supporting long-range educational programs
that cannot easily be assayed. Among these is support for teachers of
quality, with preparation approaching or equal in amount to that possessed by members of other recognized professions.

Running through much of the literature on American education one
will find discussed the question of how much preparation is essential to
ensure success in teaching. In medicine and law the number of years required for admission to those callings has been rather well standardized,
allowing for some variations related to certain specializations. But comparable standards have not yet been accepted and prescribed for teaching.

A fourth important influence of recent vintage has been the appearance of Sputnik and the rivalry between Russia and the United States on
all matters relating to military and economic strength. Discussions of educational practices and the strengths and weaknesses of our system in
comparison with the Russian system have spread to every village and
hamlet in the U.S.A. The background preparation of teachers has received considerable attention in these discussions. It is too early to predict just what effect Russian accomplishments and practices will eventually have on our program here in the United States. The Federal Government, judging by recent Congressional debates and actions, seems unlikely to modify its "hands off" policy on the major problems related to
teacher preparation. The fact that education is a state function has
served to provide political—and economy-minded—legislators in Washington with the argument that the support of teacher education and
teachers' salaries should be left on the shoulders of local and state governments.

But, despite the apparent short-sightedness of Congress with respect
to providing generous support for public education and thereby meeting
the Russian threat, developments in the latter country have had signifi-

cant effects. The emphasis on science and mathematics growing out of Soviet achievements in both the nuclear and space fields has led educators to place greater stress on these subjects in the program of teacher preparation. What is perhaps equally important, the Federal Government has provided some financial support for in-service education programs in science, mathematics, and foreign languages. Many universities are now offering special classes for teachers responsible for each of these three fields and receive some government subsidy to enable them to provide appropriate instruction. Still another evidence of Russian influence lies in the fact that many educators have been sent to Russia at public or foundation expense to study educational developments there. While there is little, if any, proof that our system of teacher preparation is being fashioned after the Soviet model, the effect has been to place greater emphasis upon subject-matter mastery and, in general, to uplift standards.

Despite the confusion and the apathy of the public with respect to teacher education, one can point to a number of changes and trends that make the last fifty years significant in the history of teacher education in the United States. First of all, there has been a marked trend in the direction of added preparation. From two years (in many instances less) of training which represented the amount of preparation commonly required for certification to teach in 1910, a steady advance with considerable acceleration since 1940 has been made in the training of elementary school teachers. Today a bachelor's degree representing four years' preparation beyond high school is almost universally required. While the upward trend in the preparation of high school teachers has been less observable, several states are moving rapidly towards a five-year requirement or one year of graduate study beyond the bachelor's degree.

Whereas admission requirements to normal schools were formerly low, calling for two years or less of high-school preparation, the standards were lifted in the 1920's as a result of action taken by the American Association of Teachers Colleges and Normal Schools. In 1923 this association adopted a standard of four years of high school preparation for admission to a teacher training program. While the association's standards were not always recognized, the general effect was to increase the total amount of education acquired by teachers and presumably to add to their stock of knowledge.

Teacher certification standards have moved upwards by one whole year of preparation during each of the last two decades. If this trend continues, the level of teacher training seems certain to approach the current standards established for several of the older professions. It is quite conceivable that a point of diminishing returns may be reached soon in the number of years required for certification. Unless and until the institutions which prepare teachers develop programs that can demonstrably increase teaching efficiency, the upward trend in the amount of pre-service preparation may be slowed considerably.

A second change in the preparation of teachers is related to the type of institution providing the training. In 1910, two-year normal schools with meager offerings were typical. By 1930, normal schools were quite generally being supplanted by teachers' colleges organized to provide three- and four-year programs. By 1950 the normal school was practically extinct. Interestingly enough the teachers' colleges which emerged during the first three decades of this century are now also undergoing transformation. They are being rapidly converted into multi-purpose institutions offering in addition to teacher education programs, work in liberal arts and specialization in such fields as business, art, music, pre-engineering, pre-law and pre-medicine. Many of these schools are offering a fifth year of graduate work.

This trend towards a more liberal program for teachers has been favorably received by both lay and professional groups. It should be pointed out, however, that the role of teachers' colleges in the preparation of prospective teachers is not as great in this country as one might well imagine. Only about 20 per cent of teachers new to the schools receive their training in what may be classed strictly as teachers' colleges. Public general colleges, of which the converted teacher's colleges constitute a sizeable proportion, together with universities prepare by far the largest proportion of America's teachers (approximately 50 per cent). The other institutions involved are private colleges and universities.

There are today nearly 1,200 separate institutions offering teacher education programs. As might be expected, the range in standards is extremely wide, due to differences in facilities, number and qualifications of staff members, and to state certification requirements. In some cases the location of the preparing institution and the environmental conditions surrounding it are limiting factors. Historically, normal schools were located without reference to cultural setting, and while modern transportation and educational media have tended to reduce the environmental differences somewhat, many of the 1,200 institutions involved in teacher preparation still provide meager opportunities for enlightened living.

One of the major problems now confronting teacher education stems from the transformation of teachers' colleges into multi-purpose institutions designed to offer a much wider program and provide for a more heterogeneous student body. Desirable as the trend may be, it has often been accomplished with inadequate facilities and staff. Moreover, standards of admission have frequently been relatively low in comparison with the better liberal arts colleges. Time will undoubtedly remedy this situation.

Fortunately a national accrediting association has been formed, and through its efforts to raise standards to a defensible height the future for teacher preparation appears hopeful. This association, known as *The National Council for Accreditation of Teacher Education,* was established in 1952. It is an autonomous, voluntary accrediting body devoted exclusively to the evaluation and accreditation of teacher education programs. While the task of elevating the standards of 1,200 diversified institutional programs or eliminating some of them altogether is a colossal one, considerable improvements are to be anticipated. Up to the present time approximately one-third of the 1,200 have been accredited by the National Council. It is estimated that these institutions now prepare 80 per cent of the teachers for the public schools.

Other agencies also are exerting influence on teacher education standards. Specifically, state departments of education have the responsibility for approving programs designed for the preparation of elementary and secondary school teachers. That these have proved less than adequate is indicated by the formation of the national accrediting association just mentioned. Among other groups which are having an influence on the quality of the programs offered are the National Education Association, the American Council on Education, and educational foundations. Indirectly, their studies and pronouncements have had some impact upon the type and quality of program offered.

One interesting fact regarding teacher education in the United States is that both elementary- and secondary-teachers are frequently prepared in the same institution. The pros and cons of this have been discussed widely, but where the facilities are adequate and programs well conceived, the advantages seem greatly to outweigh the disadvantages.

Not only is there diversity in the type of institution in which teachers receive their preparation in the United States, but there is considerable diversity in patterns of what is taught. In some respects this is the greatest bone of contention among educators and interested laymen since what is taught will obviously set certain limits on what students learn. There is considerable agreement among educators that teachers, regardless of the level of the educational program in which they are assigned, should be broadly educated and a large part of every four- or five-year program should be devoted to general or liberal education. It is also agreed that a significant proportion of the preparatory program should be given over to study of the subject-matter to be taught. Finally, because teaching is viewed as a profession with a unique body of knowledge and skills essential to its effective practice, the program of teacher preparation should include what is commonly referred to as professional education.

As can well be imagined, a serious problem arises in determining the relative amounts of time to be assigned to these agreed components of a teacher preparatory program as well as their sequence in the program. While no single diagram can adequately portray the practices extant in the United States, examination of the chart [shown on this page] will give the reader some notion of current patterns.

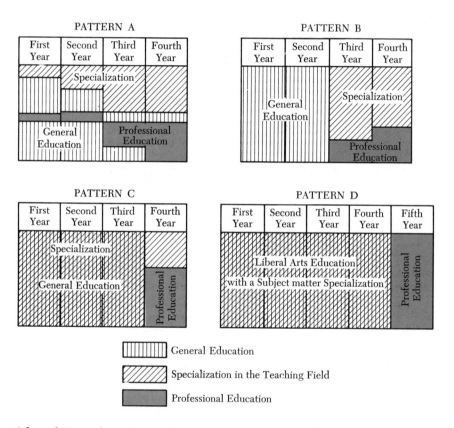

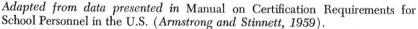

Adapted from data presented in Manual on Certification Requirements for School Personnel in the U.S. (*Armstrong and Stinnett, 1959*).

While no one seems to know for certain just what knowledge a teacher needs to possess in order to be most efficient, there is less controversy over the program of general education and subject-matter specialization than over the amount and type of professional education needed by teachers. A fact which has contributed to the confusion is that most people are ignorant with regard to current practice. The cry of critics is

that too much time and attention is being devoted to professional education. The latter is not always clearly defined, but usually it is interpreted
to include methods courses, educational psychology, history and philosophy of education, classroom management, and certain other courses
that do not always lend themselves to classification. Contrary to the notions held by the critics, this segment of the teacher's preparation is relatively small compared with the curricula required by other professional
schools. Thus, prospective elementary teachers receive on the average 36
per cent of their total instruction in courses directly related to their professional work and secondary teachers about 17 per cent. Schools of
agriculture, business administration, engineering, music, nursing, and
pharmacy equal or exceed teaching in the proportion of undergraduate
subject-matter that is purely professional in character.

There are, of course, many individual college programs which surpass the average in the number of courses offered of a strictly professional type. Some of these are subject to just criticism since there is considerable duplication of subject-matter and much of questionable worth
contained in the program. As frequently happens, some critics have
based their attacks on teacher preparatory efforts on the assumption that
all institutional programs were of this poor substance and quality.

There are some current approaches to teacher education sponsored
by one or more foundations which appear to emphasize the desirability
of more liberal education for teachers than has generally been provided
and a reduction in the amount of time required to complete the program
of study. Experiments are now being carried on with foundation support
in a number of liberal arts colleges in co-operation with selected school
systems, in which training on the job is being provided simultaneously
with a study program in the college. A very limited amount of professional content is offered and a great reliance is placed on an internship
and the ability of the young student teacher to develop the necessary
skills under the supervision of local employers and college instructors assigned to the project.

Coupled with this approach are attempts to modify certification requirements so as to admit to teaching many college graduates who are
now debarred because they had few, if any, courses related to methodology and other professional content.

While this shortening process may have some desirable immediate
effects, there is considerable scepticism among educators that the solution is to be found in this approach. While there is room for dissatisfaction with existing arrangements, there appears to be little justification for
any diminution in the professional subject-matter required of those who
plan to teach. The problem arises because the profession itself has been
slow in formulating a sound, long-term program and, in place of the expert, lay influences have assumed the leadership.

Without doubt, the weakest point in the current situation is the relatively low standards which obtain in many of the 1,200 institutions which prepare teachers. The staffing problem has been extremely difficult, due to low salaries and low prestige. The ablest men and women have been reluctant to accept positions in teacher training institutions because of the low esteem in which teacher education has been held. With improvements in salary and public support, there is reason to believe that a significant upgrading in the quality of instruction will soon take place. While this obviously cannot be achieved overnight, there are strong forces at work both within and outside the profession in the hopes of achieving high standards of teacher preparation. The problem is at last being recognized as one related to national security and welfare. Hence, it seems certain that there will be no let up in the move to accomplish this objective.

CONCLUSIONS

In conclusion, it would appear that barring some major war or national catastrophe, teacher education in the United States will make forward strides in the years which lie immediately ahead. That there is much left to be done cannot be questioned. Perhaps the greatest weakness relates to the low standards which obtain in too many of the institutional programs. The solution would seem to lie in two directions—one to eliminate through accreditation procedures those which give little promise of high quality and raise the level of efficiency of those equipped to fulfil their mission. In a country where local autonomy and decentralization of authority are highly prized, the achievement of this objective will be difficult. But both the profession and the public are ready to give strong support to the effort to improve standards. Hence, it seems realistic to assume that one of the major limitations in the current situation will be overcome during the next quarter-century.

A second problem, not especially unique to the United States, is the confusion regarding the qualities and traits which make for success in teaching. Research has contributed little to our knowledge of the ingredients of good teaching. This is partly due to differences in philosophy on the part of educators and partly to the absence of reliable measuring devices and the need to rely largely on subjective judgments in making assessments of teacher achievements. But it is imperative if real gains are to be made in education that we identify the characteristics that are inherent in good teaching.

Related to this is the absence of clear national goals bearing on education. Recent efforts to clarify what we are aiming at with respect to both individual development and our society generally, reveal an awareness of this problem and hence give some assurance that progress can be logically anticipated.

Much of the controversy over the proper components of a teacher education program will undoubtedly be settled as educators continue to assess the validity of the arguments advanced. As was pointed out earlier, there is a great deal of ignorance extant regarding the time and attention given to the purely professional aspects of teaching. Improved communication should do much to place this in proper perspective. The relatively small number of institutions which have badly balanced curricula will undoubtedly soon be brought into line or be compelled to close their doors.

It is comforting to note the gains made in teacher education since the first normal schools were established around 1840, a period of only 120 years. In view of the titanic struggles of the American people to provide an education at public expense for every boy and girl in a country that has witnessed unprecedented growth, the success achieved in supplying schools with teachers having as much preparation as they now possess deserves high commendation. The teaching profession is still young and its future promising.

PHYSICAL, INTELLECTUAL, MORAL, AND RELIGIOUS EDUCATION

Horace Mann (1796–1859) was one of the most capable educational reformers of the nineteenth century. In 1827, Mann was elected to the Massachusetts Legislature, and when this body established a board of education eight years later, he was appointed its secretary. In 1848, he was elected to Congress. He became president of Antioch College in 1853, and it was here that he told a graduation class, "Be ashamed to die until you have won some victory for humanity," oft-quoted words that accurately describe his spirit. As Secretary of the Massachusetts Board of Education, Mann vigorously and eloquently argued his educational beliefs in a series of twelve annual reports submitted to the Board. The following selection is composed of excerpts from his Twelfth Annual Report, and, as in the preceding reports it is possible to see why Mann is considered to be the father of the free "common" school in America. Throughout this selection the reader is exposed to Mann's characteristic zeal for developing an educational system that would foster equality not only in public education but in society as a whole. Although the Twelfth Annual Report ranges over a variety of educational problems which are as important today as they were in Mann's time, the section on religious education is singularly outstanding for its current relevance. Mann was an outspoken proponent of nonsectarianism in public education, and the student should have little difficulty in seeing the cogency of his arguments to the important court decisions in this century regarding the church-state relationships to the schools.

Horace Mann

Excerpts taken from The Twelfth Annual Report of 1848 (*Boston: Lee and Shepard, 1891*), pp. 377–389.

Without undervaluing any other human agency, it may be safely affirmed that the common school, improved and energized as it can easily be, may become the most effective and benignant of all the forces of civilization. Two reasons sustain this position. In the first place, there is a universality in its operation, which can be affirmed of no other institution whatever. If administered in the spirit of justice and conciliation, all the rising generation may be brought within the circle of its reformatory and elevating influences. And, in the second place, the materials upon which it operates are so pliant and ductile as to be susceptible of assuming a greater variety of forms than any other earthly work of the Creator. The inflexibility and ruggedness of the oak, when compared with the lithe sapling or the tender germ, are but feeble emblems to typify the docility of childhood when contrasted with the obduracy and intractableness of man. It is these inherent advantages of the common school, which, in our own state, have produced results so striking, from a system so imperfect, and an administration so feeble. In teaching the blind and the deaf and dumb, in kindling the latent spark of intelligence that lurks in an idiot's mind, and in the more holy work of reforming abandoned and outcast children, education has proved what it can do by glorious experiments. These wonders it has done in its infancy, and with the lights of a limited experience; but when its faculties shall be fully developed, when it shall be trained to wield its mighty energies for the protection of society against the giant vices which now invade and torment it—against intemperance, avarice, war, slavery, bigotry, the woes of want, and the wickedness of waste—then there will not be a height to which these enemies of the race can escape which it will not scale, nor a Titan among them all whom it will not slay.

I proceed, then, in endeavoring to show how the true business of the schoolroom connects itself, and becomes identical, with the great interests of society. The former is the infant, immature state of those interests; the latter their developed adult state. As "the child is father to the man," so may the training of the schoolroom expand into the institutions and fortunes of the state. . . .

PHYSICAL EDUCATION

My general conclusion, then, under this head is that it is the duty of all the governing minds in society—whether in office or out of it—to diffuse a knowledge of these beautiful and beneficent laws of health and life throughout the length and breadth of the state; to popularize them; to make them, in the first place, the common acquisition of all, and through education and custom the common inheritance of all, so that the healthful habits naturally growing out of their observance shall be inbred in the people, exemplified in the personal regime of each individual, incorporated into the economy of every household, observable in all private dwellings, and in all public edifices, especially in those buildings which are erected by capitalists for the residence of their work-people, or for renting to the poorer classes; obeyed by supplying cities with pure water; by providing public baths, public walks, and public squares; by rural cemeteries; by the drainage and sewerage of populous towns, and by whatever else may promote the general salubrity of the atmosphere: in fine, by a religious observance of all those sanitary regulations with which modern science has blessed the world.

For this thorough diffusion of sanitary intelligence, the common school is the only agency. It is, however, an adequate agency. Let human physiology be introduced as an indispensable branch of study into our public schools; let no teacher be approved who is not master of its leading principles, and of their applications to the varying circumstances of life; let all the older classes in the schools be regularly and rigidly examined upon this study by the school-committees—and a speedy change would come over our personal habits, over our domestic usages, and over the public arrangements of society. Temperance and moderation would not be such strangers at the table. Fashion, like European sovereigns, if not compelled to abdicate and fly, would be forced to compromise for the continual possession of her throne by the surrender to her subjects of many of their natural rights. A sixth order of architecture would be invented—the hygienic—which, without subtracting at all from the beauty of any other order, would add a new element of utility to them all. The "health regulations" of cities would be issued in a revised code —a code that would bear the scrutiny of science. And, as the result and reward of all, a race of men and women, loftier in statute, firmer in structure, fairer in form, and better able to perform the duties and bear the burdens of life, would revisit the earth. The minikin specimens of the race, who now go on dwindling and tapering from parent to child, would reascend to manhood and womanhood. Just in proportion as the laws of health and life were discovered and obeyed, would pain, disease, insanity, and untimely death, cease from among men. Consumption would remain; but it would be consumption in the active sense.

INTELLECTUAL EDUCATION

Another cardinal object which the government of Massachusetts, and all the influential men in the state, should propose to themselves, is the physical well-being of all the people—the sufficiency, comfort, competence, of every individual in regard to food, raiment, and shelter. And these necessaries and conveniences of life should be obtained by each individual for himself, or by each family for themselves, rather than accepted from the hand of charity or extorted by poor laws. It is not averred that this most desirable result can, in all instances, be obtained; but it is, nevertheless, the end to be aimed at.

True statesmanship and true political economy, not less than true philanthropy, present this perfect theory as the goal, to be more and more closely approximated by our imperfect practice. The desire to achieve such a result cannot be regarded as an unreasonable ambition; for, though all mankind were well fed, well clothed, and well housed, they might still be but half civilized.

Our ambition as a state should trace itself to a different origin, and propose to itself a different object. Its flame should be lighted at the skies. Its radiance and its warmth should reach the darkest and the coldest abodes of men. It should seek the solution of such problems as these: To what extent can competence displace pauperism? How nearly can we free ourselves from the low-minded and the vicious, not by their expatriation, but by their elevation? To what extent can the resources and power of nature be converted into human welfare, the peaceful arts of life be advanced, and the vast treasures of human talent and genius be developed? How much of suffering, in all its forms, can be relieved? or, what is better than relief, how much can be prevented? Cannot the classes of crimes be lessened and the number of criminals in each class be diminished? Our exemplars, both for public and for private imitation, should be the parables of the lost sheep and of the lost piece of silver.

When we have spread competence through all the abodes of poverty, when we have substituted knowledge for ignorance in the minds of the whole people, when we have reformed the vicious and reclaimed the criminal, then may we invite all neighboring nations to behold the spectacle, and say to them, in the conscious elation of virtue, "Rejoice with me," for I have found that which was lost. Until that day shall arrive, our duties will not be wholly fulfilled, and our ambition will have new honors to win. . . .

Surely nothing but universal education can counterwork this tendency to the domination of capital and the servility of labor. If one class possesses all the wealth and education, while the residue of society is ignorant and poor, it matters not by what name the relation between them may be called; the latter, in fact and in truth, will be the servile dependants and subjects of the former. But, if education be equably diffused, it will draw property after it by the strongest of all attractions; for such a thing never did happen, and never can happen, as that an intelligent and practical body of men should be permanently poor. Property and labor in different classes are essentially antagonistic; but property and labor in the same class are essentially fraternal. The people of Massachusetts have, in some degree, appreciated the truth, that the unexampled prosperity of the state—its comfort, its competence, its general intelligence and virtue—is attributable to the education, more or less perfect, which all its people have received; but are they sensible of a fact equally important, namely, that it is to this same education that two-thirds of the people are indebted for not being today the vassals of as severe a tyranny, in the form of capital, as the lower classes of Europe are bound to in the form of brute force?

Education, then, beyond all other devices of human origin, is the greater equalizer of the conditions of men—the balance-wheel of the social machinery. I do not here mean that it so elevates the moral nature as to make men disdain and abhor the oppression of their fellow-men. This idea pertains to another of its attributes. But I mean that it gives each man the independence and the means by which he can resist the selfishness of other men. It does better than to disarm the poor of their hostility towards the rich: it prevents being poor. Agrarianism is the revenge of poverty against wealth. The wanton destruction of the property of others—the burning of hay-ricks and corn-ricks, the demolition of machinery because it supersedes hand-labor, the sprinkling of vitriol on rich dresses—is only agrarianism run mad. Education prevents both the revenge and the madness. On the other hand, a fellow-feeling for one's class or caste is the common instinct of hearts not wholly sunk in selfish regards for person or family. The spread of education, by enlarging the cultivated class or caste, will open a wider area over which the social feelings will expand; and, if this education should be universal and complete, it would do more than all things else to obliterate factitious distinctions in society. . . .

I hold all past achievements of the human mind to be rather in the nature of prophecy than of fulfillment—the first-fruits of the beneficence of God in endowing us with the faculties of perception, comparison, calculation, and causality, rather than the full harvest of their eventual development. For look at the magnificent creation into which we have been brought, and at the adaptation of our faculties to understand, admire, and use it. All around us are works worthy of an infinite God; and we are led, by irresistible evidence, to believe that, just so far as we acquire this knowledge, we shall be endued with his power. From history and from consciousness, we find ourselves capable of ever-onward improvement: and therefore it seems to be a denial of first principles—it seems no better than impiety—to suppose that we shall ever become such finished scholars, that the works of the All-wise will have no new problem for our solution, and will, therefore, be able to teach us no longer.

Nor is it any less than impiety to suppose that we shall ever so completely enlist the powers of Nature in our service, that exhausted Omnipotence can reward our industry with no further bounties. This would be to suppose that we shall arrive at a period when our active and progressive natures will become passive and stationary; when we shall have nothing to do but to sit in indolent and inglorious contemplation of past achievements; and when, all aspirations having been lost in fruition, we shall have outlived the joys of hope and the rewards of effort, and no new glories will beckon us onward to new felicities.

MORAL EDUCATION

Moral education is a primal necessity of social existence. The unrestrained passions of men are not only homicidal, but suicidal; and a community without a conscience would soon extinguish itself. Even with a natural conscience, how often has evil triumphed over good! From the beginning of time, wrong has followed right, as the shadow, the substance. As the relations of men become more complex, and the business of the world more extended, new opportunities and new temptations for wrong-doing have been created. With the endearing relations of parent and child came also the possibility of infanticide and parricide; and the first domestic altar that brothers ever reared was stained with fratricidal blood. Following close upon the obligations to truth came falsehood and perjury, and closer still upon the duty of obedience to the divine law came disobedience. With the existence of private relations between men came fraud; and with the existence of public relations between nations came aggression, war, and slavery. And so, just in proportion as the relations of life became more numerous, and the interests of society more various and manifold, the range of possible and of actual offenses has been continually enlarging. As for every new substance there may be a new shadow, so for every new law there may be a new transgression. . . .

The race has existed long enough to try many experiments for the solution of this greatest problem ever submitted to its hands; and the race has experimented, without stint of time or circumscription of space to mar or modify legitimate results. Mankind have tried despotisms, monarchies, and republican forms of government. They have tried the extremes of anarchy and of autocracy. They have tried Draconian codes of law, and for the lightest offenses have extinguished the life of the offender. They have established theological standards, claiming for them the sanction of divine authority, and the attributes of a perfect and infallible law; and then they have imprisoned, burnt, massacred, not individuals only, but whole communities at a time, for not bowing down to idols which ecclesiastical authority had set up. These and other great systems of measures have been adopted as barriers against error and guilt: they have been extended over empires, prolonged through centuries, and administered with terrible energy; and yet the great ocean of vice and crime overleaps every embankment, pours down upon our heads, saps the foundations under our feet, and sweeps away the securities of social order, of property, liberty, and life. . . .

But to all doubters, disbelievers, or despairers in human progress, it may still be said, there is one experiment which has never yet been tried. It is an experiment which, even before its inception, offers the highest authority for its ultimate success. Its formula is intelligible to all; and it is as legible as though written in starry letters on an azure sky. It is expressed in these few simple words: *"Train up a child in the way he should go; and when he is old, he will not depart from it."* This declaration is positive. If the conditions are complied with, it makes no provision for a failure. Though pertaining to morals, yet, if the terms of the direction are observed, there is no more reason to doubt the result than there would be in an optical or a chemical experiment.

But this experiment has never yet been tried. Education has never yet been brought to bear with one-hundredth part of its potential force upon the natures of children, and through them upon the character of men and of the race. In all the attempts to reform mankind which have hitherto been made, whether by changing the frame of government, by aggravating or softening the severity of the penal code, or by substituting a government—created for a God-created religion—in all these attempts, the infantile and youthful mind, its amenability to influences, and the enduring and self-operating character of the influences it receives, have been almost wholly unrecognized. Here, then, is a new agency, whose powers are but just beginning to be understood, and whose mighty energies hitherto have been but feebly invoked; and yet, from our experience, limited and imperfect as it is, we do know that, far beyond any other earthly instrumentality, it is comprehensive and decisive. . . .

Is any high-minded, exemplary, and conscientious man disposed to believe that this substantial extirpation of social vices and crimes is a Utopian idea, is more than we have any reason to expect while human nature remains as it is, let me use the *ad hominem* argument to refute him. Let me refer him to himself, and ask him why the same influences which have saved him from gaming, intemperance, dissoluteness, falsehood, dishonesty, violence, and their kindred offenses, and have made him a man of sobriety, frugality, and probity, why the same influences which have saved him from ruin, might not, if brought to bear upon others, save them also. So far as human instrumentalities are concerned, we have abundant means for surrounding every child in the state with preservative and moral influences as extensive and as efficient as those under which the present industrious, worthy, and virtuous members of the community were reared. And as to all those things in regard to which we are directly dependent upon the divine favor, have we not the promise, explicit and unconditional, that the men *shall not* depart from the way in which they should go, if the children are trained up in it? It has been overlooked that this promise is not restricted to parents, but seems to be addressed indiscriminately to all, whether parents, communities, states, or mankind.

RELIGIOUS EDUCATION

. . . On this subject, I propose to speak with freedom and plainness, and more at length than I should feel required to do, but for the peculiar circumstances in which I have been placed. It is matter of notoriety, that the views of the Board of Education—and my own, perhaps still more than those of the Board—on the subject of religious instruction in our Public Schools, have been subjected to animadversion. Grave charges have been made against us, that our purpose was to exclude religion; and to exclude that, too, which is the common exponent of religion—the Bible—from the Common Schools of the State; or, at least, to derogate from its authority, and destroy its influence in them. Whatever prevalence a suspicion of the truth of these imputations may have heretofore had, I have reason to believe that further inquiry and examination have done much to disabuse the too credulous recipients of so groundless a charge. Still, amongst a people so commendably sensitive on the subject of religion, as are the people of Massachusetts, any suspicion of irreligious tendencies, will greatly prejudice any cause, and, so far as any cause may otherwise have the power of doing good, will greatly impair that power.

It is known, too, that our noble system of Free Schools for the whole people, is strenuously opposed—by a few persons in our own State, and by no inconsiderable numbers in some of the other states of this Union —and that a rival system of "Parochial" or "Sectarian Schools," is now urged upon the public by a numerous, a powerful, and a well-organized body of men. It has pleased the advocates of this rival system, in various public addresses, in reports, and through periodicals devoted to their cause, to denounce our system as irreligious and anti-Christian. They do not trouble themselves to describe what our system is, but adopt a more summary way to forestall public opinion against it, by using general epithets of reproach, and signals of alarm. . . .

. . . The truth of a proposition may be established, by showing the falsity or absurdity of all conflicting propositions. So far as this method can be applied to moral questions, its aid may safely be invoked here.

What are the other courses, which the State of Massachusetts might adopt or sanction, in relation to the education of its youth? They are these four:

1. It might establish schools, but expressly exclude all religious instruction from them—making them merely schools for secular instruction.

2. It might adopt a course, directly the reverse of this. It might define and prescribe a system of religion for the schools, and appoint the teachers and officers, whose duty it should be to carry out that system.

3. It might establish schools by law, and empower each religious sect, whenever and wherever it could get a majority, to determine what religious faith should be taught in them. And,

4. It might expressly disclaim and refuse all interference with the education of the young, and abandon the whole work to the hazards of private enterprise, or to parental will, ability, or caprice.

1. A system of schools from which all religious instruction should be excluded might properly be called un-Christian, or, rather, non-Christian, in the same sense in which it could be called non-Jewish, or non-Mahommedan; that is, as having no connection with either. I do not suppose a man can be found in Massachusetts, who would declare such a system to be his first choice.

2. Were the State to establish schools, and prescribe a system of religion to be taught in them, and appoint the teachers and officers to superintend it, could there be any better definition or exemplification of an Ecclesiastical Establishment? . . .

For any human government, then, to attempt to coerce and predetermine the religious opinions of children, by law, and contrary to the will of their parents, is unspeakably more criminal than the usurpation of such control over the opinions of men. The latter is treason against truth; but the former is sacrilege. As the worst of all crimes against chastity are those which debauch the infant victim before she knows what chastity is; so the worst of all crimes against religious truth, are those which forcibly close up the avenues, and bar the doors, that lead to the forum of reason and conscience. The spirit of ecclesiastical domination, in modern times, finding that the principles of men are too strong for it, is attempting the seduction of children. Fearing the opinions that may be developed by mature reflection, it anticipates and forestalls those opinions; and seeks to imprint, upon the ignorance and receptiveness of childhood, the convictions which it could never fasten upon the minds of men in their maturity. . . .

3. As a third method, the government might establish schools by law, and empower each religious sect, whenever and wherever it could get a majority, to determine what religious faith should be taught in them.

Under such a system, each sect would demand that its own faith should be inculcated in all the schools—and this, on the clear and simple ground that such faith is the only true one. Each differing faith, believed in by all the other sects, must, of course, be excluded from the schools —and this, on the equally clear and simple ground, that there can be but one true faith; and which that is, has already been determined, and is no longer an open question. Under such a system, it will not suffice to have the Bible in the schools, to speak for itself. Each sect will rise up and virtually say, "Although the Bible from Genesis to Revelation is in the schools, yet its true meaning and doctrines are not there; Christianity is not there, unless our commentary, our creed, or our catechism, is there also. A revelation from God is not sufficient. Our commentary, or our teacher, must go with it, to reveal what the revelation means. . . . Your schools may be like the noble Bereans, searching the Scriptures daily, but unless the result of those searchings have our countersign and endorsement, those schools are un-Christian and anti-Christian."

Now, it is almost too obvious to be mentioned, that such a claim as the above, reduces society at once to this dilemma: If one religious sect is authorized to advance it, for itself, then all other sects are equally authorized to do the same thing, for themselves. The right being equal among all the sects, and each sect being equally certain and equally determined; what shall be done? Will not each sect, acting under religious impulses—which are the strongest impulses that ever animate the breast of man—will not each sect do its utmost to establish its supremacy in all the schools? Will not the heats and animosities engendered in families, and among neighbors, burst forth with a devouring fire, in the primary, or district school meetings; and when the inflammable materials of all the district meetings are gathered together in the town meeting, what can quell or quench the flames, till the zealots, themselves, are consumed in the conflagration they have kindled? Why would not all those machinations and oppressions be restored to, in order to obtain the ascendancy, if religious proselytism should be legalized in the schools, which would be resorted to, as I have endeavored, in a preceding part of this report, to explain, if political proselytism were permitted in the schools? . . .

4. One other system—if it may be so called—is supposable; and this exhausts the number of those which stand in direct conflict with ours. It is this: Government might expressly disclaim and refuse all interference with the education of the young, abandoning the whole work to the hazards of private enterprise, or to parental will, ability, or caprice. . . .

If, then, a government would recognize and protect the rights of religious freedom, it must abstain from subjugating the capacities of its children to any legal standard of religious faith, with as great fidelity as it abstains from controlling the opinions of men. It must meet the unquestionable fact, that the old spirit of religious domination is adopting new measures to accomplish its work—measures, which, if successful, will be as fatal to the liberties of mankind, as those which were practiced in by-gone days of violence and terror. These new measures are aimed at children instead of men. They propose to supersede the necessity of subduing free thought, *in the mind of the adult, by forestalling* the development of any capacity of free thought, *in the mind of the child.*

TOWARD A NATIONWIDE
EDUCATIONAL POLICY

After reading Mann, it is a valuable contrast for the student to read the appeals of a contemporary educational reformer in order to witness the differences and similarities in the causes espoused. James Bryant Conant, a former president of Harvard University and the author of several highly respected books on American education (The American High School Today; The Comprehensive High School), *advocates the need for the development of a national educational policy. He describes the road to the establishment of such a policy and formulates seven premises for American education which would serve as a framework for an interstate commission working toward the development of this national policy. It is important to note that even though Mann was reiterating his conviction in the common school and outlining its goals, and Conant is concerned about the need for a coordinated national effort in education, both are in essence appealing for equality and excellence in educating all American youth. What other similarities and differences can the student detect in both selections?*

James Bryant Conant

Excerpt from "Nationwide Educational Policy," Shaping Educational Policy (New York: McGraw-Hill, 1964), pp. 121–131. Reprinted by permission of the copyright owner, A Study of American Education, Princeton, N.J.

In general I am convinced that educational systems cannot be exported or imported either as a whole or in part. Nevertheless I cannot help raising the question whether we do not need in the United States to create some sort of organization which will have the confidence of the state governments on the one hand, and on the other can bring to a focus a discussion of the important topics in education. Indeed I would hope there would be eventually not only a discussion but interstate cooperation.

An initial step along such a road was taken in 1949 with the establishment by sixteen states of the Southern Regional Education Board. Later (in 1953) came the formation of the Western Interstate Commission for Higher Education (thirteen states) and still later the New England Board of Higher Education (six states). Two of these regional boards or commissions are based on formal interstate compacts approved by Congress. Originally it was planned to have the Southern Regional Board also based on an interstate compact approved by Congress, but the idea was abandoned and its status is now that of an interstate agreement. All three agencies now embrace thirty-five states, leaving only twelve Midwestern states, in addition to New York, New Jersey, and Pennsylvania, outside any regional compact. A resolution urging the exploration of proposals for an interstate compact was adopted in 1954 by the Midwestern Regional Conference of the Council of State Governments. But in 1955 the committee reported against the proposal. Three years later eleven of the leading universities in the same area (including two private universities) formed the private voluntary organization known as the Committee on Institutional Cooperation. The chief purpose of this committee is to "improve the educational and public services offered by its member institutions while minimizing the cost of these services by fostering cooperation in instruction and research, particularly at the graduate level."

Clearly, both organizations created by agreement only and by interstate compact have a wider aim than can be possible for the association

of a small group of universities. Indeed, one of the prime motives for the
formation of these regional interstate planning commissions was the idea
of improving and increasing educational opportunities for all the youth
in the states involved. This it is hoped will be accomplished by the establishment of coordinated educational programs. As one person has well
said, "We believed that we could better meet some of the problems in
higher education by cooperation between the states rather than by competition."

The boards created by these interstate compacts are in theory at
least regional planning agencies for higher education. None, I believe,
has any authority or control over state activities or other educational institutions. However, by gathering facts and figures and identifying problems, the members of the staff can acquaint educators, legislators, and
the public with the problems the region faces; expert consultants can
recommend solutions. What has been achieved has been through persuasion, since no authority by coercion is even implied in the arrangement.

An example provided by the New England Board is typical of the
good that may be accomplished in this manner. Facts made available to
a university president in one state made it possible for him to withstand
local pressures to establish a new program in a specialized area. He
could point out that a similar program in the university in another state
was already well developed and available. The objective is to prevent
(by persuasion) a proliferation of programs and curricula when the
needs of the region do not require them. The New England Board endeavors to bring into conferences legislative leaders as well as governors,
budget officers, and educators to discuss programs throughout the area.

The work of these interstate boards is clearly only in its first stages,
but the results, at least in some cases, show much promise. At the post-
high-school level, where state differences are so great, at least some coordination of the diverse interests in a region may be possible. It is interesting to note that in all these interstate activities the emphasis is on
education beyond the high school—indeed in most instances exclusively
in this area. The reasons are evident. The forces I have already referred
to have produced a considerable degree of uniformity in the schools. Out
of this uniformity within each state has come a belief that the financing
of the schools, in contrast to the state colleges and universities, was
largely a matter of teachers' salaries. And the teachers' organizations
have operated to reinforce this idea. The consequence has been that at
least until recently there has appeared to be no reason for any official arrangement for the exchange of information about school problems and
school finances between the states.

The states that have entered into these interstate compacts have certainly taken important steps in the direction of a rational approach to

our educational problems. But one is still bound to ask: Are these regional pacts enough? They are excellent in principle and could be most effective in operation, but why only regional agreements? Why not a new venture in cooperative federalism? Why not a compact between *all* the states?

To be quite specific, let me be bold and make a suggestion for a possible way by which the road to the development of a nationwide educational policy might be opened up. *Let the fifty states, or at least fifteen to twenty of the more populous states, enter into a compact for the creation of an "Interstate Commission for Planning a Nationwide Educational Policy."* The compact would have to be drawn up by the states and approved by Congress. The document would provide for the membership of the commission and provide the guidelines for its operation. Each state would be represented, though a group of less populous states might decide to be represented by one person. Each state would be ready to listen to any conclusions of the commission but, of course, would not be bound to follow its recommendations.

Since such an interstate commission would be concerned with the drawing up of plans, *not* with administration, I see no constitutional or legal reason against a state legislature authorizing one or more persons to participate in it. Nor do I see any obstacles to a legislature expressing its willingness to examine any reports coming from such a group. The matter of finances might raise issues. It might be difficult to get any considerable number of state legislatures to appropriate the money; but I hope not, for if it were proposed that the Congress of the United States do so, certainly the cry of states' rights might be raised. Yet I would hope the commission would invite the chief United States school officer, the Commissioner of Education, as well as other Federal officials to attend each conference.

The whole commission, of course, would meet only from time to time. The real work would be done by special committees appointed by the commission, which might be called working parties. I suggest as a motto for all the working parties: "More facts, fewer slogans." And to get the facts and set them forth clearly on a state-by-state basis is a task, I submit, that has not yet been performed. For example, an interesting study published by the National Science Foundation (*The Duration of Formal Education for High Ability Youth*, NSF 61—36) indicates that on a national basis an alarmingly small percentage of able boys and girls go on to education in college and finish college. The study was preliminary and the statistics were obtained on a sampling basis. What is badly needed is more adequate data state by state. Such information would be basic to the work of *all* the working parties. In some states the most pressing need in terms of recruiting the academically talented students for the professions is to insure that more of this group finish high school and at least enter college. Throughout the preceding pages I have mentioned our lack of statistical information about the education of professional people state by state and their subsequent employment. We also lack in any one document a collection of the facts about scholarships and loans and the location of centers for study beyond the A.B. degree in relation to the distribution of the population. The increasing costs of education underlines the importance of providing undergraduate and graduate education within commuting distance of home for as many young people as possible. There seems no doubt that the proximity of institutions of higher education is a factor in determining the level of college and university attendance. Some of the information needed, particularly about the impact of Federal spending, would be made available to the commission as a whole at first and used by the separate working parties as might be needed.

I am well aware there is no novelty in suggesting the appointment of a national body to plan for the future of American education. It is a time-honored scheme to have the President of the United States appoint a commission of educators and well-known laymen. This was done by President Hoover in 1930. His committee was charged as follows: "In view of the considerable differences of opinion as to policies which should be pursued by the Federal government with respect to education, I have appointed a committee representative of the important educational associations and others to investigate and present recommendations" (Annual Message to Congress, December 3, 1929).

The committee was chaired by the Secretary of the Interior, Ray Lyman Wilbur, who was president of Stanford University on leave of absence. Three volumes of findings were published of which the last was entitled *Education in the States* and contained a wealth of statistical information. The recommendations, however, following the Presidential directive, were confined to action by the Federal government. It is ironical that the key recommendation, which found wide support among public school people then and now, has been blindly ignored by the national executive and Congress alike. The recommendation, in essence, was that no additional laws be passed "to grant federal financial aid to the States in support of special types of education."

The committee recognized that much good had been accomplished in the past by the special appropriations such as those for vocational education and to the land-grant colleges. Nevertheless they recommended that after a period of years all future grants of Federal money should be in "aid of education in general expendable by each state for any or all educational purposes as the state itself may direct." This was a statesmanlike but totally unrealistic recommendation, as the history of the next thirty years was to demonstrate. If accepted it would have blocked all efforts of reformers to use the power of Congress to appropriate money to promote the projects dear to their own hearts. Indeed, without the creation of some new coordinating political machinery, it would have so decentralized planning for education as to have made impossible many advances we now all praise. Nevertheless, as far as elementary and secondary education is concerned, I think the nation would have been better off if the views of the committee had prevailed. What became known as "general Federal aid for the public schools" was in line with the thinking of the members of Hoover's committee. The idea has been pushed for over thirty years by the NEA. There have been difficulties in deciding on what basis such general aid should be distributed to the states, but the chief opposition has come from the supporters of the church-connected elementary and secondary schools who wished to have their schools included. I have always been one of those strongly opposed to the use of taxpayers' money for private elementary and secondary schools (whether church-connected or not), because I believe it would lead to a fragmentation of our public schools as instruments for strengthening our democracy. The same argument does not apply to education beyond the high school, for our private colleges already enroll a large percentage of our youth. Furthermore, unlike the comprehensive high school, they have rarely set out to promote an understanding between cultural and economic groups within a local community.

Another Presidential committee was appointed by President Truman and still another by President Eisenhower. Both committees worked industriously and produced interesting, forward-looking documents, but one must use a microscope to find any evidence today of the effects of their recommendations. There exists in the statute books today authorization for the appointment of a national committee and there was recently introduced into Congress a bipartisan bill to authorize a "National Advisory Council on Education." Congressman Lindsay in speaking of the bill said, "We need to know what kind of educational programs are most vital to the welfare of America and most essential at this time." To which I venture to agree wholeheartedly and add we must know the programs in detail and how they can conceivably be implemented state by state. For example, the Congressman goes on to say that what the American people want to know are what kinds of priorities should be established among the many proposals requiring public funds—for example, youth employment, vocational education training, quality education, technical education, etc. Again I agree, but to me such priorities cannot be realistically determined except on a state-by-state basis. What Vermont has and what Vermont needs is very different in many areas from what California needs, which is different again from New Jersey. Therefore I suggest that Congress appoint first a National Advisory Committee to explore the workings of the present interstate compacts and to list the problems to be met. I am frank to say that I believe the report of such a preliminary survey would lead to the formation of the type of commission I have recommended based on an interstate compact.

I must admit that the record of national committees on education, however authorized and however appointed, is not such as to lead one to be optimistic about the results to be accomplished by still another committee. Yet the creation of a national commission which would be an interstate educational planning commission whose existence was the result of a compact between the states would be something quite new. It differs from schemes for appointing a Presidential or Congressional advisory commission in several respects. In the first place, because the commission would be an interstate commission, the reports of the working parties would be automatically concerned with state-by-state variations and would recognize the realities of the conditions in each state. In the second place, the recommendations would be directed to the state legislatures or state boards of education and would be considered by the state authorities because each state had been involved in the creation of the undertaking. In the third place, the magnitude and detailed nature of the financial demands required would be spelled out in such a way that Congress (through its own committees) and the Office of Education (through its own staff) could explore the significance of each item in terms of the function of the Federal governmental agencies.

Each working party would have to start with certain premises agreed upon by the commission. Within the framework thus established, the working party would be required first to make an exhaustive factual study of the structure state by state, second to come up with specific recommendations to the state authorities (the chief state school officer, the state school board, or the legislature). There might well be dissenting opinions on many points. The right to public dissent would be inherent in accepting an appointment on the working party. The more controversial the area, the more necessary would be such a provision.

Admittedly, in setting up any working party, the most difficult task for the interstate commission would be an agreement on what I have called the framework. And to let a working party loose in any controversial area without some guidelines would be to insure catastrophic failure at the onset. Certain premises could be agreed on without much difficulty. These would constitute part of the framework for all of the working parties. In my opinion, these premises might be formulated somewhat as follows:

1. It is assumed that our present form of government should be perpetuated; to that end all future citizens of the nation should receive an education that will prepare them to function as responsible members of a

free society, as intelligent voters and, if appointed or elected to public office, as honest reliable servants of the nation, state, or locality.

2. It is assumed that each state is committed to the proposition of providing free schooling to all the children in the state through twelve grades. (Though the Federal government has no power to proclaim the doctrine of free schools, practically the action of all the states during the last 100 years enables the interstate commission to declare that providing free public schooling is a nationwide policy of the United States.)

3. It is assumed that in every state the parents have a right to send their children to private schools, colleges, and universities instead of to the publicly supported institutions. This assumption follows from the interpretation of the Federal Constitution by the Supreme Court on more than one occasion.

4. It is assumed that each state *desires* to have all normal children in the state attend school at least five hours a day, 150 days a year, at least until they reach the age of 18, but that the states differ and will continue to differ in regard to the laws requiring school attendance and the way special provisions are provided for physically and mentally handicapped children.

5. It is assumed that each state accepts the responsibility of providing for the education of at least some of its youth beyond high school; the organization and financing of such education, however, differs and will continue to differ state by state; in each state opportunities for education beyond high school now includes at least one university chartered by the state and largely supported by public funds; the continuation of such universities as centers of research, advanced study, and above all, fearless free inquiry is essential to the welfare of the state and the nation.

6. It is assumed that the education provided in high school and beyond by public institutions is designed to develop the potentialities of all the youth to fit them for employment in a highly industrialized society.

7. The financing of education, including research and scholarly work in the universities, is a concern of private universities, the states, and the Federal government.

The declaration of some such set of premises by an interstate commission would be the first step in shaping a nationwide educational policy. If each state legislature would pass a resolution accepting such a declaration, we should for the first time as a nation be officially committed to certain basic principles of educational policy. We now assume these principles to be valid, but in fact they have never been promulgated by representative assemblies and could not be promulgated by the Congress.

After formulating the premises of American education (the framework, as I have called it), the commission would determine what subjects to explore and name the working parties. Then many months later the commission would reconvene to receive the reports of the working parties, discuss them, and pass them on with comment to the legislatures of all the states represented. The working committees should be what the name implies. Their composition should be such as to represent diverse views of experts, and unanimous reports would *not* be expected. The layman's criticism would best come, I should think, from the interstate planning commission, which I envisage as being made up of distinguished citizens of each state who are *not* educators (the sort of person one finds on boards of trustees of our most famous universities). An alternate scheme in which the working parties contained laymen as well as educators need not be excluded.

THE NINETEENTH CENTURY AMERICAN TEACHER: *Country Schoolmaster of Long Ago*

Change in culture is always confronted by society as a mixed blessing. There are those who would have us believe the "good old days" were golden and present day life is wracked by decadence. Thomas Woody (1891–1960), who was a professor of education at the University of Pennsylvania, believed this nostalgia is a common human affliction which has a special meaning to teachers when the remembrance is turned back to the little red schoolhouses of yesteryear and the teachers who "kept" school in them. This is a story based upon the recollections of a nineteenth century schoolmaster, as personally told to Professor Woody. In addition to vividly recounting memorable experiences in his teaching career, the old schoolmaster also tells about his own education as a child during the 1870s and 1880s.

Thomas Woody

"Country Schoolmaster of Long Ago," History of Education Journal, **5** (Winter 1954), 41–53, by permission of the editor. This journal is now entitled History of Education Quarterly.

Every generation has those who cry against its decadence. In one sense, and to a degree, they are always right: in life there is death; social growth entails destruction; but this is not the view of those who lament.

Growth and destruction, especially at times of marked acceleration, occasion emotional reactions—apprehension for the future, nostalgia for the past. This nostalgia is a common affliction of parents, newspaper editors, clerics, teachers—and occasionally students. Others experience attacks now and then, but they are less articulate.

Schools and teachers throughout the ages have been blamed for the evils of the new day, as though they created societies. In this respect, 1954 is not unlike fifth century Athens before the Christian era, and the last century of the Roman Republic. Names have changed, certainly: then it was philosophers and orators; today, it is scientists, and pedagogues who study their profession, who are blamed—for philosophers have retired from active duty, and orators are seldom heard.

Reflecting thus upon the nostalgic temper of modern prophets of pedagogical and social doom that awaits us, unless we return speedily to the good old days, the image of an old master and his school came to mind. The image is particular, the master real. The writer tells the story as he heard it. The general may dwell in the particular, but no effort is intended to draw it forth. If it should occur to any who come upon this fragment, however, that on balance they prefer the new school—learning without larruping; reading without tears—such occurrence may be put down to personal idiosyncrasy; and if others, at this glimpse of the old school, find their longing for the past enhanced, let them be nostalgic still.

D. S. Domer, who attended a far away class, should have published his own story, which he was persuaded to tell the writer. Since he did not find the opportunity, it is hoped that, though belatedly and much shortened, his desire may be partially realized; and, at the same time, remembrance may be kept of a master of the old school.

> It is now [1929] fifty-five years ago that I first entered the public schools of Pennsylvania, in the little village of Springville, now Florin. The experiences related of going to school in the early seventies and eighties, the trials of teaching, the methods, discipline, buildings, mode of recitation, the teachers who taught me, and other matters, are vivid memories and can be verified.[1]
>
> The village was mainly Pennsylvania Dutch, of whom I am a descendant. At the age of six I was scarcely able to speak a word of English. We lived about a block from the school. The building was an old moss-covered structure, built long before my entry. It was of brick and had three windows on each side and a door at one end. There were no cloak rooms, but a row of hooks to the right and left of the

[1] Mr. Domer showed me documents which he had preserved, to vouch for some of them.

door, where hats and coats were hung, often three deep. If one kept his own wearing apparel for the whole term, he was lucky.

The seats were plain pine board benches; the desks, of the same material, had plain tops, with backs raised about two inches above the top. Legs were two by four uprights, fastened to the floor. Two sat at each desk; a partition inside it was designed to keep books and materials of pupils separate. The floor was oak boards, split and rough hewn. Walls were partly wainscoting. The "blackboard" was painted on the walls; slate, just coming into use, was opposed as a too expensive luxury. The rest of the walls and the ceiling were plastered with a mixture of lime, sand and clay, and whitewashed about twice a year, at the beginning of the term in autumn and again at holidays. There were no blinds; but outside shutters, partly closed, kept out sun-glare; when entirely closed, to keep out cold and wind, the room was so dark, it was almost impossible to see to work, unless the oil lamps hanging on the wall were lit.

The school had forty or fifty pupils. The boys sat on one side of a wide aisle, the girls on the other. A platform ran across the front of the room. Long benches stood against the wall, where the class reciting was seated. The teacher usually turned his back to the recitation he was hearing; it was not safe to turn his back to the rest of the school, for some culprit would try "heathen tricks" on him; and if he went to the other end of the room, the reciting class would make trouble. Teaching by moral influence had not yet superseded the hickory rod.

Little pedagogy and less psychology were used. A recitation— geography, for example, covering the United States, its location, extent, and development—was conducted as follows: the lesson was assigned; questions, numbering often twenty or thirty, came at the end of the chapter. If the class had ten pupils, it was easy for us to learn the lesson. The pupil at the head of the class learned No. 1, the next one No. 2, and so on to the tenth; the first then studies No. 11, and so on through the entire list. Each had his question and answer well studied, and a perfect recitation could be recorded. It seems not to have occurred to the teacher to vary the order of the recitation. Routine dominated method; it went over big, it was easiest for teacher and pupil alike; it was followed in all subjects having questions and answers. That was the day of formal teaching, variations were avoided, originality was frowned upon. Promiscuous asking of questions was taboo; the child had no right to think; he was to do just what the teacher said.

In a school where 31 classes were heard in about 300 minutes— an average of about 10 minutes to a class—little more could be expected than a rapid question and answer method. The same routine obtained in all classes. In arithmetic the pupil solved his problem, read it from the board, was excused, another was called on, and so on to the end; a new lesson was assigned, and the class was dismissed, either by taps on a bell or counting one, two, three—stand, pass, sit. Seldom did the teacher explain the lesson; his object was to get through the day and cover all the ground. This continued throughout the year; at the end of six months we had often "gone through" the book twice. In one term we even "went through" the same book three times.

Until I was fifteen, while I was at this type of school, I had "gone through" my grammar, arithmetic, geography, speller, and the rest, a dozen times or more. There were no "grades" or "promotions" then. You were placed by the book you were reading. In my first three years I had completed my Third Reader; at twelve or thirteen I reached the Fifth and Sixth. We used Sander's, McGuffey's and Swinton's readers; Appleton's were more difficult, and I read the Fifth Reader several years. Tests or examinations were never held. If we did what was in the book, it was a mark of perfect scholarship, and that was all that was required.

When eight years old, I was afflicted with a malady which crippled me badly, so I could not play games, or move rapidly. It grew worse; I had to use crutches; for seven years there seemed no prospect of recovery, and I was threatened with spinal paralysis. Finally, after much deliberation and opposition, an operation at Jefferson Hospital saved me from the blighting effects of deformity, and enabled me to carry on my profession, though always incapacitated for physical labor.

Due to poverty, I was compelled to learn some trade; and my illness dictated that it should be something I could do with my hands while my body remained quiet. My cousin, A. B. Kreider, was both teacher and cigar-maker—which was not contrary to the ethics of that time. After long consultation with my mother, it was decided I should become his ward, attend his school, and learn cigar-making at the same time. I began the trade in the Spring of 1884, and entered his school that Fall. I worked morning, noon, and night, attending school from 9 to 12 and 1 to 4. After supper I applied myself to my books by the kitchen stove, with the aid of a kerosene lamp, often till one and two o'clock next morning. Summers, I spent the day in the shop, and read at night, chiefly history, for my benefactor had a good library for that time. Thus I was occupied from 1884 to 1888.

It was at Salunga Public School, under the solicitous teaching of my cousin, that I prepared, during the winter of 1887–1888, to become a teacher. I remained in his school till I was twenty. For three months I went to night school. In day school I studied the common branches; at night school, I read and recited pedagogy and several advanced studies. After school closed in March, I was tutored for my first county teachers examination, which came in June, 1888.[2]

On my way to the examination I met the County Superintendent, M. J. Brecht. We walked a half mile together from the train, and I have no doubt I won his sympathy, which may have stood me in good stead. There were then no uniform State examinations. The County Superintendent, chosen by the trustees of the school districts, was the sole authority. At nine o'clock, the mill began to grind—operated by one-man power, the Superintendent. The first subject was arithmetic. The Superintendent read a set of questions, prepared in advance in his office or propounded extemporaneously. About 40 minutes were allowed to solve them. There were problems in mental arithmetic, to be solved on the spot, and on one's feet. Sometimes only the method of solution was called for. When each candidate finished one examination, his papers were taken up, read, and graded then and there by the official. All the nine common branches were treated the same way during the day.

At last the end approached. At four o'clock we would know our fate. If one passed, his name was called, and a certificate was handed him. If he failed, his named was not called, which saved some embarrassment. The subjects were rated 1, very good; 2, good; 3, middling.[3] If the sum total were more than 24, no certificate could be issued. Per cent grades were not then popularized in Lancaster County. Later, when I followed Greeley's advice and went West, my Ohio certificate, issued in 1891, used per cents. My total the first time was 23¾. If I had added a quarter to my total, my hopes would have received a rude shock; but I lowered my integers and raised my standard enough so that I was on the road I longed to travel. I still treasure my first three certificates.

Thus armed, I was ready, whether "qualified" or not, to enter upon the noblest work of man. The preparation I then had at the age of twenty might now be matched by a pupil in Junior High School. My first school was a man's job—64 pupils, ranging from 6 to 20, more than half being under 10 years of age—but I set to work with serious intent to apply my little store of pedagogy and psychology.

Getting my first school proved to be an experience never to be forgotten. After receiving a certificate, one looked for a school—unless it had been promised earlier on condition of passing. I had no such

[2] Mr. Domer's memory slipped here; his first certificate shows May.

[3] Mr. Domer's memory varied from the documents later shown me, which are followed here.

promise, but the County Superintendent suggested several places to look up. I selected one and notified the Board I would present myself.

A word on the administration of common schools may be useful. Lancaster County had township organization. The township I first taught in had forty districts, all under the direction of six school trustees, chosen annually. Each trustee had an area, or number of schools under his oversight, and he reported to the Board each month. At such meetings the trustees also examined teachers' reports and paid their salaries. The Board could be quite autocratic, might disregard even the suggestions of the County Superintendent, for he himself held office at their pleasure.

The Board I approached wanted a "man" teacher. They met on a Saturday in August (1888), 20 days before the beginning of school, to hire the teacher. These six representatives of the community were indeed an august body—but their names are all forgotten now, save those of the president and one other. It was with some trepidation that I came before this body, for they met in the back end of a barroom in the village of Schoeneck. As I entered the room, I met the gaze, the inspection, and then the quiz of these patriarchs of education.

I had applied in writing for a school a short way from the village, and the application was filed here with others. When I was seated at one end of the long table around which the Board sat, I was asked by the chairman whether I believed in the "three R's"; but he, to relieve me of any fear, at once assured me they stood for "Radcliffe's Ready Relief." Of course, they had already read the applications and had really decided by a previous vote to let me have the school at the munificent salary of $28.00 [4] a month for a term of six months. I was to be my own janitor, sweep out, and keep fires going. But before I was to sign the contract, a surprise awaited me.

"Mr. Domer," the President began, "we have decided to give you the M—— School, and we think you are all right. Now since one good turn deserves another, we think you ought to set up the drinks to us for the favor; so if you want to sign the contract, go and bring a bottle of whiskey and six glasses for us, and we will then close the deal." The Almighty was witness to such an act, no doubt. With disgust and dejection I acted on the suggestion of the venerable President of the Board. That a body of men could be so enslaved to drinking on all occasions, and to bind a contract by treating a set of men in the deal, was indeed dumbfounding to me, an incident in my young life that I can never erase. For I had been under the tutelage of a radical prohi-

[4] The County Superintendent rated teachers "1 plus, 1, 1—, 2 plus, 2, and 2—." From "2—" up each grade meant a $5.00 raise. I was raised to $33.00 the second year, and received $40.00 the third.

bitionist, and had signed the temperance pledge on the sixth of May, 1886, which I have kept all these years.

Nevertheless, I turned on my heel and went to the barroom; there, across the bar were handed me a bottle and six small glasses. Returning to the room with the loaded tray, I placed it on the table in front of the President of the Board. He acted as host to the rest of them, poured six glasses full, passed one to each of the members, and all drank to my success as a teacher, swallowing all at one gulp, without even a twitch of the mouth, so habituated to liquor were these men. When they had all drunk, I took the tray-load back to the bartender, who took my word for it that only six glasses full were used. I paid him 60 cents for the drinks, the price of my contract. When I returned, they told me I was a good sport, and could now sign the contract, as they had already done. Seating myself next to the clerk of the Board, I attached my signature. Many reflections have come and gone since I traded six glasses of whiskey for a teacher's contract. Nothing like it has happened to me from that day to this. Whether it happened so to other young men who sought positions, I do not know. The moral effect on me was profound. Raised in a home which was opposed to strong drink of any kind, and tutored by a man who was a leader in the anti-whiskey forces, I felt I had done wrong; but as I was not a professing Christian at the time, and I was anxious to get a school, I soon cleared my conscience and started on the first Monday in September to teach school.

I chose a place to room and board a few days in advance of opening school. It was about ¾ of a mile away, and I covered the distance, walking, or catching a ride when possible. In sloppy weather I wore high top rubber boots, changed to shoes at school, and wore the boots home in the evening. Board, room, and washing cost $10.00 a month.[5] It was an old-fashioned farm home, and one lived with the family. There was plenty to eat, a good bed (a wooden bedstead, rope springs, straw mattress, feather ticks, and blankets), and woven carpets on the floor. Wood and an old-fashioned cookstove furnished heat for kitchen, dining room, and all the rest of the house, upstairs and down. Hot water was provided by a tea kettle and a reservoir in the stove itself.

I went to the schoolhouse alone the Saturday before school began. The building, located on an acre for a playground, was not significantly different from the one where I first went to school. It was of brick, dirt cheap, burned in a nearby kiln for the purpose. Aesthetics

[5] The salary of $28.00 was really far more than it seems now, for prices were low; a suit cost $8.00 to $10.00; hat $1.00 to $1.50; shoes, made to order, $4.50 to $5.00.

had not yet taken root among patrons, trustees, or teachers. The inside was as dull as a leaden sky in December, save as it was sometimes brightened by leaves in autumn, or some pictures could be borrowed from the pupils' homes. The desks were a little better than I had first used at school, but single seats had not yet appeared. The double-seated desks were a source of trouble: they induced whispering, idle mischief, neglect and dishonesty in studies; books got mixed up, articles were stolen, and property destroyed. I counted the seats, made up a tentative programme, set the clock, put shoe mats in place, had two water buckets (one for waste, for there was no drain) and two tin cups ready for thirsty children. Sanitary rules were then unknown in country districts, and often in small towns, too. Water was brought from the nearest farmer's well. With 60 children, a bucket full would not last long. Sometimes trustees paid a monthly tax to the farmer for the water used at school. Toilets were outdoors, and exposed to public view. A partition separated boys and girls. Obscenity was bound to result from such conditions. More than one problem arose from this source to confront me in my early teaching.

Monday, the first day of school, came. It was with no little emotion that I faced a small army of motley-dressed boys and girls. They had arranged themselves in two rows of about equal length along the pathway, and I had to run the gauntlet of inspection. No sooner was the door opened than a rush for seats was made; for it was customary there, that the first arrivals should have the choice of seats. One can imagine the tumult: about 60 pupils, six to twenty, dashing through the door before I could say "Stop!" Such a scramble meant that half the seats were unsuitable to those who first claimed them, so teacher's job, and a lot of trouble it was, too, loomed before him. But with a show of being master, after an hour's work the "seating" of the school was completed, the small ones up front, the rest, according to size, reaching back to the rear.

Classifying pupils was the next task that taxed my ingenuity. I had them write their names, if they could, and the Reader they were "in" at the previous school term. This showed me at once who were the writers. Some who could not write, printed their names. The beginners were interviewed personally, to get their names. These would be the A B C class. Placing the others was more difficult. Some brought an advanced Reader, but could not read it at all, when put to the test. The promotions and demotions made some parents glad and others mad; mothers came and wanted their children changed. I made enemies the first day. I was obdurate; I was running the school, and I would not change pupils unless I was convinced they could do the work that was assigned them. I handled some cases by calling the pupils to read in the presence of their parents, who could then see and hear the child could not read, or do the other work of the class they had wanted to enter. The oldest pupils, whose records I could learn from the register left by my predecessor, I simply directed to the programme placed earlier on the blackboard.

The programme went like this: I opened with Bible reading, repeating the Lord's prayer, and singing a familiar song. Then came, first, the beginners; then arithmetic; reading classes; grammar, elementary and advanced; geography; history; physiology; and finally three or four spelling classes. The beginners recited three or four times a day; altogether thirty-three classes were heard in about 310 minutes, an average of less than 10 minutes to each.

Rules, all of which I thought very necessary at the time, were posted in a conspicuous place for the observation of all. Among them were: no whispering, sharpening pencils, throwing stones, name-calling. They were to raise their hands when anything was wanted; they were to stand, pass, and be seated, as I counted one, two, three, or tapped a small bell. All seemed sensible then, but they appear nonsensical now. The most ridiculous rule I made was that no German should be spoken on the playground at recess; and no swearing, either in German or English, would be permitted. My intentions were good, I tried to enforce the rules I made; but my pedagogy was bad, I went at teaching character the wrong way. I soon saw my entire code was out of place, and I learned to put children on their honor more and more, charging them with only two things: Do right; and make life worth while. These I tried to exemplify before them. But the public moral atmosphere was very much lower then than it is today. Children's conduct was not so well looked after as it is now; and pupils were not so independent and self-reliant as they are today.

The school classified, programme and rules posted, I was ready to teach. One of my first difficult problems was due to the community, which was Pennsylvania Dutch. More than half the children were unable to speak a word of English, and did not understand them even when they read English words. How could it be otherwise? They spoke Dutch or German at home; and all the religion they knew was in German. Doubtless many a Pennsylvania German felt as did the old man who insisted, *Der Herr Gott war ja Deitsch*—The Lord God was indeed German. To the beginners, then, I was the interpreter of a foreign tongue, not just a teacher of written forms for a language already known by daily use. I devised my own method. As I happened to be a good artist, I would draw pictures on the "board"—a hat, a fly, a moth, a ball, a knife, etc., write the Pennsylvania Dutch names shouted by the pupils (they seemed to like the pictures) and then the

English terms. Thus I helped each one to the English for various objects, increasing their vocabulary.[6]

As for other teaching, I followed a method my mother had used forty years earlier, the same by which I had myself been taught. We memorized the alphabet and the abs—combining all the vowels with the twenty-two consonants, thus: ab, eb, ob, ub; ac, ec, ic, oc, uc; ad, ed, id, od, ud; and so on through the alphabet. However nonsensical it may seem now, it was then considered a splendid method, and was exhibited on the pages of many a textbook. This was formal discipline with a vengeance; if a child could remember this, he could very well remember a lesson in spelling, reading, history, or any other fundamental subject. As a good method, it had the stamp of approval of the County Superintendent and other pedagogical leaders of the day, though it seems "devilish" to critics now.

When ab, eb, ec, and so on had been learned, pupils went to the First Reader, and learned to use words in sentences. The name of the letter was essential then. When "A" was put on the "board" it meant "A," and not another sound. O, Y, T meant O, Y, and T. If a child saw T O Y on the board, he spelled it out, naming the letters, and then pronounced the word. Phonics were unknown; if we had tried to introduce such "tomfoolery," it would have brought the wrath of parents on our heads. In every word he built, the pupil must know the letters; no one was allowed to read unless he knew his letters forward, backward, and crosswise. Reading was not dramatized, one read to increase vocabulary, and to see who could read farthest without a mistake, noticing all the *marks*.

In geography the question and answer method was thought the best. Map study was an art. Every town, city, river, mountain peak, bay, gulf, lake, island, straight, isthmus, peninsula, and sea were hunted up. It was a contest in acquiring information. "Trapping" was a game in every class; the one who could stand at the head of the class longest was the best scholar. History was a matter of chronology, as many old textbooks show. Arithmetic was extremely formal; the one who got the answers to the most problems was the best mathematician. I myself committed almost all the problems of a Mental Arithmetic to memory, together with the answers for each. It was a feat to be proud of! It was a day of memorizing; not much reasoning was sought or developed.

[6] Mr. Domer seems not to have known Sander's *Bilder Fibel*. This book (1846) showed pictures, gave German and English in parallel columns and pages, and thus facilitated transition from the tongue of family and community to the idiom of the school room. It was to be an introduction to Sander's First Reader.

Grammar was chiefly the committing of the parts of speech, conjugations, and paradigms to memory. We went through the modes and tenses of every regular and irregular verb. Parsing and diagramming were a mental acrobatic stunt. It was pure memory drill. Writing compositions was a Friday afternoon exercise, not a regular curriculum subject. It was chiefly to increase vocabulary, not for literary value. No one thought of having children read good books, tell stories, write narratives, or descriptions, or dramatize a scene from life. Such things, if tried, would have been criticised violently and reported to the School Board as proof of a lack of sense and the qualifications of a good teacher. Children went to school to "learn," not to be entertained.

Penmanship was simply drill in following a copy. Each pupil had a Spencerian copybook, or the teacher wrote a "copy" to follow—often a very fine model, expressing good moral precepts to be followed in later life. The Palmer system came into use later, then the vertical system—and a ruinous system it was. Finally there came scales to measure the quality of writing.

Thus my first three years were spent practicing what I thought was common sense in teaching, committing the rules of grammar, the rules of arithmetic and of spelling, and the location of every mountain and molehill in the United States to memory. I knew little or nothing of principles of pedagogy or laws of psychology, except the little gained from reading a few books. While pedagogy classes were offered in Normal School, I had not attended such an institution before beginning to teach. Hence my knowledge was extremely limited. I passed from the rural school to the small town school, where "grades," "method," and "psychological teaching" were unknown. It was just a question of the smartest pupil going on to higher classes as fast as he could make them.

Discipline was a large part of the old school. No other phase of teaching has undergone such a thorough change. Discipline, when I began teaching, depended more on physical strength, the ability and the will to give punishment, than any other thing. One of the first questions I was asked upon applying for the school, was whether I believed in "licking," and whether I was afraid of the boys in school. A negative answer to the first question, or an affirmative answer to the second, would have ended my career then and there.

The kind of school one had was a reflection of the government and discipline he employed. In my own school days it was not uncommon to see a large bundle of "hickories" behind the teacher's desk, ready for use. I can not even estimate the number of punishments I received with the "rod"; but I can well remember some of them, administered by a strong arm, justly or unjustly. It was not uncommon forty or fifty years ago for a master to wear out a heavy "hickory" on an obstreperous boy, or even a girl, as I have seen. I vividly recall one occasion, a real fight between a teacher and a pupil, resulting from the teacher's attempting to thrash a large boy. Teacher and pupil both "went to the mat," and fought from the desk to the door, while smaller children crouched in fright under seats, or ran to the older ones for protection. The teacher came out second best, with bruised face, torn clothes, while the bully walked out of the room with an oath on his lips. Nothing was done to either pupil or teacher; it was purely a matter of discipline; if the teacher could not "handle" the boys, he must resign; and if a boy did not like the teacher's rule he could take a licking or leave school. But sometimes he did neither. This particular young ruffian never came back to school.

As for my own school, much of my time was spent showing boys, and girls too, how strong I was, and what feats of strength I could perform. It was a day of weight-lifting. I became adept at lifting with my arms and gripping with teeth and hands. It was no small trick to place a twenty-five pound bag of shot on my left shoulder, and then reach my right hand over my head and lift the weight single handed to the right shoulder. I moved the big stove around the school room, held pupils in or out of the room by bracing myself against them in the doorway; let the pupils hang on my arm, extended against the wall; had pupils strike my chest; lifted heavy objects on the school grounds, and did feats of strength at neighborhood gatherings, such as lifting bags of wheat with my teeth, and wheeling heavy loads in a wheelbarrow. These I did when "living round" with patrons of a district.

By such demonstrations I showed I would be physically able to punish boys as old and big as I was, and the girls too, for they were sometimes hard to keep obedient to the rules laid down. It was sometimes necessary to demonstrate competence. I did not hold to the notion that it was always necessary to thrash pupils to make them mind, but it was sometimes necessary, seemed a fairly effective remedy, and, in fact, was mandatory from headquarters. Several teachers had been run out before I came. Laws governing conduct of pupils in the late eighties, save by such means as have been named, were not thought of, and the teacher had to be a law unto himself when emergencies demanded quick action.

The last school I taught in Pennsylvania was chiefly of boys, and they were hard to handle. Coming, as they did, from a community that had little culture, and composed mostly of pioneers and sons of first and second generations, it was necessary for me to do more fighting and to use more physical punishments in this school than I had in the two years before. Some boys came from homes of veriest ruffians. Belligerent and rebellious towards school discipline, I could not have dared to show the white feather. They would not hesitate to "double team" the teacher, as they had the year before. But I was on guard. With vigilant eye, I was constantly on watch for any concerted action of these fellows.

One day, towards the middle of the term, I saw a move was on foot to play horse with me in a spelling class. Every word that came to a group of boys was misspelled; after the second round, I pronounced the same word to the same boys, and they all misspelled it again. I then told them that if they missed another word during that recitation, I would thrash every one of them individually. I meant what I said, I placed a large "gad" where I could reach it, and I put the stovepoker next to it, to let them know that I would be boss, even if I had to kill some of them. Things moved along very quietly after that, and I finished the term "to the satisfaction of the trustees."

But I could not reconcile myself to such teaching, where one had to declare war on incorrigibles. Patrons offered to make up five dollars extra pay, over the regular salary of forty dollars; but I had "Western fever," and turned down all inducements. I exercised such discipline for three years in the public schools of Pennsylvania, never lacking the courage to put it into execution when needed. But times have now changed; no more does a teacher have to be a branch of the War Department to teach successfully.

THE TWENTIETH CENTURY AMERICAN
TEACHER: *Busy as a Classroom Teacher*

What is it really like to be a teacher? This is a frequent question asked by prospective teachers. To answer, a close-up of the life of a successful teacher is presented by Jane Priwer, a correspondent for the London Times Educational Supplement. *In this vividly written article the author acquaints the reader with Mrs. Ellern, a sixth-grade teacher in the Vogt School in Ferguson, Missouri. The author describes in detail how Mrs. Ellern creates a favorable classroom environment and how she helps her students become interested in and responsible for their own learning. In order to give a composite picture of Mrs. Ellern, her family life and professional activities are also related. The student may find it valuable to compare her modern teaching techniques with those used in Mr. Domer's time, described in the previous selection. What other changes have occurred in the teaching process since the nineteenth century? What are some of the educational, sociological, and psychological assumptions underlying these changes?*

Jane Priwer

> *"Busy as a Classroom Teacher!,"* NEA Journal (*March 1959*), 29–32. *Reprinted by permission of the publisher.*

The atmosphere in Room 207 of Vogt School is tense. The sixth-grade class meeting has reached an impasse from which, it seems, only Sam Rayburn himself could extricate it. There are three motions on the floor at once, and no one wants to withdraw any of them. The class president, Wayne, is worried, and Judy, the secretary, is pink and a little flustered. Gene, the sergeant-at-arms, has a wary eye cocked for incipient disorder.

At this point, a slight person in a pink dress raises her hand and is recognized.

"People," she asks quietly, "do you know how to get yourselves out of this awkward situation you're in?"

The speaker is Edna Linn Ellern, dark-haired, attractive, married, the mother of two teen-agers, and sixth-grade elementary-school teacher. The skill with which she unties the procedural knot, drawing on *Robert's Rules of Order* as well as on experience in a half-dozen civic groups, typifies all of Mrs. Ellern's activities as a teacher. An unusual, highly individual person, Mrs. Ellern represents, in the intelligence and enthusiasm she devotes to her work, the best ideas of her chosen profession.

What makes a good teacher? The heart of the matter must surely be found in the classroom.

Room 207 is probably not the neatest of the 13 classrooms in the Vogt School in Ferguson, Missouri. Mrs. Ellern's classroom is too well stocked for strict order. There are two wall-size bulletin boards, one covered with newspaper clippings and the other gay with pictures and charts triumphantly labeled in Spanish.

Under the tall windows three bookcases hold encyclopedias, *National Geographic Magazines,* and a lending library collected and managed by the children. A large Webster's dictionary is used under the supervision of a boy called Ron, who must explain not only the subtle difference in meaning between words like *imminent* and *impending,* but their different derivations also.

Maps, a globe, a chess set for rainy days, and a typewriter, which the children are learning to use, complete the décor—that is, except for the 28 sixth-graders of assorted sizes and shapes. If they are more alert-looking than most, it is not surprising, for they belong to the 15%–20% of the nation's children who are academically talented.

Two years ago, to the great credit of Superintendent V. C. McCluer and his staff, this hard-pressed suburban school district north of St. Louis decided to set up an enrichment program for its brightest grade-school children. There are four rapid-learning classes; all four (two sixth- and two seventh-grade rooms) are at Vogt School. Mrs. Ellern was selected to teach one of these groups.

The atmosphere in Mrs. Ellern's classroom is that of an intellectual voyage of discovery, with an inspiring captain and no reluctant crew members. Strict standards of cooperation and courtesy are observed. Here are 28 bright, articulate, naturally competitive youngsters working, often for the first time, with children of similar intelligence.

They are learning the give-and-take of constructive criticism. No one is criticized for a petty error. No one, least of all the teacher, minds admitting a mistake. Keen critical faculties are used, not to make hamburger of rivals, but to raise group standards.

No one on this voyage gets bored. Mrs. Ellern is a flexible, imaginative teacher, varying projects within a carefully planned, long-range framework. One day art may be emphasized, as the children mould Halloween papier-mâché masks over giant balloons. Another time music is stressed.

Before every concert given by the St. Louis Symphony Orchestra for elementary-school children, Mrs. Ellern draws on her wide musical background and superb record collection to give the children insight into the music which they will hear.

Mrs. Ellern loves to enliven the standard sixth-grade study of Latin America. Recently she invited both sixth-grade rapid-learning classes to an illustrated lecture on South America at the St. Louis County Library. It was a nasty January evening, but 46 of 56 children attended—a tribute to the teachers and to the interested parents who chauffeured their offspring.

In January, the Cuban revolution was thoroughly studied via press clippings. The class became almost convinced that Señor Castro had engineered the uprising purposely to illustrate their study of Cuba. For days, fathers nursed mutilated newspapers, while their children discussed every phase of the revolt.

Science projects of this class have included a study of weather and of elementary geology.

During reading class, Mrs. Ellern uses the basic reader, but supplements it with three other texts and numerous classics. Drill books are replaced by class discussion, dramatizations, and written essays and summaries of the material.

Additional writing work may include "tall tales" or other stories written by the children as part of creative-writing lessons given over KSLH, the radio station operated by the St. Louis Board of Education. Each child writes five book reports a term, of which only one may be on a work of fiction.

All this writing adds to a grading load which occupies Mrs. Ellern at least an hour every night and three or four hours on week ends. The children's homework load, on the other hand, is not oppressively heavy. Mrs. Ellern does not believe that enrichment is "more of the same old stuff," as her pupils might put it. Against the usual laws of probability, Mrs. Ellern's pupils have been known to do extra work for fun!

While varied and interesting, the material used in Mrs. Ellern's classes is always appropriate for 11-year-old minds. A sound knowledge of the theory of thrust in flight comes before the latest wrinkle about the newest jet.

Nor do her pupils indulge in rocketry or send formulas for new solid fuels to Washington. Her husband, in his position as a research director for the Armament Division of Universal Match Corporation in Ferguson, receives so many letters from schoolboy rocketeers that he has composed a form letter saying, in effect, "Before you blow your heads off with rockets, study physics and chemistry!" This philosophy has been passed on by Mrs. Ellern to her classes.

Dr. Ellern, incidentally, is more interested in his wife's work than he is likely to admit. Educated in the German style, with a doctorate in inorganic chemistry from the Friedrich Wilhelm University in Germany, he acts as his wife's educational encyclopedia and presents her with all the best books on education, picked up on his frequent trips to Washington and other points of the compass.

Dr. Ellern is just completing a book on military pyrotechnics. This project filled many of his week ends and vacation periods during the last three years. All it needs now, he states wryly, is an enterprising publisher.

Mrs. Ellern puts to use in her classroom ideas for enrichment gleaned from books and from magazines like the *Scientific American.* In addition, many of her best ideas for handling bright children have come from 17 years of experience in providing an enrichment program for her son, James, who entered the University of Illinois last fall with advanced placement in chemistry and rhetoric. In his senior year at Ferguson High, Jim was not only graduated as valedictorian in a class of over 300, but won the American Chemical Society prize over all St. Louis-area high-school students and placed in percentile 99 of the National Merit Scholarship Qualifying Tests.

Soon after his sixth birthday, Jim was doing experiments in chemistry on the kitchen table. Believing in a well-rounded development for all children, Mrs. Ellern has encouraged him not only in his scientific bent, but also in activities such as wrestling, scouting, and debating, in all of which he has done well.

Mrs. Ellern's feelings about the importance of enrichment may be partly due to early, and not too happy, experience with acceleration. Double promoted twice in the grades, she attended grade-school graduation in knee socks—a diminutive 12-year-old among sophisticated maidens of 14.

Graduating from Harris Teachers College, St. Louis, as one of a bright group with little funds, calling themselves "the Brain Trust," her first teaching post was at the St. Louis Training School, which in those depression days was being staffed by new Harris graduates at 75% of base pay.

After their marriage in 1938, Mr. and Mrs. Ellern lived in Baltimore and Los Angeles. When they settled again in Ferguson, Mrs. Ellern devoted herself to a young family and to groups like the League of Women Voters, the PTA, and the Unitarian Church.

Many friends made at that time have since become active in the school-oriented citizens groups which are an encouraging part of the educational picture in the St. Louis area. Accordingly, after returning to full-time teaching in 1954, Mrs. Ellern often found herself acting as unofficial liaison between the schools and school-minded lay people.

She takes particular pains to champion the rapid-learning program, knowing that in some areas these projects have failed not so much in the classrooms as in the community, through jealousy, misunderstanding, and the habit some parents have of beating one another over the head with their children's intelligence quotients.

The daily schedule of Edna Ellern, teacher, would be considered strenuous for anyone, let alone a woman who weighs some 115 pounds when dressed for winter playground duty. She rises at 6:30 in her three-bedroom ranch home on a hillside in Ferguson. (She painted it herself only last summer.) Before breakfast she listens to a televised physics course.

During breakfast, the whole family absorbs the national and local news and feature interviews on TV. After breakfast, Mrs. Ellern makes the beds, her husband gives the dishes a chemical dousing, and they leave in separate cars—a recent luxury.

Mrs. Ellern drives her car to school, while her husband hops in his tiny English auto and takes daughter Elizabeth and a neighborhood friend to their sophomore high-school classes. By 7:35 the only one left at 25 Shireford Lane is Woofie, an improbable blend of German shepherd and cocker.

According to Herbert A. White, Vogt principal, Mrs. Ellern gets to school an hour before classes begin and has not missed a day all year.

After the day's round of teaching, interspersed with playground duty, preparation, and parent conferences, Mrs. Ellern attends numerous teachers meetings. Known to her colleagues as co-operative, enthusiastic, never given to shirking, Mrs. Ellern is active in nearly all local professional and inservice activities.

In the wider field, she was the school system's delegate to the 1957 NEA centennial convention. As a member of NEA's Department of Classroom Teachers, she is currently spending Saturdays helping to plan the 1959 NEA convention to be held in St. Louis.

College courses take up much of her time. Studying more for her own improvement than for a master's degree, Mrs. Ellern has, in recent years, taken three postgraduate courses, including an inservice music course she is working on now, a class in education of the exceptional, and the first TV course offered in St. Louis on comparative religion.

The Ellerns do a good deal of week-end entertaining and are much in demand socially. Their evening hours are busy ones. Mrs. Ellern sets a good table, with no short cuts—her husband is quite outspoken in his preference for German potato pancakes over frozen French fries. She has marketing, sewing, and housework to do, especially at present, when the family's two-day-a-week helper, Louise, is on maternity leave. And, of course, there are always papers to be graded.

A close-knit group, the Ellerns are fond of poking fun at themselves and each other. Dr. Ellern, 14 years older than his young-looking wife, may moan lugubriously, "I told Edna she should have married a younger man. Now they're mistaking me for her grandfather." Or Elizabeth, asked where she got her beautiful hair, may answer, "From my father! He gave me all of his!"

It would be easy to amass personal tributes to Edna Ellern from her many friends. Relaxed in manner, with an infectious laugh and an intelligent, expressive face, she is deeply interested in other people. She does not give the impression (given by some busy women) that she is riding a nonstop merry-go-round, quite insulated from the wonders of the outside world by the noise of her own personal calliope.

The final tribute to a teacher must come, however, from students. When Mrs. Ellern's pupils wrote their autobiographies, several of them mentioned inclusion in the rapid-learning class as the most important thing that ever happened to them.

It is probably this kind of unsolicited appreciation which has decided Mrs. Ellern's daughter to pay her mother the compliment of following in her footsteps. A member of NEA's Future Teachers of America, Elizabeth recently urged her classmates in an essay: "If you are in-

terested in teaching, by all means become a teacher. You will always be
wanted and welcomed."

FACTORS INFLUENCING THE COURSE
OF AMERICAN EDUCATION

*The previous selections have provided the student with an over-
view of American educational history. In the following selection
the authors review the major historical factors which have contributed to the shaping of modern education in America. An understanding of these factors can help the student comprehend
the interrelationship of society and education and analyze our
contemporary educational practices and problems in the light of
the past, for history is a continuing process, and many of the factors which left their impact on education yesterday, and are influencing education today, can still have an effect on education
tomorrow.*

*In this selection the following historical factors which have
had a notable influence on American education will be discussed: (1) European background, (2) spirit of equality, (3)
industrial expansion, (4) legal foundations, and (5) the role of
the United States in world affairs. Looking into the future, which
of these factors is likely to exert an important influence on chart-
ing the course of the American school in the years to come?*

Kalil I. Gezi and James E. Myers

Prepared especially for this volume.

EUROPEAN BACKGROUND

When the colonists came to New England, their patterns of living and
behavior were strongly influenced by their European background. That
background was evidenced in a common language, a well-developed literature, a religious tradition, a socio-political-legal system, and their experiences in a European educational system that spanned from the primary grades to the university.

Thus, in the seventeenth century when the colonists established their
first schools, these institutions were patterned after European schools. It
is significant to note that the colonial primary school and the colonial
Latin grammar school resembled greatly their English counterparts. If

one takes the early colonial and the English Latin grammar schools as an example, he would find they had the same curriculum with its heavy emphasis on Latin, a student body composed of boys only, fees for admission to most students, a strong church affiliation, and the same goals of preparing students for college, which in turn prepared them for an "enlightened clergy." As an early settler put it,

> After God had carried us safe to New England, and we had builded our houses, provided necessaries for our livelihood, rear'd convenient places for God's worship, and settled the Civil Government; one of the next things we longed for, and looked after was to advance learning, and perpetuate it to Posterity, dreading to leave an illiterate Ministry to the churches, when our present Ministers shall lie in the Dust.[1]

The development of the common school in New England was aided by the fact that the early settlers there belonged to one church, the Congregational church, and hence there was agreement on the kind of religious instruction to be offered by the school to all children.

As for the Southern colonies, the colonists exhibited and developed considerably a well-defined and rigid class structure similar to that of Europe, which tended to slow the development of the common school in the South. The aristocratic class of wealthy landholders and higher clergy felt, as did the aristocratic class in England, that any parent desiring education for his own children should provide such an education by his own means.

The lower classes—tenants, servants, and slaves—were for the most part unable to pay for the education of their children. However, pauper schools supported by the colonies and apprenticeship to trades were available.

In the middle colonies, the development of the common school was hampered by the fact that the settlers belonged to various religious denominations which disagreed on the type of religious instruction to be offered in a common school for all children.

In the eighteenth century, it became more apparent to many colonists that a rapidly developing frontier required them to modify their system of education to better serve the growing and emerging needs. However, European education continued to be a source of influence on American education. The work of such European educators as Rousseau, Pestalozzi, Froebel, and Herbart found supporters in America during the nineteenth century. For example, Froebel's kindergarten spurred interest in this country in providing education for children below the common-school level.

[1] Quoted in E. P. Cubberley, *Readings in Public Education in the United States* (Boston: Houghton Mifflin Company, 1934), p. 13.

During the nineteenth century, a large number of American scholars attended European universities and returned to this country to espouse the virtues of higher education in Europe. Several American universities were established or reorganized after European models. Johns Hopkins University, founded in 1876 in Baltimore, was the first American university to be established along the lines of German universities. The student will recall that Harvard, our first institution of higher learning, was modeled in the tradition of the English university. Even in the present time, the University of California at Santa Cruz is planning to pattern itself after Oxford University.

The questions of whether we should shape our educational institutions after those of Europe and which institutions are better, Europe's or ours, are still voiced today. Indeed, the advent of Sputnik has raised many questions concerning the adequacy of our educational system and has stimulated further our interest in European education.

THE SPIRIT OF EQUALITY

The western frontier provided an environment which tended to nurture democracy. Its vast lands, resources, and opportunities encouraged men to rely on their individual skills, initiative, and courage to achieve success.

Hence, in such a frontier milieu a spirit of equality was developed and maintained, and was destined to pervade the whole country. This spirit of equality moved de Tocqueville, a French scholar who appraised American democracy in 1835, to observe "the prodigious influence" which this spirit had "on the whole course of (American) society." He declared that the spirit of equality in this country

> . . . gives a peculiar direction to public opinion and a peculiar tenor to the laws; it imparts new maxims to the governing authorities, and peculiar habits to the governed. . . . [T]he more I advanced in the study of American society, the more I perceived that this equality of conditions is the fundamental fact from which all others seemed to be derived. . . .[2]

The concept of equality influenced not only the political, social, and economic spheres of society but also the educational realm. This concept strengthened the notion that education should be provided for all American youth, that the common school should be free, that it be publicly controlled and supported, that it be nonsectarian, and that women have opportunities for education equal with men.

[2] Tocqueville, Alexis de, *Democracy in America* (New York: Alfred A. Knopf, 1946), p. 3.

While equality affected education, education in turn augmented equality. In this regard, Horace Mann believed, as evidenced from his essay reprinted in this book (p. 53), "Education, then, beyond all other devices of human origin, is the greater equalizer of the conditions of men. . . ." He went on to say,

> . . . The spread of education, by enlarging the cultivated class or caste, will open a wider area over which the social feelings will expand; and, if this education should be universal and complete, it would do more than all things else to obliterate factitious distinctions in society. . . .

INDUSTRIAL EXPANSION

Students in education are aware of the mutual relationship between the school and society. While the school tends to reflect the conditions and trends in society, society can also be influenced by what goes on in the schools. One of the greatest forces in American society since its inception is the growth of business and industry. Therefore, it is not surprising to discover that such a force has left its impact on education in this country. In the early part of colonial history, the school curriculum was narrow and it failed to prepare most students for an emerging society. With the growth of trade with Europe and the West Indies, the western movement, and the ever expanding number of tasks in the frontier that required more skills and knowledge, the school had to expand its curriculum and re-examine its goals. In 1749, Benjamin Franklin proposed a new school, the academy, which would teach a practical type of education to its students—an education that is useful in daily living.

The curriculums of the academy, and later of the high school, provided new subjects along with their classical offerings. A list of such new subjects included bookkeeping, chemistry, commerce, engineering, mapping, navigation, political economy, Spanish, and surveying.

In the nineteenth century, the business and industrial boom in this country put a mounting pressure on the school to reorganize its curriculum to meet the new needs of a technological and scientific revolution. This boom brought with it a host of new problems to the schools. In the large industrial cities, for instance, classrooms became overcrowded because of the great number of people who converged on these cities seeking employment. Several social problems accompanied the migration to cities, such as the development of slums, delinquency, and the deterioration of sanitary conditions. City schools now enrolled a more heterogeneous group of children, who came from various regions and from underprivileged homes, to whom the traditional curriculum was not equally meaningful.

In addition to migration to large cities, this country witnessed an increased immigration largely because of the new job opportunities created by an industrial America. The immigrants and their children posed new cultural and linguistic problems to the schools.

Since the turn of the twentieth century, with child-labor and compulsory-attendance laws, and with the phenomenal growth of business and industry, the school has been under an even greater pressure to reevaluate itself.

Industrial expansion has been associated with certain significant problems which had their impact on society and education. For instance, automation made certain jobs obsolete, and the task of training those whose jobs were eliminated fell on educational institutions. Another problem is that the increased need by industry for highly trained people in specialized fields has caused schools and colleges to include in their curriculum the new areas of specialization. Increased leisure time, growing employment of women, and part-time employment of school-age youth are some of the many areas that posed new problems for the school.

The tremendous rate of industrial development has also brought many advances which benefit society and the school. Increased prosperity, for instance, which is one of the results of industrial economy in this country, has made it possible for more parents to send their children to educational institutions beyond the age of compulsory attendance. The presence of industry in a community tends also to contribute to the financial resources of the school system. Furthermore, new industrial techniques and products—such as educational television and other audiovisual devices, programed instruction, teaching machines, data processing and computer technology, and advanced techniques and materials used in school construction—have found their way into educational use.

In brief, the school responded to the influence of industry by changing continuously its curriculum to meet the new needs of a flourishing industrial society. Such emerging fields as nuclear physics, atomic energy studies, and space exploration have made themselves felt in the curriculums of many colleges and even high schools.

In an industrial society, the school has had to shoulder new responsibilities. With the increasing employment of women, for instance, the school had assumed some of the functions held previously by the home such as sex education and home economics. Another new responsibility of the school is its commitment to adult education and to continuation education.

As a direct result of the growth of industry, business, and science and the challenges they have created, increased research has been undertaken by many colleges and universities. This research was given an added impetus by the financial encouragement granted to it by industry.

LEGAL FOUNDATIONS

From the time of this country's beginnings up to the present, the laws of the land have had a marked influence on the course of American education. As early as 1642, the Massachusetts Bay Colony passed the first compulsory education law, which required parents to see that their children were taught to read, learn the major laws, and know catechism. Fines were to be assessed against parents who did not obey this law. In 1647, the "Old Deluder Satan" Act in Massachusetts required towns to appoint a teacher when they reached a population of fifty households, and, when they expanded to one hundred households, to set up a Latin grammar school and hire a teacher. Education, which relied on the teaching of the Bible, was to safeguard the youth of the colony from being deluded by Satan.

When the federal Constitution was drafted, there was no direct mention of education in it. The Tenth Amendment reserved indirectly the responsibility for education to the state; therefore, education is considered primarily to be a state function. However, the preamble to the Constitution affirms the duty of the federal government to "promote the general welfare." Also, Section Eight under "Powers Granted to Congress," states that Congress has the power "to lay and collect taxes . . . and to provide for the common defense and the general welfare of the United States." It is long agreed that education in American society is vitally important to the general welfare of the country. Thomas Jefferson observed this when he said, "If a nation expects to be ignorant and free in a state of civilization, it expects what never was and never will be." The constitutional reference to the federal government's responsibility to the general welfare thus sanctioned the government's role to induce the states to provide for the national welfare which involves education.

It would be helpful to trace the various contributions of the federal government to education. Here are the landmarks in federal legislation in this area: [3]

1785 *Northwest Ordinance*   Commencement of aid for education to territories and later to States by endowment of schools with public lands. Stipulated that "there shall be reserved the lot number 16

[3] Summary of landmarks in federal legislation for education up to 1962 adapted from National Education Association, Division of Federal Relations, *It's Older than the Constitution* (Washington, D.C.: The Association, 1962), by permission of the publisher.

of every township for the maintenance of public schools within said township."

1787 *Northwest Ordinance* Commencement of endowment of public institutions of higher education with public lands.

1800 *Congressional Library* The first appropriation for books, which became the nucleus of the Library of Congress.

1802 *Military Academy* The first federal institution of higher education established at West Point.

1802 *Ohio Enabling Act* Granted section 16 of each township in the states carved from the public domain to the township inhabitants for the support of schools.

1803 *Ohio Enabling Act Amendment* Granted a township to Ohio for a seminary of learning and stipulated that all educational land grants were to be "for schools and for no other use, intent or purposes whatever." Similar grants extended to other states carved from the public domain.

1862 *The Morrill Land Grant Act* Granted to each state an amount of thirty thousand acres of public land (or its equivalent in scrip) per congressman for the support of a college which would have as its primary purpose the teaching of "such branches of learning as are related to agriculture and the mechanic arts. . . ." Provision was also made for military training. The Morrill Act of 1890, the Nelson Amendment of 1905, and the Bankhead-Jones Act of 1935 increased this support for these institutions.

1867 *Office of Education* A federal Department of Education created —now the U.S. Office of Education. (Collects and diffuses information, administers programs approved by Congress.)

1917 *Smith-Hughes Act* Provided grants for promoting vocational training in the public schools and for encouraging special education for teachers of vocational subjects.

1920 *Smith-Bankhead Act* Initiated a policy of federal-state cooperation in vocational rehabilitation, including education.

1936 *George-Deen Act* Extended Smith-Hughes Act to include education in distributive occupations.

1941 *Lanham Act* Provided federal assistance for school building aid for communities adversely affected by federal activities.

1944 *The "G.I. Bill of Rights"* Provided educational training benefits for veterans. Extended in 1952 to include veterans who served between 1950 and 1955.

1944 *Surplus Property Act* A broad policy governing surplus property disposal for educational, health, and civil defense purposes enacted.

1946   *George-Barden Act*   Strengthened federal-state cooperation in vocational education. Programs for practical nursing and fishery education authorized by 1956 amendments.

1946   *Fulbright Act*   Provided for the use of some currencies and credits of other countries acquired by the United States through sale of surplus property abroad to be used for international educational exchanges.

1946   *National School Lunch Act*   Provided for the distribution of funds and federally purchased foods to public and nonpublic schools. In 1954 provided for an accompanying School Milk Program.

1948   *Smith-Mundt Act*   A broad program of international educational exchanges established.

1950   *Housing Act*   Included loans for college housing. Extended and enlarged in 1961.

1950   *Impacted Area Aid (P.L. 815 and P.L. 874)*   Public laws 815 and 874 provided assistance for school construction and maintenance and operation in federally affected areas. Extended in 1961 for two years.

1956   *Rural Libraries Act*   Established a five-year program of federal grants to the states for extension of library services in rural areas. Extended in 1960 for another five years.

1958   *National Defense Education Act*   Authorized funds over a period of four years to strengthen critical areas in education. Includes assistance for science, mathematics, foreign languages; counseling, testing, guidance; graduate fellowships; research and experimentation in modern teaching tools (TV, films, and so forth); and improvement in statistical and information services. Extended for two years in 1961.

1958   *Fogarty-McGovern Act*   Authorized federal grants to train teachers for the mentally retarded.

1961   *Exceptional Children (Deaf)*   Funds provided to train teachers of deaf children and to make available to them speech pathologists and audiologists.

1961   *Peace Corps Act*   Establishment of a permanent Peace Corps to supply American teachers and technicians to underdeveloped nations.

1962   *Manpower Development and Training Act*   Provides for a program of occupational training and retraining of the nation's labor force. The Department of Labor and the Department of Health, Education, and Welfare are jointly responsible for the training programs, institutions, and state and local agencies.

1962 *Educational TV Act; All-Channel TV Act* Authorizes federal grants to educational institutions or nonprofit groups to assist in building educational television stations; requires manufacturers, beginning January 1, 1964, to equip TV sets to receive all 82 channels. (The latter Act has significance for American education because two-thirds of the 263 channels reserved for education are in the UHF part of the spectrum.)

1964 *Civil Rights Act* Authorized the U.S. Office of Education to give technical and financial assistance to local public school systems planning or going through the process of desegregation. It also barred discrimination under federally assisted programs.

1964 *Economic Opportunity Act* (Anti-Poverty Law) This education-oriented measure was designed to stimulate local, state, and federal governments to cooperate in establishing programs to aid public schools. The titles of the act, most of which are of great significance to education, are: youth programs, urban and rural community action programs, special programs to combat poverty in rural areas, employment and investment incentives, work experience programs, and volunteers in service to America.

1964 *NDEA and Impacted Areas Programs Extended* National Defense Education Act was extended until 1968, and aid to federally "impacted" school areas was extended to 1966.

1965 *Elementary-Secondary Education Act* A comprehensive federal aid to public schools which provided: A three-year $1.06 billion program of federal moneys to school districts with predominantly low-income families. Upon the approval of the state and federal authorities, each district can determine how its funds would be expended; five-year programs for the development of supplementary education centers, for the purchase of textbooks and encouragement of school library resources and instructional material, and for the improvement of educational research and the state departments of education; and a two-year extension of federal aid to school districts which are affected by the presence of federal installations.

1965 *Higher Education Act* Provides undergraduate scholarships and fellowships for experienced or prospective teachers and authorizes a Teacher Corps trained to serve in urban and rural poverty areas.

1966 *International Education Act* Authorizes expenditures to further graduate and undergraduate efforts in international education or special programs or studies in related fields.

The federal government's involvement in education includes also the establishment and operation of military academies, schools for Indians, overseas schools for children of service personnel, and educational institutions in the District of Columbia.

In the absence of a clear constitutional definition of a federal role in education, many questions have risen regarding the legality of certain educational practices. Several of these questions involving such constitutional provisions as the church-state relationship and equal protection of the law were of such magnitude that they were brought before the Supreme Court of the United States. Here are some of the major decisions of the Supreme Court that have influenced the course of education in this country:

1816   *The Trustees of Dartmouth College v. Woodward*   When in 1819 the New Hampshire legislature converted Dartmouth College from a private institution to a university controlled by the state, a question of legality arose. Three years later, the Supreme Court held "that a charter granted to a private college is in the nature of a contract and cannot be revoked or altered by a state legislature without the consent of those to whom it was granted."

1896   *Plessy v. Ferguson*   The Supreme Court found the practice of "separate but equal" valid. Although this case was in regards to transportation, the principle of "separate but equal" applied also to public schools where segregation was considered to be legal if separate and equal schools for Negroes were established and maintained.

1925   *Pierce et al. v. The Society of Sisters*   The Oregon law of 1922 which required parents to send their children to public schools only was found by the Supreme Court to be in violation of the Fourteenth Amendment. This decision sanctioned the parents' right to send their children to either private or public schools.

1930   *Cochran v. Board of Education*   The Louisiana practice of supplying free textbooks to children in private schools was judged to be constitutional by the Supreme Court. The Court advanced the "child-benefit" principle, which contended that the benefit from these free materials accrued to the children and the state but not to the church.

1947   *Everson v. Board of Education*   The Supreme Court validated a New Jersey statute permitting local school boards to reimburse parents the cost of bussing their children to parochial schools. This decision gave the implication that public moneys can be expended on other services for children attending private schools, thus furthering the "child-benefit" principle.

1948   *McCullum v. Board of Education*   The Supreme Court rejected the Champaign (Illinois) plan of providing and supervising released time for sectarian instruction on it public school premises. The Court found this plan to be in violation of the separation-of-church-and-state and of the due-process-of-law clauses of the First and Fourteenth amendments.

1952   *Zorach v. Clawson*   The Supreme Court held constitutional the program of released time in New York City public schools by which students were permitted to leave school premises to receive sectarian instruction given them by their respective church authorities.

1954   *Brown et al. v. Board of Education of Topeka*   The Supreme Court, by a unanimous vote, ruled that segregation in public schools is unconstitutional and that it must be ended by the states "with all deliberate speed." In delivering the Court's opinion on this case, Chief Justice Warren declared:

> To separate them (Negroes) from others of similar age and qualifications solely because of their race generates a feeling of inferiority as to their status in the community that may affect their hearts and minds in a way unlikely ever to be undone. . . . We conclude that in the field of public education the doctrine of "separate but equal" has no place. Separate educational facilities are inherently unequal.

1962   *Engle v. Vitale*   The Supreme Court found unconstitutional the recitation in New York public schools of official prayers composed by the New York Board of Regents. The Court ruled that "each separate government in this country should stay out of the business of writing or sanctioning official prayers."

1963   *School District of Abington (Pa.) v. Schempp et al.* and *Murray v. Curlett (Md.)*   The Supreme Court declared unconstitutional the reading of the Bible and the recitation of the Lord's Prayer in public schools. Justice Clark, in his majority opinion, reaffirmed the principle that "[in] the relationship between man and religion, the state is firmly committed to a position of neutrality."

THE ROLE OF THE UNITED STATES IN WORLD AFFAIRS

Education has been an important instrument in perpetuating national pride and worthy citizenship. In the United States, effective citizenship was one of the Seven Cardinal Objectives of Education formulated in 1918 by the Commission on the Reorganization of Secondary Education. Citizenship was also included in one of the four Purposes of Education in American Democracy which were enunciated by the NEA's Educational Policies Commission in 1938. The curriculum of the American school today reflects its enduring emphasis on preparing students for civic responsibility.

But as the political, economic, and cultural role of the United States became more prominent in world affairs, American schools began to expand their teaching in the international field and to add to the goal of citizenship the goal of international understanding and cooperation. Such new subject areas as Russian, human geography, cultural anthropology, and teaching about communism are now included in the curriculum of some of the nation's schools. Established subjects such as world history, current events, and foreign languages have been given more emphasis in most American schools. On the college and university levels, international studies have long constituted an important and expanding part of the curriculum.

The phenomenal advances in rapid transportation and mass communications, along with increased interest in international understanding, encouraged a greater number of faculty and students from various nations to study and teach abroad.[4] Programs of faculty and student exchanges, scholarships and fellowships for research in international studies, and assistance to foreign students have been encouraged by government and private organizations not only in the United States but in several other countries as well.

In this country, a public discussion of nationwide proportion on the United Nations, UNESCO, and our involvement with other nations has erupted on particular occasions and continues to be a favorite topic of the mass media and of many groups and individuals.

To summarize, the rise of this country to a role of leadership in the modern world has had an inevitable influence on the kind and extent of curricular offerings in the schools. This influence is destined to remain with us, for a leading nation cannot exercise its leadership function unless it knows, understands, and can help those who seek its leadership.

After discussing the major factors affecting education, the student may better see the interrelationship between the past and the present in education. It is important to note that the kinds of problems, issues, and criticisms that we have now in American education are to an extent not

---

[4] In 1965–1966, 91,909 foreign students and faculty were in American schools and colleges, and in 1964–1965, 22,154 American students and faculty were in educational institutions abroad. Data from Institute of International Education, *Open Doors* (New York: The Institute, 1966), pp. 4, 11, 12, 13.

unlike those of the past. Since colonial times, the public and educators have raised basic questions regarding the goals of the schools, the content of their curriculums, the methods of teaching, the kinds of standards for admitting and promoting students, the qualifications for teaching, the control and support of the schools, and the types of school buildings and facilities which are best suited for educating students.

The student can also find, however, that many of these questions have been asked throughout history. As Aristotle astutely observed:

> There are doubts concerning the business (of education) since all people do not agree in those things which they would have a child taught, both with respect to improvement in virtue and a happy life; nor is it clear whether the object of it should be to improve the reason or rectify the morals. From the present mode of education we cannot determine with certainty to which men incline, or what tends to virtue, or what is excellent; for all these things have their separate defenders.[5]

Let us consider now some of the criticisms of education and of youth in the past and see how they resemble some of our current criticisms. For instance, the perennial outcry for adequate teacher salaries was heard more than two-thousand years ago in Rome. Juvenal (60–140), the Roman poet and satirist, complained that teaching is "A barren and fruitless employment" and that the teacher's salary for a year is no more than a charioteer receives for winning a single race.
Here are other examples:

> The most promising of our young men are wasting their youth in drinking-bouts, in parties, in soft living and childish folly, to the neglect of all efforts to improve themselves; while those of grosser nature are engaged from morning until night in extremes of dissipations which in former days an honest slave would have despised. You see some of them chilling their wine at the "Nine-fountains"; others, drinking in taverns; others, tossing dice in gambling dens; and many, hanging about the training-schools of the flute-girls.[6]   ISOCRATES (436–338 B.C.)

> When we were boys, boys had to do a little work in school. They were not coaxed; they were hammered. Spelling, writing, and arithmetic were not electives, and you had to learn. In these more fortunate

[5] Quoted by Mark Van Doren, *Liberal Education* (New York: Holt, Rinehart and Winston, Inc., 1943), pp. 2–3.

[6] Quoted by Patrick J. Ryan, *Historical Foundations of Public Education in America* (Dubuque, Iowa: W. A. Brown, 1965), pp. 22–23.

times, elementary education has become in many places a vaudeville show. The child must be kept amused, and learns what he pleases. Many sage teachers scorn the old-fashioned rudiments, and it seems to be regarded as between a misfortune and a crime for a child to learn to read.[7]   EDITORIAL IN *New York Sun*, OCTOBER 5, 1902.

To say that many of the criticisms of education throughout history are alike is not to imply that great progress has not taken place in education. Our modern knowledge of the psychological, physiological, and socio-cultural dimensions of the student's life has increased our effectiveness in the teaching-learning process. Great progress is being made in educational theory, methods, measurement and evaluation of student growth, the utilization of audio-visual aids, school design, and educational legislation.

Controversy in education should be viewed as a healthy manifestation of the public's interest in education. The American public has not only the right but also the responsibility to engage itself in determining the course of education in this country. For education is the most important foundation of a democratic society whose people are entrusted with making decisions affecting their destiny and even the destiny of the world.

[7] Quoted by Marian G. Valentine, in *School and Society*, **75** (June 7, 1952), p. 354.

2

SOCIO-ANTHROPOLOGICAL
PERSPECTIVES

INTRODUCTION

*Sociologists and anthropologists have made many contributions
to the study of education. Late in the nineteenth century, Emile
Durkheim emphasized the need for a sociological perspective on
the process of education. Historically, sociologists have become
more involved in the study of the school and the process of education than have anthropologists. Over the years, the cross-
fertilization between education and sociology has grown to the
extent that we find numerous publications, including a number
of journals, in educational sociology. There is also an increasing
number of professors holding dual appointments in education
and sociology. Among the many writers in the field of sociology
of education are Talcott Parsons, Burton Clark, Martin Trow,
Robert Havighurst, Wilber Brookover, David Gottlieb, Lloyd
Warner, James Coleman and Allison Davis.*

*One of the earliest anthropologists to write on education
was Edgar Hewett, whose article "Anthropology and Education"
was published in 1904 in the* American Anthropologist. *In the
area of anthropology and education, valuable work has been
done by such scholars as George Spindler, Jules Henry, Solon
Kimball, Theodore Brameld, Margaret Mead, Robert Redfield,
John Gillen, and Dorothy Lee.*

*Since education may be viewed as an instrument by which
culture is transmitted and perpetuated, the main contribution of
sociology and anthropology has been helping students gain cultural awareness—awareness of the school as a social agency operating in a unique cultural milieu. Researchers in these two
fields have explored such topics as the influence of social class
and cultural background on personality and achievement, the
effect of cultural change and value conflicts on the process of*

99

*education, and, conversely, the influence of the school on cul-
ture. Because of the work of sociologists and anthropologists, the
school is better understood as a separate social and cultural system, and the social roles of teachers, students, and parents are
more clearly delineated. The work of these scholars has also
helped us understand the influence on children by social agencies other than the school, such as the family, peer groups, community organizations, and mass media of communications. Research in sociology and anthropology has also made teachers
more aware of the plight of the culturally disadvantaged student
in the middle-class-oriented school.*

*This chapter begins with an analysis of the influence of so-
cial class on education by Brookover and Gottlieb. Next, Spindler discusses the value conflicts that arise in a rapidly changing
American culture. Bronfenbrenner analyzes the changing relationship between parents and children in the United States over
the past twenty-five years and the effect of these relationships on
the behavior of children. Coleman examines the contributions of
the school in developing the personality of adolescents in American culture, while Ginzberg discusses some of the most important issues the school faces in a rapidly changing economy. Margaret Mead questions the suitability of our current pattern of
education in meeting the emerging needs of the changing American culture. The chapter ends with an article in which Myers
and Gezi discuss the problems of disadvantaged youth and explore ways of teaching these students.*

SOCIAL CLASS AND EDUCATION

*In the following selection two sociologists analyze the meaning
of social class and its relationship to school attendance, level of
education, and achievement. The influence of social class on
education can hardly be ignored, but it is the overemphasis on
social class as a single factor affecting students that the authors
of the following selection question. They also point out that
teachers more than any other group have helped and encouraged
lower-class students. The authors conclude that there are three
alternatives for future educational policy in relation to social
class. The school can prepare students to live in their own social
class, can stress social mobility, or can re-enforce a class system
and stimulate class mobility at the same time. The authors are
sociologists and educators; David Gottlieb served as Program
Director for the Job Corps in 1967.*

Wilbur Brookover
David Gottlieb

> *Excerpt from* A Sociology of Education *(2d ed.; New York: American Book Company, 1964), pp. 153–174 and 188–192. Reprinted by permission of the publisher.*

There are few sociological reports or texts which do not deal with the question of social class in American society. The importance of the class structure is widely accepted. Through mass media we are told how the middle class lives, what it drives, what it wears, and what it eats. We are reminded that if we want to be identified as an "influential" we should read such and such a book or magazine. Entertainers are cautioned by their agents to maintain a certain kind of "image" or risk the possibility of alienating a certain social class. Concern with how class background affects the consumer's habits has led to the pre-testing of popular music, movies, food items, and so on. There is general agreement that if we are to understand the dynamics of the family, voting behavior, socialization processes, and countless other behavioral phenomena, we cannot go far without considering social class as a crucial variable.

Education has not escaped this influence. Much of this concern undoubtedly arises from the American belief in a democratic society, with a relatively fluid social structure, and the common assumption that education is the means by which equality of opportunity and social mobility are guaranteed. Hence, though much is yet to be learned about the social-class system in American society, there is some basis for considering the relationship between the class structure and the educational system. But before we examine this relationship, we should consider the nature of the social-class structure in America.

THE NATURE OF SOCIAL CLASSES IN AMERICA

The concept *social class* has many diverse meanings, all of which have to do with differentiation in the population of a society. A critical examination of the numerous bases for differentiation and of the development of a theory of social class is not intended,[1] but some general considerations may be mentioned.

[1] For some of these analyses, see Max Weber in Talcott Parsons (ed.), *The Theory of Social and Economic Organization* (New York: Oxford University Press, 1947); Kingsley Davis, "A Conceptual Analysis of Stratification," *American Sociological Review,* 7 (1942): 309–321; Talcott Parsons, "An Analytical Approach to the Theory of Social Stratification," *American Journal of*

At least three bases for differentiation of class groups can be noted. Perhaps the most common is classification according to *status* and *prestige*. A second, which is closely related, but not identical, is differentiation by *power*. Persons or groups, such as American labor leaders, may have much power in the community, but they have relatively low status or prestige. A third basis is by *sentiments* and *interests*. In this sense a social class is a broad group of people with relatively similar sentiments and interests distinguishable from those of another class.

Much difficulty and confusion in the conceptualization of social-class theory arises because the above criteria, distinguishable in the abstract, are not so distinguishable in the minds of the people who make up the class system. Differences in status, power, and sentiments are in reality almost always involved in a total complex of differences.

One means of avoiding this problem in defining the nature of class differences is to have the people of a community delineate the different classes and identify the members of each. Warner and his associates have made most extensive use of this technique without actually defining the basis on which the differentiation is made.[2] This concept of social class ignores the theoretical basis for class differentiation and attempts to determine the stratification existing in the interaction among the people, for it is assumed that "they are the final authorities about the realities of American social class."[3]

This technique, which Warner calls *evaluated participation*, makes no attempt to distinguish between differences in status and differences in power or sentiments. It may be assumed that these are interrelated to some extent, and that all are involved in the stratification which members of the group conceive among themselves. But people in one com-

Sociology, **45** (1940): 841–862; Lucio Mendieta y Nunez, "The Social Classes," *American Sociological Review*, **11** (1946): 166–176; Charles H. Cooley, *Social Organization* (New York: Charles Scribner's Sons, 1929); Herbert Goldhamer and Edward Shils, "Type of Power and Status," *American Journal of Sociology*, **45** (1939): 171–182; John F. Cuber and William F. Kenkel, *Social Stratification in United States* (New York: Appleton-Century-Crofts, 1954); Milton Gordon, *Social Class* (Durham, N. C.: Duke University Press, 1958); Joseph Kahl, *The American Class Structure* (New York: Holt, Rinehart and Winston, Inc., 1957). Numerous other items may be found in Reinhard Bendix and Seymour Lipset, *Class, Status and Power: A Reader in Social Stratification* (New York: Crowell-Collier and Macmillan, 1953).

[2] W. Lloyd Warner, Marchia Meeker, and Kenneth Eells, *Social Class in America* (Chicago: Science Research Associates, 1949), gives the most recent and detailed account of the process used in the identification of the various classes. This volume also contains a bibliography of other works by this group and other studies of social class.

[3] Warner, Meeker, and Eells, p. 38.

munity may stratify on a different basis than those in another. For this reason it is difficult to equate the class system delineated by this method in one community with that of another. Much of the research on education and social class is based on Warner's method.

Other studies have used various socio-economic criteria commonly correlated with social class position. Among these are occupation, amount and source of income, levels of educational attainment, religious affiliation, quality and size of house, area in which the residence is located, family origin, participation in organizational activities, and numerous other symbols of position. There is no universally accepted method of identifying the social class of a person or family. Perhaps no particular criterion or combination of criteria is equally valid for all communities. In some cases, particularly in rural communities, it is difficult to delineate the class structure. In other cases there may be two or more parallel systems of stratification. Stone and Form report such a situation in Vansburg.[4] In this community the older residents and the newcomers were stratified in two distinguishable systems. These were sometimes confused and difficult to recognize. It may be added that the farm people living in the surrounding area interacted in a third, ill-defined but emerging, class system. This community demonstrates the possible error in positing a single hierarchical class system. It indicated also that there are varying systems of class stratification in American communities.

Analyses of American communities have been made according to several sets of social classes. In Middletown the classification included the business class and the working class.[5] In Yankee City, Warner and his associates delineated six classes: the upper-upper, lower-upper, upper-middle, lower-middle, upper-lower, and the lower-lower. In other communities they found that the two upper groups are indistinguishable.[6] In another community study designed to determine the extent to which children recognize the class system, Stendler discovered three main classes, with a subdivided lower class and a very small upper class.[7] Using the terms common to the people of the community, she called these

[4] Gregory P. Stone and William Form, "Instabilities in Status: The Problem of Hierarchy in the Community Study of Status Arrangement," *American Sociological Review*, 18 (1953): 149–162.

[5] Robert S. Lynd and Helen M. Lynd, *Middletown*, and *Middletown in Transition* (New York: Harcourt, Brace & World, 1929, 1937).

[6] W. Lloyd Warner and Paul S. Lunt, *Yankee City Series*, Vols. I and II, particularly Vol. II, *The Status System of a Modern Community* (New Haven: Yale University Press, 1942); and Warner, Meeker, and Eells; and Warner *et al.*, *Democracy in Jonesville* (New York: Harper & Row, Publishers, 1949).

[7] Celia Burns Stendler, *Children in Brasstown* (Urbana: University of Illinois Press, 1949).

the upper-middle or cream-of-the-middle class, the white-collar class, and the working class. The brief description which she gives each of these is indicative of the broad class types common to American city and town communities.

Brasstown had an upper class, small and exclusive, typified by the Rockwells. They were "old family"; in their day they had given much to the town. A bridge, the town hall, the public library, all were memorials to members of Brasstown's first family. Renoirs in the Rockwells' possession were loaned to the Metropolitan Museum in New York upon occasion. They were not the richest family in town, but they were able to maintain a residence in Brasstown and one in quiet, secluded Long Acres, whose upper class claimed them as members. The Rockwells and others like them had little communication with Brasstown society; their wives held themselves aloof from the women's clubs, and their children did not attend the public schools.

The upper-middle class represented a professional, managerial, or large business group and included both new and old factions in the town. The McDowells were described as good, comfortable, salt-of-the-earth kind of people, staunch church members. He was president of the local bank, but the family lived simply and unassumingly, although in the best section of town. The Pebles and the Loomises on the other hand, were considered to be "flashy." Each had started a little plant or business of his own on a shoestring in the twenties and exemplified the typical American success story of moving up the ladder, making good through cheap labor and poor working conditions. These were the people who built the big houses, who had the big cars with license plates spelling out their initials, whose socially ambitious wives were the clubwomen of the town. Then there were the Campbells, men with doctorate degrees in chemistry, who were in high managerial positions in the local factories. These men were comparative newcomers in town, but by adopting the symbols of the upper-middle class they were able to assume their places in it.

Clerks, schoolteachers, small proprietors, and the skilled craftsmen made another large class, the white-collar group, generally described by one of its members as including "people like you and I," good self-respecting honest Americans who recognize the importance of trying to get ahead. "Like the Barnetts; they're a good example. A nice little family. She was a Rogers from Rockville before she was married—studied music. He's a steamfitter up at Eastern foundry, belongs to the Elks. They have a nice little home up on Pine Street Extension."

The working class consisted mainly of operators on conveyors or those in comparable jobs, people who were "all right" but "ordinary," who might not have finished their schooling, or, above all, . . . had escaped the middle class zeal of forging upward. This group also included foreigners who were "trying to be good Americans" and any large group of industrial workers newly imported from other communities. The description of the Strieskis is typical of many others. "They're dull, stolid, thrifty, Poles who've saved enough to buy a little house up on Grosvenor Street. They're ordinary people—they both work on conveyors down in the Brass Shop—both rather ignorant, but they want their kids to get along, and they're raising them to be good Americans."

There was a subdivision of this lower group, sometimes referred to as the "lower fringe," comparatively easy to identify. There was no particular section in which this subdivision lived, and no particular name consistently used to describe it, such as the Riverbrookers of Yankee City, but being poor and living in a certain way could place one in this group. Some of its members were "queer" couples who lived on the outskirts of town in unions which had failed to be blessed by church or state, raising broods of "queer" children. Moral or cultural reasons also help to decide membership. If one drank too much and was also poor, had a dirty home and no "standards" one was in the "lower fringe." If one "ran around with niggers" or was a recently-arrived "Porkchop" (Portuguese), the chances were one would be assigned a place at the bottom of the scale. "Take the O'Shaughnessys, for example. They live in clusters—a rough, tough, and hard-boiled lot. Father works down at the chemical plant—makes about $50.00 a week with overtime, but drinks it all up. He was arrested a couple of times for being a Peeping Tom." [8]

Stendler's subdivision of the working class and the upper class is similar to the five-class system reported by Warner in Jonesville. It is also comparable to the class structure of Johnstown.[9] Johnstown's old families were hardly distinguishable from the upper-middle class group; the "lower fringe" was commonly identified as the "no-counts."

All the communities we have mentioned are either cities or smaller towns of various sizes. There is some similarity in their class structures. It must be recognized, however, that other communities may be stratified in a quite different manner. This is particularly true of open-country

[8] Stendler, pp. 21–22. Reprinted by permission of the University of Illinois Press.

[9] W. B. Brookover and John Holland, unpublished study of minorities in a Midwestern rural community (East Lansing: Michigan State University, Social Research Service, 1950).

farm groups. Relatively limited analysis of rural class systems has been made, but there is evidence that a much less clearly differentiated system of classes is emerging in the farm society.

Analysis of the social structure in a Midwestern cornbelt community, identified as Maple County, reveals two distinct social systems among the people living on the land.[10] One consists of nonfarmers who live on the land but have little interaction with the farmers and are identified primarily with the town or city society. Even in typical cornbelt farm communities, they represent an increasing proportion of the residents. The other is composed of farmers and part-time farmers who have some interaction in the farm group. These systems in Maple County seemed to include five distinguishable but overlapping strata: (1) the Big Farmers, who hold such large acreage that they are primarily managers rather than farm operators; (2) the Real or Commercial Farmers, who have modern equipment and farm sizable acreages; (3) the Traditional Farmers, who retain many of the characteristics of the smaller subsistence farm families; (4) the part-time or Weekend Farmers, who have other jobs but engage in some farm operations; and (5) the Outcasts, who are found on the land as well as in the towns—the "No-counts."

REVIEW OF COMMUNITY STUDIES [11]

A brief review of three sociological classics dealing with social stratification and education will provide a foundation for our later analysis.

Middletown

During 1924 and 1925 the Lynds, using the techniques of the cultural anthropologist, carried on a detailed investigation of Middletown, a Midwestern industrial city of about 38,000 population.[12] The Middletown study included, among other areas, a social analysis of "training the young."

The Lynds found that the people of Middletown were very much concerned about education. They note that "no less than 45% of all money expended by the city in 1925 was devoted to its schools." [13] This

[10] Brookover and Holland. See also Warner *et al.*, ch. 14 (by Evan Vogt, Jr.).

[11] Portions of the material in this chapter are included in Brookover and Gottlieb, "Social Class and Education," Section I of W. W. Charters, Jr. and N. L. Gage (eds.), *Readings in the Social Psychology of Education* (Boston: Allyn and Bacon, 1963). The material is used here with permission of the editors and publisher.

[12] Robert S. Lynd and Helen M. Lynd, *Middletown: A Study in American Culture* (New York: Harcourt, Brace & World, 1929).

[13] Lynd and Lynd, *Middletown*, p. 182.

concern with education was not limited to elementary and secondary schools, parents wanted their children to go on to college. This desire for education was so great that the researchers give special attention to school drop-outs. They found that one important element in school continuance was the economic status of a child's family. This was indicated by the comments of several Middletown working-class mothers:

> A number of mothers who said that a child had left school because "he didn't like it" finally explained with great reluctance, "We couldn't dress him like we'd ought to and he felt out of it," or, "The two boys and the oldest girl all quit because they hated Central High School. They all loved the Junior High School down here, but up there they're so snobbish. If you don't dress right you haven't any friends." [14]

While the evidence for difference in attitude toward education on the part of business and working class was not systematic, the Lynds do say:

> If education is oftentimes taken for granted by the business class, it is no exaggeration to say that it evokes the fervor of a religion, a means of salvation, among a large section of the working class.[15]

They go on to discuss how the school system, a product of middle-class values, operates to suppress the educational aspirations of lower social class children.

Two major conclusions may be drawn from the study of Middletown. The first is that lower-class parents, even though they too recognize the value of schooling, are less likely than middle-class parents to instill in their children a desire for a formal education. The second is that lower-class children are penalized within the school system, since they do not possess the symbols, attitudes, and behavior characteristics valued by the dominant class group.

Who shall be educated?

The extensive research on social prestige conducted by W. L. Warner and those who were later to become identified with Warner began in the early 1930's. The first study of "Yankee City" [16] in New England was

[14] Lynd and Lynd, *Middletown*, pp. 185–186.

[15] Lynd and Lynd, *Middletown*, p. 187.

[16] W. Lloyd Warner and Paul S. Lunt, *The Social Life of a Modern Community* (New Haven: Yale University Press, 1941); W. Lloyd Warner and Paul S. Lunt, *The Status System of a Modern Community* (New Haven: Yale University Press, 1942); W. Lloyd Warner and Leo Srole, *The Social Systems of American Ethnic Groups* (New Haven: Yale University Press, 1945); W. Lloyd Warner and J. O. Low, *The Social System of a Modern Factory* (New Haven: Yale University Press, 1947).

followed by *Deep South* [17] and a Midwestern study, *Democracy in Jonesville*.[18] From these studies Warner, Havighurst, and Loeb wrote *Who Shall Be Educated?* in which they conclude that American schools have a social class screening device which generally keeps upward mobility at a minimum.

> This book describes how our schools, functioning in a society with basic inequalities, facilitates the rise of a few from lower to higher levels but continue to serve the social system by keeping down many people who try for higher places. The teacher, the school administrator, the school board, as well as the students, themselves, play their roles to hold people in their places in our structure.[19]

The authors note that education is one of several potential elevators in moving people from one status position to another, but they add that the elevator does not travel upward for all people. The school curriculum, administrators, and teachers—all, according to the authors, products of middle-class values—are viewed as playing a role in keeping lower-class students at the same status position held by their parents.

The authors describe the educational institutions' function to be that of sorting students, rejecting some and re-routing others:

> One large group is almost immediately brushed off into a bin labeled "non-readers," "first-grade repeaters," or "opportunity class," where they stay for eight or ten years and are then released through a chute to the outside world to become "hewers of wood and drawers of water." [20]

The intricate conveyor belt continues through high school and college, at each grade level a bit more selective and certainly less democratic in rejecting and accepting.

> The young people are inspected not only for brains and learning ability, but also for skin color, pronunciation, cut of clothes, table manners, parental bank account.[21]

Evidence to support the conveyor-belt hypothesis comes in the form of two tables which show that the larger the students' parental income,

[17] Allison Davis, Burleigh B. Gardner, and Mary R. Gardner, *Deep South* (Chicago: University of Chicago Press, 1941).

[18] W. Lloyd Warner and Wilfrid C. Bailey, *Democracy in Jonesville* (New York: Harper & Row, Publishers, 1949).

[19] W. Lloyd Warner, Robert J. Havighurst, and Martin B. Loeb, *Who Shall Be Educated?* (New York: Harper & Row, Publishers, 1944), p. xi.

[20] Warner, Havighurst, and Loeb, p. 49.

[21] Warner, Havighurst, and Loeb, p. 50.

the greater the likelihood that he will go to college. In each case it is noted that IQ is not the vital factor in variations in educational attainment. The authors note, however, that it should not be assumed from these figures that members of the lower class are not interested in higher education for their children. On the contrary, they indicate that lack of money is a reason frequently given by poorer people for the withdrawal of their children from school. In this connection it is significant that, with the establishment of the National Youth Administration student-aid program of 1935, there was a sharp increase in high-school and college enrollment.

It is in their discussion of the school curriculum that Warner and his colleagues are perhaps most emphatic in their statements about the non-democratic aspects of American public schools.

> The evidence is clear that the social class system of Yankee City definitely exercises a control over the pupils' choice of curricula.
>
> The children of the two upper and the upper-middle classes, in overwhelming percentages, were learning and being taught a way of life which would fit them into higher statuses. On the other hand, the lower-middle and the lower-class children, in their studies in the high school, were learning a way of life which would help adjust them to the rank in which they were born.[22]

Nor is the teacher spared.

> Teachers represent middle-class attitudes and enforce middle-class values and manners. In playing this role, teachers do two things. They train or seek to train children in middle-class manners and skills. And they select those children from the middle and lower classes who appear to be the best candidates for promotion in the social hierarchy.[23]

We can summarize the material presented in *Who Shall Be Educated?* as follows:

1. Upper class people ordinarily send their children to private schools, especially at the high-school level.

2. For others in the community, the school may act as a means of social mobility by teaching skills essential for occupational advancement and the middle-class values and attitudes.

3. In high schools there is a relationship between the student's socio-economic status and the curriculum in which he is enrolled, and, when intelligence is constant, the proportion of high school graduates that go on to college decreases with socio-economic status.

4. The type of school curriculum determines, in part, the quality of

[22] Warner, Havighurst, and Loeb, p. 62.
[23] Warner, Havighurst, and Loeb, p. 107.

education, for teachers and administrators assign less prestige to vocational training programs than to college-oriented courses.

5. Children from the lower socio-economic groups are penalized in the social life of the school because the do not conform to the school's middle-class standards.

Elmtown's youth

Hollingshead focused on the relationship of adolescents to the social structure in a Midwestern community.[24]

The analysis involved 390 high-school students, 345 who had withdrawn from the school, and the 535 families of these adolescents.

The study gave major attention to the relationship of class level to patterns of school attendance, attrition, dating, school activity, employment, career expectations, and peer association. Significant differences in social class for each of the variables noted above were presented. This data, supplemented by case histories, provided the foundations for the conclusion that opportunities for the attainment of desirable rewards and values (those held by members of the middle class) vary positively with the individual's position on the social class ladder.

Hollingshead proposes two explanations for the failure of the lower-class adolescent to rise in status. The first is that the socialization process in the lower class does not fit the working-class adolescent for satisfactory educational and occupational adjustment. The second is that middle-class adults in the school enforce their class values by "putting down" lower-class adolescents.

Hollingshead presents evidence to support his initial hypothesis that youngsters reflect within the social structure of the school the attitudes, values, and behavior patterns characteristic of their parents in the larger society.

The above studies were selected for particular attention because each has had and continues to have a great impact on educators' views of our schools.

These studies have been criticized on the grounds that the relatively small communities analyzed are inadequate samples from which to make generalizations about American society as a whole. Furthermore, the data do not fully support the hypothesis that variations in school dropout, curriculum selection, friendship choices, extracurricular participation, and other variables relevant to education are determined by social-class position or by unjust school policies. It is difficult to pinpoint just

[24] August Hollingshead, *Elmtown's Youth* (New York: John Wiley & Sons, 1949).

what causal relationships exist. Generally the authors fail to consider other factors once a relationship is found to exist between social class and some dependent variable.

Hollingshead's discussion of social class and patterns of friendship among Elmtown's high-school youth illustrates the limitations of his analysis. He shows that most students maintain clique associations within their own social-class group, but he also finds that freshmen are more likely to maintain friendship ties with other freshmen, sophomores with sophomores, juniors with juniors, and seniors with seniors. Thus both social class and school class are related to clique associations. Since dropouts increase with years in school and are highest for the lower classes, it should not be surprising to find that social class is related to friendship patterns. We cannot, however, be certain whether the differences result from social-class discrimination or from the fact that over time there are fewer and fewer lower-class students around to choose as friends. A better analysis would have examined the correlation between social class and clique relationships with year in school (freshman, sophomore, and so on) controlled. We would speculate that, in time, social-class differences become less important in determining friendship choices than post-high school plans, school activity involvement, and academic interests, or other reference-group variables.

These studies also fail to make clear just what there is in the student's socio-economic status that leads to variations in attitudes, norms, and behavior. Is it, for example, finances alone? Will capable lower-class students who are given financial assistance express as strong an interest in college as students from more affluent families? Is it the values stressed by parents from the different class groups? To what extent do members of lower classes use the middle class as a reference group for educational matters and, hence, hold educational values and attitudes like those of the middle class? Could difference in educational success be due simply to differences in educational sophistication among individuals from the various social strata? Because of their own college experiences and community positions, middle-class parents may have a better understanding of how schools operate, where to get information, with whom to speak in the academic bureaucracy, how to fill out applications, and so on.

Probably each of these factors is present in the total operation of social class and education. The problem is to determine the saliency of each and to measure its impact as the student moves through the various stages of the educational program.

Finally, and here the authors of the works cited above cannot be held accountable, there have been many changes in our schools and communities during the past three decades. Given these changes as well as the recent innovations in methods and techniques of social research, it is necessary to review the more current research in this field.

Any analysis of the relationship between class position and education must include variations in the amount and kind of formal school experience obtained by children from different strata. These will be examined in the light of school attendance, differences in the type of education provided, differences in educational aptitude, and teachers' classroom behavior in relation to children from different class levels.

School attendance and social-class position

School attendance has been correlated with social-class position. In many studies the highest grade level attained has been used as an index of social position. Warner, for example, found that the levels of school attainment and social class as determined by his *evaluated participation* technique were related to the extent of a 0.78 coefficient of correlation.[25] Although not in itself predictive of social-class position without consideration of other factors, the highest level of school attended is definitely related to class. The correlation does not prove, however, as it is sometimes interpreted, that the acquisition of a higher level of education automatically provides the youth with a ticket to higher status. But on the average, persons with higher social position go farther in the formal school grades than those in lower classes. This relationship is also reflected in the high correlation between level of education and other indices of social class. Occupation, amount and source of income, residential area, self-evaluation of social class, and various symbols of class are all related to the level of educational attendance.[26]

At the elementary level there is little class difference in the proportion of children who attend school, but as the non-compulsory school-attendance age is approached, differences occur.

Table 1 shows the proportion of a given age group dropping out of high school, graduating, and entering college in a Midwestern city of 45,000. Nearly 90 percent of the drop outs are from lower-class families. And less than one third of the 27.5 percent who entered college came from such families. A larger proportion of the young people in many communities enter college than in this River City group, and the proportion from each class may not be representative of the nation as a whole.

[25] Warner, Havighurst, and Loeb, pp. 165–169.

[26] Warner, Havighurst, and Loeb, pp. 169–175. See also Brookover and Holland.

Table 1 HIGHEST EDUCATIONAL LEVEL OF AN AGE-
GROUP OF RIVER CITY YOUTH [a] (PERCENT-
AGES OF AGE-GROUP)

Social Class	High-School Drop-outs	High-School Graduates	College Entrants
Upper and upper-middle	0.5	1.5	7.5
Lower-middle	3.5	12.5	11.5
Upper-lower	15.0	15.5	8.0
Lower-lower	16.5	7.5	0.5
All classes	35.5	37.0	27.5

[a] From Robert J. Havighurst, "Social Class Influences on American Education," in *Social Forces Influencing American Education,* 60th Year-book, National Society for the Study of Education (Nelson Henry, ed.; Chicago: University of Chicago Press, 1961), p. 122. Reprinted by permission of the University of Chicago Press.

The proportion attaining higher levels of education has been increasing rapidly in recent years, and most of the increase must come from lower- and lower-middle-class families. The data in Table 2, though based on estimates, gives an indication of this trend. Although lower-class youth have not commonly completed high school or attended college in the

Table 2 THE RELATION BETWEEN TRENDS IN COLLEGE EN-
TRANCE AND THE SOCIAL CLASS OF THE EN-
TRANTS' PARENTS [a]

Social Class	Percent in Population	1920	1940	1948	1958		1960	
		Males	Males	Males	Males	Females	Males	Females
Upper and upper-middle	10	40	80	80	75	70	85	70
Lower-middle	30	10	20	50	45	32	55	35
Upper-lower	40	2	5	15	20	17	25	18
Lower-lower	20	0	0	6	6	0	10	5

Percent of a Given Social-Class Group Who Enter College

[a] From Robert J. Havighurst, "Social Class Influences on American Education," in *Social Forces Influencing American Education,* 60th yearbook, National Society for the Study of Education (Nelson Henry, ed.; Chicago: University of Chicago Press, 1961), p. 123. Reprinted by permission of the University of Chicago Press.

past, the estimates in Table 2 indicate that college entrants from lower-class families now outnumber those from upper-middle and upper-class families, even though a much smaller proportion of the lower class go this far. Continuation of this trend will either modify the correlation between educational level and social class or alter the social-class distribution in our society.

Class differences in type of education

The expansion of the secondary school through the attendance of youth from all class levels and interests has presented another source of class differentiation. The early high-school curriculum was designed for the predominantly higher-class youth who expected to enter the professions. The traditional classical curriculum was not well adapted to the tremendous numbers from all levels who came into the secondary schools with the advent of compulsory education. New curricula were designed to meet the needs of those who did not intend to go on to college and professional schools. The resulting curricula have a variety of content and titles. Among these are commercial, general, vocational, and home-making.

The college-preparatory curriculum is most likely to be taken by higher-status youth. The significant correlation, indicated by the distribution in Table 3, between class position and curricula shows that the re-

Table 3   PERCENTAGE OF EACH SOCIAL CLASS IN ELMTOWN HIGH SCHOOL ENROLLED IN EACH OF THREE CURRICULA [a]

Curriculum	Social Class [b]			
	I-II	III	IV	V
College preparatory	64	27	9	4
General	36	51	58	58
Commercial	0	21	33	38

I-II—Upper Class
III—Middle Class
IV—Upper-Lower Class
V—Lower-Lower Class

[a] Adapted from A. B. Hollingshead, *Elmtown's Youth*, p. 462. Reprinted by permission of John Wiley & Sons, Inc.
[b] The classification here is similar to that of Warner, Havighurst, and Loeb.

lationship is present in at least one Midwestern community. Further-more, it seems that "the prestige bias in the different courses is particularly clear among the girls." [27] One Elmtown senior gave a concise description of the social orientation of the various curricula.

> If you take the college preparatory course, you're better than those who take the general course. Those who take a general course are neither here nor there. If you take a commercial course, you don't rate. It's a funny thing, those who take college preparatory set them-selves up as better than the other kids. Those that take the college preparatory course run the place. I remember when I was a freshman, mother wanted me to take home economics, but I didn't want to. I knew I couldn't rate. You could take typing and shorthand and still rate, but if you took a straight commercial course, you couldn't rate.
>
> You see you're rated by the teacher according to the course you take. They rate you in the first six weeks. The teachers type you in a small school and you're made in classes before you get there. College preparatory kids get good grades and the others take what's left. The teachers get together and talk, and if you are not in college prepara-tory, you haven't got a chance.[28]

This high-school senior would find it rather difficult to adjust to the general or commercial course if she were straining to acquire high status or if she were a member of a high-status family. Even more difficult might be the adjustment of her parents if they felt as she does. Parents who envision high-status positions for their children generally insist on their enrolling in the college-preparatory course. These parents may con-sider the general curriculum satisfactory for the children who are not likely to go to college and may even believe that lower-status children should be directed into such programs. Yet they insist that their own children must prepare for college.

The teachers also provide the model for status differentiation be-tween curricula. Teachers, except some in trade or vocational schools, always have had college training, and they place high value on the type of education which enabled them to attain their positions. It is therefore not unusual for the teacher of English, mathematics, languages, or sci-ence to look with disdain on both teachers and students in the vocational courses. They may regard these students as inferior in both ability and status to those who concentrate in their fields of interest. Although the teachers of vocational subjects may have a somewhat different view, many of them also consider their students inferior. Frequently, a voca-tional teacher can command a higher salary because fewer persons are

[27] Havighurst, p. 168.
[28] Hollingshead, *Elmstown's Youth,* pp. 169–170.

willing to accept positions in which they are expected to teach the lower-status courses. It is not unusual for cleavage to develop between the two groups of teachers over differences in status and salary. These disagreements and the differential evaluation of curricula made by teachers are readily recognized by students.

EDUCATIONAL APTITUDE, ACHIEVEMENT, AND SOCIAL CLASS

Many maintain that differences in secondary-school curricula are necessary because they are based on inherent differences in aptitude. The cold-war concern about talent waste has increased the emphasis on special curricula and even separate schools for those students thought to be endowed with superior "gifts." Much of this attention has been directed to the discovery of talent at an early age, on the assumption that the factors producing high achievement and success are relatively stable. The validity of this assumption is limited by evidence that measured abilities, aptitudes, attitudes, motivation, and other aspects of behavior change over time—either these factors are less stable than is commonly believed or our methods for measuring them are unreliable.

It is generally accepted that there is some correlation, though limited, between ability as measured by intelligence tests and school achievement, on one hand, and adult accomplishment, on the other. But the variation in both IQ and school grades from time to time and the other factors associated with adult achievement make early talent identification extremely difficult. Social-class and other family-background differences in emphasizing the factors associated with achievement are among the basic considerations in this area.

A number of investigators have noted that eventual expression of talent may be a product of differences in child-rearing practices. These investigators point out that need for achievement is strongly affected by parental attitudes and values. Exactly what there is in the family structure that may account for these differences in achievement need is not clearly established. Rosen discusses an "achievement syndrome," which he finds more prevalent in middle-class than in lower-class families.[29] He attributes variations in achievement need and intensity to differences in the values held by parents in the social-class groups. Middle-class parents are seen to place greater emphasis on mobility and success; hence their children are more likely to embrace achievement-oriented behavior. Strodtbeck concludes from his study of differences in achievement and

[29] Bernard Rosen, "The Achievement Syndrome," *American Sociological Review*, **21** (1956): 203–211.

incentive between boys of Italian and Jewish extraction that the higher motivation of the Jewish youth can be explained by family-power structure, cultural traditions, and parental attitudes.[30] These and other studies suggest that ethnic or religious values may cut across social-class lines and reduce the importance of the social-economic background.

What, then, can be said about the importance of socio-economic background as a factor related to achievement? At this point, it would seem, not much. McClelland makes the following observation about socio-economic status, IQ, and achievement:

> Since probably no other single assumption is so widely held among both scientists and laymen as that intelligence, as such, regardless of background, is linearly associated with success both in school and in life, the importance of clarifying the whole issue is crucial. It should be accorded high priority in any set of research projects undertaken to improve the predictive efficiency of test scores.[31]

Numerous studies indicate a limited relationship between family-social status and both intelligence-test scores and school grades.[32] In recognition of this, the fact that these correlations are relatively low is sometimes overlooked.

The data in Tables 4 and 5 show a typical relationship between social class and both measured intelligence and grade-point average. The children from higher-status families have higher IQ's and higher school grades on the average than the children from lower-status families. At the same time, it must be noted that over 30 percent of the lower-status students are high achievers. Furthermore, the high achievement of nearly 40 percent of the lower-class children in the high-achievement category was attained in spite of below-average IQ scores. This indicates that factors other than social-class are affecting school achievement and suggests the avenue which lower-class youth can follow for upward mobility. In spite of the limited educational attainment and lower occupational status of their parents, a sizable proportion of youth from lower-class families are excelling in school.

Social stratification and school segregation

The patterns of social stratification in many communities is reflected in separate schools for students of different strata. Americans have been

[30] Fred L. Strodtbeck, "Family Interaction, Values and Achievement," in David C. McClelland et al. (eds.), Talent and Society (Princeton, N.J.: D. Van Nostrand, 1958).

[31] McClelland et al., Talent and Society, p. 14.

[32] W. W. Charters, Jr., "Social Class Differences in Measured Intelligence," in Charters and Gage.

Table 4   MEAN INTELLIGENCE-TEST SCORES, MEAN GRADE-
POINT AVERAGES, AND FREQUENCY DISTRIBUTION
OF SEVENTH-GRADE MALES IN A MIDWESTERN CITY
BY SOCIAL CLASS OF FAMILY AND ACHIEVEMENT
CATEGORIES [a]

Achievement Category	Social Class									Total N
	Higher			Middle			Lower			
	Mean IQ	Mean GPA	N	Mean IQ	Mean GPA	N	Mean IQ	Mean GPA	N	
High	123	3.27	85	117	3.17	104	111	3.14	58	247
Average	110	2.47	25	109	2.43	39	104	2.45	14	78
Low	101	1.93	37	96	1.73	109	97	1.58	93	239
Total										
Group	115	2.77	147	107	2.44	252	103	2.21	165	564

[a] The data are from a current study of school achievement directed by the senior author. The average achievement category includes only those students with grade point averages within the range of one standard error of measurement above and below the total mean. Social class is based on father's occupation.

Table 5   MEAN INTELLIGENCE-TEST SCORES, MEAN GRADE-
POINT AVERAGES, AND FREQUENCY DISTRIBUTION
OF SEVENTH-GRADE FEMALES IN A MIDWESTERN CITY
BY SOCIAL CLASS OF FAMILY AND ACHIEVEMENT
CATEGORIES [a]

Achievement Category	Social Class									Total N
	Higher			Middle			Lower			
	Mean IQ	Mean GPA	N	Mean IQ	Mean GPA	N	Mean IQ	Mean GPA	N	
High	119	3.48	92	115	3.45	119	112	3.45	53	264
Average	107	2.86	22	108	2.79	37	110	2.76	17	76
Low	102	2.23	32	99	2.08	118	98	1.96	97	247
Total										
Group	114	3.14	146	107	2.77	274	104	2.51	167	587

[a] The data are from a current study of school achievement directed by the senior author. The average achievement category includes only those students with grade point averages within the range of one standard error of measurement above and below the total mean. Social class is based on father's occupation.

most conscious of the racially segregated school systems which have prevailed in the South. School-attendance districts which follow racial or
socio-economic class lines are also common in large cities and in metropolitan areas throughout the country. Many central city school-attendance districts are almost 100 percent lower-class and sometimes have a
high proportion of racial and ethnic minorities. Many other areas, particularly the suburban, are essentially 100 percent upper and upper-middle
class. Although some school systems have attempted to overcome this
ecological segregation of social strata in the schools, the residential areas,
coupled with the traditional neighborhood school-attendance districts,
have produced schools segregated on socio-economic and racial or ethnic
bases in the metropolitan areas. Such segregation is less likely in smaller
cities and towns, where a school district generally includes people from
several strata.

Class differences in academic interest, measured ability, and school
achievement may be exaggerated in such schools. The lack of cross-class
motivation and the inferior educational programs generally provided in
underprivileged areas increases rather than decreases the difference. In a
study of a large Midwestern city, Sexton found that average school
achievement was significantly lower in low-income area schools than in
high-income area schools.[33] Furthermore, she notes that the difference
increased from the fourth to the eighth grade.

There is ample evidence that in the city studied by Sexton, as in
other metropolitan areas, school programs do not operate to equalize the
achievement and opportunities of lower-strata youth. Many assume that
this difference in achievement reflects inherent differences in ability to
learn. They cite intelligence-test scores to support such contention, but
the evidence that these tests have a strong class bias makes such an assumption untenable. . . .

IMPLICATIONS OF SOCIAL-CLASS ANALYSIS
FOR EDUCATIONAL POLICY

There is ample evidence that social classes exist in American communities. This fact is increasingly recognized, but there is still an inclination to ignore the implications of class structure for educational policy
and to think of a school program as if it were independent of society.
Every study of the school clearly indicates that it is part of the social system and must function within its structure and culture. Regardless of the
function that education is to assume in relation to the class system, it
must always operate in relation to other forces in the society. It cannot

[33] Patricia C. Sexton, *Education and Income* (New York: The Viking
Press, 1961), pp. 25–28.

extricate itself from society, nor can it function as a molder of social structure, except as it functions within the framework of that society.

Many Americans expect mass education to maintain approximate equality of opportunity in American society. This implies a relatively low degree of social stratification, low visibility of barriers between classes, and a high degree of mobility within the social structure. The educational expectation is based on the belief that equality of opportunity depends on educational opportunities. Consideration of such expectations of education, when compared with the actual role of the school in relation to the class system, causes one to ask: What are the social-class goals of education? [34]

One answer to this question is that the educator must accept the class system as it is and organize the schools to prepare youth to live in it as effectively and as happily as possible. This position is a realistic one for the educator who is clearly aware of the difficulties involved in organizing an educational system which could achieve the traditional aims of equality and mobility. Many frankly believe that the school can have little or no impact on the social-class structure. This does not mean that the class system does not change. Neither does it imply that the present class system is rigid. This position is based on the belief that education can change the social structure very little. . . . If the educator is to accept it, his task becomes one of designing a school system which will prepare youth to function in roles which their status makes available to them. There are, however, some difficulties involved in this program.[35]

First, such a program would require a major change in one of the most valued sentiments in our society—that we can provide for mobility and equality of opportunity. If it is difficult for education to modify the class system, it may be even more difficult for education to modify the belief that the schools should continually strive to counteract the development of class barriers. The advisability of such an educational program may be questioned on another basis. It is possible that the control and direction of American society may shift in future generations to those who would, in the present situation, be educated for lower-class positions. If labor, for example, were to assume a managerial function in society, it would seem unwise to educate its members for a laborer's role only. Although it may seem logical to prepare youth to live in their own

[34] See W. B. Brookover, "The Implication of Social Class Analysis for a Social Theory of Education," *Journal of Educational Theory*, 1 (1951): 97–105, for a more elaborate discussion of this problem. The material in this section draws heavily from that paper.

[35] Foster McMurray, "Who Shall Be Educated for What?", *Progressive Education*, 27 (1950): 111–116, gives a pointed analysis of the difficulties and unlikelihood of this position prevailing.

class, there are forces which make it difficult and perhaps unwise, even in a highly stratified society. Such a program assumes that the society will remain stratified on the same basis. This is unlikely in a society that changes as rapidly as ours.

The second alternative for educational policy as it relates to class goals is to attempt to maintain low class barriers and to increase social mobility. This has been the traditional verbalized aim of education for decades. The difficulty involved in counter-acting the other forces which tend to stratify society is so great that education can achieve only limited success in this direction. The design of an educational system that would function successfully in this way has not yet been produced. Any program that would attain a more fluid class system would necessitate drastic changes in the present educational program. If education is to modify the class structure, much more fundamental knowledge of the function of education in society and of the nature of the experience provided by the schools will be required. At this point we have little basis on which to design a system of educational control, the type of curricula, or the methods of teacher selection and training which would insure equality of opportunity in America.

The third alternative is a continuation of the policy in which the values of equality and mobility are verbalized and diffused as widely as possible, while the educational and noneducational process of stratification continues. We have seen how both processes have operated side-by-side in the schools: perpetuation and reinforcement of the class system, on one hand, and stimulation for mobility, on the other. This assumes that we can continue to teach the ideal of equality in a social system in which it has only limited applicability. The difficulties involved in the other two alternatives and the momentum of long practice suggest this as the probable future of educational policy.

EDUCATION IN A TRANSFORMING AMERICAN CULTURE

George D. Spindler is one of the leading anthropologists in America today. To educators his writings are of special significance because he has utilized an anthropological approach in the analysis of the educational process. He and his wife, Dr. Louise Spindler, have served as editors of the American Anthropologist. *In the following article Spindler explores how conflicting values which exist side-by-side in American culture affect education. In order to do so, he studied a sample of several hundred students in professional education classes at Stanford University over an eight-year period. He determined what values these students held and what influences their values would have on their classroom behavior. The results of the study confirmed his idea that there has been a shift in our culture from traditional to emergent values and that the value conflict between students, teachers, school board members, and parents can account for most of the attacks on the schools. The student may wish to ponder such questions as: What is the role of the teacher in this value conflict? What should he do when his values are in conflict with those of his students or of the majority of the parents?*

George D. Spindler

Harvard Educational Review, **25** (1955), 145–146. *Reprinted with permission of the author and* Harvard Educational Review.

The American public school system, and the professional educators who operate it, have been subjected to increasingly strident attacks from both the lay (non-educationist) public, and from within the ranks. My premise is that these attacks can best be understood as symptoms of an American culture that is undergoing transformation—a transformation that produces serious conflict. I shall discuss this transformation as a problem in culture change that directly affects all of education, and everyone identified with it.

The notion of social and cultural change is used persuasively, if carelessly, by too many writers to explain too much. Generalized allusions to technological change, cultural lag, the atomic age, and mass society, are more suggestive than clarifying. We must strike to the core of the change. And my argument is that this core can best be conceived as a radical shift in values.

The anthropologist, and I speak as one but not for all, sees culture as a goal-oriented system.[1] These goals are expressed, patterned, lived out by people in their behaviors and aspirations in the form of values— objects or possessions, conditions or existence, personality or characterological features, and states of mind, that are conceived as desirable, and act as motivating determinants of behaviors. It is the shifts in what I believe are the core values in American culture, and the effect of these

[1] The relationship between anthropology and education is a relatively new one. For further information on the connections and applications between the two see *Education and Anthropology*, edited by G. D. Spindler, Stanford University Press, 1955.

shifts on education today, that I wish to discuss. I will present these shifts in values as the conditions of life to which education and educators, whether progressives, experimentalists, conservatives, or in-betweens, must adapt—and to which they are adapting, albeit confusedly. My emphasis within the value frame-work will be upon shifts in the conception of the desirable character type, since education can never be freed from the obligation to support, if not produce, the kind of personality, or social character deemed desirable in society.

But first I must specify what sources are to be used as the factual baseline for generalization, even though there is no avoiding the necessity of going beyond these facts in the discussion to follow. There is a body of literature on American culture, as a culture, and the changes within it. I have drawn most heavily from the anthropologists, like Margaret Mead (4), Clyde and Florence Kluckhohn (2, 3), Gregory Bateson (6), Lloyd Warner (8), and Geoffrey Gorer (1), and a few sociologists, like David Riesman (5). Their writings range from the highly intuitive to the relatively observation-based. Though there is concensus, and a surprising degree of it, on the part of these students of American culture, little they say can be or is intended by them to be taken as proven.

These writings are useful, but most emphasize static patterning in values more than change in values. To extend my factual baseline I have been collecting relevant data from college students for the past four years. The sample consists of several hundred students, ranging in age from 19 to 57 years, mainly graduates in professional education courses, and representing socio-economic strata describable as lower-middle to upper-middle class. The sample is as representative of this professional group and these economic strata as any regionally biased sample can be. I have used two simple value-projective techniques. The aim has been to find out what features of social character (the term I will use to designate those personality elements that are most relevant to social action) the students in the sample hold as being valuable and that presumably determine much of their behavior in classrooms. The first of these techniques is a series of 24 open-ended statements, such as "The individual is———," "Intellectuals should ————," "All men are born ————." The second of these techniques is to require each student to write one brief paragraph describing his (or her) conception of the "Ideal American Boy."

The various qualifications, problems, and discrepancies in analysis appearing in the treatment of the results cannot be discussed here. Let it suffice to say that I have subjected the responses of the students in the sample to a straight-forward content analysis—counting numbers of responses that fall into certain categories appearing from the data themselves.[2] Perhaps some examples will illustrate both the techniques and the kinds of materials from which I am going to draw in the rest of this article.

From the open-ended sentence value-projective technique, results like these have been obtained: "All men are born ———," "equal" (70% of all responses), "wolves," "stupid," "dopes," "hot-blooded" (a miscellaneous negative category of 28%—provided mainly by females in the sample); "Artists are ———," "queer," "perverted," "nuts," "effeminate" (a negative-hostile category of 38% of all responses), "different," "people," "few" (a neutral category of 35%), "creative," "smart," "original," "interesting" (a positive category of 25%); "Intellectuals should ———," "be more sociable," "be more practical," "get down to earth" (a mildly derogative category of 36%), "keep it under cover," "drop dead," "shut up" (an openly hostile category 20%), "apply their intellect," "study," "create," "think" (a neutral to positive category of 40%); Nudity is ———, "vulgar," "obscene," "profane," "repulsive" (a negative-moralistic category of 43%), "pleasant," "self-expressive," "beautiful," "healthy" (an enthusiastic-positive category of 20%), "depends on how interpreted," "alright in some places," "depends on who is looking" (a relativistic category of 30%).[3]

The values are self-evident, and do not call for discussion, as such, for the moment. What is more important is that this fairly homogeneous sample of students provides a wide range of response to each of these statements, excepting for the purposefully stereotyped "All men are born———." And not only is there a wide range of response evidenced, but many of the categories of response to a single statement can be considered as contradictions with respect to each other. This suggests that although there are clear modalites of values in this sample, there are also differences between people and groups of people in respect to what they believe is good.

The material gathered together as results from the "Ideal American Boy" technique are even more suggestive. A sentence-content analysis procedure reveals that the desirable features of character are ranked in the following order, from highest number of mentions, to lowest number: He should be *sociable*, like people, and get along well with them; he must be *popular*, be liked by others; he is to be *well-rounded*, he can do many things quite well, but is not an expert at anything in particular; he should be *athletic* (but not a star), and *healthy* (no qualifications);

[2] The analysis is still in process and will be subject to modifications in procedure. The statements in this article are based on a preliminary analysis of 328 individual protocols.

[3] Where percentages do not total 100 it is because various miscellanea are omitted.

he should be *ambitious* to succeed, and have clear goals, but these must be acceptable within limited norms; he must be *considerate of others,* ever-sensitive to their feelings about him and about events; he should be a *clean-cut Christian,* moral and respectful of God and parents; he should be *patriotic;* and he should demonstrate *average academic ability,* and *average intellectual capacity.*

These are the characteristics of the ideal American boy seen as most important by the students in the sample. Leadership, independence, high intelligence, high academic ability, individuality, are mentioned relatively infrequently (in about 20% of the descriptive paragraphs). But individuals do vary in the pattern of characteristics that are combined in the paragraph. Some emphasize the high achievement and individualized characteristics just mentioned. Some include elements from the modal list and combine them with these latter items. But the majority emphasize the sociable, well-rounded, average characteristics ranked above.

The implications seem clear. The keynote to the character type regarded as most desirable, and therefore constituting a complex of values, is *balance, outward-orientedness, sociability,* and *conformity* for the sake of harmony. Individuality and creativity, or even mere originality, are not stressed in this conception of values. Introspective behavior is devaluated (even intellectuals are suspicioned by many). Deviancy, it seems, is to be tolerated only within the narrow limits of sociability, of general outwardness, of conformity for harmony ("Artists are perverts"). The All-American boy is altogether average.

The materials just cited not only serve to illustrate the technique, but more important for present purposes, indicate rather clearly the fabric of the value pattern that I believe to be emerging as the dominant core of the social character values in American culture (providing one can assume, as I am here, that the middle-class culture is the core of our way of life—the pattern of norms against which lower and upper class cultures are seen as deviations). From this point on, I shall use the implications of this data, along with the content of anthropological and sociological writings on American culture, without further reference to the factual baseline itself. The purpose is to sketch in bold strokes the major dimensions of culture change in our American society and relate them in explanatory style to the contretemps of modern public education and educators.

In doing this, I cannot indicate all of the logical and analytic steps between data and generalization, since this is not a research report. The statements I will make now about American values, their shift, and the effect on education, are based upon the varying responses of different age groups in the sample, upon person-to-person variation in responses, and upon variations in response and particularly contradictions of response within single individual protocols (the total set of responses for a single individual).

On the basis of these kinds of data, and in the light of the perceptive works of the fore-mentioned writers on American Culture, I believe it is clear that a major shift in American values has, and is taking place.[4] I find it convenient to label this shift as being from *traditional* to *emergent*. The values thus dichotomized are listed under their respective headings below, with explanatory statements in parentheses.

Traditional Values	Emergent Values
Puritan morality (Respectability, thrift, self-denial, sexual constraint; a puritan is someone who can have anything he wants, as long as he doesn't enjoy it!)	*Sociability* (As described above. One should like people and get along well with them. Suspicion of solitary activities is characteristic.)
Work-Success ethic (Successful people worked hard to become so. Anyone can get to the top if he tries hard enough. So people who are not successful are lazy, or stupid, or both. People must work desperately and continuously to convince themselves of their worth.)	*Relativistic moral attitude* (Absolutes in right and wrong are questionable. Morality is what the group thinks is right. Shame, rather than guilt-oriented personality is appropriate.)
Individualism (The individual is sacred, and always more important than the group. In one extreme form, the value sanctions egocentricity, expediency, and disregard for other people's rights. In its healthier form the value sanctions independence and originality.)	*Consideration for others* (Everything one does should be done with regard for others and their feelings. The individual has a built-in radar that alerts him to others' feelings. Tolerance for the other person's point of view and behaviors is regarded as desirable, so long as the harmony of the group is not disrupted.)
Achievement orientation (Success is a constant goal. There is no resting on past glories. If one makes $9,000 this year he must make $10,000 next year. Coupled with the work-success ethic, this value keeps people moving, and tense.)	

[4] I have been particularly influenced by the writings of David Riesman and particularly his *The Lonely Crowd*, now available in a Doubleday Anchor Book edition, 1953, (with Nathan Glazer and Reuel Denny).

Traditional Values	Emergent Values
Future-time orientation (The future, not the past, or even the present, is most important. There is a "pot of gold at the end of the rainbow." Time is valuable, and cannot be wasted. Present needs must be denied for satisfactions to be gained in the future.)	*Hedonistic, present-time orientation* (No one can tell what the future will hold, therefore one should enjoy the present—but within the limits of the well-rounded, balanced personality and group.)
	Conformity to the group (Implied in the other emergent values. Everything is relative to the group. Group harmony is the ultimate goal. Leadership consists of group-machinery lubrication.)

I believe American Culture is undergoing a transformation, and a rapid one producing many disjunctions and conflicts, from the traditional to the emergent value systems outlined above. It is probable that both value systems have been present and operating in American Culture for some time, perhaps since the birth of the nation. But recently, and under the impetus of World Wars, atomic insecurities, and a past history of "boom and bust," the heretofore latent tendencies in the emergent direction have gathered strength and appear to be on the way towards becoming the dominant value system of American Culture.

Like all major shifts in culture, this one has consequences for people. Culturally transitional populations, as anthropologists know from their studies of acculturating Indian tribes, Hindu villages, and Samoan communities (among others), are characterized by conflict, and in most severe form—demoralization and disorganization. Institutions and people are in a state of flux. Contradictory views of life are held by different groups and persons within the society. Hostilities are displaced, attacks are made on one group by another. And this applies as well to the condition of American Culture—the context of American education.

The traditionalist views the emergentist as "socialistic," "communistic," "spineless and weak-headed," or downright "immoral." The emergentist regards the traditionalist as "hidebound," "reactionary," "selfish," or "neurotically compulsive." Most of what representatives of either viewpoint do may be regarded as insidious and destructive from the point of view of the other. The conflict goes beyond groups or institutions, because individuals in our transitional society are likely to hold elements of both value systems concomitantly. This is characteristic, as a matter of fact, of most students included in the sample described previously. There are few "pure" types. The social character of most is split, calling for different responses in different situations, and with respect to different symbols. So an ingredient of personal confusion is added that intensifies social and institutional conflict.

I hypothesize that the attacks upon education, which were our starting point, and the confusion and failure of nerve characterizing educators today, can be seen in clear and helpful perspective in the light of the conflict of traditional and emergent values that has been described. It is the heart of the matter. The task then becomes one of placing groups, institutions, and persons on a continuum of transformation from the one value system to the other. Without prior explanation, I should like to provide a simple diagram that will aid at least the visual-minded to comprehension of what is meant. With this accomplished I will provide the rationale for such placement and discuss the implications of it in greater detail.

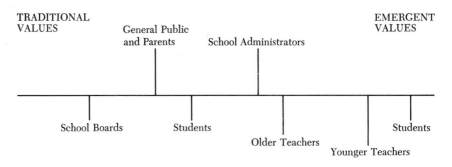

The diagram is meant to convey the information that different groups operating in the context of relations between school and community, educator and public, occupy different positions on the value continuum, with varying degrees and mixtures of traditional and emergent orientations. It should be understood that the placements indicate hypothecated tendencies, that no one group representing any particular institution ever consists of "pure" value types, but that there is probably a modal tendency for the groups indicated to place on the transformation, or continuum line, in the way expressed in the diagram.

The rationale for the placement of the various groups on the value continuum is fairly complex, but let me try to explain some salient points. School boards are placed nearest the *traditional* end of the continuum because such boards are usually composed of persons representing the power, *status-quo,* elements of the community, and of persons in the higher age ranges. They are therefore people who have a stake in keeping things as they are, who gained their successes within the framework of the traditional value system and consequently believe it to be good, and who, by virtue of their age, grew up and acquired their value sets during a period of time when American Culture was presumably more tradition-oriented than it is today.

The general public and parent group, of course, contains many elements of varying value predilection. It is therefore unrealistic to place this public at any particular point in the value continuum. But I hypothesize that the public *tends* to be more conservative in its social philosophy than the professional education set. The placement to the left of center of the continuum ("left" being "right" in the usual sense) takes on further validity if it is seen as a placement of that part of the public that is most vocal in its criticism of educators and education—since most of the criticisms made appear to spring out of value conflicts between traditionalist and emergentist positions. Parents complain that their children are not being taught the "three R's" (even when they are), that educators want to "socialize" the competitive system by eliminating report cards, that children are not taught the meaning of hard work. These all sound, irrespective of the question of their justification or lack of it, like traditionalist responses to change in an "emergent" direction.

Students are placed at two points on the transformation line because it is clear that those coming from traditionalist family environments will tend to hold traditionalistic values, but hold them less securely than will their parents (if our hypothesis for over-all change is valid), while other students who come from emergent-oriented families will tend to place even further, as a function of their age and peer groups, towards the emergent end of the line than their parents would. This is only partially true, indeed, for such a rationale does not account for the fact that offspring in revolt (and many American children from 6 to 16 are in a state of revolt against parental dictums) may go to extremes in either direction.

School administrators, older, and younger teachers, place at varying points on the emergent half of the transformation line. I have placed them there because I believe that the professional education culture (every institution has its own way of life, in this sense) that they have acquired in the schools and colleges of education has a clear bias towards an emergent-oriented ethos. Many of my educationist colleagues will reject this interpretation, and indeed, such interpretations are always guilty of over-generalization. Others of my colleagues will welcome such a characterization, but still question its validity. My case must rest on the basis of contemporary educational philosophy, theory, and practice. The emphasis is on the "social adjustment" of the individual, upon his role as a member of the group and community. Most of the values listed under the *emergent* heading are explicitly stated in educational literature as goals. Some of them, such as conformity to the group, are implicit. This value, in particular, grows out of the others, is more or less unintended, and constitutes a *covert* or *latent* value, by definition. This is, admittedly, a little like accusing a man of hating his mother, but not knowing it, and such accusations are usually rejected, or rationalized out of existence. But I believe that it is literally impossible to hold the other values in this system and avoid placing a strong emphasis on group harmony, and group control of the individual. My data, at least, gathered largely from graduate students in professional education courses, indicate that this is the case.

But educators and schools do not all come off the same shelf in the supermarket. Older teachers will tend, I hypothesize, to hold relatively traditionalist views by virtue of their age, and time of their childhood training (when they acquired their basic values)—a period in American culture when the traditionalist values were relatively more certain and supported than they are at present. Younger teachers were not only children and acquired their personal culture during a relatively more emergent oriented period of American history, but they have been (I hypothesize) exposed to a professional education culture that has become rapidly more emergent-oriented in its value position. They are therefore placed near the extreme of the transformation line in the emergent direction.

School administrators come from a different shelf in the same section of the supermarket. They, to be sure, range in age from young to old, come from different family backgrounds, and have been exposed in varying degrees to the professional education culture. But sociological and anthropological studies of the influence of status and role on behavior and perception indicate that these factors tend to over-ride others, and produce certain uniformities of outlook. The school administrator's role is a precarious one—as any school principal or superintendent knows. He faces towards several different audiences, each with different sets of demands—school boards, parents, power groups, teachers, and students—as well as other administrators. He has to play his role appropriately in the light of all these demands. The fact that many cannot, accounts for the increasingly short tenure of personages like school superintendents. But to the extent that he plays *across the board* he will place somewhere towards the center of the line of transformation. Furthermore, his dependence upon the school board, and the power groups in the community, in many cases will tend to make his outlook relatively more conservative, and probably more traditionalistic, than that of his teachers—at least the younger ones. There are many exceptions, of course. I am only claiming *tendencies*.

My thesis, I hope, is clear by now. I am attempting to explain, or help explain, the increasingly bitter and strident attacks on schools and educators, and the conflict and confusion within the ranks. I have claimed that this situation can better be understood as a series of complex but very real conflicts in core values. And I have tried to show the direction of the values shift in American culture and place the various actors in the drama upon a transformation line within this shift.

In this perspective, many conflicts between parents and teachers, school boards and educators, parents and children, and between the various personages and groups within the school system (teachers against teachers, administrators against teachers, and so on) can be understood as conflicts that grow out of sharp differences in values that mirror social and cultural transformation of tremendous scope—and for which none of the actors in the situation can be held personally accountable. This is the real, and perhaps only contribution of this analysis. If these conflicts can be seen as emerging out of great sociocultural shifts—out of a veritable transformation of a way of life—they will lose some of their sting. To understand, the psychiatrist says, is to forgive.

But now, though it seems indeed improper at this point, permit me to add another complication to an already complicated picture. I have tried to make it clear that not only are there variations in values held by groups and different parts of the social body and school institutions, but that there are also various values, some of them contradictory, held by single individuals as diverse streams of influence in their own systems. This is always true in rapid culture-change situations, as the anthropologist and philosopher know.

This means that the situation is not only confused by groups battling each other, but that individuals are fighting themselves. This has certain predicatable results, if the anthropological studies of personal adaptation to culture change have any validity. And I believe that those results can be detected in the behaviors of most, if not all, of the actors in the scene. Let me try to clarify this.

I will deal only with teachers, as one of the most important sets of actors on this particular stage. I hypothesize that the child training of most of the people who become teachers has been more tradition than emergent value-oriented. They are drawn largely from middle to lower-middle social class groups in American society, and this segment of the class structure is the stronghold of the work-success ethic and moral respectability values in our culture (even in a culture that is shifting away from these values). Furthermore, it seems probable that a selective process is operating to draw a relatively puritanistic element into the public school teaching as an occupation. Self-denial, altruism, a moralistic self-concept, seem to be functional prerequisites for the historically-derived role of school teacher in American society (I might have said "school-marm").

If this can be granted, then only one other ingredient needs to be added to explain several persistent types of personal adaptation to value conflicts observable among school teachers. That ingredient is one already spelled out—the relatively heavy emphasis, within the professional education culture, on the emergent-oriented value system. Teachers-to-be acquire their personal culture in a more tradition-oriented familiar environment, but they encounter a new kind of culture when in training to become school teachers—in the teacher-training institutions. There is, in this experience, what the anthropologist would call a discontinuity in the *enculturation* of the individual.[5] This is a particular kind of culture-conflict situation that anthropologists have recently begun to study, but mostly in non-western societies undergoing rapid change towards a western way of life.

On the basis of observations of a fair sample of teachers in coastal communities and in the middle west, I hypothesize that three types of adaptation to this personal culture-conflict situation and experience are characteristic.

Ambivalent: This type is characterized by contradictory and vacillating behavior, particularly with respect to the exercise of discipline and authority. The type tends to be *laissez-faire* in some classroom situations, and authoritarian in others, depending upon which behavior is called into being as a defense against threat of loss of control.

Compensatory: This type is characterized by one of two modes of behavior. The teacher overcompensates consistently either in the direction of the emergent or the tradition-centered values. In the first mode he (or she) tends to become a member of a *group-thinkism* cult—a perversion of progressive educational philosophy in action. The total stress is placed on social adjustment. Individuality is not sanctioned to any significant degree. Conformity to the group becomes the key to success. The type, in its extreme form, is a caricature of the better features of the emergent-centered values set. The second type compensates for internal culture-conflict in the opposite direction, and becomes an outright authoritarian. Tight dominance is maintained over children. All relationships with them are formalized and rigid. No deviation is allowed, so curiously enough, there is a convergence in the end-results of both types. This type is a caricature of the better features of the tradition-centered values set.

Adapted: This type can be either traditional or emergent value oriented. But the compensatory and ambivalent mechanisms operating in the first two types are much less intense, or absent. The teacher of this

[5] *Enculturation* is a new, but useful term being used by social scientists. It stands for the process through which the individual acquires the culture of his group or society.

type has come to terms with the value conflict situation and experience, and has chosen (consciously or unconsciously) to act within the framework of one or the other value set. There is consequently a consistency of behavior, and the mode of classroom management and teacher-student relationship is not a caricature of either value system.

No one is in a position to say which of these types is represented in greatest numbers among American public school teachers today, and there are few "pure" types. Certainly there are many traditional and emergent-oriented teachers who have adapted successfully to the personal culture-conflict situation and discontinuity of enculturative experience described. But equally certainly there are many school teachers who fall more clearly into one or the other typologies. It would be asking too much to suppose that a cultural values-conflict situation as intense as the one transforming American culture could be handled without strain by the key agent of the culture-transmission process—the school teacher. But again, to understand is to forgive.

In any event, it seems clear that if conditions are even partially of the nature described, the group culture-conflict situation resulting in attacks by representatives of those groups upon each other is intensified and at the same time confused by the personal culture-conflict problem. Both processes must be seen, and understood, as resultants of a larger culture-transformation process.

In conclusion to this by-far unfinished analysis (the next 20 years may tell the more complete story), let me make it clear that I am not castigating either the emergentists, or the traditionalists. Value systems must always be functional in terms of the demands of the social and economic structure of a people. The traditional mode has much that is good about it. There is a staunchness, and a virility in it that many of us may view with considerable nostalgia in some future time. But rugged individualism (in its expedient, ego-centered form), and rigid moralism (with its capacity for displaced hate) become non-functional in a society where people are rubbing shoulders in polyglot masses, and playing with a technology that may destroy, or save, with a pushing of buttons. The emergentist position seems to be growing in strength. Social adaptability, relativistic outlooks, sensitivity to the needs and opinions of others, and of the group, seem functional in this new age. But perhaps we need, as people, educators, anthropologists, and parents, to examine our premises more closely. The emergentist can become a group conformist—an average man proud of his well-rounded averageness—without really meaning to at all.

And lastly I would like to reiterate the basic theme of this article. Conflicts between groups centering on issues of educational relevance, and confusions within the rank and file of educators, can be understood best, I believe, in the perspective of the transformation of American culture that proceeds without regard for personal fortune or institutional survival. This transformation, it is true, can be guided and shaped to a considerable degree by the human actors on the scene. But they cannot guide and shape their destiny within this transformation if their energies are expended in knifing attacks on each other in such a central arena as education, or if their energies are dissipated in personal confusions. I am arguing, therefore, for the functional utility of understanding, and of insight into the all-encompassing transformation of American culture and its educational-social resultants.

REFERENCES

1. Gorer, Geoffrey. *The American People.* New York: W. W. Norton & Company, 1948.
2. Kluckhohn, Clyde. *Mirror for Man.* New York: McGraw-Hill, 1949.
3. Kluckhohn, Clyde, and Florence Kluckhohn. "American Culture: Generalized Orientations and Class Patterns," in *Conflicts of Power in Modern Culture, Seventh Symposium of the Conference on Science, Philosophy, and Religion.* New York: Harper & Row, Publishers, 1947.
4. Mead, Margaret. *And Keep Your Powder Dry.* New York: William Morrow, 1942.
5. Riesman, David, Nathan Glazer, and Reuel Denney. *The Lonely Crowd.* New York: Doubleday and Company, 1953.
6. Ruesch, Jurgen, and Gregory Bateson. *Communication: The Social Matrix of Psychiatry.* New York: W. W. Norton & Company, 1951.
7. Spindler, George D. (ed.). *Education and Anthropology.* Stanford, Calif.: Stanford University Press, 1955.
8. Warner, W. Lloyd. *American Life: Dream and Reality.* Chicago: University of Chicago Press, 1953.

THE CHANGING AMERICAN CHILD:
A Speculative Analysis

Over the past twenty-five years, American families have become more democratic and have relied more upon love-oriented techniques in dealing with their children. While most people may welcome this change in the American family, Urie Bronfenbrenner, a professor of psychology and child development and family relationships, thinks that the democratic family "tends to produce young people who do not take initiative, look to others for direction and decision and cannot be counted upon to fulfill obligations." Since high achievement motivation is encouraged in a family that uses nonpermissive, explicit discipline techniques, then our modern democratic family does not contribute to getting ahead as much as to getting along. However, in achievement-oriented homes children may excel in performance, but Bronfenbrenner cautions that the overemphasis on performance "may entail some sobering social costs."

Urie Bronfenbrenner

The Journal of Social Issues, **17** (*1961*), 6–18. *Reprinted by permission of The Society for the Psychological Study of Social Issues. This paper draws heavily on results from a program of research being conducted by the author in collaboration with Edward C. Devereux and George J. Suci. The contribution of these colleagues to facts and ideas presented in this paper is gratefully acknowledged. The research program is supported in part with grants from the National Science Foundation and the National Institutes of Health.*

A QUESTION OF MOMENT

It is now a matter of scientific record that patterns of child rearing in the United States have changed appreciably over the past twenty-five years (Bronfenbrenner, 1958). Middle class parents especially have moved away from the more rigid and strict styles of care and discipline advocated in the early Twenties and Thirties toward modes of response involving greater tolerance of the child's impulses and desires, freer expression of affection, and increased reliance on "psychological" methods of discipline, such as reasoning and appeals to guilt, as distinguished from more direct techniques like physical punishment. At the same time, the gap between the social classes in their goals and methods of child rearing appears to be narrowing, with working class parents beginning to adopt both the values and techniques of the middle class. Finally, there is dramatic correspondence between these observed shifts in parental values and behavior and the changing character of the attitudes and practices advocated in successive editions of such widely read manuals as the Children's Bureau bulletin on *Infant Care* and Spock's *Baby and Child Care*. Such correspondence should not be taken to mean that the expert has now become the principal instigator and instrument of social change, since the ideas of scientists and professional workers themselves reflect in part the operation of deep-rooted cultural processes. Nevertheless, the fact remains that changes in values and practices advocated by prestigeful professional figures can be substantially accelerated by rapid and widespread dissemination through the press, mass media of communication, and public discussion.

Given these facts, it becomes especially important to gauge the effect of the changes that are advocated and adopted. Nowhere is this issue more significant, both scientifically and socially, than in the sphere of familial values and behavior. It is certainly no trivial matter to ask whether the changes that have occurred in the attitudes and actions of parents over the past twenty-five years have been such as to affect the personality development of their children, so that the boys and girls of today are somewhat different in character structure from those of a decade or more ago. Or, to put the question more succinctly: has the changing American parent produced a changing American child?

A STRATEGY OF INFERENCE

Do we have any basis for answering this intriguing question? To begin with, do we have any evidence of changes in the behavior of children in successive decades analogous to those we have already been able to find for parents? If so, we could take an important first step toward a solution of the problem. Unfortunately, in contrast to his gratifying experience in seeking and finding appropriate data on parents, the present writer has, to date, been unable to locate enough instances in which comparable methods of behavioral assessment have been employed with different groups of children of similar ages over an extended period of time. Although the absence of such material precludes any direct and unequivocal approach to the question at hand, it is nevertheless possible, through a series of inferences from facts already known, to arrive at some estimate of what the answer might be. Specifically, although as yet we have no comparable data on the relation between parental and child behavior for different families at successive points in time, we do have facts on the influence of parental treatment on child behavior at a given point in time; that is, we know that certain variations in parental behavior tend to be accompanied by systematic differences in the personality characteristics of children. If we are willing to assume that these same relationships obtained not only at a given moment but across different points in time, we are in a position to infer the possible effects on children of changing patterns of child rearing over the years. It is this strategy that we propose to follow.

THE CHANGING AMERICAN PARENT

We have already noted the major changes in parental behavior discerned in a recent analysis of data reported over a twenty-five year period. These secular trends may be summarized as follows:

1. Greater permissiveness toward the child's spontaneous desires
2. Freer expression of affection
3. Increased reliance on indirect "psychological" techniques of discipline (such as reasoning or appeals to guilt) vs. direct methods (like physical punishment, scolding, or threats)
4. In consequence of the above shifts in the direction of what are predominantly middle class values and techniques, a narrowing of the gap between social classes in their patterns of child rearing.

Since the above analysis was published, a new study has documented an additional trend. Bronson, Katten, and Livson (1959) have compared patterns of paternal and maternal authority and affection in two generations of families from the California Guidance Study. Unfortunately, the time span surveyed overlaps only partially with the twenty-five year period covered in our own analysis, the first California generation having been raised in the early 1900's and the second in the late '20's and early '30's. Accordingly, if we are to consider the California results along with the others cited above, we must make the somewhat risky assumption that a trend discerned in the first three decades of the century has continued in the same direction through the early 1950's. With this important qualification, an examination of the data cited by Bronson et al. (1959) points to still another, secular trend—a shift over the years in the pattern of parental role differentiation within the family. Specifically:

5. In succeeding generations the relative position of the father vis-à-vis the mother is shifting with the former becoming increasingly more affectionate and less authoritarian, and the latter becoming relatively more important as the agent of discipline, especially for boys.

"PSYCHOLOGICAL" TECHNIQUES OF DISCIPLINE
AND THEIR EFFECTS

In pursuing our analytic strategy, we next seek evidence of the effects on the behavior of children of variations in parental treatment of the type noted in our inventory. We may begin by noting that the variables involved in the first three secular trends constitute a complex that has received considerable attention in recent research in parent-child relationships. Within the last three years, two sets of investigators, working independently, have called attention to the greater efficacy of "love-oriented" or "psychological" techniques in bringing about desired behavior in the child (Sears, Maccoby, and Levin, 1957; Miller and Swanson, 1958; 1960). The present writer, noting that such methods are especially favored by middle class parents, offered the following analysis of the nature of these techniques and the reasons for their effectiveness.

Such parents are, in the first place, more likely to overlook offenses, and when they do punish, they are less likely to ridicule or inflict physical pain. Instead, they reason with the youngster, isolate him, appeal to guilt, show disappointment—in short, convey in a variety of ways, on the one hand, the kind of behavior that is expected of the child; on the other, the realization that transgression means the interruption of a mutually valued relationship. . . .

These findings [of greater efficacy] mean that middle class parents, though in one sense more lenient in their discipline techniques, are using methods that are actually more compelling. Moreover, the compelling power of these practices is probably enhanced by the more permissive treatment accorded to middle class children in the early years of life. The successful use of withdrawal of love as a discipline technique implies the prior existence of a gratifying relationship; the more love present in the first instance, the greater the threat implied in its withdrawal (Bronfenbrenner, 1958).

It is now a well established fact that children from middle class families tend to excel those from lower class in many characteristics ordinarily regarded as desirable, such as self-control, achievement, responsibility, leadership, popularity, and adjustment in general.[1] If, as seems plausible, such differences in behavior are attributable at least in part to class-linked variations in parental treatment, the strategy of inference we have adopted would appear on first blush to lead to a rather optimistic conclusion. Since, over the years, increasing numbers of parents have been adopting the more effective socialization techniques typically employed by the middle class, does it not follow that successive generations of children should show gains in the development of effective behavior and desirable personality characteristics?

Unfortunately, this welcome conclusion, however logical, is premature, for it fails to take into account all of the available facts.

[1] For a summary of findings on social class differences in children's behavior and personality characteristics, see Mussen, P. H., and Conger, J. J., *Child Development and Personality.* New York: Harper & Row, Publishers, 1956.

SEX, SOCIALIZATION, AND SOCIAL CLASS

To begin with, the parental behaviors we have been discussing are differentially distributed not only by socio-economic status but also by sex. As we have pointed out elsewhere (Bronfenbrenner, 1961), girls are exposed to more affection and less punishment than boys, but at the same time are more likely to be subjected to "love-oriented" discipline of the type which encourages the development of internalized controls. And, consistent with our line of reasoning, girls are found repeatedly to be "more obedient, cooperative, and in general better socialized than boys at comparable age levels." But this is not the whole story.

. . . At the same time, the research results indicate that girls tend to be more anxious, timid, dependent, and sensitive to rejection. If these differences are a function of differential treatment by parents, then it would seem that the more "efficient" methods of child rearing employed with girls involve some risk of what might be called "oversocialization" (Bronfenbrenner, 1961).

One could argue, of course, that the contrasting behaviors of boys and girls have less to do with differential parental treatment than with genetically-based maturational influences. Nevertheless, two independent lines of evidence suggest that socialization techniques do contribute to individual differences, *within the same sex,* precisely in the types of personality characteristics noted above. In the first place, variations in child behavior and parental treatment strikingly similar to those we have cited for the two sexes are reported in a recent comprehensive study of differences between first and later born children (Schachter, 1959). Like girls, first children receive more attention, are more likely to be exposed to "psychological" discipline, and end up more anxious and dependent, whereas later children, like boys, are more aggressive and self-confident.

A second line of evidence comes from our own current research. We have been concerned with the role of parents in the development of such "constructive" personality characteristics as responsibility and leadership among adolescent boys and girls. Our findings reveal not only the usual differences in adolescents' and parents' behaviors associated with the sex of the child, but also a striking contrast in the relationship between parental and child behaviors for the two sexes. To start on firm and familiar ground, girls are rated by their teachers as more responsible than boys, whereas the latter obtain higher scores on leadership. Expected differences similarly appear in the realm of parental behavior: girls receive more affection, praise, and companionship; boys are subjected to more physical punishment and achievement demands. Quite unanticipated, however, at least by us, was the finding that both parental affection and discipline appeared to facilitate effective psychological functioning in boys, but to impede the development of such constructive behavior in girls. Closer examination of our data indicated that both extremes of either affection or discipline were deleterious for all children, but that the process of socialization entailed somewhat different risks for the two sexes. Girls were especially susceptible to the detrimental influence of over-protection; boys to the ill effects of insufficient parental discipline and support. Or, to put it in more colloquial terms: boys suffered more often from too little taming, girls from too much.

In an attempt to account for this contrasting pattern of relationships, we proposed the notion of differential optimal levels of affection and authority for the two sexes.

The qualities of independence, initiative, and self-sufficiency, which are especially valued for boys in our culture, apparently require for their development a somewhat different balance of authority and affection than is found in the "love-oriented" strategy characteristically applied with girls. While an affectional context is important for the socialization of boys, it must evidently be accompanied by and be compatible with a strong component of parental discipline. Otherwise, the boy finds himself in the same situation as the girl, who, having received greater affection, is more sensitive to its withdrawal, with the result that a little discipline goes a long way and strong authority is constricting rather than constructive (Bronfenbrenner, 1960).

What is more, available data suggest that this very process may already be operating for boys from upper middle class homes. To begin with, differential treatment of the sexes is at a minimum for these families. Contrasting parental attitudes and behaviors toward boys and girls are pronounced only at lower class levels, and decrease as one moves up the socio-economic scale (Kohn, 1959; Bronfenbrenner, 1960). Thus our own results show that it is primarily at lower middle class levels that boys get more punishment than girls, and the latter receive greater warmth and attention. With an increase in the family's social position, direct discipline drops off, especially for boys, and indulgence and protectiveness decrease for girls. As a result, patterns of parental treatment for the two sexes begin to converge. In like manner, we find that the diffential effects of parental behavior on the two sexes are marked only in the lower middle class. It is here that girls especially risk being over-protected and boys not receiving sufficient discipline and support. In upper middle class the picture changes. Girls are not as readily debilitated by parental affection and power; nor is parental discipline as effective in fostering the development of responsibility and leadership in boys.

All these trends point to the conclusion that the "risks" experienced by each sex during the process of socialization tend to be somewhat different at different social class levels. Thus the danger of overprotection for girls is especially great in lower class families, but lower in upper middle class because of the decreased likelihood of overprotection. Analogously, boys are in greater danger of suffering from inadequate discipline and support in lower middle than in upper middle class. But the upper middle class boy, unlike the girl, exchanges one hazard for another. Since at this upper level the more potent "psychological" techniques of discipline are likely to be employed with both sexes, the boy presumably now too runs the risk of being "oversocialized," of losing some of his capacity for independent aggressive accomplishment.

Accordingly, if our line of reasoning is correct, we should expect a changing pattern of sex differences at successive socio-economic levels. Specifically, aspects of effective psychological functioning favoring girls should be most pronounced in the upper middle class; those favoring boys in the lower middle. A recent analysis of some of our data bears out this expectation. Girls excel boys on such variables as *responsibility* and *social acceptance* primarily at the higher socio-economic levels. In contrast, boys surpass girls on such traits as *leadership, level of aspiration,* and *competitiveness* almost exclusively in lower middle class. Indeed, with a rise in a family's social position, the differences tend to reverse themselves with girls now excelling boys.[2]

TRENDS IN PERSONALITY DEVELOPMENT:
A FIRST APPROXIMATION

The implications for our original line of inquiry are clear. We are suggesting that the "love-oriented" socialization techniques, which over the past twenty-five years have been employed in increasing degree by American middle class families, may have negative as well as constructive aspects. While fostering the internalization of adult standards and the development of socialized behavior, they may also have the effect of undermining capacities for initiative and independence, particularly in boys. Males exposed to this "modern" pattern of child rearing might be expected to differ from their counterparts of a quarter century ago in being somewhat more conforming and anxious, less enterprising and self-sufficient, and, in general, possessing more of the virtues and liabilities commonly associated with feminine character structure.[3]

[2] These shifts in sex difference with a rise in class status are significant at the 5% level of confidence (one-tailed test).

[3] Strikingly similar conclusions were reached almost fifteen years ago in a provocative essay by Arnold Green ("The Middle Class Male Child and Neurosis," *American Sociological Review,* 1946, 11, 31–41). With little to go on be-

At long last, then, our strategy of inference has led us to a first major conclusion. The term "major" is appropriate since the conclusion takes as its points of departure and return four of the secular trends which served as the impetus for our inquiry. Specifically, through a series of empirical links and theoretical extrapolations, we have arrived at an estimate of the effects on children of the tendency of successive generations of parents to become progressively more permissive, to express affection more freely, to utilize "psychological" techniques of discipline, and, by moving in these directions to narrow the gap between the social classes in their patterns of child rearing.

FAMILY STRUCTURE
AND PERSONALITY DEVELOPMENT

But one other secular trend remains to be considered: what of the changing pattern of parental role differentiation during the first three decades of the century? If our extrapolation is correct, the balance of power within the family has continued to shift with fathers yielding parental authority to mothers and taking on some of the nurturant and affectional functions traditionally associated with the maternal role. Again we have no direct evidence of the effects of such secular changes on successive generations of children, and must look for leads to analogous data on contemporaneous relationships.

We may begin by considering the contribution of each parent to the socialization processes we have examined thus far. Our data indicate that it is primarily mothers who tend to employ "love-oriented" techniques of discipline and fathers who rely on more direct methods like physical punishment. The above statement must be qualified, however, by reference to the sex of the child, for it is only in relation to boys that fathers use direct punishment more than mothers. More generally, . . . the results reveal a tendency for each parent to be somewhat more active, firm, and demanding with a child of the same sex, more lenient and indulgent with a child of the opposite sex. . . . The reversal is most complete with respect to discipline, with fathers being stricter with boys, mothers with girls. In the spheres of affection and protectiveness, there is no actual shift in preference, but the tendency to be especially warm and solicitous with girls is much more pronounced among fathers than among mothers. In fact, generally speaking, it is the father who is more likely to treat children of the two sexes differently (Bronfenbrenner, 1960).

yond scattered clinical observations and impressions, Green was able to detect many of the same trends which we have begun to discern in more recent systematic empirical data.

Consistent with this pattern of results, it is primarily the behavior of fathers that accounts for the differential effects of parental behavior on the two sexes and for the individual differences within each sex. In other words, it is paternal authority and affection that tend especially to be salutary for sons but detrimental for daughters. But as might be anticipated from what we already know, these trends are pronounced only in the lower middle class; with a rise in the family's social status, both parents tend to have similar effects on their children, both within and across sexes. Such a trend is entirely to be expected since parental role differentiation tends to decrease markedly as one ascends the socio-economic ladder. It is almost exclusively in lower middle class homes that fathers are more strict with boys and mothers with girls. To the extent that direct discipline is employed in upper middle class families, it tends to be exercised by both parents equally. Here again we see a parallelism between shifts in parental behavior across time and social class in the direction of forms (in this instance of family structure) favored by the upper middle class group.

What kinds of children, then, can we expect to develop in families in which the father plays a predominantly affectionate role, and a relatively low level of discipline is exercised equally by both parents? A tentative answer to this question is supplied by a preliminary analysis of our data in which the relation between parental role structure and adolescent behavior was examined with controls for the family's social class position. The results of this analysis are summarized as follows: . . . Both responsibility and leadership are fostered by the relatively greater salience of the parent of the same sex. . . . Boys tend to be more responsible when the father rather than the mother is the principal disciplinarian; girls are more dependable when the mother is the major authority figure. . . . In short, boys thrive in a patriarchal context, girls in a matriarchal. . . . The most dependent and least dependable adolescents describe family arrangements that are neither patriarchal nor matriarchal, but equalitarian. To state the issue in more provocative form, our data suggest that the democratic family, which for so many years has been held up and aspired to as a model by professionals and enlightened laymen, tends to produce young people who "do not take initiative," "look to others for direction and decision," and "cannot be counted on to fulfill obligations" (Bronfenbrenner, 1960).

In the wake of so sweeping a conclusion, it is important to call attention to the tentative, if not tenuous character of our findings. The results were based on a single study employing crude questionnaire methods and rating scales. Also, our interpretation is limited by the somewhat "attenuated" character of most of the families classified as patriarchal or matriarchal in our sample. Extreme concentrations of power in one or another parent were comparatively rare. Had they been more frequent, we suspect the data would have shown that such extreme asymmetrical patterns of authority were detrimental rather than salutary for effective psychological development, perhaps even more disorganizing than equalitarian forms.

Nevertheless, our findings do find some peripheral support in the work of others. A number of investigations, for example, point to the special importance of the father in the socialization of boys (Bandura and Walters, 1959; Mussen and Distler, 1959). Further corroborative evidence appears in the growing series of studies of effects of paternal absence (Bach, 1946; Sears, Pintler and Sears, 1946; Lynn and Sawrey, 1959; Tiller, 1958). The absence of the father apparently not only affects the behavior of the child directly but also influences the mother in the direction of greater over-protectiveness. The effect of both these tendencies is especially critical for male children; boys from father-absent homes tend to be markedly more submissive and dependent. Studies dealing explicitly with the influence of parental role structure in intact families are few and far between. Papanek (1957), in an unpublished doctoral dissertation, reports greater sex-role differentiation among children from homes in which the parental roles were differentiated. And in a carefully controlled study, Kohn and Clausen (1956) find that "schizophrenic patients more frequently than normal persons report that their mothers played a very strong authority role and the father a very weak authority role." Finally, what might best be called complementary evidence for our inferences regarding trends in family structure and their effects comes from the work of Miller, Swanson, and their associates (1958; 1960) on the differing patterns of behavior exhibited by families from *bureaucratic* and *entrepreneurial* work settings. These investigators argue that the entrepreneurial-bureaucratic dichotomy represents a new cleavage in American social structure that cuts across and overrides social class influences and carries with it its own characteristic patterns of family structure and socialization. Thus one investigation (Gold and Slater, 1958) contrasts the exercise of power in families of husbands employed in two kinds of job situations: a) those working in large organizations with three or more levels of supervision; b) those self-employed or working in small organizations with few levels of supervision. With appropriate controls for social class, equalitarian families were found more frequently in the bureaucratic groups; patriarchal and, to a lesser extent, matriarchal in the entrepreneurial setting. Another study (Miller and Swanson, 1958) shows that, in line with Miller and Swanson's hypotheses, parents from these same two groups tend to favor rather different ends and means of socialization, with entrepreneurial families putting considerably more emphasis on the development of independence and mastery and on the use of "psychological" techniques of discipline. These differences appear at both upper and lower middle class levels but are less pronounced in higher socio-economic strata. It is Miller and Swanson's belief, however, that the trend is toward the bureaucratic way of life, with its less structured patterns of family organization and child rearing. The evidence we have cited on secular changes in family structure and the inferences we have drawn regarding their possible effects on personality development are on the whole consistent with their views.

LOOKING FORWARD

If Miller and Swanson are correct in the prediction that America is moving toward a bureaucratic society that emphasizes, to put it colloquially, "getting along" rather than "getting ahead," then presumably we can look forward to ever increasing numbers of equalitarian families who, in turn, will produce successive generations of ever more adaptable but unaggressive "organization men." But recent signs do not all point in this direction. In our review of secular trends in child rearing practices we detected in the data from the more recent studies a slowing up in the headlong rush toward greater permissiveness and toward reliance on indirect methods of discipline. We pointed out also that if the most recent editions of well-thumbed guidebooks on child care are as reliable harbingers of the future as they have been in the past, we can anticipate something of a return to the more explicit discipline techniques of an earlier era. Perhaps the most important forces, however, acting to redirect both the aims and methods of child rearing in America emanate from behind the Iron Curtain. With the firing of the first Sputnik, Achievement began to replace Adjustment as the highest goal of the American way of life. We have become concerned—perhaps even obsessed—with "education for excellence" and the maximal utilization of our intellectual resources. Already, ability grouping, and the guidance counsellor who is its prophet, have moved down from the junior high to the elementary school, and parents can be counted on to do their part in preparing their youngsters for survival in the new competitive world of applications and achievement tests.

But if a new trend in parental behavior is to develop, it must do so in the context of changes already under way. And if the focus of parental authority is shifting from husband to wife, then perhaps we should anticipate that pressures for achievement will be imposed primarily by mothers rather than fathers. Moreover, the mother's continuing strong emotional investment in the child should provide her with a powerful lever for evoking desired performance. It is noteworthy in this connection that recent studies of the familial origins of need-achievement point to the matriarchy as the optimal context for development of the motive to excel (Strodtbeck, 1958; Rosen and D'Andrade, 1959).

The prospect of a society in which socialization techniques are directed toward maximizing achievement drive is not altogether a pleasant one. As a number of investigators have shown (Baldwin, Kalhorn and Breese, 1945; Baldwin, 1948; Haggard, 1957; Winterbottom, 1958; Rosen and D'Andrade, 1959), high achievement motivation appears to flourish in a family atmosphere of "cold democracy" in which initial high levels of maternal involvement are followed by pressures for independence and accomplishment.[4] Nor does the product of this process give ground for reassurance. True, children from achievement-oriented homes excel in planfulness and performance, but they are also more aggressive, tense, domineering, and cruel (Baldwin, Kalhorn and Breese, 1945; Baldwin, 1948; Haggard, 1957). It would appear that education for excellence if pursued single-mindedly may entail some sobering social costs.

But by now we are in danger of having stretched our chain of inference beyond the strength of its weakest link. Our speculative analysis has become far more speculative than analytic and to pursue it further would bring us past the bounds of science into the realms of science fiction. In concluding our discussion, we would re-emphasize that speculations should, by their very nature, be held suspect. It is for good reason that, like "damn Yankees" they too carry their almost inseparable sobriquets: speculations are either "idle" or "wild." Given the scientific and social importance of the issues we have raised, we would dismiss the first of these labels out of hand, but the second cannot be disposed of so easily. Like the impetuous child, the "wild" speculation responds best to the sobering influence of friendly but firm discipline, in this instance from the hand of the behavioral scientist. As we look ahead to the next twenty-five years of human socialization, let us hope that the "optimal levels" of involvement and discipline can be achieved not only by the parent who is unavoidably engaged in the process, but also by the scientist who attempts to understand its working, and who—also unavoidably—contributes to shaping its course.

[4] Cold democracy under female administration appears to foster the development of achievement not only in the home but in the classroom as well. In a review of research on teaching effectiveness, Ackerman reports that teachers most successful in bringing about gains in achievement scores for their pupils were judged "least considerate," while those thought friendly and congenial were least effective. (Ackerman, W. I., "Teacher Competence and Pupil Change," *Harvard Educational Review*, 1954, **24**, 273–289.)

REFERENCES

1. Bach, G. R. "Father-Fantasies and Father-Typing in Father-Separated Children," *Child Development,* 1946, **17,** 63–79.
2. Baldwin, A. L., J. Kalhorn, and F. H. Breese. "The Appraisal of Parent Behavior," *Psychological Monographs,* 1945, **58,** No. 3 (Whole No. 268).
3. Baldwin, A. L. "Socialization and the Parent-Child Relationship," *Child Development,* 1948, **19,** 127–136.
4. Bandura, A., and R. H. Walters. *Adolescent Aggression.* New York: The Ronald Press Company, 1959.
5. Bronfenbrenner, U. "Socialization and Social Class through Time and Space," in E. E. Maccoby, T. M. Newcomb, and E. L. Hartley, *Readings in Social Psychology,* third ed.: New York: Holt, Rinehart, and Winston, 1958, 400–425.
6. Bronfenbrenner, U. "Some Familial Antecedents of Responsibility and Leadership in Adolescents," in L. Petrullo and B. M. Bass, *Leadership and Interpersonal Behavior.* New York: Holt, Rinehart and Winston, 1961.
7. Bronson, W. C., E. S. Katten, and N. Livson. "Patterns of Authority and Affection in Two Generations," *Journal of Abnormal and Social Psychology,* 1959, **58,** 143–152.
8. Gold, M., and C. Slater. "Office, Factory, Store—and Family: A Study of Integration Setting," *American Sociological Review,* 1959, **23,** 64–74.
9. Haggard, E. A. "Socialization, Personality, and Academic Achievement in Gifted Children," *The School Review,* 1957, **65,** 388–414.
10. Kohn, M. L., and J. A. Clausen. "Parental Authority Behavior and Schizophrenia," *American Journal of Orthopsychiatry,* 1956, **26,** 297–313.
11. Kohn, M. L. "Social Class and Parental Values," *American Journal of Sociology,* 1959, **44,** 337–351.
12. Lynn, D. B., and W. L. Sawrey. "The Effects of Father-Absence on Norwegian Boys and Girls," *Journal of Abnormal and Social Psychology,* 1959, **59,** 258–262.
13. Miller, D. R., and G. E. Swanson. *The Changing American Parent.* New York: John Wiley & Sons, 1958.
14. Miller, D. R., and G. E. Swanson. *Inner Conflict and Defense.* New York: Holt, Rinehart and Winston, 1960.
15. Mussen, P., and L. Distler. "Masculinity, Identification, and Father-Son Relationships," *Journal of Abnormal and Social Psychology,* 1959, **59,** 350–356.

16. Papanek, M. *Authority and Interpersonal Relations in the Family.* Unpublished doctoral dissertation on file at the Radcliffe College Library, 1957.
17. Rosen, B. L., and R. D'Andrade. "The Psychosocial Origins of Achievement Motivation," *Sociometry,* 1959, **22,** 185–217.
18. Schachter, S. *The Psychology of Affiliation.* Stanford, Calif.: Stanford University Press, 1959.
19. Sears, R. R., M. H. Pintler, and P. S. Sears. "Effects of Father-Separation on Preschool Children's Doll Play Aggression," *Child Development,* 1946, **17,** 219–243.
20. Sears, R. R., Eleanor E. Maccoby, and M. Levin. *Patterns of Child Rearing.* New York: Harper & Row, Publishers, 1957.
21. Strodtbeck, F. L. "Family Interaction, Values, and Achievement," in D. C. McClelland, A. L. Baldwin, U. Bronfenbrenner, and F. L. Strodtbeck, *Talent and Society.* Princeton, N.J.: D. Van Nostrand Company, 1958, pp. 135–194.
22. Tiller, P. O. "Father-Absence and Personality Development of Children in Sailor Families," *Nordisk Psykologis Monograph Series,* 1958, **9.**
23. Winterbottom, M. R. "The Relation of Need Achievement to Learning Experiences in Independence and Mastery," in J. W. Atkinson, *Motives in Fantasy, Action, and Society.* Princeton, N.J.: D. Van Nostrand Company, 1958, pp. 453–494.

RESEARCH IN AUTONOMY AND RESPONSIBILITY IN ADOLESCENTS

The following article was adapted from an address given by James S. Coleman to the 1964 convention of the National Association of Women Deans and Counselors. The author is a professor of social relations and a recognized authority on adolescence. In The Adolescent Society *he analyzed the subcultures of students in ten high schools. His research,* Equality of Educational Opportunity, *published in 1966, is a massive study of segregation in American schools. In the article presented here Coleman discusses the attributes required of adults in societies at three different levels of complexity: face-to-face relations, secondary relations, and tertiary relations. He explores the various alternatives used by the school in an attempt to develop self-responsibility and autonomy among adolescents. Has the school been able to develop these qualities among its students? Coleman responds negatively and suggests certain ways in which the school may be able to achieve these objectives.*

James S. Coleman

Journal of the National Association of Women Deans and Counselors (*Fall 1964*), 2–9. *Reprinted by permission of the* Journal.

In Charles Dickens' time, children had no easy time of it. A child could be physically broken by work before he was 14. He knew no period of adolescence, no insouciant years in which he was free of the cares of the world. Early in life he had thrust upon him brutalizing work, and he was not relieved of that work until he approached his grave.

In our time, children do have an easy time of it. The evils of child labor have passed; the exploitation of children is no longer one of society's faults. In almost every way, the life of a child has been transformed since that time. Children in our society are highly protected, not only by child labor laws and other legal safeguards to ensure their well being, but also by their parents, who seek for them "the advantages I never had." Children share in the affluence of their parents; popular music and clothes and movies and sports and dancing are their pastimes.

In Dickens' time, a society could not afford the "luxury of adolescence." Children became adults for good or ill by the rude shock of facing the adult world as a child. Today the opposite is true: Instead of dire want, we have the luxury of a period for bringing young people slowly into adulthood. How should this period of adolescence be spent?

First we must ask what attributes a given society requires of its adults. Then we can proceed to ask how these are, or might be, acquired.

It is useful to think of societies at three points along a continuum of complexity. The first is a communal, face-to-face society in which a man knows personally all the members of his relevant social environment. The second is a society that includes relations-at-a-distance, or what some sociologists call secondary relations. In such societies, a man's daily activities include interactions, both economic and social, with persons he does not know personally. A nonindustrial society of craftsmen, merchants, and farmers, spread over a geographic area with travel between different towns, exemplifies such a society, and America of the eighteenth and early nineteenth centuries, and preindustrialized Europe are good examples.

The third point on the continuum of complexity is a society that includes not only primary and secondary relations, but also what might be called tertiary relations—relations with large institutions. Industrialization, the growth of the corporation, and the development of the modern state with all its agencies have combined to reconstruct society into a vast complex of these organizations, with individuals qua individuals in the interstices between them. Many of the activities in the society involve the legal or economic interaction between these large constructs. In addition to the primary or secondary relations among people, there are relations between people and these large organizations. In industrial society, finding a job, purchasing, dealing with the law, registering a political opinion, all involve this tertiary form of interaction that is not interaction with other people at all, but with large institutions.

For each of these kinds of societies, certain kinds of socialization are necessary for the making of an adult. As the level of complexity increases, the newly needed attributes are not *substituted for* the ones previously necessary; they are *added to* them. Thus as the complexity of society increases, the complexity of socialization increases as well.

In the communal, face-to-face society, the basic elements that are necessary for socialization derive directly from the nature of face-to-face relations. An adult must be able to establish relations, develop expectations, and live up to the expectations governing the relationship. Two essentials are necessary, one a pure skill and the other a personality attribute. The skill is spoken language; it is necessary to communicate with the other in order to establish and maintain the relationship. The personality attribute may be called "the acquisition of norms governing the interaction," but I prefer to call it "the ability to identify with the other." It is the shift from a totally egocentric world, the attribute G. H. Mead called "the ability to take the role of the other," the attribute Adam Smith called "sympathy" in his *Theory of Moral Sentiments*, the attribute we often call "empathy" today. Whatever it is called, it is the ability to enter into a social interaction, be governed by it, and accept the constraints on behavior that such a relationship demands. There are always some persons in society who are not socialized in this way; autistic persons are perhaps the best example.

In the secondary society, which includes relations-at-a-distance, the additional attributes necessary for adequate socialization derive directly from the new form of relation. The skills necessary are those of classical education: the three R's of reading, 'riting, and 'rithmetic. For when relations are at a distance, spoken language is no longer sufficient, and direct trading of physical objects is not possible. Written symbols must serve in their place, and mental calculations must replace direct manipulation of objects. Until society includes such relations-at-a-distance, neither written language nor arithmetic calculations are necessary; but when it does, the adult must have these skills in order to perform as a member of society.

The additional skills necessary for occupational performance in such a society derive directly from the new occupations created. For most persons, the occupational skills are no different from those of a communal society, but in addition, the roles of lawyer, teacher, merchant, and others that characterize a nonindustrial society of towns and villages arise. Only in training for these roles is it necessary for the skills acquired to go beyond those of the three R's.

In such a society, the personality attribute necessary is an extension of the ability to identify with the other and thus establish a stable personal relation. It is the ability to internalize the attitudes of those whom one has never seen, who are not particular persons but categories of persons; to realize that those in another town or another nation are not wholly foreign, but behave from motives similar to one's own. It is the ability to recognize and see as legitimate the interests of others one does not know personally and at the same time to be able to protect one's own interests in such extended relations. It is useful to note that country people are often characterized by two attributes that show the lack of each of these parts of the socialization—suspiciousness of strangers and gullibility to sophisticated urbanites. Thus we may say that just as the primary society requires a shift from a totally *egocentric* world view, the secondary society requires a shift from a totally *ethnocentric* world view. A part of what is called citizenship education in schools today is an attempt to bring about this shift.

In the society with tertiary relations, that is, relations with large institutions, the attributes necessary for an adult expand enormously. The skills and the personality attributes required are no longer so distinct. What is necessary is to perform effectively in relations with these large institutions, which means such diverse things as obeying formal laws laid down by large governments, knowing how to keep from getting gypped in a sale, knowing whether to buy insurance, knowing how to resist advertising, knowing how to find a desirable job, how to make one's voice felt in government, how to tell good products from inferior ones, how to deal with employers, how to rent or buy a house, how to have a telephone installed, how to pay the correct amount of taxes, how to use welfare services provided in the community. To carry out all of these tasks well, an adult in such a society needs many skills: greatly increased calculating ability in order to manage finances and keep oneself from personal bankruptcy, knowledge of where one can turn for specific needs, knowledge of the laws and the consequences of not obeying them, knowledge of how government operates, a picture of what different jobs are like. A boy or girl in such a society faces a vast and complex machinery and is required to deal with parts of that machinery whose sophistication and power (and sometimes cunning) far outweigh his own.

Thus the task of socializing agencies in such a society becomes an extremely difficult one. Some of the tasks are not possible through socialization: trade unions have developed to deal collectively with employers, consumers' information magazines give product advice, and laws have been developed to protect individuals against unscrupulous organizations. But many of the tasks must be carried out as part of socialization.

In all of these kinds of societies, we may think of the task of socialization as that of creating from an infant a "self-regulating" and "self-generating" entity. Early in life, a child's behavior is totally governed by parents, and he acts under their authority, both in his constraints and in his positive actions. But when he is an adult in a democratic society, he must be autonomous, self-regulating, self-motivating, having internalized those aspects of the society with which he must interact. The question of how a society, particularly a complex one composed of large institutions, can bring about this internalization is the critical problem of education.

The task of socialization for primary relations occurs quite early in childhood, principally within the family. To be sure, there is an extremely wide range of variation in the quality of socialization that occurs, and until an effective substitute for the family in early childhood is found, it seems unlikely that this range of variation will diminish greatly. Therefore, a potentially fruitful problem does remain: How to ensure that primary socialization processes are carried out well in society.

In contrast to the socialization of primary relations, specific skills such as reading, writing, arithmetic and further skills and information, as well as other aspects of socialization for secondary and tertiary relations, are taught in formal institutions and seem likely to remain so. Why is this true? The existence of television and printed media makes it technically simple to present to all children in a modern society the same information they now receive from teachers in schools, at a fraction of the cost to the society.Yet there is no suggestion that schools be disbanded and education take place in the home.

This means that there is something important about the *institution* apart from the content of knowledge that it presents to children. The most obvious added element is the authority that such an institution has over the child. Without this authority, and the schedule of activities imposed on every child, it is easy to conjecture that for many children little learning would take place. There are many more interesting activities for a child than practicing writing or reading or addition when he is left to his own devices.

Yet perhaps the most difficult learning of all, that of language, is accomplished by these same children, at an earlier age, wholly without the aid of an external institution. Why cannot these simple skills be learned in the same way? What is it about them that requires the crutch of an institution with compelling authority?

The difference lies, I think, in the different role that secondary relations play in social behavior. The ability to function in primary relations is necessary to the child from an early age, if he is to cope with his environment at all. For his environment consists of both a physical world and a social world, and that social world consists wholly of face-to-face contacts with a relatively stable set of persons.

The socialization tasks of the school, in contrast, are those concerned with secondary relations, relations-at-a-distance. These relations are not part of a child's everyday existence. He need not write or read or calculate or know about faraway places in order to get along in his family and with his friends. It is only the artificial demands of the school that make him do so. He may need these skills as an adult, but as a child he is still living in a communal society composed of primary relations. Thus one solution to this problem is to commit children to an institution, the school, to use the authority still held by adults to coerce learning of these as yet unimportant activities.

It is reasonable, however, to consider other institutional mechanisms. It is evident that many things are wrong with this one solution which uses adult authority to coerce learning. Perhaps the major defect is that the learning just does not occur very well. Neither the skills nor the internalization of society that is required for secondary and tertiary relations are well learned or efficiently learned, when compared to the learning of language and empathy in primary relations.

One of these alternatives employs the following hypothesis: If every vestige of authority and constraint employed by adults is removed from children, they will no longer react against the constraints, but must necessarily set up their own, which then constitute self-regulation. The thesis is based on the premise that most norms and constraints of society (or at least all that should be transmitted to the young) derive from the necessity of maintaining social order, and that children will learn these constraints when they must themselves establish such norms to maintain social order among themselves.

This thesis (on which the social therapeutic technique of role-playing also depends) is an eminently reasonable one. From it one would deduce that children learn more about norms and about internalization of the role of the other through their own social games (which break down if the rules are not obeyed) than from their parents, teachers, or other adults.

There is one example of this thesis having been put into practice. The practitioner is A. S. Neil, an Englishman, who a number of years ago established a community of children and a school without rules, compulsion, or requirements for attendance.[1] There has never been a se-

[1] A. S. Neil, *Summerhill* (New York: Hart Publishing Company, 1960).

rious evaluation of this experiment, but it should be taken quite seriously. The indications are that the hypothesis is correct and that under certain conditions the process works. Whether such conditions are compatible with other institutions of modern society is an open question.

Neil's experiment includes a second hypothesis: Without adult compulsion, children will come to learn the attributes required for secondary and tertiary relations, that is, all the things that are "taught" in ordinary schools. If school subjects are available, they will be sought after and learned. The results from Neil's community-school leave considerable doubt that this is true, at least in the conditions that he established. It seems, on the basis of scanty evidence, that so long as these relations are of little importance in children's everyday lives, they do not seek, on their own, to learn them. As Neil says of his own experiment, the children of Summerhill do not seem much interested in book learning.

A second alternative is one presently being studied by a sociologist, O. K. Moore.[2] The general hypothesis is this: Children respond to the internal satisfaction of success, of accomplishing an activity. If the activity is structured correctly, without the external rewards and punishments meted out in ordinary learning situations in school, children will both seek it out and learn very rapidly. The activity is "autotelic," that is, it provides its intrinsic satisfactions, and only these are required for optimal learning. Moore's experiments are with preschool children, learning to read by typing on a typewriter and hearing the sound corresponding to the visual symbol. The results of Moore's work to date are impressive: The children *do* learn rapidly and are eager to carry out the activity. The applicability to other kinds of learning, to other age groups, and to other than small experimental settings remains unexplored. But the initial success is there.

As with Neil's experiment with the self-regulated child, this work depends on the child carrying out an activity under his own motive power, and proposes that such self-generated activity will produce a more nearly self-regulated and autonomous adult than activity carried out under adult-imposed authority.

A third alternative is one based on the following hypothesis: A child will learn those things he must learn to perform effectively in his present environment. He will not learn things that are only useful in the far future, for he cannot project himself into future roles and activities. With this hypothesis as a basis, the experiment that would follow is the constriction of such environments, bringing future roles into the present, requiring a child to perform in these roles, rather than merely those that naturally befall him as a child or adolescent.

[2] Professor Moore's work is being carried out at Yale University on an experimental basis. Published reports on it are not yet available.

This thesis is closely akin to Dewey's thesis of "bringing the community into the school," making the school a microcosmic community. The extracurricular activities of many high schools constitute a movement in this direction. The results of these developments are ambiguous. It is quite clear that some things have gone as expected: Work as editor of a school newspaper has led many boys into careers of journalism and made many other adolescents far more aware of the functioning of society than they would otherwise have been. But other such activities have led away from the development of responsible adults, or been quite irrelevant to it, though they may be the most sought-after positions in the community (e.g., cheerleader, prom queen, fraternity member). It seems in some schools, in fact, that the "community of adolescents" which the school has become has come to have many of the worst qualities of small, ingrown communities of adults: tightly-knit and exclusive cliques, a powerful status system, ridiculing of certain useful or harmless activities, and worshipping others. In addition, it has certain foibles of its own, such as rigid norms that may be set up to *disrupt* the order imposed by adults rather than establish order. In sum, it can hardly be said that the experiment has worked well. Yet this does not negate the hypothesis on which the experiment is based, for it seems likely that little attention has been given to the establishment of such environments. It seems quite likely that sociology can make important contributions to education in precisely this area—in designing the kind of educational environment in which the attributes of secondary and tertiary relations can be learned.

Perhaps the single most crucial quality that must be learned for such societies is that of self-responsibility. In a society of tertiary relations, a man is alone, on his own, in a way that he never was in a communal society, where the master of the household was responsible for all. Our tertiary society, with its freedom and its mobility, requires of each man that he attend to his own interests, that he be autonomous and responsible for himself (This may well be a major reason why American Negroes have had so much more difficult a time accommodating to an urban society than have other immigrant groups. They have so very recently left an environment in which they had neither authority over nor responsibility for their own destiny. Suddenly given the authority for their destiny in urban society, many lack the resources necessary for taking the responsibility.) Yet a school is in its very essence precisely the wrong environment for encouraging self-responsibility. Because it is confining and compulsory, school leaves little room for self-responsibility, and instead invites its opposite.

The creation of environments that generate self-responsibility has occurred sporadically, in private schools, in summer work camps, and elsewhere, such as the Peace Corps. The examples are frequent enough only to show that it can be done—not frequent enough as yet to have a significant impact on our educational system and thus on the generations of adolescents that flow through it.

I would like to describe an approach which falls somewhat short of this goal, yet reaches in that direction. It is the explicit creation of artificial or "simulated" environments for secondary education. These environments serve as the context within which adolescents play games, acting as they might in later life situations. The simplified prototype which give a flavor of this approach is Monopoly. It is easy to see how Monopoly, somewhat elaborated, could serve as a game for learning certain economic activities. Management games, as a kind of elaborated Monopoly, are presently used in many schools of business administration and many businesses, to induct future managers into those environments requiring responsible action which they will face in the future.

One high school, Nova High School in Florida, is taking seriously to these simulated environments and the games embedded within them. This school is planning to use such games as an integral part of its curriculum, allowing its students to learn about their future activities through the play and practice that a game provides, in generating in these students the self-responsibility that comes from an awareness of the consequences of one's action.

We have developed several such games in research at Johns Hopkins,[3] which are presently being tested and modified in high schools. One is in the area of political behavior, one is a legislative game; both are designed to bring far-distant environments into the direct experience of an adolescent. Other social scientists are currently developing similar games in various realms of politics. One set of games is particularly relevant to the teenager—career games. We are currently devising two such games, each rich with factual detail about colleges, occupations, and opportunities. Perhaps more than any others, such games can act to bring the far-distant future close to the adolescent, to show him the probable consequences of present actions, to aid him in acting responsibly toward his future.

These games with simulated environments are merely one approach designed to allow young people to acquire the qualities that our complex urban society will require of them. Many such approaches are necessary;

[3] See for example: Sarane S. Boocock, "Simulation Games: Bringing the World into the Classroom," *Vassar Alumnae Magazine* 49:20–22 (June 1964); "Playing Politics in the Classroom," *The Johns Hopkins Magazine* 15:14–20, (October 1963).

two others were described earlier. The major point is that we have the opportunity, for the first time in history, to use the period of adolescence in the service of an adolescent's future life, rather than in the service of existing society. Our attempts today show defects, but the opportunity is mothering inventions so that the future of adolescence appears far brighter than its past, whether in Dickens' day or our own.

JOBS, DROPOUTS, AND AUTOMATION

A distinguished group of educators and laymen were invited to the White House Conference on Education in July 1965, in order to seek answers to the question: "How can a growing nation in an increasingly complex world provide education of the highest quality for all of its people?" Among the participants in this conference was economist and educator Eli Ginzberg. In his paper, presented here, he analyzes some of the most important questions confronting education as it relates to the world of work. He poses such basic questions as: What have been some of the major changes in the relationship between education and employment, and what are they likely to be in the near future? How has the school responded to the changing demands of employers? What are the possible solutions to the dilemma of the dropout? What are the consequences of automation? What are the possible roles the school can play in meeting the demands of a growing and changing economy? His analysis of these questions is of great value to all of those who are involved in preparing students to live and work effectively in our society.

Eli Ginzberg

"Jobs, Dropouts and Automation," from Whitney M. Young, Jr., "Education and the World of Work," in Contemporary Issues in American Education (U.S. Office of Education Bulletin 1966, No. 3 [Washington, D.C.: U.S. Government Printing Press, 1965]), pp. 7–13.

INTRODUCTION

During the past century our young people have spent an increasing number of years in school preparatory to starting work. The patterns of schooling have differed in various regions of the country, and access to and use of the available schooling has differed among various groups in the population. But beneath these diversities have been certain general trends: Children and young people have tended to spend more years in school; the school year has been lengthened; the quality of the staff has been improved; the curriculum has been broadened and deepened to better meet the needs of an increasingly diversified school population; more and more young people have been graduating from high school and going on to college.

Today about four out of every six young people earn a high school diploma, and approximately half of these enter college. Once again, about half who enter college eventually earn their baccalaureate degree —that is, about one in every six in the age group. Put negatively, five out of six young people do not graduate from college; two leave high school; two stop with a high school diploma; one more leaves at some time in college.

In comparison, in 1900, only 17 in 100 earned a high school diploma; only seven in 100, a college degree. In 1930, the comparable figures were 35 in 100 and 13 in 100. For a great variety of reasons, including the belief that education is a good in itself, it is a mainspring of our democracy because it creates a literate electorate; it underpins our dynamic economy by helping to develop the potential and skill of future workers; it is a cornerstone of a mobile society because it offers the opportunity to youngsters born into low income families to acquire the prerequisities by which they will be able to move up the occupational ladder—for these and other reasons, the American people have been willing to spend increasing sums on education and have been willing to delay the time when young people begin to work.

THE SCHOOL AS TRAINER

Our society has long considered the primary task of the school to be instruction in basic knowledge and reinforcement of basic social values. The school has the responsibility of the second stage of the socialization process—the family has responsibility for the initial effort. The school is the transitional environment between the sheltered family and the competitive work place. With this role, the school has always served as a preparatory training ground for employment.

In addition to instructing children in the use of language and numbers and in familiarizing them with certain basic facts about the natural and social world, the school provides training in discipline, routines, cooperation, leadership and the other basic facets of adult life, particularly those reflected in the world of work.

THE CHANGING OCCUPATIONAL STRUCTURE

Whenever a basic social institution such as the public school has multiple functions to perform, it is inevitable that the professional leadership as well as concerned citizens will disagree about the exact emphasis which the institution should place on the accomplishment of one or another objective. No decade has been free of disagreements about the responsibility of the schools for preparing young people for gainful employment nor about the best ways to discharge this responsibility.

Rather than enter upon a review of this never-ending controversy, it might be more useful to make explicit some of the major changes in the relationship between education and employment that have characterized the recent past and those that are likely to be upon us before very long. First, with regard to the changes in the economy: The number of jobs which require little more than a strong back and a willingness to work long and hard has been declining rapidly. One generality that can be safely ventured here is that whenever a machine is invented that is capable of doing the tasks formerly performed by large numbers of persons, it is likely to be installed—even if the machine is costly and even if the workers were paid a low wage. The last several decades have seen more and more routine laboring jobs eliminated in agriculture, mining, construction, manufacturing and in the service sector of the economy.

At the same time, the economy has created opportunities for an increasing proportion of persons with professional, technical, or managerial skills—that is, individuals who have completed higher education.

Another development has been the rapid expansion of white collar jobs below the professional and technical level—that is, in clerical and sales occupations. These are the jobs for which a high school diploma or junior college degree have increasingly become prerequisite.

THE RESPONSE OF THE SCHOOLS

We have noted that there has been a steady expansion in higher education reflected in the growing proportion of the population which attends and graduates from college. These are the young people who are filling the rapidly expanding professional and technical occupations. We also referred to the steady increases in the proportion who complete high school but do not go beyond—the source of supply for the rapidly expanding white collar sector of the economy. For both of these groups, the schools have done well: they have been able to attract, hold, and educate an increasing proportion of the population for those occupational areas which have been undergoing the most rapid expansion.

But what about the one out of three young persons who leaves high school and then faces a relative and even absolute decline in the number of laboring positions available? The school-leaving age in most states remains 16, although a few legal states require attendance until 17 or 18. In contrast, in some states young people can still get working papers at 14. In light of the steady upward drift in the educational and skill requirements for new workers, the question must be asked whether the educational authorities have been slow to respond to the changing demands of employers. The answer to this question hinges in considerable measure on the characteristics of the young people who now leave high school as soon as legally possible.

THE DROPOUTS

The number of years that a young person must remain in school is determined by law. But the number of years that he is able to profit from education is a function of a great many other variables, including his genetic potential, his developed intelligence, his value structure, the influences exerted on him by family, community and peers, and by special circumstances that may dominate his life—such as trouble with the police, early parenthood, emotional instability.

The considerable effort that has been made in recent years to study the "dropout" has provided many, if not all, of the answers to the question of why a significant proportion of young people fail to complete high school. By far the most important reason is that by the time they reach school-leaving age, usually 16, many of them are several years behind schedule. Instead of being ready to enter the 11th grade, they may be in the 8th or 9th grade. This usually reflects an early difficulty in mastering the curriculum which, in turn, caused the youngster to develop negative attitudes toward the school. Classes become uninteresting and the discipline increasingly burdensome. Small wonder that this group takes the first opportunity to escape from these constraints.

Another large group of dropouts are young men and women who have been able to make normal progress in their studies but have never become really interested in learning and do not see much point in prolonging this experience until they acquire a diploma. Many of these young people are growing up in communities which place little importance on educational achievement, where the facilities and teaching staff are often inadequate; usually they are not encouraged by family or friends to continue in school. Their early withdrawal usually reflects a pervasive lack of interest.

The third group is a much more heterogeneous assemblage of young people, including some with special talents, who have major problems which make it difficult or impossible for them to continue in school. Some have run afoul of the law and are already in custodial institutions. Others are so disturbed that they cannot control themselves sufficiently to meet the minimum requirements of the educational system. A considerable number of young women withdraw because of marriage or pregnancy. Others, usually boys, are determined to get away from home at the earliest possible moment. Some young people from very low income families are under pressure to become wage earners as early as possible. These groups, and other distinguishable groups of young people, when given the opportunity, prefer to leave school.

THE PRESENT DILEMMA

The term "dropout" has an insidious connotation until one realizes that in earlier generations it could have been applied to youngsters who did not complete elementary school, and that it is beginning to be applied to those who enter college but do not stay to earn a degree.

Despite the increasing public clamor for all young people to remain in high school until they graduate, the following realistic factors must be confronted. There is no point in forcing young people to remain in school if they have not acquired the skills with which to learn; and, if they cannot relate their school experiences to their present or future life, they therefore do not make any effort to learn.

The ambitious national effort which would be required to insure that all young people graduate from high school can be justified only if the knowledge and skills they would acquire between their 17th and 19th years would significantly enhance their opportunities for employment or would add to their individual and social performance as adults. The incremental education—which would be about 20 percent more than they now have—might or might not prove worthwhile.

Moreover, the question must be faced whether the present reliance of many employers on a high school diploma as prerequisite for employment for new workers is an inexpensive screening device which has the additional effect of reducing the number of potential applicants from minority groups, or whether the knowledge and skills acquired in the last two years of high school actually add a necessary increment to the young person's personal capital. If under-employment prosperity, which has characterized the American economy since shortly after the end of the Korean War continues, it is likely that employers who must select new workers from among high school and post-high school graduates will simply raise their criterion; and the young man with only a high school diploma will still be at the end of the queue.

It is not a high school diploma per se that qualifies a young person for work and for responsible citizenship. Rather, it is his acquisition during the years that he is growing up of a value orientation, social competences, intellectual knowledge and skills, and study and work habits that will enable him to find a place within our highly differentiated economy and society. Therefore, to appreciate the challenge to the schools it is necessary to look more closely at emerging social and economic trends.

In a very few years the vast majority of the American people will be living in metropolitan areas. The modern city does not provide the type of protective environment that for a long time was characteristic of rural America, where the uneducated could survive at a modest level. Many of our most acute problems reflect the transfer of the rural population, white and Negro, from the low income farm areas of the Southeast into the large urban centers.

We are suddenly becoming aware of a two generational gap between the education and skills of the new migrants and that of the settled urban population. It may not be necessary for the urban dweller of the future to be a high school graduate but it is difficult to see how he will be able to make his way unless he has the equivalent of at least ten years of effective schooling back of him. . . .

The word "automation," like the word "dropout," is highly charged. Some writers proclaim that we are in the early stages of a revolution that will soon result in making work or workers obsolete. The new automated machines, with the help of a few programmers and maintenance workers, they say, will be able to turn out all the goods we need or desire. The critical questions, they claim, will be how to distribute income so that there will be an effective demand of all these goods, and how to turn our new leisure into constructive channels.

Others hold that nothing has changed; there is no revolution, nor is there likely to be one. They claim that a tremendous gap remains between what we want and need as individuals and as a society and our ability to produce the required goods and services. Prophecy is a poor platform for policy. The future will certainly be different from the past and yet the past gives us our best clue to the shape of the future, especially the near future. On this basis, we can reasonably be sure that agriculture will provide relatively few jobs and fewer will utilize unskilled labor. The President's First Report on Manpower indicated that nine out of ten young people now growing up on farms will have to find employment in other sectors of the economy.

The outlook for manufacturing is less clear. We know, however, that it was not until this year that total employment exceeded the peak

reached in 1943, and that the proportion of blue collar workers in manufacturing is considerably lower than in the early forties. A cautious estimate would see no significant absolute and surely no relative increases in
manufacturing employment in the years ahead and would forecast, in
any case, a shrinkage in semi-skilled jobs.

Technological advances in construction have been steady if not
spectacular, and this is the way it is likely to continue—although there is
always the possibilty of a radical breakthrough in prefabrication which
would lead to a substantial substitution of machinery for labor.

Currently, two out of every three persons in the labor force are employed, not in the goods-producing sector, but in the service sector; that
is, in trade, transportation and public utilities, finance, insurance and real
estate, government services, and other services. While it is unlikely that
the machine will be able to displace labor at a rapid rate in some of
these service fields, the potentiality of rapid development in others cannot be ruled out; in fact, it must be anticipated in light of the potency of
the computer. Moreover, the machine is not the only factor that operates
to economize in the use of labor; the growth of enterprises and markets,
improvements in managerial effort, and the upgrading of the work force
itself all have this potential.

While the foregoing summary statement does not imply any extreme
position about tremendous disemployment as a result of automation, it
does point to the probability of a relative, and possibly even an absolute,
reduction in unskilled jobs and a relative decline in the proportion of
semi-skilled jobs. There is another aspect to automation that should be
briefly mentioned. Although the substantially enlarged resources being
devoted to research and development will certainly result in the more
rapid obsolescence of knowledge and skill; this creates a concomitant
need for the expansion of educational and training opportunities for
adults if the nation is to have a vital work force.

The outlook, then, is for further relative and even absolute declines
in the unskilled and semi-skilled blue collar jobs; a probable slowing up
in the expansion of white collar jobs in those sectors where the computer
can be installed; a continued growth in professional and technical workers; a possible growing gap between the total number of jobs available,
and the total number of younger and older persons available for and interested in working.

THE OPTIONS WE CONFRONT

1. Acknowledging that the amount of education an individual has
acquired has a significant influence on his prospects for employment,
should we assume that all young people coming of working age will be

employed if they have earned a high school diploma? If education is only one of the determinants of employability, how much effort should society devote to attempting to keep the dropout in high school? How much to other approaches aimed at expanding the demand for workers with limited competence?

2. To what extent can the high school solve the dropout problem, even with substantially enlarged resources? May it not be necessary to seek fundamental improvements much earlier in the schooling process so that all young people acquire the reading and other skills which they will need if they are to make constructive use of four years of secondary education?

3. Since many high school students with average or even above average ability drop out because they are not interested in their classes and do not understand the importance of acquiring additional education, could some of this group be encouraged to continue to graduation if more work-study programs were available? Would their exposure to real jobs, their association with adults, their earning of money provide the stimulation and incentive which are now lacking? How practical is it for the schools to seek the cooperation of employers and trade unions to explore this dimension?

4. No matter what efforts are made to hold all adolescents in school or in school-corrected programs until they earn a high school diploma, some will continue to drop out. To what extent do these young people now have the opportunity to return to school or otherwise acquire a diploma? What steps might be taken to broaden their opportunities for a "second chance"?

5. Many employers have established the requirement of a high school diploma for all new members of their work force. Is this a reasonable requirement? If not, should efforts be made to encourage them to restudy this requirement in order to increase the opportunities of dropouts to obtain employment?

6. In light of the probable speedier obsolescence of knowledge and skills in the years ahead, what actions should be recommended to individuals, employers, and communities so that more adults will have the opportunity to continue their education and training?

7. The probable increasing proportion of jobs in professional and technical occupations in the future raises the question of whether there are serious barriers to entrance to college, junior college, or other post-high school educational and training facilities for some qualified young people and what types of action may be recommended to reduce or eliminate these barriers.

8. Is there any danger that, as a result of the current concern with the future employability of many young people, the high schools will

slight or ignore other important goals? What, if anything, can be done to assure that this does not occur?

9. If more and more adults will need access to educational and training facilities, what steps should be taken by employers, governmental agencies, and other strategic groups in our society to help assure that the required facilities and personnel will be made available?

10. What actions can narrow the marked differences among regions in their ability and willingness to support education and the substantial differences between urban and rural communities within the same region, as well as between the central cities and the suburban areas of large metropolitan centers? What additional actions are required to assure that each child has a reasonable opportunity to get a solid educational preparation for his later work and life?

11. The school builds on the foundation that the family lays. What special efforts should be made by the school systems in communities in which large numbers of children and young people are growing up under handicapping circumstances, including the particular handicap of not living with both parents? Should school boards attempt to persuade the American people that they should spend more money on children from low income homes than on children from more privileged families? If this policy is sound, what adjustments are required in our system of taxation to accomplish this end? What programs are most likely to prove productive?

12. If the American people can be persuaded to make additional resources available for education in general and for secondary education in particular, what adjustments are called for in the present variegated patterning of secondary education which includes academic, vocational, and general curricula in comprehensive and specialized high schools?

CONCLUDING OBSERVATIONS

Many of the issues posed above are of long standing. Some go back to the earliest days of public education. But there are several new dimensions that should be borne in mind as these problems are studied, for the solutions must be attuned to them.

Educational preparation has come to play an increasingly important part in determining the work and careers of the population. This means that any serious deficiencies in the schools will have increasingly serious consequences for the productivity of the economy and the stability of the society. A significant minority of the population grows up in a family and community setting which fails to prepare them to profit from what the school has to offer. Hence, the school faces a special challenge to meet the needs of this disadvantaged minority.

No matter how effectively the schools discharge their responsibilities, not all of their graduates will necessarily secure employment. Full employment will be easier to appproach if gross differences in educational background are reduced, but even if these differences are eliminated, to achieve full employment now requires additional changes.

But if the schools are to make their optimal contribution to the preparation of the population for work and life, they must meet the overriding challenge of awakening in all of their pupils an interest in learning and teaching them the basic skill of reading on which a lifetime of continued learning ultimately rests.

A REDEFINITION OF EDUCATION

Margaret Mead is an internationally known anthropologist and a prolific writer in both anthropology and education (Coming of Age in Samoa, Growing Up in New Guinea, The School in American Culture, New Lives for Old). *In the article presented here she examines and offers valuable insights into the process of the transmission of knowledge in school and society. Failing to grasp the tremendous rate of change, the American school has traditionally been preoccupied with what Mead calls the vertical transmission of knowledge instead of the lateral transmission. She urges that the entire pattern of American schooling be redefined so that it might accomplish its new function of "education for rapid and self-conscious adaptation to a changing world."*

Margaret Mead

NEA Journal (*October 1959*), *15–17. Reprinted by permission of the author and the NEA Journal.*

When we look realistically at today's world and become aware of what the actual problems of learning are, our conception of education changes radically. Although the educational system remains basically unchanged, we are no longer dealing primarily with the vertical transmission of the tried and true by the old, mature, and experienced teacher to the young, immature, and inexperienced pupil in the classroom.

This was the system of education developed in a stable, slowly changing culture. By itself, vertical transmission of knowledge no longer adequately serves the purposes of education in a world of rapid change.

What is needed and what we are already moving toward is the inclusion of another whole dimension of learning: the lateral transmission, to every sentient member of society, of what has just been discovered, invented, created, manufactured, or marketed.

This need for lateral transmission exists no less in the classroom and laboratory than it does on the assembly line with its working force of experienced and raw workmen. The man who teaches another individual the new mathematics or the use of a newly invented tool is not sharing knowledge he acquired years ago. He learned what was new yesterday, and his pupil must learn it today.

The whole teaching-and-learning continuum, once tied in an orderly and productive way to the passing of generations and the growth of the child into a man, has exploded in our faces. Yet even as we try to catch hold of and patch up the pieces, we fail to recognize what has happened.

We have moved into a period in which the break with the past provides an opportunity for creating a new framework for activity in almost every field—but in each field the fact that there has been a break must be rediscovered. In education there has been up to now no real recognition of the extent to which our present system is outmoded.

Historians point sagely to the last two educational crises—the first of which ended with the establishment of the universal elementary school and the second with the establishment of the universal high school—and with remarkable logic and lack of imagination they predict that the present crisis will follow the same pattern.

According to such predictions, the crisis will last until 1970, when it will end with the establishment of universal college education, accessible in principle to all young Americans.

Implicit in this prediction is a series of other dubious assumptions, such as these:

1. Our educational system has fallen behind in something and should therefore arrange to catch up.

2. Our difficulties are due to the "bulge," the host of babies that tricked the statisticians.

3. The pendulum is swinging back to sense—to discipline and dunce caps, switches, and multiplication tables.

But in the midst of the incessant discussion and the search for scapegoats to take the blame for what everyone admits is a parlous state, extraordinarily little attention is being paid to basic issues. Everyone simply wants more of what we already have: more children in more schools for more hours studying more of something.

Likewise, scant attention is paid to the fact that two great new educational agencies, the armed services and industry, have entered the field, and there is little awareness of the ways in which operations in these institutions are altering traditional education.

But most important, the pattern itself is hardly questioned, for we think we know what education is and what a good education ought to be. However deficient we may be as a people, as taxpayers, or as educators, we may be actualizing our ideals.

An occasional iconoclast can ask: "Wouldn't it be fine if we could scrap our whole school system and start anew?" But he gets no hearing because everyone knows that what he is saying is nonsense. Wishful dreams of starting anew are obviously impractical, but this does not mean that someone should not ask these crucial questions:

Is our present historic idea of education suitable for people in the mid-twentieth century, who have a life expectancy of 70 years, and who live in a world of automation and global communication, ready to begin space exploration and aware of the possibility of bringing about the suicide of the entire human species?

Is it not possible that the problem of the educational system's obsolescence goes beyond such issues as methods of teaching reading or physics, or the most desirable age for leaving school, or the payment of teachers, or the length of summer holidays, or the number of years best devoted to college?

Is not the break between past and present—and so the whole problem of outdating in our educational system—related to a change in the rate of change? For change has become so rapid that adjustment cannot be left to the next generation. Adults must—not once, but continually—take in, adjust to, use, and make innovations in a steady stream of discovery and new conditions.

Is it not possible that an educational system that was designed to teach what was known to little children and to a selected few young men may not fit a world in which the most important factors in everyone's life are those things that are not yet, but soon will be known?

Is it not equally possible that our present definition of a pupil or a student is out of date when we define the learner as a child (or at best an immature person) who is entitled to moral protection and subsistence in a dependency position and who is denied the moral autonomy that is accorded to an adult?

Looking at our educational system today, we can see that in various ways it combines these different functions:

1. The protection of the child against exploitation and the protection of society against precocity and inexperience

2. The maintenance of learners in a state of moral and economic dependency

3. Giving to all children the special, wider education once reserved for those of privileged groups, in an attempt to form the citizen of a democracy as once the son of a noble house was formed

4. The teaching of complex and specialized skills which, under our complex system of division of labor, is too difficult and time-consuming for each set of parents to master or to hand on to their own children

5. The transmission of something which the parents' generation does not know (in the case of immigrants with varied cultural and linguistic backgrounds) to children whom the authorities or the parents wish to have educated.

To these multiple functions of an educational system, which in a slowly changing society were variously performed, we have added slowly and reluctantly a quite new function: education for rapid and self-conscious adaptation to a changing world.

That we have as yet failed to recognize the new character of change is apparent in a thousand ways. Despite the fact that a subject taught to college freshmen may have altered basically by the time the same students are seniors, it is still said that colleges are able to give students "a good education"—finished, wrapped, sealed with a degree.

Upon getting a bachelor's degree, a student can decide to "go on" to a higher degree because he has not as yet "completed" his education, that is, the lump of the known which he has decided to bite off. But a student who has once let a year go by after he is "out of school" does not "go on," but rather "goes back" to school.

And as we treat education as the right of a minor who has not yet completed high school, just so we equate marriage and parenthood with getting a diploma; both indicate that one's education is "finished."

Consistent with our conception of what a student is, our educational institutions are places where we keep "children" for a shorter or longer period. The length of time depends in part on their intelligence and motivation and in part on their parents' incomes and the immediately recognized national needs for particular skills or types of training.

Once they have left, we regard them as in some sense finished, neither capable of nor in need of further "education," for we still believe that education should come all in one piece, or rather, in a series of connected pieces, each presented as a whole at the elementary, secondary, and the college level. All other behaviors are aberrant.

So we speak of "interrupted" education—that is, education which has been broken into by sickness, delinquency, or military service—and we attempt to find means of repairing this interruption. Indeed, the whole GI bill, which in a magnificent way gave millions of young men a chance for a different kind of education than they would otherwise have got, was conceived of primarily as a means of compensating young men for an unsought but unavoidable interruption.

Thus we avoid facing the most vivid truth of the new age: No one will live all his life in the world into which he was born, and no one will die in the world in which he worked in his maturity.

For those who work on the growing edge of science, technology, or the arts, contemporary life changes at even shorter intervals. Often, only a few months may elapse before something which previously was easily taken for granted must be unlearned or transformed to fit the new state of knowledge or practice.

In today's world, no one can "complete an education." The students we need are not just children who are learning to read and write, plus older students, conceived of as minors, who are either "going on" with or "going back" to specialized education. Rather, we need children and adolescents and young and mature and "senior" adults, each of whom is learning at the appropriate pace and with all the special advantages and disadvantages of experience peculiar to his own age.

Each and every one of these is a learner, not only of the old and tried—the alphabet or multiplication tables or Latin declensions or French irregular verbs or the binomial theorem—but of new, hardly tried theories and methods: pattern analysis, general system theory, space lattices, cybernetics, and so on.

Learning of this kind must go on, not only at special times and in special places, but all through production and consumption—from the technician who must handle a new machine to the factory supervisor who must introduce its use, the union representative who must interpret it to the men, the foreman who must keep the men working, the salesman who must service a new device or find markets for it, the housewife who must understand how to care for a new material, the mother who must answer the questions of a four-year-old child.

In this world, the age of the teacher is no longer necessarily relevant. For instance, children teach grandparents how to manage TV, young expediters come into the factory along with the new equipment, and young men invent automatic programing for computers over which their seniors struggle.

This, then, is what we call the lateral transmission of knowledge. It is not an outpouring of knowledge from the "wise old teacher" into the minds of young pupils, as in vertical transmission. Rather, it is sharing of knowledge by the informed with the uninformed, whatever their ages. The primary prerequisite for the learner is the desire to know.

To facilitate this lateral transmission of knowledge, we need to redefine what we mean by primary and secondary education. We need to stop thinking that free and, when necessary, subsidized education is appropriate only when it is preliminary to an individual's work experience.

Instead of adding more and more years of compulsory education (which would further confuse the meaning of education and the purpose of schools), we need to separate primary and secondary education in an entirely new way:

By primary education we would mean the stage of education in which all children are taught what they need to know in order to be fully human in the world in which they are growing up—including the basic skills of reading and writing and a basic knowledge of numbers, money, geography, transportation and communication, the law, and the nations of the world.

By secondary education we would mean an education that is based on primary education, and that can be obtained in any amount and at any period during the individual's whole lifetime.

After agreeing upon this redefinition, we could begin to deal effectively with the vast new demands that are being made on us. The high schools would be relieved of the nonlearners. (It would be essential, of course, that industry, government, or some other social group accept the responsibility of employing or otherwise occupying these persons).

But more important, men and women, instead of preparing for a single career to which—for lack of any alternative—they must stick during their entire active lives, would realize that they might learn something else. Women, after their children became older, could be educated for particular new tasks, instead of facing the rejection that today is related to fear about the difficulty of acquiring new learning in middle age.

Whatever their age, those obtaining a secondary education at any level (high school, college, or beyond) would be in school because they wanted to learn and wanted to be there at that time.

In an educational system of this kind, we could give primary education and protection to children as well as protection and sensitive supervision to adolescents. We could back up to the hilt the potentiality of every human being—of whatever age—to learn at any level.

The right to obtain secondary education when and where the individual could use it would include not only the right of access to existing conventional types of schools but also the right of access to types of work training not yet or only now being developed—new kinds of apprenticeship and also new kinds of work teams.

In thinking about an effective educational system, we should recognize that the adolescent's need and right to work is as great as (perhaps greater than) his immediate need and right to study. And we must recognize that the adult's need and right to study more is as great as (perhaps greater than) his need and right to hold the same job until he is 65.

We cannot accomplish the essential educational task merely by keeping children and young adults—whom we treat like children—in school longer. We can do it by creating an educational system in which all individuals will be assured of the secondary and higher education they want and can use any time throughout their entire lives.

TEACHING THE CULTURALLY DISADVANTAGED

One of the most challenging problems in American education today is the problem of the culturally disadvantaged student. In the following essay the authors analyze the characteristics of disadvantaged children, describe their environment, and give certain suggestions which have been found by experience and research to be valuable in helping these children. The authors urge the teacher of the disadvantaged "to begin where the child is instead of penalizing him for being there." Myers and Gezi have served as consultants to school districts and to several NDEA-supported Institutes for Teachers of the Culturally Deprived at Chico State College. They have had extensive teaching experience with disadvantaged students in California.

James E. Myers
Kalil I. Gezi

   Prepared especially for this volume.

The plight of the disadvantaged American has become more acute today with the urban conditions which have resulted in slums and ghettos in our large cities. An increasing number of the school population in these cities can be termed culturally disadvantaged, thereby underscoring the urgent need for preparing teachers who can work successfully with these children.

WHO ARE THE DISADVANTAGED?

With the publication of Riessman's *The Culturally Deprived Child* in 1962, the term "culturally deprived" gained popularity. The difficulty with this term is that it assumes that there are some people who are deprived, yet it is impossible to deprive an individual of his own culture. The Mexican-American is not deprived of his Mexican heritage, but he is at a disadvantage in comparison with middle-class Americans in terms of living and working successfully in American society.

California's McAteer Act of 1963, a compensatory-education act, defined the culturally disadvantaged child as "one who, although potentially capable of graduating from the public schools, is hindered from doing so by cultural, socio-economic, and environmental handicaps." Although this is a well-meaning definition, its all-inclusiveness renders it useless in identifying culturally disadvantaged children until they drop out of school.

Havighurst uses the term "socially disadvantaged" to mean "disadvantaged for living competently in an urban, industrial, and democratic society." The difficulty with this definition is that it sets successful living in an urban, industrial milieu as a prerequisite for being socially advantaged. According to this definition, middle-class farmers who are living successfully in rural America are socially disadvantaged. It is hard to see how such middle-class Americans who have adequate educational opportunities can be designated as socially disadvantaged; but it is apparent that social class is the key factor in distinguishing between those who are advantaged and those who are not. The school and the teachers have traditionally reflected the values and aspirations of middle-class Americans. Therefore, when lower-class children enter the school, they have greater problems of adjustment than do middle-class children. These children are clearly at an advantage when the teacher insists upon such values as punctuality, cleanliness, thrift, and correct language because these values have been transmitted in their environment. Furthermore, it is evident that in America there is an increasing tendency to distinguish people more on the basis of their social class than on their religion, ethnic background, or color. This conclusion has been supported by many studies. For instance, Kerckhoff and Gould, in their study of fifth-grade children, discovered that children were more accepting "of children of a different race than they were of children of a different social class." [1]

In this discussion the term "culturally disadvantaged" will be used to denote those persons whose environment has failed to transmit to them the values necessary for success in the school and society. The majority of these persons come from the lower classes and from certain minority groups to whom full socioeconomic opportunities are not available, the disadvantaged in this country being composed, for the most part, of Negroes, Mexicans, Puerto Ricans, Indians, and poor whites. But regardless of which definition of the culturally disadvantaged child is used, it is necessary, for a fuller understanding of this child, to describe the specific characteristics which distinguish him from the culturally advantaged.

[1] R. Kerckhoff and F. Gould, "Developing the Sixth Sense: The Sense of Community," *The PTA Magazine*, 57 (October 1962), 30–32.

CHARACTERISTICS OF THE CULTURALLY DISADVANTAGED
AND HIS ENVIRONMENT

Poverty

The overwhelming majority of the culturally disadvantaged are poor. Who are the poor? As Galbraith has pointed out, there seems to be no precise definition of poverty in the United States. The difficulty stems not only from its nature but also from changing social conceptions of it over the years. However, when poverty is determined by family annual income, the most frequent figure used has been the minimum of $3000 for a family. This figure was used by the Council of Economic Advisors in their 1964 "Economic Report of the President." [2]

Using this as a base level, 9.3 percent of the forty-seven-million American families, which comprises 20 percent of the total population, were poor in 1962. Harrington estimates the poor of the United States to be between forty to fifty million individuals, which is 20 to 25 percent of the total population.[3] Many of these families have annual incomes far below the $3000 level.

Associated with low level income are many social, psychological, health, and educational disadvantages. When four slum areas in Chicago were compared with four non-slum areas in the same city, the results indicated that the slum areas had "twenty times as much juvenile delinquency, twelve times as much mortality from tuberculosis, four times as much mortality from pneumonia, three times as much truancy, and more than twice as much infant mortality. . . ." [4] Psychologically, lower-class children were found by Wylie to estimate their ability to do school work more modestly than students in higher classes. Other studies tend also to substantiate the finding that lower-class children have lower aspirations, lower self-esteem, and a greater withdrawal tendency than middle or upper-class children. As for education, there is evidence indicating a strong relationship between low income and the amount of schooling. Table 1 shows that the lower the income of the family, the fewer years of schooling completed by its head. Table 2 illustrates the relationship of school dropouts to family income.

[2] Council of Economic Advisors, "Economic Report of the President together with the Annual Report of the Council of Economic Advisors" (Washington, D.C., 1964).

[3] Michael Harrington, *The Other America* (Baltimore: Penguin Books, Inc., 1965), p. 178.

[4] Midcentury White House Conference on Children and Youth, "Children and Youth at Midcentury" (Washington, D.C., 1950), Chart 29.

Table 1   FAMILY INCOME AND
            MEDIAN YEARS OF
            SCHOOL, 1964 [a]

Median Total Family Income	Median Years of School Completed by Head of Family
Under $1000	8.8
$1000–1999	8.3
$2000–2999	8.7
$3000–3999	9.7
$4000–4999	10.8
$5000–5999	11.6
$6000–6999	12.1
$7000–7999	12.2
$8000–9999	12.3
$10,000–14,999	12.5
$15,000–24,999	13.5
$25,000 and over	15.0

[a] U.S. Department of Commerce, Bureau of the Census, *Income of Families and Persons in the United States,* (Current Population Reports, Consumer Income, Series P-60, No. 47. [Washington, D.C., 1965]), Table 7, p. 27.

Table 2   SCHOOL DROPOUTS BY FAMILY
            INCOME, OCTOBER 1964 [a]

Family Income	Percent of 16–24-Year-Olds	
	Total	*Dropouts* [b]
Under $2000	9.6%	20.3%
$2000–2999	8.1	14.3
$3000–4999	20.9	29.8
$5000–7999	24.7	18.8
$7500–9999	14.4	6.3
$10,000 and over	15.5	4.0
Income not reported	6.8	6.5

[a] U.S. Department of Commerce, Bureau of the Census, *School Enrollments, October, 1964,* (Current Population Report, Population Characteristics, Series P-20, No. 148 [Washington, D.C., 1966]), p. 1.

[b] Persons not enrolled in school in October 1964, and not high school graduates.

Home environment

In the preschool years home environment is probably the most significant influence on the child. Studies have shown important differences in the home environment of disadvantaged and advantaged children.[5] The homes of the disadvantaged tend to be more crowded, lacking in magazines, newspapers, records, toys, and other objects that are likely to help in the cultural development of the child. Disadvantaged parents give little language encouragement to their children, have less direct interaction with them, take less interest in their learning, maintain closed and rigid relationships with them, and administer more physical punishment.

Riessman pointed out some attributes of the disadvantaged home, such as the security offered by the cooperation among the members of the extended family, but on the whole this kind of home environment is not conducive to the development of many attitudes, values, and experiences which are necessary for success in our middle-class-oriented schools. Indeed, substantial doubt has been cast on whether disadvantaged children are superior in any respect to the members of the middle and upper classes.[6] There is no question that discrimination has a detrimental effect on the individual. The children who are the object of discrimination, whether racial, ethnic, religious, or class, are made to feel that they are not as good as children from the dominant group, and that they have fewer opportunities to advance themselves educationally, socially, and economically. In many areas of the United States disadvantaged children are forced by *de facto* segregation to live in ghettos where they attend poorly staffed and equipped slum schools and where they are limited to interacting with other disadvantaged children. Their feelings of inferiority may, in the words, of Chief Justice Earl Warren, "affect their hearts and minds in a way unlikely ever to be undone."

Language

One of basic prerequisites for achievement in school is the acquisition of an adequate level of language proficiency. Comparative studies of the development of language skills among lower- and middle-class children indicate that there are some basic differences. On the whole, the lan-

---

[5] For a summary of research in this area, see Edmund W. Gordon, "Characteristics of Socially Disadvantaged Children," *Review of Educational Research,* 35 (December, 1965), 377–388.

[6] Robert Havighurst, "Who Are the Socially Disadvantaged?", *The Journal of Negro Education,* 33 (Summer 1964), 210–217.

guage of the middle-class child tends to be elaborate, while the speech of the disadvantaged child is usually restricted.

After summarizing important research on language development in socially disadvantaged children, Raph concluded that these children, in comparison with middle-class students, are more subject: a) to a lack of vocal stimulation during infancy; b) to a paucity of experiences in conversation with more verbally mature adults in the first three or four years of life; c) to severe limitations in the opportunities to develop mature cognitive behavior; d) to the types of emotional encounters which result in the restricting of the children's conceptual and verbal skills.[7]

What, however, are the specific characteristics of the restricted language of the lower-class child in comparison with the elaborated language of his middle-class counterpart? Bernstein typifies the restricted language environment of the disadvantaged child by: "a) short, grammatically simple, often unfinished sentences with a poor syntactical form; b) simple and repetitive use of conjunctions (so, then, and, because); c) little use of subordinate clauses used to break down the initial categories of the dominant subject; d) inability to hold a formal subject through a speech sequence, thus facilitating a dislocated informational content; e) rigid and limited use of adjectives and adverbs; f) infrequent use of impersonal pronouns as subjects of conditional clauses or sentences, for example, "one"; g) frequent use of statements where the reason and the conclusion are confounded to produce a categoric utterance; h) a large number of statements and phrases that signal a requirement for the previous speech sequence to be reinforced; for example, "Wouldn't it," "You see," "Just fancy," a process termed "sympathetic circularity"; i) frequent occurrence of individual selection from a group of idiomatic sequences; j) individual qualification implicit in the sentence organization: It is a language of implicit meaning." [8]

Thus, the middle-class child finds much less difficulty in understanding the language used by his teachers than the disadvantaged child with his restricted language background. This child is likely to fall behind in the primary grades because of his language deficiency, and is destined to experience a widening gap between his language and that of his teacher and his middle-class peers as the school studies become progressively more demanding. For an interesting example of the gap between the language of Negro inmates and that of the standard English, see Table 3.

[7] Jane Beasley Raph, "Language Development in Socially Disadvantaged Children," *Review of Educational Research,* **35** (December 1965), 389–400.

[8] Basil Bernstein, "Social Class and Linguistic Development: A Theory of Social Learning," in *Education, Economy, and Society,* ed. A. H. Halsey *et al.*, (New York: Crowell-Collier and Macmillan, 1961).

Table 3   THE LANGUAGE USED BY NEGRO INMATES
WITHIN THE CALIFORNIA PRISON SYSTEM [a]

MELON:	The head.
MIATE:	A negro.
MUSLIM:	A negro sect, supposedly religious.
GUNSEL:	One who tries to be a bully.
MAKE A MOVE:	A decision or some type of action.
MACE:	A spice used as a stimulant.
MULE:	One who will bring contraband into the institution.
KNUCKLE THERAPY:	To give or take a beating with the fists.
NEEDLE:	Hypodermic needle.
NOD:	The dropping of one's head, usually from the use of narcotics, sleep.
NUTMEG:	A spice use as a stimulant.
OLD LADY:	Wife, sweetheart, mother, or a homosexual partner.
OLD MAN:	Father, or a homosexual partner.
ON THE ERIE:	Listening for something or eavesdropping.
OUT OF MY CORD:	Out of his head, usually from anger or a narcotic, same as wiped out.
PADDLE:	A type of count made in the blocks after a mis-count.
PUT DOWN:	No longer considered a friend by a friend.
PANIC:	To make an unwise move at the wrong time.
PUNK:	A homosexual.
PRESSURE:	To force another to one's wants or desires—usually canteen items or homosexual favors.
HANG A JACKET:	To label one as a stool pigeon or pervert.
PIPE:	A length of pipe or other item used to strike another with.
PICKETS:	The teeth.
PAD:	House, apartment, or cell.
PADDY:	Anyone of the Caucasian race.
PILL:	Any form of narcotics. Also designating the lethal gas pills used in Legal executions.
PORCH:	The Captain's Office.
PSYCH:	Anyone considered mentally unbalanced.
PAPER HANGER:	Bad check artist.
PACK:	A package of cigarettes.
PASS:	Not to be punished for an infraction.
NICKLE:	A five dollar bill.
RIDE A BEEF:	To accept punishment for an infraction of the rules.
RAP:	Type of crime or infraction of the rules.
ROTUNDA:	The area one enters when going into a block before entering the main unit.
RAT PACK:	A group using strong-arm tactics or threats.
RUNNER:	An inmate or Officer who delivers articles to the various units.

ROACH:	Butt of a marijuana cigarette.
RADIO:	Be quiet.
ROMEOS:	A type of condom.
ROUTE:	An established area for illegal transactions.
ROW:	Condemned Row—Death Row—Men awaiting the Death Penalty.
RIP OFF:	To take without the other's consent.
STUFF:	Narcotics—A knife or other weapon—A homosexual.
SHANK:	A knife.
SHORT:	Short period of time left before release.
SNIVEL:	To gripe or plead—to feel sorry for oneself.
SHELF:	Isolation.
SUEDE:	Any negro.
SPOOK:	Any negro.
SNITCH:	An informer.
STUCK:	To be stabbed or to be in debt.
SWING WITH:	To steal.
SHUCK:	A fake.
SNIFFER:	One who sniffs glues or other materials for intoxication.
SCREW:	Any Correctional Officer.
SPIKE:	A hypodermic needle. Also keys for the cell doors.
SEGREGATION:	A Unit for protective custody inmates.
SHORT LINE:	A group of workers who eat before the mainline so there is no slow down in production on certain assignments.
SPREAD:	To treat others to goodies. Also in a shakedown, the spreading of the cheeks or the buttocks for inspection.
STASH:	A hiding place or a reserve of some kind.
STRUNG OUT:	Sometimes concerning narcotics—sometimes designating "In Love."
STAND POINT:	To watch out for Officers when an associate is doing something illegal.
SPLIT:	To leave.
SOMETHING ELSE:	Could refer to something very good or something very bad. Also, something rare.
SNAP:	To comprehend.
SPOT:	An area for illegal activities—usually homosexual.
WRITE UP:	To receive a disciplinary report.
WIRED UP:	To be in love. Also, set up for a frame-up or all keyed up mentally.
SHIV:	A knife.
SPOON:	A spoon used for cooking narcotics.
SHADES:	Sun Glasses.
SWISH:	To walk like a woman—usually a homosexual.
SNIFFINS:	Sniffing material.
STINGER:	A device to heat water or coffee.

Table 3 (*continued*)

SHAKEDOWN:	To be searched.
SET UP:	To be framed.
STREETS:	The outside.
SHIT CAN:	A garbage can.
SHITTERS:	Toilets.
SKIN SHAKE:	To be stripped and searched.
SOUNDS:	Music.
QUIET CELL:	A cell in isolation that is separated from other cells.
HUSSLE:	An illegal gainful activity.
HORNING:	Sniffing narcotics through the nose.
TURN OUT:	To become a homosexual or a snitch.
SING:	Inform.
THREE FOR TWO:	To lend out two of an item for three in return.
THE MAN:	Any Correctional Officer.
TAKE CARE OF:	To take care of a friend or settle an argument.
TRIP:	To relate an experience or to Day-Dream.
TIER TENDER:	A worker in the cell block who is responsible for the cleanliness of a designated tier(s) and who issues hot water to the inmates celled in his tier(s).
WHITES:	Tee shirts, shorts & towels.
WHEELER & DEALER:	One who traffics in gainful illegal activities.
WASTER:	To be intoxicated or under the influence of a narcotic. Dead.
YA:	One sentenced by the Youth Authority. Not charged as adult.
FOUR POST:	The Yard Office.
ONE-FIFTEEN:	A disciplinary report.
ONE-TWENTY-EIGHT:	A good or bad report on an individual. 128-A.
JUICE:	Home Brew. Also, in good standing with an Official.
DUST:	State-issued cigarette tobacco. Also to kill.

ª From a list of words commonly used by Negro inmates in California prisons collected and supplied to the authors by Jarriet W. Warner, a teacher in Richmond, California.

Bilingual children, who number about twenty-two million in the United States, face even greater problems in the school. This is especially true of bilingual children who come from disadvantaged homes, such as Puerto Rican, Mexican-American, and Indian children.

Intelligence, Cognition, and Achievement

Intelligence   Evidence from studies of intelligence and socio-economic status has indicated that intelligence scores of disadvantaged children as measured by IQ tests tended to be lower than those of children from advantaged homes. However, there is also evidence that these differences in intelligence may be attributed to an impoverished environment rather than to a inherent lack of ability. Klineberg could not find any scientific support for the notion that ethnic groups are intellectually inferior. Furthermore, he found that Negro children who migrated to New York City from the South tended to improve their IQ scores as a result of improving their environment.[9]

There are some serious problems underlying the validity of our methods of determining the intelligence of the culturally disadvantaged child. First, the traditional IQ tests will discriminate against children from impoverished backgrounds because they are usually oriented toward middle-class norms. Second, since most of the IQ tests rely on verbal ability, the disadvantaged child with a restricted language background is likely to obtain lower scores than the advantaged student with an elaborate language environment. Third, school work, including test taking, is facilitated in advantaged homes by introducing the child early to educational toys, games, and other experiences which tend to give him an educational head start. Adjustment to school work is further enhanced in these homes by reinforcement of values such as promptness, speed, efficiency, and industry.

The disadvantaged child from the bilingual home presents an even greater problem in the assessment of his intelligence. In addition to the problems cited above, the bilingual child from a Mexican or a Puerto Rican background, for example, has a cultural background manifesting greater disparities with the American middle-class culture than the disadvantaged child whose sole language at home is English.

Cognition   Like intelligence, the level of cognition in disadvantaged children seems to be lower than that of privileged children. This is not surprising, in view of the fact that concept formation is based in part on a wide background of experiences, intellectual stimulation, and language competency. The disadvantaged child lags in each of these areas. Riessman characterized concept formation among the disadvantaged as being content centered instead of form centered, and more inductive than deductive.[10]

[9] Otto Klineburg, "Negro-White Differences in Intelligence Tests Performances: A New Look at an Old Problem," *American Psychologist*, 18 (April 1963), 198–203.

[10] Frank Riessman, "The Culturally Deprived Child: A New View," *Programs for the Educationally Disadvantaged* (U.S. Dept. of Health, Education, and Welfare, Office of Education, Bulletin, 1963, No. 17 [Washington, D.C., 1963]), pp. 3–10.

Achievement   Hampered by an impoverished environment, it is inevitable that the disadvantaged child's achievement in school is far below that of his classmates. For instance, the Watts Report by the Governor's Commission on the Lost Angeles riots of 1965, showed that students in the disadvantaged areas of Los Angeles were distressingly lower in achievement-test scores than those of city wide and advantaged area students. Table 4 attests to the great disparity between advantaged and

Table 4 AVERAGE READING PERFORMANCE
IN COMPARISON AREAS—GRADE B5 [a]

Area	Reading Vocabulary Ranking Percentile	Reading Comprehension Ranking Percentile
Citywide (Los Angeles)	48	48
Advantaged Area	81	75
Disadvantaged Area—Watts	20	24
Disadvantaged Area—Avalon	20	21
Disadvantaged Area—Boyle Heights	18	19
Disadvantaged Area—East Los Angeles	18	24

[a] *Violence in the City—An End or a Beginning?*, A Report by the Governor's Commission on the Los Angeles Riots, December 2, 1965.

disadvantaged students in reading vocabulary and comprehension. It can be clearly seen that students in disadvantaged areas were between the eighteenth- and twenty-fourth-percentile of the national fifth-grade reading-test population. In comparison with the achievement of students in these disadvantaged areas, 80 percent and 76 percent of the national fifth-grade population scored higher in reading vocabulary and reading comprehension respectively.

The Watts Report authors found the average fifth grader in disadvantaged areas to be "unable to read and understand a daily newspaper, or to make use of reading and writing for ordinary purposes in his life."

It is also evident in this report that the differences in achievement between the disadvantaged and advantaged children become increasingly greater as time moves on.

Attitudes and Motivation

In middle- and upper-class homes, in comparison with those in the lower class, children are more prone to have high levels of aspiration and positive attitudes which enhance their chances of achievement in school work.[11]

Lower-class children tend to underestimate their abilities in the school and to form low self-concepts. Favorable self-concepts have been shown to be related to better performance in school.[12]

The negative self-image, the low level of self-confidence, and the feeling of persecution have disturbing effects on the personality of the disadvantaged child. Because of his frustrating experiences in the school, he is more likely to become a dropout. For example, in three Los Angeles schools located in disadvantaged areas, according to the Watts Report, about two-thirds of the students drop out before high school graduation.[13]

REFLECTIONS OF A TEACHER CANDIDATE
WITH A LOWER-CLASS BACKGROUND

There are numerous examples illustrative of the problems inherent in the value discrepancies between lower and middle classes. The example selected here has a special poignance for teachers and students in education because it conveys the frustrations of a prospective teacher who sees the middle-class school through a lower-class perspective.

A STUDENT SPEAKS OUT [14]

After observing and working at ——— elementary school, I can honestly say that I wouldn't teach grammar school for love or money. I have never met so many small, trite, petty and bigoted people in my life as I found out at ———. Their biggest delight was to yell, scream, shake and threaten the children (Little Children). It seems to fill them with some ecstatic feeling.

During lunch I don't believe the conversation ever rose above the level of a moron. It went like this: "My my, they certainly gave the pews a nice varnish," or "Have you heard about so and so," or "Have you eaten in that new exotic restaurant in ———? Isn't the desert

[11] A. N. Hieronymus, "A Study of Social Class Motivation: Relationships between Anxiety for Education and Certain Socio-Economic and Intellectual Variables," *Journal of Educational Psychology,* 42 (April 1951), 193–205.

[12] Wilber Brookover *et al.,* "Self-Concept of Ability and School Achievement," *Sociology of Education,* 37 (Spring 1964), 271.

[13] *Violence in the City,* p. 52.

[14] These comments were written by a student in a Social Foundations of Education class at Chico State College.

marvelous!" If a person tries to interject something intellectual into the conversation, they look at him as if he were mad.

Really, the books on Education that are trying to raise the values of the lower class to those of the middle class have the values backward. It would be better if the middle class adopted the social values of the "lower class." Sure I ran with a gang in high school, but let me tell you there was a true friendship, loyalty and sincerity among us that you will never find among the middle class children. We ditched high school. Why? Because we liked to organize our own fun, do our own thinking, make decisions.

I think some of our best times were spent playing street football, baseball, kick-the-can, but whatever we did, we organized or created it ourselves. We used to play ball in an old vacant lot. There were big kids, skinny kids, crippled kids, and ordinary kids that used to play there, until one day one of those dirty, slimy little leagues started taking over. I remember sloppy, fat, pallid businessmen that wanted to be buddies to their sons instead of fathers. They organized the little league for their bubble gum sons. They said I could play, but my friend Max couldn't play anymore because he was crippled, and the game had to be taken seriously. The other third of my friends couldn't play because they were girls. I told them to shove it!

We used to play in some old abandoned tenement houses; we took chances on high places, played follow-the-leader through difficult and dangerous mazes. Sometimes we played in these old tenement houses from dark till daylight. It was adventurous, and most of all it was not supervised by some mealy-mouthed adult. One day a wrecking crew came and tore down the old tenement houses, and they asphalted a square of ground. They erected skinny, cold, impersonal aluminum slides, swings, monkey bars and a couple of sandboxes. They stuck a one-inch foreheader in the playground. He looked like a Cro-Magnon; he wore a t-shirt with "playground supervisor" written on it. He had a butch and huge muscles to compensate for his mind. He was in his glory. They gave him a new chrome-plated whistle. I honestly believe that tooting on that shiny whistle gave him some sort of sexual satisfaction. What I am saying is, if we want to educate the kids to be real people, genuine persons, we have got to get rid of about half of the do-gooder, honey-eyed, effeminate teaching staff.

I observed a math class at ——— high school. I went into the classroom at eight and was prepared to stay until noon, but at ten o'clock classes broke up for a fifteen-minute coffee break. I asked the instructor how this worked; he said great, both the students and the teachers were refreshed. At the elementary school I told them about the kids getting a coffee break; these are the answers I got: "They probably smoke, too." "They probably make out in cars." "It's horrible, I just can't imagine kids drinking coffee." One of these teachers that was giving these answers looked like a road runner wearing telephone insulators for glasses. She informed me that her husband was the minister of the ———— church.

Hell, there is probably just as much despotic teaching going on today as there was fifty years ago. We should rid the schools of bigoted, puritanical values and petty rules that dominate the classroom. They don't leave enough room for thinking. We should place a greater emphasis on friendliness, loyalty, kindness and sincerity, and a hell of a lot less on "Cleanliness is next to Godliness," and "Authority makes right."

I might add they were doing one thing at ———— that appalled me. They encouraged the children to tell on each other. I told each child that tattled to me in a vindictive tone that I hated tattling worse than anything on this earth. The middle class seems to emphasize Orwell's *1984* as well as the sick *Brave New World*.

WHAT CAN TEACHERS DO TO HELP THE CULTURALLY DISADVANTAGED CHILD?

Recommendations and suggestions for teaching disadvantaged children are many and varied. One of the problems in suggesting a particular course of action stems from the fact that not all disadvantaged children have the same disadvantages. The problems of a white lower-class child living in an inner city slum are different from those of a Mexican-American child whose family follows the crops. Similarly, the difficulties facing the ghetto Negro child are not the same as the ones confronted by an American Indian child attending an off-reservation school.

Another major problem in recommending a particular pattern for teaching disadvantaged children is that not all teachers can adapt to a given way of dealing with these children because of their unique background, temperament, and styles of teaching.

Therefore, in making the following suggestions in respect to the disadvantaged child in the classroom, it is important to remember that these are not prescriptions that will work for every teacher with every child in all situations, but are rather suggestions that were found to be helpful by the authors in teaching disadvantaged children.

1. The teacher should establish a warm classroom climate based on accepting, appreciating, and respecting each individual, without sacrificing his authority as a teacher. Understanding children and treating them with respect does not mean that a laissez-faire attitude will prevail

in the classroom. Conversely, setting down and enforcing limits of behavior need not presuppose an authoritarian classroom atmosphere.

An accepting classroom environment can help the disadvantaged child develop a positive self-concept and foster a good attitude toward the teacher, other students, and the school.

2. The teacher should become familiar with the subcultures of the disadvantaged. An understanding of the child's family structure, home environment, modes of behavior, cultural traditions and values, can help the teacher guide the child's learning more effectively. For instance, by realizing that the tempo of living in Mexico is slower than in America, the teacher may not place a premium on speed in evaluating the work of the Mexican-American child.

By understanding the culture of disadvantaged students, the teacher can enhance his effectiveness in communicating with them and eventually break down the barriers of mutual rejection.

3. The teacher can help his students understand the dynamics of prejudice and its implications for minority groups. Students from both the minority and dominant groups can benefit from such an understanding. Students from the majority group may be able to analyze the basis of their prejudices and rely instead upon rational approaches in their relationships with minority group students. Students from minority groups, who have been the objects of prejudice, may be able to understand why others have negative attitudes toward them.

It is mandatory for the teacher of disadvantaged children to understand his own prejudices so that they will not hamper him in teaching these children.

4. The teacher should use methods specifically attuned to the needs of disadvantaged children. He must understand the "hip" language used by these children, start with what they know, and move progressively toward an enriched vocabulary. Role-playing also can be used effectively because it seems to be "much more congenial with the low-income person's style; physical (action oriented; do vs. talk); down to earth, concrete, problem directed; *externally oriented rather than introspective;* group centered; gamelike rather than test oriented; easy, informal tempo." [15] Emphasis should also be placed on auditory and visual aids to teaching. Textbooks should be selected which contain stories, pictures, and examples with which the inner city lower-class child can identify. Classroom activities should help the student experience a certain degree of success so that he can acquire some satisfaction from his classwork and develop a positive attitude toward school. Motivitating the disad-

[15] Frank Riessman, "Education of the Culturally Deprived Child," *The Science Teacher,* 32 (November 1965) 14–16.

vantaged child should be oriented, at least in the beginning, toward what he considers most important to him. Special evaluative methods should be designed to focus on comparing his present progress with his past achievement instead of comparing his achievement against middle-class students.

5. In order to meet the human relations problem in the class, the teacher must be sensitive to his students. Sensitivity is especially important for the teacher of the culturally disadvantaged. The sensitive teacher is able to predict what a student is likely to feel, to say and to do about the teacher, himself, and others. To develop sensitivity, teachers and administrators should be open to experience, genuinely motivated to understand people, interested in involving students in the learning process and in the evaluation of the learning experience.

In examining the foregoing suggestions, it is important for the teacher of the disadvantaged to begin where the child is instead of penalizing him for being there. As Riessman cautioned, we must "distinguish between ignorance and stupidity and make it clear that ignorance and many other limitations can be reversed." [16] It is toward this reversal that the school in American culture has a primary obligation.

[16] Riessman, "Education of the Culturally Deprived Child," p. 16.

3

CROSS-CULTURAL PERSPECTIVES

INTRODUCTION

In recent years, this country has witnessed an increasing interest in the study of cross-cultural education. Some of the major factors underlying this interest are the country's expanding role in world affairs, the increasing interdependence among nations, the mounting pressure of competition from abroad, and the urgent need to resolve world conflict and preserve peace. One of the most striking examples of how the achievements of a country can spur a re-evaluation of the educational system of another country is the Russian advances in space exploration since 1957. Russia's successes brought about an immediate outcry in America, forcing educators, school boards, and legislatures to re-examine the American system of education.

The American interest in international education can be seen in many of the activities that have been undertaken by this country since World War II. The United States has staunchly supported the objectives of the United Nations Educational, Scientific and Cultural Organization (UNESCO), namely, the diffusion of knowledge among all people, the stimulation of nations to provide a basic education for their people, and the increase in scholarly communication and cooperation among all countries. By embracing the goals of UNESCO, the United States has committed itself to supporting international education as a means of rationally solving world conflict; as the preamble to UNESCO's constitution states, "Since wars begin in the minds of men, it is in the minds of men that the defenses of peace must be constructed." President Kennedy manifested the deep interest of the United States in international education and cooperation by creating the Peace Corps in March 1961. President Johnson described this country's vital interest in cross-cultural education by saying,

For we know today that certain truths are self-evident in every nation on this earth:

That ideas, not armaments, will shape our lasting prospects for peace.

That the conduct of our foreign policy will advance no faster than the curriculum of our classrooms.

That the knowledge of our citizens is the one treasure that grows only when it is shared.

It would profit us little to limit the World's exchange to those who can afford it. We must extend the treasure to those lands where learning is still a luxury for the few. . . .

Unless the world can find a way to extend the light, the force of . . . darkness may engulf us all.[1]

Given this interest in comparative education, what are the specific values of this field to the classroom teacher? First, in order to study any society and its goals, one has to understand how the young are educated, for education is the major instrument by which a society achieves its objectives. Second, by studying systems of education of other lands one can learn much from their practices. It is true that a system of education cannot be transplanted from one country to another, but there are numerous common problems which exist in many cultures, such as the relationship between education and politics, the school's role in culture change, and the educational provisions for exceptional children. By studying how other educational systems endeavor to meet such common problems, we can better understand our problems and the approaches we pursue toward their solutions. Third, learning about the process of education in other societies can be an important step in fostering international understanding.

The values of comparative education have never been more apparent than today. No day passes without someone making hasty comparisons between other systems of education and ours. We are told that if this country is to survive we must adopt the educational patterns of Switzerland, Britain, Germany, the Soviet Union, and other nations. Clearly, what we need is more objective comparative analyses of foreign educational systems in terms of their value for their particular cultures at a given time in history.

[1] From a speech by President Lyndon Johnson at the Smithsonian Institution Bicentennial Celebration, September 16, 1965.

In comparing educational systems, two questions must be asked at the outset. First, what are the significant needs of the people in the country? Second, how is the educational system attempting to meet these needs? In order to answer the first question, areas such as the following should be explored: 1) the social and cultural context: values, traditions, religions; 2) culture change and conflict: economy, ideology, family, intergroup relations; 3) the impact of culture and ideology on education: democracy, communism, imperialism, and nationalism.

In order to respond to the second question, a study should be made of such aspects of each educational system: 1) aims and objectives, 2) support of public and private schools, 3) control of education, 4) organization and administration, 5) curriculum development, 6) classroom practices, 7) teacher preparation and recruitment, 8) critical issues and promising trends.

The selections in this chapter have been chosen to represent samples of education in several societies at various stages of development. Watkins opens the chapter with a description of the "bush" school in West Africa. Kimball follows with a discussion of Brazilian primary education. Two analyses of certain aspects of education in Communist China and Russia are offered by Hu and Bronfenbrenner, respectively. Bowles compares a number of specific areas in European and American education. Schickele reflects on his experiences as a Peace Corps volunteer in Nigeria. Gezi, in concluding this chapter, explores the influence of four factors on the adjustment of Middle Eastern students in a cross-cultural contact situation.

THE WEST AFRICAN "BUSH" SCHOOL

Mark Hanna Watkins portrays in the following article a vivid picture of how a preliterate society attempts to transmit its culture to its youth so that they can be responsible members of their tribes. The writer explores objectively the many strengths of the West African "bush" school in relation to its own culture. The student is made aware of the lack of cultural gaps, useless knowledge, and contrived learning situations in the native school. Although some of the activities and subject matter in this school might be questioned by American teachers, the author urges the reader to consider the system with sympathetic appreciation and judge it only in terms of whether it has succeeded in preparing youth to be functioning members of their native com-

munities. The author, an anthropologist and educator, has done field work in Haiti, Guatemala, and Africa.

Mark Hanna Watkins

American Journal of Sociology, *48 (1943), 1661–1675. Reprinted by permission of the University of Chicago Press, copyright, 1943, University of Chicago.*

The social anthropologists and the sociologist consider education in its broadest aspects to be coterminous with the cultural process in which, over successive generations, the young and unassimilated members of a group are incorporated by their sharing of the social heritage. Education from this point of view thus is directed by the group in the daily interaction of its members as well as by specialized functionaries or subgroups, and in the process the cultural patterns are transmitted and the socially accepted values realized.

The social values of a group are those phenomena which it recognizes as constituting the active or potential factors in the promotion of its welfare or which, when not properly controlled, create dysphoric conditions. Thus there are, on the one hand, positive social values, as food, shelter, health, and the fundamental necessities of life, as well as other socially desirable ends defined by the culture, and, on the other hand, negative social values, as crime, disease, death, witchcraft. These constitute in a large measure the social environment and determine the characteristic activities of a society. It is in relation to them that we may therefore speak of the function of education. This function is not to be confused with purpose, although in social life the two are often closely related; for the function of anything is simply what it does, and we speak of the function of objects which have no purposes, as, for example, that of the sunlight. Moreover, in attempting to achieve the goals which are proposed, a people often attain quite different ends, as in the case of the teacher who, desirous of creating friendship, makes two boys embrace after a fight, but only intensifies their enmity; or of the Volstead Act, which created a wave of vice and crime instead of a nation of temperate citizens.

Hence, while the function of social life, in general, is that of passing on the cultural heritage, it may be recognized that not every social example is worthy to be copied and preserved. Every group struggles to maintain only its ideals, along with the technology and skills needed for providing subsistence. Thus, while education is identical with life in a particular society, it is obligatory that in every group there should be imposed upon certain institutions the duty of making deliberate efforts toward fostering the best in the cultural heritage, in regard both to the objective world of materials and techniques and to their subjective counterpart of sentiments, interests, and attitudes. In short, the incidental educative function of social life is supplemented by a more or less self-conscious purpose, superimposed upon one or more fundamental institutions or carried out by a special educational organization. This purpose involves the conservation, extension, and transmission of all the culturally accepted values and ideals to the succeeding generations so as to insure their continuity as they are defined in the local group and thus to perpetuate its life. There generally is required a more or less special emphasis determined by national or local aims. There also are the problems of adjusting the group to the larger world in which it lives and of accommodating the individual so that his efforts to realize his wishes may not conflict too seriously with the needs of his society.

The formulation of an educational program for any group therefore is dependent upon two general factors: the nature and needs of the child, which determine the methods of procedure, and the nature and needs of the society, which determine the goals.

In the very simplest societies, as that of the Andaman Islanders, the Sakai of the Malay Peninsula, an Eskimo village, or other similar groups, informal education, in which the individual learns incidentally by direct participation and imitation, is relatively adequate for social continuity. The learning that goes on under such conditions is genuine; for the patterns of life are presented to the individual in their immediate setting, and what he learns is close to his interests and put into direct use; in fact, he learns by doing. In such a society, where there is only a meager differentiation of vocations, with no complex technology, and in which the system of beliefs and practices is comparatively simple, the gap between the growing child and the adult world is relatively narrow and may be spanned without a long period of special preparation. Here the inculcation of the social values is achieved with a minimum of self-conscious purpose; that is to say, it is not abstracted from the daily life. In more complex social orders, where only the general designs of life are accessible to the young, the educative process must take on some degree of specific and separate organization; the social heritage must be broken up into assimilable portions and simplified, so that education as a purposive endeavor becomes differentiated from the educative function of daily life. Some form of specialized educational institution develops, and the passing-on of selected social ideals takes place in a relatively distinctive and artificial environment. But this differentiation entails certain problems, for the social values tend to become somewhat impersonal to the learner, are not immediate and vital in character, and are likely to be hidden in symbols. In such a situation learning may degenerate to mere acceptance of preformulated matter, to rote memory without understanding or responsibility. It becomes more and more difficult to relate the experiences acquired under such formal circumstances to those obtained in direct association, to distinguish between intrinsic and mediate values, and for the learner to understand the mediate values associated with his contemporary activity.

From the foregoing remarks it would appear that the adequacy of any deliberate and formalized educational system may be tested by considering the extent to which it is representative of the cultural heritage and its achievement in so relating the activities of the more or less specialized environment to those of the practical social world of which it is a part that the two may be contiguous.

It seems permissible and profitable to describe and study the "bush" school of West Africa on the basis of this framework, although that educational system may not be regarded as formal on a par with the schools among westernized peoples. The "bush" school, as will be seen, has the characteristics of a deliberate and purposive procedure in a specialized environment.

The training of youth in West Africa is accomplished through one of the types of secret societies common in the area. In these societies, as in many other affairs, the sexes are segregated. The name which is now in general usage for he boys' society is *poro*—in the Vai language, *pólô* or *póró* (with open *o*).[1] This form, or some dialectic variant of it, is found over a relatively wide area in Liberia, Sierra Leone, and other areas over which the Mandingo languages are spoken. The name for the corresponding girls' society is *bondo*, Vai *bòndó* (*o* closed), or, more correctly, *sàndì* (with open *i*). There is little variation in the organization and activities of these societies as they occur among the Mende, Vai, Kpelle, Krima, Gola, and other related groups. The description given here refers to them as they are established among the Mende and Vai, the data being obtained primarily from Miss Fatima Massaquoi, a native Vai student at Fisk University, including notes in correspondence with her brother, Mr. S. Ciaka Massaquoi, of Pendembu, Sierra Leone. *Poro*

[1] For sake of economy, the few native (Vai) words included have not been transcribed in phonetic script, with the exception that the tones are shown by the grave accent (for low) and the acute accent (for the high register). There are at least three significant tonal distinctions (tonemes) in this language, but the middle tone does not appear in any of the words employed here. The vowel qualities have been described briefly in parentheses following the first occurence of each word. The Vai *a* is invariably a low back vowel, while *i,e,* and *o* may be open or closed. A colon following a vowel indicates that the vowel is long. The consonants have practically the same qualities as in English.

seems to be a generic term which once was and still may be applied to the societies without regard to the sex of the participants and which in-cludes similar associations among men and women, the adult group being political and civic rather than distinctively educational in aim.

> The most widely distributed and probably also the oldest name of the society is *poro*, strictly speaking, *polo*, thus with open *o* in both in-stances. Dapper, in the seventeenth century, called it *paaro*, so that perhaps the stem originally contained an *a*. (Westermann: 236).

The adult groups are not strictly germane to the subject presented here and therefore may be omitted.

The original meaning of the word *poro* is not known clearly. Westermann, (1921:236n) quoting two other authors, makes the follow-ing statement: [2]

> Wallis (p. 183) says *poro* means literally "law" or "one word"; also Alldridge, *A Transformed Colony* (p. 194), speaks of "the order of the Poro or law." If this translation is not etymologically correct, it is nev-ertheless expressive of the power of the *poro* for legal discipline.

These societies are of fundamental importance in the local culture, and every youth, male or female, must receive such training before being considered worthy to assume the responsibilities of an adult. With the growing influence of Mohammedanism, Christianity, and European cul-ture, the significance of the *poro* in native life is waning, along with de-tribalization and the general modification of aboriginal culture.

The boys' society or school may be described first. In the Vai lan-guage, the specific name for this institution is *bélì*, and a person who has been inducted into it is known as a *bélì kàì*, "initiated man." (The *e* of *bélì* is open, the *i* closed; in *kàì* the *a* is a low back vowel and the *i* is closed.)

The sessions of this school are not held in the towns or villages proper, but a permanent place is selected in the forest not far distant from the principal or capital town of a chiefdom or district. This special section of forest is called *bélì fìlà* (*fìlà* pronounced with closed *i*, low back *a*), "*bélì* forest," and is never used for other purposes, although all the structures are burned at the close of each term. Every district or sub-chiefdom has its own school and special reserved forest for the purpose.

Once boys have entered the forest, they are at no time allowed to return to the towns until their training is complete; nor under any cir-cumstances are female visitors tolerated. No one except members of the

---

[2] The writers quoted by Westermann are Braithwaite Wallis, "The Poro of the Mendi," *Journal of the African Society*, 4 (1904–5), 181–189, and T. J. Alldridge, *A Transformed Colony: Sierra Leone as It Was and Is* (London, 1910).

society is permitted entrance to the area. If uninitiated persons approach it, they must make their presence known so that none of its secrets will be exposed. If a man trespasses, he will be initiated, while a woman under such circumstances will be killed. During the period in which the school is in session the forest is said to be the special possession of the principal official of the institution, and not even the chief is permitted to enter without the permission of this man. Thus, in a physical and spatial sense, the "bush" school is a special or distinctive environment.

The principal official of the school is the *dá zò:* (*a* low back, *o* closed and long), "the leader who stands at the mouth or head," who is endowed with wisdom and mystic power in a superlative degree. He has a majestic status in the society, is respected by the chief and elders of the tribe, and is honored with intense devotion by the youth of the land. In personal characteristics he must be chivalrous, courteous, public-spirited, law-abiding, and fearless. He must have a full knowledge of all the native lore, arts, and crafts, must be well versed in the history and traditions of his people and an authentic judge of all matters affecting their welfare. Other men of good repute who are specialists in various fields of activity serve as his assistants and as teachers of the novices.

For the institution among the Kpelle the characteristics and role of the leader have been described in the following words:

> The grandmaster, *ṅamū*, is, of course, a human being and is known as such by the members. At the same time, he possesses attributes which raise him above the merely human. He himself is immortal; that is, his death is kept a secret, and the choice of the successor takes place in the strictest secrecy and in the narrow circle of the outstanding members; and he has the power to kill people and restore them to life. This refers, of course, actually to the secret sojourn of the *poro* youths in the *poro* bush and their later re-entrance into the community of village companions. They are thought of as having been dead and restored to life, actually swallowed by the grandmaster and reborn, which, however, the usual popular opinion quite generally conceives of as the ability of the *ṅamū* to revive the dead.
>
> It is only natural that the imagination of the folk is vigorously occupied with the *ṅamū* and attributes to him the supernatural. He is seen surrounded by the beings [people] in the village, since he moves about just as other people, but he also flies through the air. Thus near Densu [place name] there is pointed out a large, slender tree with fantastically projecting boughs, on which the *ṅamū* takes rest when on his journeys through the air on which he meets the grandmistress of the *sande* society.
>
> On his visits to the towns the grandmaster always makes his appear-

ance surrounded by a group of initiated, who protect him from strange glances [glances of the uninitiated]. He generally goes unclothed. Only to the initiated is he visible: upon his appearance in the village all the uninitiated—women, children, and strangers—must retire to the huts and close the doors.

On festive occasions the ñamū wears a gala costume which consists of wide trousers extending over the knees; a short-sleeved, close-fitting waistcoat; and a headdress which is a type of cylindrical hat made of small metal plate, ornamented on the upper portion of the front with the head of a plumed raven [*Hornraben*], and trimmed with cowrie shells and white otter or ape fur; over the brow a white band; around the neck a large ruffle made of projecting leather pieces (leopard and antelope skin), three to five centimeters wide and ten centimeters long, trimmed with white fur and cowrie shell; a medicine bag and other magic hung around the neck; in one hand a large fan decked with many pieces of skin underneath and little bells above and in the other hand a horsetail or cowtail.

A ñamū can conduct several schools at the same time—as many as three—which often are located some distance apart. In this case he spends alternately some time in each one and intrusts the remaining part of the development to his assistants, one of whom always carries out the inspection of a school. The journeys of the ñamū from one school to another are kept secret, and the students learn hardly anything of his absence; therefrom originates the belief that he may be in several places simultaneously and is bound to no locality. Often agreements are made between various headmasters for the purpose of conducting a course interchangeably. The headmasters then hold a conference in the capital of the oldest, and the latter presides. (Westermann: 238–240).

The period during which a session is to be held is determined by a council consisting of the leader, his assistants, and the elders of the tribe. The term in length varies from group to group. Among the Gola, in the old days, the session is said to have had a duration of from four to eight years; among the Krima, or Krim, it was three to five years; while among the Mende and the Vai the time was from two to three years. Westermann gives the length of the term as recorded by himself and others for a number of tribes. His figures vary from two months among the Kru to ten years for the Temne, although he adds the statement that "many of the figures given above may be more ideal than actual" (Westermann: 234–235).

At present, under the influence of new ideas and the gradual Europeanization of the region, there is a general desire for opportunity to acquire knowledge which the "bush" school alone cannot provide, so that the periods have been progressively reduced. Thus the term among the Vai and the Mende is now approximately eighteen months only, while it is about two years among the Krima and from two to three years among the Gola.

When the time arrives for the school to convene, parents who wish their boys to be initiated make known their desires to the tribal elders who in turn inform the paramount chief. The latter passes the informtion on to the leader and other officials of the school. Then the news circulates rapidly throughout the land, and the boys begin to gather, coming in from all parts of the chiefdom. There is no established regulation covering the age limits for membership. However, it is generally believed that human beings are more tractable and teachable when young than when fully mature, so that boys are expected to enter usually between the ages of approximately seven to nineteen years. In exceptional cases, however, the authorities do not generally object.

At the beginning of the session all the boys who have not been circumcised already are given this treatment. The number of boys who are circumcised at this time is dependent upon the age distribution, as the older ones will have received the operation prior to entrance. It appears that in years before the influence of the West was so great, most of the novices were quite young and consequently were uncircumcised at the opening of the term.

Circumcision constitutes a sanitary measure, although there were no social diseases before the coming of the Europeans. It is thought, however, that less dirt will be accumulated when the skin of the male organ has been excised. An uncircumcised man, moreover, is considered to be a weakling and is despised as an inferior being.

After the circumcision rites a period of time is allowed for the healing of the wounds. Then a feast is celebrated so that the boys may be given opportunity to know one another as well as to become acquainted with the teachers. The women prepare food for this festival, but they are not permitted to bring it into the school.

Now begin the specific forms of training. The boys are divided into groups according to their ages and aptitudes and receive instruction in all the arts, crafts, and lore of native life, including a variety of games and sports, such as swimming, canoeing, hunting, trapping, acrobatic stunts, dancing, singing, drumming and the playing of other musical instruments, wrestling, climbing, etc. These are for the purpose of physical development, the acquisition of fundamental skills, the sharpening of the wits, and appreciation for native art. It is by this means that the character is molded and a youth is prepared to take his place among the generation of adults. Moreover, the continuation of all these traits is insured.

The first instruction involves a series of tests in order to determine individual differences, interests, and ambitions (to see what the boys can do) and an acquisition of the fundamental knowledge which every adult is supposed to know. Later, opportunity for demonstration of special ingenuity, skills, and originality is afforded. A youth who shows special aptitude for weaving, for example, is trained to become a master of the craft; while those who show distinctive skill and interest in carving, leatherwork, dancing, "medicines," folklore, etc., likewise are developed along these specialized lines. This early training also includes work in the erection of the structures which are used while the session lasts. The buildings constructed for the school are sufficiently numerous to constitute one or more towns. All the laws and traditions of the tribes are taught, as well as duty to the tribal chief, tribe, and elders, and the proper relations to women. Training is given in the recognition and use of various medicinal herbs, their curative powers, and various antidotes. Also, the secrets of wild animals are taught—how they live, how to recognize their spoor, and how to attack them.

All this training is tested out in the laboratory of "bush" school life. For example, instruction in warfare is accompanied by actual mock battles and skirmishes. The boys are separated into various "towns" similar in location and arrangement to those in which the general population is or has been distributed. These towns must be barricaded, defended, and attacked. Previous wars in which the tribe has been engaged are re-enacted, the boys of one group playing the role of the people under attack at a certain time, while those of another act the parts of the enemies. The ruses which the enemy employed are gone over carefully, and the attackers must carry them out with precision and dexterity. Some of the attacks are made on rainy nights, when the inhabitants are asleep; others are made when there are festivals, when the "men" are in the fields, the actual situation, with all the preoccupations, distractions, and surprises of some known war, being re-created. All this is possible because the forest is sufficiently large, covering several square miles. All the buildings, fields, and activities are the responsibility of the boys after they have received their instructions. They must live in these towns, work the fields, and carry on all the activities of normal tribal life, at the same time preparing to defend their possessions or to make attacks according to the assignment which they have received and the account which the instructors have given of the previous war. Sometimes a lapse of two or three months may occur before the plans can be executed. This makes the situation all the more genuine. The defenders are informed of the errors in judgment and tactics which were formerly committed in actual combat, and the battle is conducted upon the basis of the previous life-situation. Then the entire war game is replayed, the defenders having learned what the shortcomings were and how to correct them, and the "enemy" making special effort to succeed in the fact of the new improvements in defense. In these battles all the obstacles with which the people were once confronted in such crises are recreated. Some of the boys play the roles of women and children who must be guarded and defended, who constitute the impediment of a human cargo. The "enemy" attempts to capture and enslave these "women" and "children" just as is done in normal warfare, for it is not the custom to kill women and children in military combat.

Thus, although the "bush" school is conducted in a special environment—i.e., in one which is differentiated from the general social milieu —the degree of artificiality is not so great as it often is under the conditions of formal education among peoples of European and American cultures. The greatest amount of dissimilarity between the school situation and that of native life in the towns and villages would seem to be the absence of certain distractions in the school—the removal from normal family ties, from the direct influence of mothers and kinsmen, who tend to condone the frailties of the youths. This does not seem to constitute a disadvantage or to seclude the activities in an ivory tower. In fact, there is a general notion among these people that there should be some form of counterbalance to the intimate association between children and their immediate parents (those of the simple or biological family), for under such conditions they will be cajoled, indulged, and petted too much and in this way not prepared for the sacrifices incidental to normal social life beyond this narrow circle. For this reason, children are distributed often among the more distant relatives for various periods of time. The requirement that life in the "bush" school must involve withdrawal from such contacts appears to be an application of this fundamental principle. Indeed, a child is not expected to enter a "bush" school in which his close relative has a position of authority.

Life in the secret society is a complete *rite de passage* from the helplessness and irresponsibilities of childhood to citizenship in a world of adults. Thus a youth acquires a new name in the *béli*, according to his rank in the group and his achievements. He retains this name for life, and it is always applied to him by those who have been initiated in the school. Uninitiated persons may not use it. This latter form of life, it may be seen, is developed gradually within the confines of the institution. Entrance to the society is a symbolic death for the young, who must be reborn before returning to family and kin. Those who die from the strenuous life are considered simply not to have been reborn, and their mothers are expected not to weep or grieve for them.

It may be seen that life in the "bush" school is not a tranquil experience but rather a thorough physical, mental, and moral test in which unsuitable traits are eliminated, the individual either undergoing profound modification or meeting his death. It is said that abnormal characters experience no rebirth; weaklings, freaks, and homosexuals do not return. This has elicited some disturbance among the missionaries and humanitarians, but it should cause no lack of elation for the Hootons (See Hooton, 1937), for the natives feel that those who cannot endure the test are no loss to society.

Yet a boy is proud of his "bush" school days, and he reflects over them with fond remembrances. At the completion of the session the chief is informed privately, and he then (as during the whole period) visits the society only in the role of a private citizen. A day or two after his return he sends his representatives to meet the leader and the authorities in a highly ceremonious manner. The boys make a number of demonstrations, covering a day or more. Then there are various examinations administered by the representatives, after which they return to the chief and elders, who are informed of the impressions received. At this time preparations are made for the ceremonial return of the boys to the town. This is usually considered to be of great tribal, and in some instances intertribal, importance.

A type of pavilion is erected within the chief's compound for the reception of the boys; or, if the chief's court is sufficiently large, it may be decorated elaborately for the purpose. After all these preparations have been completed, the chief and his retinue meet with the leader and the officials of the society, when the formal presentation or return of the forest to the ruler and elders is made. This does not usually occur in the forest itself, and only responsible male citizens are present. Great speeches are made, and sentiments of appreciation are expressed to the leader. After these ceremonies the leader rises, thanks his chief and elders in a brief speech, and finally kneels before the chief (the boys of the school following his example) and, with the palm of his right hand resting on the ruler's knee, makes a statement somewhat as follows: "I pledge loyalty to you and to my tribe. Now I give back your forest. Here am I, and here are your boys." This is followed by great shouting, rejoicing, and the sounding of drums. The chief, sitting in his official chair of state (formerly a stool), lays hands on the leader and replies, "Thank you. I bid you rise." Following this, the chief is escorted to his compound with all the pomp and circumstance befitting a great ruler.

By this time the parents and relatives of the boys, the general public, friends and acquaintances from far and near, have assembled in the town in order to witness the arrival of the boys. The latter, having been ceremoniously washed and having rubbed chalk or clay on their bodies, splendidly clad in their "bush" uniforms, each bearing a long staff, are lined up near the town awaiting the signal to enter. Suddenly the report of a musket or sound of the tribal drum is heard, and amid great shouting and rejoicing the boys begin rushing immediately into all parts of the town, gazing furiously in all directions as if they were warrors anxiously in search of booty.

According to tradition, the boys have the right at this time to beat to death any animal which may be encountered as they rush about the town. Some parents deliberately leave such animals as sheep, goats, and fowl at their doors so that the boys may kill them in this manner. Wealthier people may leave even cattle for this purpose. There are at least two native explanations for the custom. One is the idea that the boys, as warriors and adventurers being permitted to enter the town, have the freedom to plunder therein, while the other notion is that they must be given the privilege to demonstrate publicly their manly and courageous spirits. It is said that at present animals other than fowl are rarely left exposed to such destruction.

After this period of license the youths are lined up again and led to a stream, where they take baths and dress in their best clothing. Then they are taken back to the "bush" quietly and secretly by way of a different route. Next they march in orderly and peaceful manner, to the accompaniment of the native guitar, drum, and singing, applauded by the jubilant and anxious spectators, to the pavilion erected for them. In this place they are met once more by their relatives and friends and enjoy the companionship of the distinguished men of the tribe. Gifts are bestowed upon them by relatives and friends. While quartered in this pavilion, they are not permitted to raise their hands to their mouths, but each is fed from a dish by a special servant, for they are considered to be babies, newly reborn. They are retained in the building for four or five days, during which time there are great feasts and much rejoicing. They have many great privileges and may call for and receive the best that can be afforded. This may constitute a burden on their proud parents, who, if they are poor, even incur debts in order to please their boys. In some instances years of preparation are required before a boy can be initiated, so heavy is the cost. This may delay the time until the boy almost reaches full manhood, or even later. However, this expense is connected entirely with the aggregation rites, as there are no fees for attendance in the school.

After these rites have been concluded and sentiments of appreciation have been expressed to the leader, chief, and elders, the boys are returned without ceremony to their parents and are finally taken to their respective homes. They are now full citizens of the society, with legal rights and responsibilities equal to those of all adults. Before being worthy of great leadership, however, a youth must have further experience in the civic and political societies, of which there are five grades.

The elaborate ritual of aggregation fulfills the function of giving effective public expression to the social sentiments associated with the cultural values which the school preserves, enlarges, and passes on to the young people. These rites are therefore educative, for it is through public expression that the sentiments are kept alive and made contagious. The behavior has inherent motivation, as it is bound up intimately with certain basic elements of human nature, such as pride, display, and heroism. Thus the activities of this group are contiguous with those of the general social order, and the *béli* may be regarded as an effective educational institution—judged of course, in the light of its cultural setting.

Attention may be directed now to the sister-organization. No great detailed consideration of it seems necessary here, for in organization and operation the *sàndì*, or "society for girls," is parallel to the *béli*. However, it is not conducted so far from the town or in so great a space as is the latter. The inclosure for the *sàndì* consists of a large fence constructed of giant forest wood, neatly plastered on both sides with clay and surrounding a spacious campus. It is usually built near one end of the town and, if possible, near a river, so that the girls may wash and bathe without having to go very far and expose themselves to public gaze. Within are constructed several temporary buildings, according to the number of inmates; and, as in the case of the school for boys, the entire structure is burned at the close of the session. The buildings and campus are the *bòndò* proper, indicating privacy, while the society itself is the *sàndì*.

The heavy construction work is done by men, after which everything is given over to the women and the men have no further concern with the institution. It is considered to be a capital crime if a man should gain knowledge of the activities or interfere with the deliberations.

At the head of the society is the *zó: bà*, "the big *zó:*," whose position, as that of the chief official of the boys' group, is hereditary. She represents the spirits of the female ancestors, who have left the institution and all the cultural values to their descendants and who are with the latter in the school. She is usually a woman of more than middle age, established in the society, and in position to break her ties with the home and domestic responsibilities during the term of the school. As a representative of the ancestral spirits she may undergo a metamorphosis and become what has been called by Europeans "the dancing devil," due to the fact that she, or a younger substitute, dances on certain occasions completely concealed by a large mask and special dress. There may thus be two persons with this title—the one who rules the school and the other who dances in the form of the spirit. The division may be necessary because the leader may be too old for the strenuous exercise required by the dance. In any case the identity of the masked dancer can never be revealed, as she is symbolically a spirit. There is a special attendant who follows the dancer, continuously praising and giving thanks to the spirit for the benefits which have accrued to the group. This attendant carries a mat, as the dead are wrapped in mats for burial. The active leader is merely the spirit having taken corporeal shape. In all these respects she is similar to the leader of the boys' society.

Next in rank to the leader is an official called the *léì gbà* (with open *e*), who holds the position of vice-leader or assistant leader. Then comes the *léì gbà kpó* (with open *o*). These constitute the leadership of the group and are called "mothers" by the girls. In addition, there is another woman, the *mámbâ* (with closed *i*), who supervises and is responsible for the cooking, washing, and general domestic affairs. Among the girls the oldest or first initiated also holds an official position. She is a type of student leader, who calls the girls together for various activities; decides, in consultation with the adult women, the program of work and recreation; and assigns the girls to various groups for these activities. She must be highly respected by her fellow-members, and she takes the lead in every important affair.

There is some uncertainty as to the time during which this society holds its session. It may very well be that the period is practically the same as that of the society for boys (which is the notion of our female informant, who herself was initiated but did not remain for a complete term). She estimates the term as varying from three to seven years, but her figures for both groups are higher than those of her youngest brother, who says: "In no case do girls remain in the *sàndì* or *bònid* for more than one year; this term has from ancient times never changed." By way of comparison, Westermann's figures for the Kpelle groups may be cited. He states that the *póró* in this tribe has a term of six years, while the *sàndì* term is only three years (Westermann: 234, 256). The differences between the social responsibilities and status of males and females may constitute an argument in favor of a briefer session for the latter.

There is not much ceremony at the beginning of the *sàndì*, although the girls must undergo clitoridectomy. It appears that the age for entrance is about the same as that for boys and that the actual time of joining likewise may vary according to circumstances.

This institution is very clearly maintained for the purpose of preparing a girl to assume her place as a wife and mother attached primarily to the domestic unit in the social order. The girls are said to be spirits, as all unborn children are, and they smear their faces with a preparation of white clay so as to simulate spirits. This clay must be replenished and replaced when washed off until the session is concluded. It is symbolic of membership in the *sàndì*, along with a necklace consisting of a small horn-shaped fruit shell in which a red berry is placed and a string of beads made of cylindrical pieces of wood and worn around the waist. These are removed at the ceremonial washing of the novices at the end of the term.

The girls are instructed in all domestic affairs, such as cooking, the various ways of preserving food, the collection of nonpoisonous mushrooms, medicinal herbs and lore, the preparation of cosmetics, spinning, embroidering, the care of children, and the elements of being good mothers and capable wives, as well as in dancing, singing, story-telling —all that which a native woman is expected to know. Like the boys, they receive new names according to their position and accomplishments in the society; and, like the boys, the weaklings may not experience rebirth.

The aggregation rites are very much the same as those at the close of the society for boys, including the special reception hall, the feasting and rejoicing (except, of course, that the girls do not rush about the town and "plunder" it as the youths do, nor do they bear staffs or wear "bush" uniforms). Upon graduation, in most instances, they are ready for marriage, although in the case of very young girls the marriages may not be consummated physically for some time. Also the girl, unlike the boy, until she has reached middle age or thereabout does not venture to offer her hand in greeting the leader of the school in which she was initiated, even for years after the session has closed. She usually bows in deep respect, resting the palm of her right hand on her knee. The leader responds by placing her hands lightly on the subordinate's shoulder.

The *sàndì*, which so closely parallels the *béli*, seems to possess the same educational characteristics and suitability as the latter, and both may be rated on equal terms.

It may appear that much of what has been described more closely approaches the ideal native cultural pattern than what is carried out in actual practice. This is no doubt true; but it would not seem to invalidate the conclusion that these institutions, considered in relation to the cultures of which they are a part, are more genuinely educative and efficient than many of the formal schools of occidental culture. There are no cultural lags and "useless knowledge" stored in symbols remote from the contemporary social order. Some of the activities and subject matter of the "bush" school may be rejected on the basis of the standards of modern civilization, but the system should be considered with sympathetic appreciation before missionary or other efforts are made to modify it fundamentally; for no criticism so severe as that which has been made of the French educational system of the recent past (and which seems largely applicable to many of our present-day schools) can readily be made of the native youth trained in the *póró* or of this institution in relation to its cultural milieu. It has been said of the French system that the primary danger of this system of education—very properly qualified as Latin—consists in the fact that it is based on the fundamental psychological error that the intelligence is developed by the learning by heart of text-books. Adopting this view, the endeavour has been made to enforce a knowledge of as many hand-books as possible. From the primary school till he leaves the university a young man does nothing but acquire books by heart without his judgment or personal initiative being ever called into play. Education consists for him in reciting by heart and obeying (Le Bon 103–104).

The experience which is gained in the "bush" school would seem to be far less spurious.

REFERENCES

1. Alldridge, T. J., 1910, *A Transformed Colony: Sierra Leone as It Was and Is.* London: Seeley and Co., Limited.
2. Hooton, Earnest A., 1937, *Apes, Men and Morons.* New York: G. P. Putnam's Sons.
3. Le Bon, Gustave, 1908, *The Crowd.* London: T. F. Unwin.
4. Wallis, B., 1904–1905, "The Poro of the Mendi." *Journal of the African Society,* 4:181–189.
5. Westermann, D., 1921, *Die Kpelle.* Göttingen, Germany: Vandenhoeck and Ruprecht.

TEACHING IN NEWLY-DEVELOPING SOCIETIES:
Primary Education in Brazil

Are there any similarities between the educational problems of a newly-emerging industrial society, such as Brazil, and those of a highly developed society such as the United States? In the following article Solon T. Kimball examines the primary schools in Brazil in relationship to the socio-economic system. Children from lower classes, who constitute about three-fourths of the population, find the middle-class Brazilian schools grossly inadequate. Shortage of qualified teachers, disruptive political activity, and a traditional family system present other problems to education in this Latin American country. Changes in the educational system have been slow and inadequate in meeting the needs of a changing Brazilian economy. Kimball, an anthropologist and the author of many articles relating anthropology to education, suggests that a new system of primary education must be created based on the culture of the "common man."

Solon T. Kimball

"Primary Education in Brazil," Comparative Education Review (*June 1960*). *Reprinted by permission of the author and* Comparative Education Review.

Brazil resembles, in some ways, other underdeveloped countries which are struggling to free themselves from the suffocating grasp of an agrarian past through the slow but steady adoption of the technology of industrialism and the transformation of their institutions. The changes, however, are not progressing evenly on all fronts. For example, its newly introduced factories and network of air transport contrast sharply with still existent primitive agricultural practices. Its traditional political processes yield slowly to new demands. And its conservative educational system, partly from neglect and partly from indifference, has failed miserably to meet the needs of an emerging industrial society.

The goal of Brazilian educational leaders is to provide a system of universal and obligatory primary education. It is also their hope to modernize teaching methods and curricula, to stimulate enthusiasm for professionalization, and to bring the salaries of teachers to a level commensurate with their status and needs. A complete program of educational reform would include many other measures such as administrative decentralization, development of citizen participation in educational matters, the construction of new facilities, and provision of classroom texts and materials. Unfortunately, any ideal plan for educational reconstruction has little chance of success. Inertia, opposition, and lack of resources are barriers sufficiently formidable to discourage even the bravest.

Such sweeping statements need qualification and explanation. Over the years there has been a gradual extension and modification of the educational system. Many men and women of good will and intelligence have devoted their energies to the task. Through training programs, experimentation, and research, the basis has been laid for modernization. But Brazil presents a curious contradiction in the acceptance of cultural innovation. There is great freedom to attempt the new, the novel, and the dynamic. But indifferent tolerance is very different from serious examination of new ideas and procedures and their eventual acceptance or rejection. Probably the politics of vested interest becomes the determining factor in social change. For this reason the incorporation of modern educational methods has been quite slow and it is doubtful if they have kept pace with other social changes or with the needs of the country.

It is necessary to know something about Brazilian culture and society to understand the reasons for existing conditions in education. A full description represents a task of great magnitude and is beyond the immediate objectives of this report. However, brief comment should be made upon industrial development and the system of social classes. Both of these aspects are of major significance in understanding the educational situation.

The process of incorporating industrial techniques and organization is progressing differentially in the several regions of Brazil. For example, the economy of the Amazon valley remains almost exclusively extractive. The Northeast, with approximately one-fourth of Brazil's population, is at a colonial stage of development and retains a subsistence and plantation agrarianism which has persisted little changed since its inception in the sixteenth century. Although cattle fazendas and sugar plantations have adopted some new practices they are very far from approximating scientific and industrial agriculture. The cities of this region are primarily administrative and commercial centers. In contrast, São Paulo and to a lesser extent adjacent states, form the core of modern Brazil with industrial cities, some modern agriculture, and developed public services. In general, the level of educational development corresponds to the economic picture. In the rural subsistence areas of the Northeast illiteracy may reach 80 per cent. In the city of São Paulo it is negligible and in other cities of the south has rapidly declined.

EDUCATION AND SOCIAL CLASS

The problem of education is also related to social class. Although it is a common practice today to speak of a middle class, the basic Brazilian pattern was a two-class system. The upper group was and is composed of the descendants of the great landowners, members of the professional classes, officers of the armed forces, the higher governmental officials, and those engaged in certain types of commercial activity. The lower group included the slaves and later their descendants, agricultural laborers and marginal rural renters or proprietors in the country, and the mechanics, artisans, laborers, and shopkeepers in the towns. Expanded occupational opportunities and a higher standard of living through urbanization and recent industrialization have tended to modify the system and favor the appearance of a middle class. Although there is no study which gives the relative proportion of the population in different social classes some rough approximation of the distribution is necessary for our purposes. Probably not more than 20 per cent of the population should be included in the middle and upper classes and in the Northeast and other agrarian areas this percentage could be halved. At least three-quarters of the population are in the lower classes and at least half of these are marginal or outside the productive system. Understanding the system of social classes is basic to understanding the educational problem. For it is in the 70 to 80 per cent in the lower classes that we find the lack of formal education as well as the great failure in educational methods.

The statistics state clearly the stark reality. Of the 12,700,000 children between the ages of seven and fourteen, 6,900,000 are in primary school, 150,000 have completed the primary course and ended their studies, 500,000 are in secondary school and 5,150,000 are not in attendance. Of the 8,200,000 children between seven and eleven, 2,500,000 or 30 per cent are not attending school. Of the 2,900,000 who matriculated in the first grade in 1957, only 1,200,000 or 44 per cent remained in school in 1958. More than half of the pupils abandoned their studies in the course of the first year. Only 18.2 per cent of those who matriculate in the first grade finish the four-year primary series.[1]

The problem is clear. Many thousands of children are denied access to education through lack of schools or fail to enter because of parental neglect. Over half of those who do enter never get beyond the first grade. Less than one-fifth finish primary education.

Secondary education has had an exceptional growth during the past quarter century. In 1930 there were 60,000 students. Today the number has reached almost a million. Even so, less than 10 per cent of Brazilian youth between the ages of twelve and eighteen years have access to these schools and of these only 7 per cent of those who enter finish the course.[2] Statistics do not classify students on the basis of social class, but simple observation and common knowledge establishes the fact that secondary school students are drawn almost entirely from the middle and upper classes. The fact that a majority of these schools are fee-charging institutions almost automatically eliminates children of the poorer classes. The children who enter the secondary school must finish the primary school successfully. Thus, the requirements of the primary school are not barriers to chidren of the upper classes. As some Brazilian critics have pointed out, the almost complete academic orientation of the primary school may be explained by its emphasis upon preparation for further education.

But it is also certain that factors other than the content and orientation of the primary curriculum may be held partially accountable for

[1] Juscelino Kubitschek de Oliveira, *Mensagem ao Congresso Nacional,* p. 216. (Rio de Janeiro, 1959.)

[2] de Oliveira, p. 220.

the lamentable situation. The middle class environment of the school may be both strange and punishing for lower-class children. The reports by Pearse [3] and Consorte [4] in Brazil, as well as that of Allison Davis in the United States, support this assumption.

The deficiency in number and professional training of teachers constitutes another problem. Within the whole of Brazil only 55 per cent of primary school teachers are normal school graduates. But the extremely favorable educational situation in the state of São Paulo heavily weights the national average. Nearly one-fourth of all teachers and students are found within this one state and of these over 95 per cent of the teachers are normal school graduates. Only Minas Gerais, Bahia, Espírito Santo, and the Federal District have more than half their teachers professionally trained. The proportion in other states varies considerably with the worst conditions in Rio Grande do Norte where only 20 per cent are *normalistas*. The situation in the private schools [5] is actually less favorable than the public for here we find that only 42 per cent have completed normal school training.

Politics and the family system create additional problems in the formation of the spirit of professionalization among primary school teachers. The study of these teachers in Rio de Janeiro shows that teaching is considered as a part-time job through which the woman, if married, contributes to family income or, if single, has taken temporary employment while awaiting marriage. [6] Under these conditions and with a large proportion of married teachers it is to be expected that family obligations take precedence over those of the school. Family needs demand occasional absences and pregnancy requires a much longer interruption. In Bahia, for example, an average of one-fifth of the primary school teachers take four months' annual leave because of pregnancy. Parents and children complain of the disturbances which such interruptions produce.

Another problem with which education must contend is that of politics. Political activity may be either harmful or beneficial. It may interfere with the discharge of professional duties, demand appointments and dismissals, or it may focus attention upon educational problems and cre-

[3] Andrew Pearse, "A Formação de Atitudes para com a Escola em Migrantes do Interior," *Educação e Ciências Sociais,* Vol. III, No. 8, pp. 9–54, August, 1959, Rio de Janeiro.

[4] Josildeth Gomes Consorte, "A Crianca Favelada e a Escola Publica," *Educação e Ciências Sociais,* Vol. V, No. 11, pp. 45–60, August, 1959, Rio de Janeiro.

[5] Ministry of Education and Culture, *Sinopse Estatística do Ensino Primário Fundamental Comum.* (Rio de Janeiro, 1958.)

[6] Consorte, *op. cit.*

ate public concern. Undoubtedly, education both benefits and suffers from political activity, but there is no study which gives any measure of its impact. Educators, however, may also use the methods of politics to advance their objectives.

The problem is further complicated by a system of federal, state, county (*município*), and private primary schools. The total number of all types of schools in 1958 was 82,953. Of these, 267 were federal, almost all of which were in the remote nonfederalised territories. State schools numbered 33,073, county schools 40,730, and private 8,893. Simple observation confirms the fact that the *ensino municipal* (county school) is more likely to be found in rural areas and that on the whole its facilities are often inadequate. Its teachers are the most poorly paid and trained. For example, 73 per cent of the teachers in state schools, but only 23 per cent of those in the county schools were normal school graduates. County schools also fail to retain as large a proportion of pupils beyond the first grade. In the state schools 70 per cent of all primary school pupils are in either the first or second grade. But for every 100 students in the first grade one finds 48 in the second. In contrast, in *ensinos municipais* 85 per cent are in the first two grades, and for every 100 in the first grade there are only 30 in the second. In both instances the first grade serves as a major barrier to further education but its effect is more pronounced among *ensinos municipais*.

CULTURAL ASPECTS

No fully satisfactory explanation of the failure of more than half the children who enter the first grade to reach the second can be offered until we have additional research. The study by Consorte on *favela* (slum) children gives us some important clues. Her findings show indifference or misunderstanding on the part of some parents, the absence of a home environment which provides home-work assistance or incentive to the child, the critical attitude of middle-class teachers toward the lower-class behavior of their pupils, inadequate preliminary preparation for entering school, and a system of school organization which permits frequent changes in teachers, and does not hold them individually responsible. An additional important item has come from the recent research by Seguin.[7] He discovered a high correlation between verbal skills and school performance and that, in general, lower-class children are markedly deficient when compared with those of the upper classes. This finding suggests a cultural deficiency in the background of the child, or, as an alter-

[7] Roger Seguin, "Promoção e Aprendizagem na Escola Primaria." *Estudos nos Fatôres Sociais*, Part II, Centro Brasileiro de Pesquisas Educacionais. (In manuscript, 1959.)

native interpretation, the curriculum and procedures of the elementary school favor children who exhibit a higher degree of verbal facility.

To these factors which militate against the success of the lower class child we may tentatively add some others. The graded system of education in Brazil is used as a device for the progressive screening of those who are unable to perform satisfactorily on examinations which test academic learning. There is an implicit philosophy that it is desirable to eliminate, as early as possible, these who show no aptitude for academic achievement. Those who succeed will have been prepared for entrance to secondary schools and eventually the university. In this sense the primary schools serve as a proving ground for eventual access to higher education, and the academic requirements of the secondary school and university determine the orientation. Such a system obviously works to the detriment of the lower-class child whose aspirations seldom go so far, or whose financial capacities do not permit such advancement.

Whether centralized administration contributes to malfunctioning of the educational system is not clear. There is an undoubted failure to adjust to local conditions because of uniform requirements in curriculum and examinations. Local administration of the schools, however, does not appear to be a solution for the entire problem. The locally financed and administered municipal schools are less successful in terms of student achievement than the state schools. These latter are better supported financially, have a better trained staff, and undoubtedly attract more students from the better situated families.

On the other hand the traditional centralization of governmental functions has worked against the development of a type of local responsibility and civic consciousness which has characterized local communities in the United States. But there are evidences of a local vitality which might be strengthened. The hotly contested elections for local political office, the exercise of certain municipal functions, the appearance of voluntary associations such as Rotary, and the old, self-regulating "brotherhoods" which function in connection with religious festivities, are all evidence of local initiative and cooperation. With rare exceptions, however, the conceptualization of an educational program as a function of community is not common.

The unconscious linkage of education with social class and family values, and to a lesser extent with religion, is a major factor in the present situation. The spirit of individual liberty which permeates Brazilian culture can operate as a deterrent to enterprises which require communal effort. Under such cultural circumstances it would not be surprising if, basically, education has not been viewed in the past much more as a problem of private decision and action rather than as a proper concern of either community or state. Certainly, the experience of the Jesuits and the educational system of the colonial period would support such a conclusion. Furthermore, there is consistency in other areas of personal behavior such as that of the code of honor which demands of the individual that he settle his problems with others directly and oftentimes apart from the restrictions of law and order.

Whatever the relevance of these aspects of Brazilian personality and culture to educational problems, the fact remains that the traditional educational system in Brazil has worked fairly well for the requirements of a semi-aristocratic agrarian civilization. It has provided education for a select minority that prepared its members to take leadership in political, economic, and cultural activities. But the statistical and other evidence leads to the conclusion that it is not the type of education that can be successfully extended to the less favored segments of the population.

If Brazilians really desire universal primary education for their children, the obvious solution is a reform of the existing system. But those who have led the fight for better education in Brazil can testify that changes come very slowly indeed. The combination of vested interest, tradition, and just enough success of the present system to serve the needs of the upper classes does not create the feeling of urgency among those who hold the power of decision. The restricted influence and indifference of the great mass of Brazilians is a contributing negative factor.

There is another possible course of action. It is to create a new system of primary education for the 70 to 80 per cent of Brazilian children for whom the present system does not work. Such a policy is not nearly as radical as the present one which attempts to force the values and cultural aspirations of a dominant class upon a lower one through the use of formalized education. The slow evolution, or disintegration, of the academically oriented system might continue undisturbed, without the calamity of imposing it upon a group which is hardly culturally prepared to receive it.

THE CONTRIBUTION OF ANTHROPOLOGY

The use of anthropological knowledge in the development of a system of education for the educationally deprived offers several possibilities. Basically, there is need to understand the culture of the "common man," his characteristic forms of social grouping, and then learn how to construct an educational program which, although it requires extensive changes in the existing system, can be accepted and understood by those for whom it operates. In this instance we cannot separate the school program from the system of family, from institutional arrangements, nor from the place of Brazil's common man in the community, whether urban or rural. Special difficulties arise because the lower classes have been outside the tradition of literacy and in the rural areas, at least, formal education has been little valued in contrast to the type of learning which came from adult members of the family for work in house and field. There is indifference, inertia, and even hostility to be overcome. An example based upon the use of indigenous patterns of cooperation will illustrate a specific contribution as well as the difficulties inherent in such a proposal.

Although traditionally the common people in Brazil have looked for protection from a *patrão* to whom they gave unwavering loyalty, there are also some cultural devices which permit cooperation among equals. These appear within the system of extended sociological kinship, the *compadresco,* and in the system of mutual help, the *mutirão.* In the plantation areas the *compadresco* united those of high and low status through implicit obligations which resembled the relations between extended kin. But the *compadresco* system also extended laterally and although one's peer might not provide the same protection as a powerful *patrão,* the network of relations across generations and between families provided security in individual crises.

There is a reported decline in the incidence of *mutirão,* but in its original form it represented the cooperative labors of a neighborhood group which, to a certain extent, cut across status factors. The fact that a traditional system of cooperation different from the vertical structure of the sugar, coffee, or cattle fazenda could bring peer groups into concerted action is of importance. Although cultural forms fall into disuse they may also be revived. In fact, existing and comparable forms of cooperation may be observed in the culturally old *irmandade* (Catholic religious brotherhoods), in the equalitarian Protestant minority sects, and in recent labor unions. More infrequently charismatic leaders such as Antonio Conselheiro win fanatic devotion. Their contemporary may be the popular demagogue.

These illustrations give emphasis to the capacity of the common people, urban and rural, for self-organization. But it should also be noted that the ruling classes, through civil and religious authorities, have viewed such movements with suspicion and on occasion have used force to suppress them. An additional negative aspect is that such spontaneous groupings have served religious, economic, and personal ends, but not those of education. Thus, even before experimentation in the adaptation of these cultural patterns to educational purposes could be attempted the approval of the ruling classes would be needed. This one illustration demonstrates that what appears to be a simple problem may actually be very complex. Nevertheless, if Brazil is to meet the educational needs of its people, its leaders must rely heavily upon planning based on social and cultural analysis, for the problems are as much sociological as they are pedagogical.

TEACHING IN COMMUNIST SOCIETIES:
Recent Trends in Chinese Education

What are some of the problems confronting education in a totalitarian society which has set national goals to be achieved in a brief period of time? The educational problems associated with China's Great Leap Forward of 1958 are analyzed by Chang-Tu Hu, a graduate of the National Fuh-Tan University in China, a professor of comparative education and the principal author of China, Its People, Its Society, Its Culture *and* Chinese Education Under Communism. *China's Great Leap was intended to bring that country to the industrial level of Britain within fifteen years. To accomplish this an overemphasis was placed on political indoctrination and the principle of "more, faster, better, cheaper" was applied to education. Hu points out that the Great Leap failed to achieve its anticipated positive results in education because quantitative development is meaningless without qualitative improvement. The recognition of this fact has brought about a shift in emphasis, placing "expertness" before "redness." This article provides a valuable object lesson of the kinds of educational problems encountered by societies moving rapidly into the industrial age.*

Chang-Tu Hu

"*Recent Trends in Chinese Education,*" International Review of Education, **10** (No. 1, 1964), 12–19. *Reprinted by permission of the author and* International Review of Education.

There is hardly a country in the world which does not nowadays seek the most rapid economic and educational advances. From Afghanistan to Zanzibar the passion for development has seized us all, and investment in human resources has all but supplanted investment in physical capital as the development consultant's favorite rostrum. Yet a number of critical issues in education and development await resolution. What specific patterns of educational investment provide the most rapid economic growth? Is the production training of students during their period of formal education a help or a hindrance for the schools, the economy, the state? How can we best solve the problems associated with the rapid increase in the number of teachers needed? Can educational development be pushed too fast? Can it be relied upon to change basic political attitudes and private motivations, molding a willing, cooperative, diligent citizenry to smooth the path to economic growth? The list of difficult problems is virtually endless.

Nowhere, perhaps, have such questions cried out more sharply and urgently for answers than in mainland China in recent years. The Great Leap Forward announced in early 1958 was supposed to vault the country in a brief period of fifteen years to the industrial level of England. The educational progress which was to go hand in hand with these prodigious plans for economic growth was based upon two primary theses; education must be combined with productive labor by students and teachers; and ideological purity and dedication (Redness) was to take precedence over the acquisition of competence and skill (Expertness).

In November, 1958, in the wake of the Great Leap Forward, an exhibition was held in the capital city of Peking to show, with charts, graphs, and visual devices of various kinds, the impressive gains and triumphs that had been achieved through the combination of education with productive labor. In a congratulatory editorial marking the opening of the exhibition, the *People's Daily*, organ of the Chinese Communist Party, reaffirmed the correctness of the Party line in stressing the principle of combining education with productive labor. Among other claims, the numbers of schools and students enrolled on all levels were reported to have increased by leaps and bounds, as indicated in the following table: (1)

	Number of Schools	Number of Students	Percentage of Increase	
			Schools	*Students*
Higher Education	1,408	790,000	515	80
Secondary Education	118,000	15,000,000	846	112
Primary Education	950,000	92,000,000	73	43

Other equally impressive "leaps" were reported to have been registered on all fronts. Citing concrete examples, the *Education Semi-Monthly* reported that the Department of Economics of Nankai University, working collectively and abiding by the principle of combining academic work with production, completed, within forty days, various research projects totalling four million words, while prior to that, over a much longer period, only less than a million words of written work had been completed. (2) In the field of steel-making, it was reported that some twenty-one thousand schools erected 14,400 steel furnaces which were expected to produce 1,590,000 tons of steel by the end of 1958. (3)

One of the most often-repeated slogans for the Great Leap Forward has been the four character adage of "To, K'uai, Hao, Sheng," meaning "more (in quantity), faster (in time), better (in quality), cheaper (in expenditure)." Applying this principle to education, schools of all types were established in all parts of China at breakneck speed. The following is a description of the manner in which educational expansion has been brought about:

> "The province of Honan has embarked upon a grandiose program of establishing technical schools. By the end of February (1960), 164 technical schools have come into existence, with an enrollment of over 46,800 students . . . Lacking capital, productive labor has been promoted by mobilizing students for labor projects, thereby earning sufficient income for the construction of school buildings. Lacking machinery, teachers and students, under the guidance of experienced workers, cooperated to build their own by making use of available local materials. Lacking teachers, short-term training courses are organized through the use of the apprenticeship method, in the meantime employing retired or active technicians." (5)

It is claimed that during the year 1958 alone, fifty-nine schools were established in Honan by means of utilizing local resources. The amount of capital outlay for one school has thus been reduced from the normal cost of three million *Yuan* to no more than one hundred thousand *Yuan*, while the majority of such schools have managed to become self-sufficient within a year's time.

At the time of publication, such claims challenged human credulity, especially when one is reminded that these gains had been achieved within the span of one year, the year 1957 being the base for comparison.

It did not take long, however, for the leaders in China to realize that the Leap had not only failed to achieve the anticipated positive results, but had given rise to problems of alarming proportions. In a communique issued in August, 1959, no less an organ than the Central Committee of the Chinese Communist Party made the admission that the 1958 production figures for all major items had been grossly overstated, necessitating, therefore, a drastic revision downward. (4) In the face of such evidence, even if we concede that educational statistics are less susceptible to such gross overestimates than agricultural yields, the impression cannot but remain that such figures as quoted by the *People's Daily* are of dubious value indeed. Nor is it necessary to point out that, in education, quantitative development has relatively little meaning unless accompanied by qualitative improvement.

Thus, in discussing the recent trends in Chinese education, the Great Leap Forward must be taken as a point of departure, for in recognition of the severely adverse effects of this campaign, which was nation-wide in scope and embraced all national endeavors, corrective measures were introduced in the field of education, as in other activities.

There can be no fundamental argument against the objective of establishing more schools at a faster speed and on a more economical basis. The key question, however, is whether schools thus created are qualitatively "good" or "better" in terms of the educational needs of the nation. By the latter part of 1959, it became obvious that the Leap in education, though impressive in quantitative terms, had not only exacted a heavy price with respect to quality but also given rise to problems of a serious nature. Since productive labor formed the cornerstone of the educational Leap, teachers and students in regular full-time institutions were required to participate in productive labor of an average period of three months, exclusive of special "crash" programs which were introduced from time to time. For part-time and spare-time schools of various types, the amount of time devoted to labor was proportionally higher. (6)

A major change of this nature in educational practices, involving millions of students and educational workers, would require an enormous amount of planning and coordination to insure that education did not suffer because of the reduction of class and study time, and to make certain that labor thus expended would prove productive. Inasmuch as the entire Leap campaign was primarily based upon a highly exaggerated estimate of both material and human resources, and an unrealistic belief in the ability of the Party's propaganda machine to generate popular enthusiasm, the campaign proved disastrous on all essential fronts. It is now common knowledge that both the agricultural and industrial sectors of the economy suffered catastrophic setbacks, attributable partly to natural calamities but more significantly to human failures of a gigantic magnitude. In the field of education, failure of the Leap provoked harsh criticisms, understandably more out-spoken among students, their parents, and certain segments of the teaching profession.

Because of the rigidity of control exercised by the Party, there have been virtually no open criticisms of the Leap expressed in publications on the mainland. But because the party has been aware of popular dissatisfactions with the new educational principle and the policies based thereupon, numerous references to such criticisms appear in official pronouncements defending the party policy. As is often the case in a totalitarian society, the vigor with which the controlling agency defends its policy is an index of the degree of popular disaffection. A review of mainland Chinese publications in the latter part of 1959 leaves one with the clear impression that there was wide-spread dissatisfaction with the educational policy then in force. Some of the most persistent criticisms stemmed from a fundamental doubt about the wisdom of emphasizing productive labor to the extent that was done at that time. The critical view which gained considerable currency was that what was lost by the Leap far outweighed the gains. According to this view, the entire program resulted in "the waste of golden youth." In specific terms, the critics charged that the practice of sending students to the rural areas deprived them of the opportunity to pursue their educational goals under trained teachers, while pitifully little was learned from the examples afforded by "Model workers." After admitting that certain beneficial results have been derived from productive labor in terms of physical development and Socialist morality, intellectual growth has suffered greatly, a situation succinctly summed up in the phrase: "Two high and one low." (7)

More importantly, the so-called merging of schools with factories and farms created a situation so chaotic that the normal educational process was seriously disrupted. Teachers were unable to follow their teaching plans while students were at a loss to know what course of action to pursue. Students suffered from a confusion concerning their identity; they were both students and workers, yet they were neither students nor workers. Under such circumstances, more and more students withdrew from schools, some of their own volition because of a loss of faith in the educational future, others at the behest of their parents. The popular view prevailed that, since the Party seemed determined to transform students into workers who, although without formal education, were comparatively well-treated, there was no longer much point in trying to seek education as a path to personal advancement. (8)

It must be borne in mind that the Leap in education formed part of a much larger movement which sought to propel China helter-skelter into the modern industrial age. Consequently, the emphasis upon productive labor can be readily appreciated in pure economic terms—to utilize a reserve of available able-bodied manpower. More important, however, was the political objective of bringing up a new generation of socialist men, dedicated to the task of building socialism according to the tenets of Marxism-Leninism-Maoism. Participation in labor was therefore considered an effective means of developing in the students a proletarian outlook and a proper respect for labor, at the same time preventing them from becoming isolated from the masses. The concern with political correctness necessitated, among other things, a firm control over education by the Communist party, whose educational cadres emphasized Redness at the expense of Expertness, resulting in a general lowering of academic standards on all levels. Further opportunities for education, as well as future careers, became dependent upon the assessment of political reliability of individual students by the party functionaries. There developed, as the Leap gathered momentum, a widespread skepticism about the need and even the wisdom of acquiring substantive knowledge, a process which was rendered increasingly difficult by the disruptive effects of productive labor. As a consequence, in addition to specific charges against the excesses in stressing labor, there was criticism of the extent to which political considerations were allowed to interfere with the educational process.

While defending the party's position on education, the Communist leadership are nonetheless aware of the many problems and criticisms. Without abandoning the slogans or changing the fundamental objectives, the party in recent years has introduced a series of corrective measures which have resulted in a tactical shift on the educational front. The recent trends in Chinese education can best be understood in reference to this shift.

Of first importance is the shift in emphasis from "redness" to "expertness," although the slogan "red and expert" still describes the goal of training and education. To have an increasingly large army of students capable of reciting worn-out Marxist-Leninist phrases and echoing party pronouncements without acquiring substantive knowledge and specialized skill will, in the long run, fail to meet the needs of national development. From 1960 on, publications on the mainland began to stress the importance of academic excellence and to exhort the students to greater scholarly efforts. On the occasion of a graduation exercise in 1961, Vice Premier Chen Yi, speaking for the Party, cautioned against undue emphasis on politics in education. He went so far as to state that, since the socialist reconstruction of China required the service of unnumbered specialists of all descriptions, each student must endeavor to demonstrate his political consciousness through the acquisition and use of special knowledge and skills, sophistication in politics in the narrow sense being a matter of secondary importance. (9) Article after article in newspapers and journals deplored the erroneous but popular notion: "Fear not nonexpertness; fear only when you are not red." (10)

The "leap" in education has exacted a tremendous price in the form of lowered academic standards, accompanied by the stultification of creativity and the stifling of personal aspirations. What the Communists have described as the "middle stream mode of thought" among students, that is, an ambivalent and negative attitude toward the entire educational process, is still quite prevalent, and it will be some time before the shift in emphasis begins to show results.

With the political line more or less redrawn and clarified, there has also been a notable change in the labor aspect of education. A considerably more rational approach has been adopted, and students now work in factories or on farms more for economic gains than for political training. Moreover, the duration and the timing of period of labor have been regulated in such a way as to minimize disruption of school work, while due consideration is given to the specialties of students in the assignment of type of labor to be performed. (11)

Organizationally, the frenzied attempt to expand at all costs has been abandoned in favor of consolidation. Such practices as elevating secondary technical schools to the rank of higher institutions, splitting one school into two, and arbitrary reshuffling of teaching personnel, all of which contributed to the chaos of the Leap, have been discontinued. At the same time, schools that existed no more than in name and were clearly of inferior quality have been either abolished or merged with others. Claims of great quantitative expansion have becomes less frequent and, when made, tend to be more reserved in tone. Since the Party's control over education is now completely assured, there is also the tendency toward granting a larger degree of autonomy in educational matters to regional and local authorities, as well as encouraging such productive organizations as communes and industrial plants to establish and maintain their own educational facilities. The fundamental objective of expanding at a fast pace but minimal cost still remains, but greater attention seems to be paid to the qualitative aspect of education now than during the initial stages of the Leap.

The consolidation and retrenchment program has some notable features which are especially indicative of recent trends in education. On the pre-school and primary level, major emphasis is still upon the universalization of primary education which seems to have achieved impressive results by the end of 1958. (12) Current efforts are in the direction of expanding primary boarding schools and raising the quality of teachers as well as the quality of primary education itself. On the level of higher education, the pace of expansion has slowed down and a re-examination of the existing institutions has taken place with a view to meeting more effectively the demand for technically competent personnel. There has been a proliferation of fields of scientific and technological specialization, but organizationally this has not resulted in the establishment of ineffectual institutions. Most of the Red and Expert colleges and universities which mushroomed during the Leap are now either extinct or reorganized. In a word, there seems to be a concerted effort to give substance to the names.

It is, however, on the secondary level that the most significant changes have been introduced. In some respects, secondary education during the Leap had proved to be a weak link between the primary phase below and the higher phase above. Regular full-time secondary schools had found it difficult to meet the needs of primary school graduates and at the same time had failed to provide higher institutions with qualified candidates in sufficient numbers. Because of this deficiency, the new trend seems to point in the direction of using the agricultural middle schools as a major remedial device.

The agricultural middle schools admit students of the 13–16 age group and operate on a half-day basis. Their curriculum is identical with that of the junior middle schoools, but in addition to regular subjects, the students are required to learn through active work on farms those technical skills which would qualify them to serve as agricultural technicians. In view of the fact that there are some thirty-seven million Chinese in the 13–17 age group, and only a little over seven million are enrolled in full-time secondary schools, the agricultural middle schools, numbering some 30,000 and with three million students in 1960, have become a very important part of the educational scene. One of the leading educational authorities in the Communist hierarchy has predicted that the development of agricultural middle schools will reach its peak in approximately ten years. Considering the new economic stress on agriculture, to which industry now plays a subordinate role, there can be little doubt that this type of middle school will continue to occupy an important position in Chinese education. (13)

It seems clear that the excesses and confusion arising from the Great Leap Forward campaign have in recent years been gradually eliminated. The all-consuming concern with economic development at a breathtaking pace has now given way to a sober reappraisal of the national capacity in terms of both material and human resources. On the educational front, the spirit of rationality, for want of a better term, seems to prevail. There is no longer the impatient quest for quantitative expansion but a genuine effort to create an educational climate in which serious academic work can proceed. Academic excellence is emphasized more than political enthusiasm, while labor, though still forming a significant part of the educational process, is now organized on a more rational basis.

The recent Chinese experience seems to provide a valuable object lesson for other societies in a similar stage of development. While it is universally acknowledged that the rate of economic growth and national development is to a large extent determined by the level of educational development, genuine progress on the educational front cannot be achieved without the requisite economic conditions. There is, so to speak, a rhythm to the whole task of modernization. Now that the Chinese have learned the bitter lesson at considerable cost and have embarked upon an educational program in a rational and pragmatic spirit, what is going to happen there will indeed deserve close attention.

REFERENCES

1. Editorial, *People's Daily*, November 1, 1958.
2. *Chiao-yu pan-yueh k'an* (Education Semi-Monthly), No. 21, 1958, p. 12.
3. *Ibid.*
4. For example, grain production for 1958 was revised downward from 525,000,000 to 275,000,000 tons; steel from 18,000,000 to 12,000,000 tons. *Peking Review*, September 1, 1959, p. 17.
5. *People's Daily*, April 14, 1960.
6. *Chiao-hsueh yu yen-chiu* (Teaching and Research), No. 1, January 1959.
7. *Ch'ien-hsien* (Front Line), No. 20, October 1959.
8. *Chung-kuo ch'ing-nien* (Chinese Youth), No. 5, March 1, 1960.
9. *Kuang-ming Daily*, Peking, September 3, 1961.
10. *Wen-hui Daily*, Shanghai, July 29, 1961.
11. *Kuang-ming Daily*, Peking, April 7, 1961.
12. *Wei-ta ti shih-nien* (Ten Great Years), People's Publishing House, Peking, 1959, p. 166.
13. Lu Ting-i's letter to the Kiangsu Provincial Committee of the Chinese Communist Party discussing the future of agricultural middle schools. *Chinese Youth Daily*, Peking, March 23, 1959.

SOVIET METHODS
OF CHARACTER EDUCATION

Since the advent of Sputnik in 1957, the United States has placed a greater emphasis on technical and scientific studies in the schools, while Russia has increased its efforts in character education. In this article Urie Bronfenbrenner examines the process of collective socialization of children in Russia, delineating the role of the teacher and giving illustrations from the elementary school. The purpose of the social collective is to provide a context in which "socialist morality" can be developed through productive activity. Bronfenbrenner, a professor of psychology and child development, has visited the Soviet Union frequently and is the Chairman of the Research Advisory Committee to UNESCO's Cross-cultural Study of Prejudice. He is an authority on the socialization of children.

Urie Bronfenbrenner

"Soviet Methods of Character Education: Some Implications for Research," Religious Education, **57** (4, Research Supplement [July–August 1962]). *Reprinted by permission of the Religious Education Association, New York, New York, copyright © 1962. Bibliographical citations have been omitted here.*

Every society faces the problem of the moral training of its youth. This is no less true of Communist society than of our own. Indeed, Communist authorities view as the primary objective of education not the learning of subject matter but the development of what they call "socialist morality." It is instructive for us in the West to examine the nature of this "socialist morality" and the manner in which it is inculcated, for to do so brings to light important differences in the ends and means of character education in the two cultures. For research workers in the field of personality development, such an examination is especially valuable, since it lays bare unrecognized assumptions and variations in approach. Accordingly, it is the purpose of this paper to provide a much-condensed account of Soviet methods of character education and to examine some of the provocative research questions that emerge from the contrast between the Soviet approach and our own.

THE WORK AND IDEAS
OF A. S. MAKARENKO

To examine Soviet methods of character training is to become acquainted with the thinking and technology developed primarily by one man—Anton Semyonovich Makarenko. Makarenko's name is virtually a household word in the Soviet Union. His popularity and influence are roughly comparable to those of Dr. Spock in the United States, but his primary concern is not with the child's physical health but with his moral upbringing. Makarenko's influence extends far beyond his own voluminous writings since there is scarcely a manual for the guidance of Communist parents, teachers, or youth workers that does not draw heavily on his methods and ideas. His works have been translated into many languages and are apparently widely read not only in the Soviet Union but throughout the Communist bloc countries, notably East Germany and Communist China. Excellent English translations of a number of his works have been published in Moscow (1949, 1953, 1959) but they are not readily available in this country.

Makarenko developed his ideas and methods over the course of a lifetime of practical work with young people. In the early 1920's, as a young school teacher and devout Communist, Makarenko was handed the assignment of setting up a rehabilitation program for some of the hundreds of homeless children who were roaming the Soviet Union after the civil wars. The first group of such children assigned to Makarenko's school, a ramshackle building far out of town, turned out to be a group of boys about 18 years of age with extensive court records of housebreaking, armed robbery, and manslaughter. For the first few months, Makarenko's school served simply as the headquarters for the band of highwaymen who were his legal wards. But gradually, through the development of his group-orientated discipline techniques, and through what can only be called the compelling power of his own moral convictions, Makarenko was able to develop a sense of group responsibility and commitment to the work program and code of conduct that he had laid out for the collective. In the end, the Gorky Commune became known throughout the Soviet Union for its high morale, discipline, and for the productivity of its fields, farms, and shops. Indeed, Makarenko's methods proved so successful that he was selected to head a new commune set up by the Ministry of Internal Affairs (then the Cheka, later to become the GPU and NKVD). In the years which followed, Makarenko's theories and techniques became widely adopted throughout the USSR and now constitute the central core of Soviet educational practice.

To turn to the ideas themselves, we may begin with an excerpt from what is possibly the most widely read of Makarenko's works, *A Book for Parents* (1959).

> But our [Soviet] family is not an accidental combination of members of society. The family is a natural collective body and, like everything natural, healthy, and normal, it can only blossom forth in socialist society, freed of those very curses from which both mankind as a whole and the individual are freeing themselves.
>
> The family becomes the natural primary cell of society, the place where the delight of human life is realized, where the triumphant forces of man are refreshed, where children—the chief joy of life—live and grow.
>
> Our parents are not without authority either, but this authority is only the reflection of societal authority. The duty of a father in our

country towards his children is a particular form of his duty towards society. It is as if our society says to parents:

You have joined together in good will and love, rejoice in your children and expect to go on rejoicing in them. That is your personal affair and concerns your own personal happiness. Within the course of this happy process you have given birth to new human beings. A time will come when these beings will cease to be solely the instruments of your happiness, and will step forth as independent members of society. For society, it is by no means a matter of indifference what kind of people they will become. In delegating to you a certain measure of societal authority the Soviet State demands from you the correct upbringing of its future citizens. Particularly it relies on you to provide certain conditions arising naturally out of your union; namely, your parental love.

If you wish to give birth to a citizen while dispensing with parental love, then be so kind as to warn society that you intend to do such a rotten thing. Human beings who are brought up without parental love are often deformed human beings (Makarenko, 1959, p. 29).

Characteristic of Makarenko's thought is the view that the parent's authority over the child is delegated to him by the state and that duty to one's children is merely a particular instance of one's broader duty towards society. A little later in his book for parents, the author makes this point even more emphatically. After telling the story of a boy who ran away from home after some differences with his mother, he concludes by affirming: "I am a great admirer of optimism and I like very much young lads who have so much faith in Soviet State that they are carried away and will not trust even their own mothers" (Makarenko, 1959, pp. 37–38). In other words, when the needs and values of the family conflict with those of society, there is no question about who gets priority. And society receives its concrete manifestation and embodiment in the *collective,* which is an organized group engaged in some socially useful enterprise.

This brings us to Makarenko's basic thesis that optimal personality development can occur only through productive activity in a social collective. The first collective is the family, but this must be supplemented early in life by other collectives specially organized in schools, neighborhoods, and other community settings. The primary function of the collective is to develop socialist morality. This aim is accomplished through an explicit regimen of activity mediated by group criticism, self-criticism, and group-oriented punishments and rewards.

Makarenko's ideas are elaborated at length in his semibiographical, semifictional accounts of life in the collective (1949, 1953). It is in these works that he describes the principles and procedures to be employed for building the collective and using it as an instrument of character education. More relevant to our purposes, however, is the manner in which these methods are applied in school settings, for it is in this form that they have become most systematized and widely used.

SOCIALIZATION IN THE SCHOOL COLLECTIVE

The account which follows is taken from a manual (Novika, 1959) for the training and guidance of "school directors, supervisors, teachers, and Young Pioneer leaders." The manual was written by staff members of the Institute on the Theory and History of Pedagogy at the Academy of Pedagogical Sciences and is typical of several others prepared under the same auspices and widely distributed throughout the USSR.

This particular volume carries the instructive title: *Socialist Competition in the Schools.* The same theme is echoed in the titles of individual chapters: "Competition in the Classroom," "Competition between Classrooms," "Competition between Schools," and so on. It is not difficult to see how Russians arrive at the notion, with which they have made us so familiar, of competition between nations and between social systems. Moreover, in the chapter titles we see already reflected the influence of dialectical materialism: Conflict at one level is resolved through synthesis at the next higher level, always in the service of the Communist collective.

Let us examine the process of collective socialization as it is initiated in the very first grade. Conveniently enough, the manual starts us off on the first day of school with the teacher standing before the newly assembled class. What should her first words be? Our text tells us:

> It is not difficult to see that a direct approach to the class with the command "All sit straight" often doesn't bring the desired effect since a demand in this form does not reach the sensibilities of the pupils and does not activate them.

How does one "reach the sensibilities of the pupils" and "activate them"? According to the manual, here is what the teacher should say: "Let's see which row can sit the straightest." This approach, we are told, has certain important psychological advantages. In response,

> The children not only try to do everything as well as possible themselves, but also take an evaluative attitude toward those who are undermining the achievement of the row. If similar measures arousing the spirit of competition in the children are systematically applied by experienced teachers in the primary classes, then gradually the chil-

dren themselves begin to monitor the behavior of their comrades and remind those of them who forget about the rules set by the teacher, who forget what needs to be done and what should not be done. The teacher soon has helpers.

The manual then goes on to describe how records are kept for each row from day to day for different types of tasks so that the young children can develop a concept of group excellence over time and over a variety of activities, including personal cleanliness, condition of notebooks, conduct in passing from one room to the other, quality of recitations in each subject matter, and so on. In these activities considerable emphasis is placed on the externals of behavior in dress, manner, and speech. There must be no spots on shirt or collar, shoes must be shined, pupils must never pass by a teacher without stopping to give greeting, there must be no talking without permission, and the like. Great charts are kept in all the schools showing the performance of each row unit in every type of activity together with their total overall standing. "Who is best?" the charts ask, but the entries are not individuals but social units—rows, and later the "cells" of the Communist youth organization which reaches down to the primary grades.

At first it is the teacher who sets the standards. But soon, still in the the first grade, a new wrinkle is introduced: Responsible monitors are designated in each row for each activity. In the beginning their job is only to keep track of the merits and demerits assigned each row by the teacher. Different children act as monitors for different activities and, if one is to believe what the manual says, the monitors become very involved in the progress of their row. Then, too, group achievement is not without its rewards. From time to time the winning row gets to be photographed "in parade uniforms" (all Soviet children must wear uniforms in school), and this photograph is published in that pervasive Soviet institution, the wall newspaper. The significance of the achievements is still further enhanced, however, by the introduction of competition between *classes* so that the winning class and the winning row are visited by delegates from other classrooms in order to learn how to attain the same standard of excellence.

Now let us look more closely at this teacher-mediated monitoring process. In the beginning, we are told, the teacher attempts to focus the attention of children on the achievements of the group; that is, in our familiar phrase, she accentuates the positive. But gradually, "it becomes necessary to take account of negative facts which interfere with the activity of the class." As an example we are given the instance of a child who despite warnings continues to enter the classroom a few minutes after the bell has rung. The teacher decides that the time has come to evoke the group process in correcting such behavior. Accordingly, the next time that Serezha is late, the teacher stops him at the door and turns to the class with this question: "Children, is it helpful or not helpful to us to have Serezha come in late?" The answers are quick in coming. "It interferes, one shouldn't be late, he ought to come on time." "Well," says the teacher, "how can we help Serezha with this problem?" There are many suggestions: get together to buy him a watch, exile him from the classroom, send him to the director's office, or even to exile him from the school. But apparently these suggestions are either not appropriate or too extreme. The teacher, our text tells us, "helps the children find the right answer." She asks for a volunteer to stop by and pick Serezha up on the way to school. Many children offer to help in this mission.

But tragedy stalks. The next day it turns out that not only Serezha is late, but also the boy who promised to pick him up. Since they are both from the same group, their unit receives two sets of demerits and falls to lowest place. Group members are keenly disappointed. "Serezha especially suffered much and felt himself responsible, but equal blame was felt by his companion who had forgotten to stop in for him."

In this way, both through concrete action and explanation, the teacher seeks to forge a spirit of group unity and responsibility. From time to time, she explains to the children the significance of what they are doing, the fact "that they have to learn to live together as one friendly family, since they will have to be learning together for all of the next ten years, and that for this reason one must learn how to help one's companions and to treat them decently."

By the time the children are in the second grade, the responsibilities expected of them are increased in complexity. For example, instead of simply recording the evaluations made by the teacher, the monitors are taught how to make the evaluations themselves. Since this is rather difficult, especially in judging homework assignments, in the beginning two monitors are assigned to every task. In this way, our text tells us, they can help each other doing a good job of evaluation.

Here is a third grade classroom:

> Class 3–B is just an ordinary class; it's not especially well disciplined nor is it outstandingly industrious. It has its lazy members and its responsible ones, quiet ones and active ones, daring, shy, and immodest ones.
>
> The teacher has led this class now for three years, and she has earned the affection, respect, and acceptance as an authority from her pupils. Her word is law for them.
>
> The bell has rung, but the teacher has not yet arrived. She has

delayed deliberately in order to check how the class will conduct itself.

In the class all is quiet. After the noisy class break, it isn't so easy to mobilize yourself and to quell the restlessness within you! Two monitors at the desk silently observe the class. On their faces is reflected the full importance and seriousness of the job they are performing. But there is no need for them to make any reprimands: the youngsters with pleasure and pride maintain scrupulous discipline; they are proud of the fact that their class conducts itself in a manner that merits the confidence of the teacher. And when the teacher enters and quietly says be seated, all understand that she deliberately refrains from praising them for the quiet and order, since in their class it could not be otherwise.

During the lesson, the teacher gives an exceptional amount of attention to collective competition between "links." (The links are the smallest unit of the Communist youth organization at this age level.) Throughout the entire lesson the youngsters are constantly hearing which link has best prepared its lesson, which link has done the best at numbers, which is the most disciplined, which has turned in the best work.

The best link not only gets a verbal positive evaluation but receives the right to leave the classroom first during the break and to have its notebooks checked before the others. As a result the links receive the benefit of collective education, common responsibility, and mutual aid.

"What are you fooling around for? You're holding up the whole link," whispers Kolya to his neighbor during the preparation period for the lesson. And during the break he teaches her how better to organize her books and pads in her knapsack.

"Count more carefully," says Olya to her girl friend. "See, on account of you our link got behind today. You come to me and we'll count together at home."

In the third grade still another innovation is introduced. The monitors are taught not only to evaluate but to state their criticisms publicly.

Here is a typical picture. It is the beginning of the lesson. In the first row the link leader reports basing his comments on information submitted by the sanitarian and other responsible monitors: "Today Valadya did the wrong problem. Masha didn't write neatly and forgot to underline the right words in her lesson, Alyoshi had a dirty shirt collar."

The other link leaders make similar reports (the Pioneers are sitting by rows).

The youngsters are not offended by this procedure: they understand that the link leaders are not just tattle-telling but simply fulfilling their duty. It doesn't even occur to the monitors and sanitarians to conceal the shortcomings of their comrades. They feel that they are doing their job well precisely when they notice one or another defect.

Also in the third grade, the teacher introduces still another procedure. She now proposes that the children enter into competition with the monitors, and see if they can beat the monitor at his own game by criticizing themselves. "The results were spectacular: if the monitor was able to talk only about four or five members of the row, there would be supplementary reports about their own shortcomings from as many as eight or ten pupils."

To what extent is this picture overdrawn? Although I have no direct evidence, the accounts I heard from participants in the process lend credence to the descriptions in the manual. For example, I recall a conversation with three elementary school teachers, all men, whom I had met by chance in a restaurant. They were curious about discipline techniques used in American schools. After I had given several examples, I was interrupted: "But how do you use the collective?" When I replied that we really did not use the classroom group in any systematic way, my three companions were puzzled. "But how do you keep discipline?"

Now it was my turn to ask for examples. "All right," came the answer. "Let us suppose that 10-year-old Vanya is pulling Anya's curls. If he doesn't stop the first time I speak to him, all I need do is mention it again in the group's presence; then I can be reasonably sure that before the class meets again the boy will be talked to by the officers of his Pioneer link. They will remind him that his behavior reflects on the reputation of the link."

"And what if he persists?"

"Then he may have to appear before his link—or even the entire collective—who will explain his misbehavior to him and determine his punishment."

"What punishment?"

"Various measures. He may just be cesured, or if his conduct is regarded as serious, he may be expelled from membership. Very often he himself will acknowledge his faults before the group."

Nor does the process of social criticism and control stop with the school. Our manual tells us, for example, that parents submit periodic reports to the school collective on the behavior of the child at home. One may wonder how parents can be depended on to turn in truthful accounts. Part of the answer was suplied to me in a conversation with a Soviet agricultural expert. In response to my questions, he explained that, no matter what a person's job, the collective at his place of work always took an active interest in his family life. Thus a representative would come to the worker's home to observe and talk with his wife and children. And if any undesirable features were noted, these would be reported back to the collective.

I asked for an example.

"Well, suppose the representative were to notice that my wife and I quarreled in front of the children [my companion shook his head]. That would be bad. They would speak to me about it and remind me of my responsibilities for training my children to be good citizens."

I pointed out how different the situation was in America where a man's home was considered a private sanctuary so that, for example, psychologists like myself often had a great deal of difficulty in getting into homes to talk with parents or to observe children.

"Yes," my companion responded. "That's one of the strange things about your system in the West. The family is separated from the rest of society. That's not good. It's bad for the family and bad for society." He paused for a moment, lost in thought. "I suppose," he went on, "if my wife didn't want to let the representative in, she could ask him to leave. But then at work, I should feel ashamed." (He hung his head to emphasize the point.) "Ivanov," they would say, "has an uncultured wife."

But it would be a mistake to conclude that Soviet methods of character education and social control are based primarily on negative criticism. On the contrary, in their approach there is as much of the carrot as the stick. But the carrot is given not merely as a reward for individual performance but explicitly for the child's contribution to group achievement. The great charts emblazoned "Who Is Best?" which bedeck the halls and walls of every classroom have as entries the names not of individual pupils but of rows and links (the link is the smallest unit of Communist youth organization, which of course reaches into every classroom, from the first grade on). It is the winning unit that gets rewarded by a pennant, a special privilege, or by having their picture taken in "parade uniforms." And when praise is given, as it frequently is, to an individual child, the group referent is always there: "Today Peter helped Kate and as a result his unit did not get behind the rest."

Helping other members of one's collective and appreciating their contributions—themes that are much stressed in Soviet character training—become matters of enlightened self-interest, since the grade that each person receives depends on the over-all performance of his unit.

Thus the good student finds it to his advantage to help the poor one. The same principle is carried over to the group level with champion rows and classes being made responsible for the performance of poorer ones.

Here, then, are the procedures employed in Soviet character education. As a result of Khrushchev's educational reforms, they may be expected to receive even wider application in the years to come, for, in connection with these reforms, several new types of educational institutions are to be developed on a massive scale. The most important of these is the "internat," or boarding school, in which youngsters are to be entered as early as three months of age with parents visiting only on weekends. The internat is described in the theses announcing the reforms as the kind of school which "creates the most favorable conditions for the education and communist upbringing of the rising generation" (Communist Party of Soviet Russia, 1958). The number of boarding schools in the USSR is to be increased during the current seven-year plan from a 1958 level of 180,000 to 2,500,000 in 1965 (figures cited in *Pravda*, November 18, 1958), and according to I. A. Kairov, head of the Academy of Pedagogical Sciences, "No one can doubt that, as material conditions are created, the usual general educational school will be supplanted by the boarding school" (Kairov, 1960).

If this prophecy is fulfilled, we may expect that in the years to come the great majority of Soviet children (and children in some other countries of the Communist bloc as well) will from the first year of life onward be spending their formative period in collective settings and will be exposed daily to the techniques of collective socialization we have been describing. It is therefore a matter of considerable practical and scientific interest to identify the salient features of these techniques and subject them to research study, insofar as this becomes possible within the framework of our own society.

GUIDING PRINCIPLES OF THE SOVIET APPROACH
TO CHARACTER TRAINING

As a first approximation, we may list the following as distinguishing characteristics or guiding principles of communist methods of character education.

1. The peer collective (under adult leadership) rivals and early surpasses the family as the principal agent of socialization.

2. Competition between groups is utilized as the principal mechanism for motivating achievement of behavior norms.

3. The behavior of the individual is evaluated primarily in terms of its relevance to the goals and achievements of the collective.

4. Rewards and punishments are frequently given on a group basis; that is to say, the entire group benefits or suffers as a consequence of the conduct of individual members.

5. As soon as possible, the tasks of evaluating the behavior of individuals and of dispensing rewards and sanctions is delegated to the members of the collective.

6. The principal methods of social control are public recognition and public criticism, with explicit training and practice being given in these activities. Specifically, each member of the collective is encouraged to observe deviant behavior by his fellows and is given opportunity to report his observations to the group. Reporting on one's peers is esteemed and rewarded as a civic duty.

7. Group criticism becomes the vehicle for training in self-criticism in the presence of one's peers. Such public self-criticism is regarded as a powerful mechanism for maintaining and enhancing commitment to approved standards of behavior, as well as the method of choice for bringing deviants back into line.

There are of course many other important features of the Soviet approach to socialization, but the seven listed above are those which present the greatest contrast to the patterns we employ in the West.

CONTRASTS IN OPPORTUNITY:
A View of European and American Education

Many comparisons have been made between the American educational system and the systems of various European countries. Some writers, especially after Sputnik in 1957, have become critical of American education and favor various European patterns of education. Other authors have defended American schools, exposing the pitfalls of inadequate cross-cultural comparisons. In the following article Frank H. Bowles examines objectively some of the major differences between education in the United States and Europe. These differences—in the selection of students for schools and colleges, in teacher preparation and school facilities, and in the total educational program—are analyzed in the context of the different instructional goals of American and European educational systems. Bowles concludes that the major problem in these systems is the important question of how to attain a balance between diversity and quality. The author, President of the College Entrance Examination Board, New York, was on leave during 1960–1962, as Director of the International Study of

*University Admissions for UNESCO and the International As-
sociation of Universities.*

Frank H. Bowles

The Bulletin of the National Association of Secondary-School Principals (*April 1963*), 118–132. *Reprinted by permission of the National
Association of Secondary-School Principals, 1963, copyright: Washington, D.C.*

This paper is an expanded version of a report made some four months
ago to the College Entrance Examination Board upon my return from a
two-year leave of absence. I have enlarged it, and am in effect presenting it a second time, because the subject matter is germane to the interests of both organizations.

The leave of absence was spent in a study, conducted under the
auspices of UNESCO and the International Association of Universities, of
the problems of access to higher education. These are problems which as
recently as twenty years ago in most countries were considered to be
solved and, therefore, to be non-existent. I do not think that we in the
United States held this view then, nor, I think, did the Russians. But the
evidence is clear that most countries did.

Today, few countries consider them solved. Some countries, particularly in Asia and Africa, have deliberately set out to overturn the solutions they inherited from a colonial past. Some, as in South America, are
doing their best to hold the problems within the framework of past solutions. Others, mainly in Europe, have admitted the need for new solutions and are undertaking an honest search for them. Only a few have
broken with tradition and tried large-scale and radically new solutions.

The need for new solutions has come out of what we may well call
the New Industrial Revolution. This may or may not be the term the historians will ultimately attach to the complex of political, social, economic, and industrial changes that have come upon us in the last half of
our century, but it does not matter. We are living with the changes and
we will, in time, find a name to categorize them. We recognize these
changes, even here in the United States. The phrase "even here in the
United States" is used deliberately, for we have seen fewer changes in
the privileges and way of life of the average man than most other parts
of the world. We have, by and large, already experienced most of those
changes. We have some to face, but that is another matter and not within
the scope of this paper. The greatest accomplished changes are evident
in Europe, but these are less remarkable than changes now taking place

in Asia and Africa. Only South America remains relatively untouched, and even there the changes ring the horizons wherever man may care or dare to look.

In the course of this study, two facts became clear. The first is obvious when stated—that the problems of access to higher education arise out of an imbalance between provision of opportunity for higher education and demand for access to opportunity. The second, less obvious, is that access to opportunity is controlled by the organization of education and that there are essentially two forms of educational organizations.

One form offers a wide variety of programs within the lower levels of education and a relatively small number at the upper levels. This is essentially the European system which, with some adaptations, prevails in most of the countries of the world. The other, which is our own system, is followed with adaptations in no more than a handful of countries, although it affects a very large number of students. It provides a fairly general program at the lower levels of education, which means that relatively few specializations are entered at that level, and a wide range of choices at the upper levels.

We may, if we like, recognize a third form, the Russian, for this is not quite either one. Briefly, defined in terms which none of my Russian and very few of my European friends would like, it is a thorough Americanization of the early nineteenth century German system, as adapted by feudal nineteenth century Russia, containing some features of all of these systems, amply rationalized in terms of Marxist dogmas, as modified by Lenin and now Khrushchev, and administered with what appears to be a kind of slap-dash dogmatism in the true educator's spirit —that it does not matter what changes are made in the rules so long as none are made in the operations. For purposes of this paper, the Russian system is best grouped with the American, with exceptions to be noted from time to time.

Given these terms of reference, this presentation of contrasts between European and American systems of secondary education actually becomes something like an introduction to a world survey. The examination of contrasts between them can be generalized and applied to educational conditions in all parts of the world, provided, of course, that due caution is exercised.

If it were necessary to base this presentation on only one major point, the point which would have to be picked would be selection, meaning the manner of determination of what students have access to what programs within systems. There are other points, and many of them are important, but nearly all of them stem from or are controlled by selections.

Selection begins early. It begins, in fact, with the provision for primary education. The American system assumes universal primary education. The European does not. Outside of Europe, in fact, it is rare. In Europe, it is provided in most, but not all countries. In most countries where it is provided, the school leaving age is 10. In countries where it is not universal, selection for primary education is determined by school location, and is essentially on the rural-urban demarkation. This is a fact which has interesting consequences for rural development and related matters such as agricultural production, but these are not concerns which can be explored here.

In our American system of six or eight years of primary school, there is, as we know, no selection at any time. Well over 90 per cent of the age group finishes primary school, and goes on into secondary school.

In the European system, by contrast, the basic primary school program is four or, at the most, six years. In many countries, selections for secondary school, based on examinations, are made at the end of the fourth grade, and in no country does it occur later than the end of the sixth grade. The important point here is that the selections are made by examination, that the examinations are tied to educational credentials, and that the educational credentials are tied to the entire employment pattern, very much as thirty years ago, American employment was tied to the high-school diploma.

The generalization that all selection for entrance to European secondary schools is by examination is so over-simplified as to be misleading. A few details are necessary to establish the pattern. These details must deal with the organization of secondary education referring back to one of the two basic contrasts already mentioned; namely, that the European system is built on a principle of early specialization, while the American is not.

The early specialization of European education is determined by three facts. First, the program which prepares for higher education is a long one which, furthermore, leads to subject matter specialization within secondary school. Second, the European labor force is fundamentally trained by apprenticeship. In technical fields, this apprenticeship is preceded by elementary technical training completed by the age of sixteen, save in a few fields recently opened, where it continues into higher technical training which is carried to age eighteen. Third, European school teachers for primary and technical schools are trained in secondary schools, much like, though probably stronger than, the American normal high school of forty years ago. In sum, most primary-school students in the European system can look forward to completing all of their formal education in some form of secondary school. The only exceptions are those who plan to enter the universities. This makes for a complicated system of secondary education.

The selections for such a complex secondary-school system are necessarily intricate. They operate on a principle of descending and narrowing range of choice. The primary-school pupil begins with a full range of choice before him. Then he takes an examination which may admit him to the university preparatory line—the familiar *gymnasia, lycee,* or *colegio.* If he fails entrance to this line, he may be placed in one of the other lines or he may take another examination to enter a teacher training or a technical school. If he fails of entry to these, he goes back to primary school, which carries him to about the equivalent of the American seventh grade.

These decisions, once made, are final. The student may shift from the *lycee* to a technical school, but he cannot shift in the other direction. The student not in the university preparatory line cannot go to the university.

The description, as given, is not completely accurate for all countries. There are individual differences, and there is a clearly discernible trend towards delaying these final decisions until the age of fourteen or fifteen by providing a common secondary program for one or two years before proceeeding to the selections. Further, many countries allow students, regardless of form of preparation to try the examinations for entry to universities, so this line is not completely closed to those students who have not followed the right program. But the pattern, as described, is basically the same for all countries.

Since we know our own system, I will not labor the contrasts at this point. The American system (and the Russian) are committed to full access to secondary school and to holding all pupils in a more or less common program after entry, for at least the first two years.

One other point of selection for secondary school—the European system admits in principle to a charge for attending the university preparatory line. The charge is small, many countries have eliminated it, others give small scholarships in case of need to cover it, others give loans, but the principle remains. This may be a powerful selective device. It is not unimportant in Europe, and outside of Europe, in Africa, Asia, and South America, it is of tremendous importance.

The contrasts in selection method continue through secondary school. The European system calls for an examination at the midpoint of secondary education for students in the university preparatory line. In practice, it has been eliminated in some countries and partially eliminated in others, but it is still kept, for example, in France, Holland, and England. These examinations constitute a major selection. The students, when they enter this line from primary school, constitute, on the average, 15 per cent of their age group. By the time they have completed this intermediate examination, their number has been reduced by one third to 10 per cent. Actually, the failure rate is higher than this figure would indicate, but many failures are redeemed by retaking examinations after repeating years.

After this selection comes the final one, when the students take their leaving examination, which is also a university entrance examination. This is a severe examination which eliminates, even after retakes, about one third of the surviving students. In other words, from entry into the university line to completion of the program, one half of the European students are eliminated by examination, having about one twelfth or 8 per cent of the age group eligible for higher education. It is important to state it this way in order to lead to a subsidiary point. These students, thus eliminated, have not been excluded from all education. In some countries, up to half of the age group finish some form of secondary schooling, an over-all figure which is about the same as the American figure for twenty years ago. But this is not true in all countries, and it is safe to say that it does not hold in any European-system country outside of Europe.

In the American system, there is, of course, a very important selection during secondary school. It is accomplished essentially by direct or indirect guidance. Students, as we know, have a choice of programs, and the programs are variously demanding. About one third of American secondary-school students choose to drop out, and not more than one half of those who remain have prepared themselves to enter higher education.

In Russia, the elimination figures are higher, but are impossible to fix with any accuracy bcause of the impenetrability of Russian statistics. However, it would appear that at least half of the Russian secondary-school students are siphoned off, mainly by school decisions, which is a form of guidance. A large number go into the Labor Reserve schools which are an euphemism for minimum training followed by apprentice employment. The others go into technical education, offered in trade schools or in the well-publicized technicums. The technicums are, by Russian definition, partly higher education, but it is worth noting that other European countries also have technicums, managed about the same way, which they do not claim as higher education.

The principle of selection by guidance is not unknown in Europe, but it is there called orientation and often has clinical overtones. Orientation clinics are often provided by the Ministry of Health, or the Ministry of Social Welfare, rather than by the Ministry of Education. The French *cycles d'orientation,* recently introduced, are in concept much like American guidance, but, in fact, are woefully short of trained personnel and have still to develop into the pattern that is expected of them.

Even when guidance is accepted as an idea, methods vary. American school systems are prone to use objective tests as faster and cheaper, providing a basis for comparison of student performance and a basis for the guidance of individual students. American tests are group tests and the psychological tests play an important part in them. The idea of group psychological testing in Europe is almost unknown, except as it is conducted for psychological experiment purposes. American tests are often used to pick out students of marked ability and to urge them into special programs, playing an important part in the whole guidance procedure. Europeans pick out students with special abilities in another way. They note them fairly early in their school career, on the basis of their performance in class and on examinations, but I think it would be fair to say that, where the Americans try to build something around students of special ability, Europeans tend to note with interest and to record for future reference. I recall seeing the grade sheet in a Dutch gymnasium for the eleven-year-old students, where one student immediately stood out on the entire page as having turned in virtually perfect performance in every subject. I asked what would happen to this student, and commented that in America we might go so far as to take him out of his class and put him in another one, and, at the very least, would give him special assignments. I was told that this was unthinkable in this school and that he would keep on with his class and in his subjects, that he would not be assigned any special work, and that no special care or consideration was going to be given to him, but that the teachers would know that he was of outstanding ability and his reputation would accompany him through his school.

In a technical sense, the important difference between the two systems is that, in the European system, the selection for higher education is made within secondary education. In the American, it is not.

There is more that could be said about selection, but it has to do with higher education, and can safely be left for another topic, another time, and another speaker.

The second point of contrast which must be presented has already received considerable, although sometimes incomplete, attention from others. This is the contrast in programs.

I think it is clear from what has already been said that this contrast is not quite as it has sometimes been presented. The comparison between a European lycee, or gymnasium, and the American comprehensive high school, to the disparagement of the latter, whether done by eminent European educators, or eminent American non-educators, simply sweeps out of sight about two thirds of the education that European systems offer on the secondary level. If we consider the whole range of education available in both systems, the picture changes considerably.

In the lower ranges of European secondary schools, many European programs simply have no American equivalent. Elementary technical training is designed to produce skills which most Americans take for granted—the use of hand tools and fundamental power tools. Elementary teacher training is not offered in the United States, save for some lingering programs in one state. Higher primary education is about the same as the minimum core program in our high schools. Higher technical training, where offered, is not above the quality level of our technical high schools. In other words, much of European secondary education is, to say the best, no better than the equivalent programs in America. At worst, it is not as good. The same could be said of Russian technical secondary education. At worst, it is less than American equivalent; at best, no better.

However, when we approach preparation for higher education, the pattern changes. The European *lycee* or *gymnasia,* or grammar school, follows a fairly standard line. The language of instruction and its literature are basic, and the literature is taught intensively and memorized copiously. The history of the country provides a winding path to the study of broader history. Science is covered broadly and descriptively, mathematics is taught with vigor and insistence. In many countries, Latin and Greek are still urged, and, for some professions, particularly law and medicine, still required. After the student has gone through the first part of this program, he may elect to follow the humanistic or the science-mathematics line, and in some countries may also choose between a technical and a commercial line. The choice determines his specialization during his last two or even three years of secondary school, a specialization which goes into better focus if it is viewed as the final specialization within general education, to be followed by entry to professional education.

This program is typically taught over six or seven years. It is taught to students who have been selected at the outset by examinations, who are tested again midway through the course, again at the end, and who are in the program in order to qualify for entry to a university where they will enter one of a half dozen faculties—law, medicine, science, letters, economics, or engineering. If they have any other objectives than these, they will not find them offered in higher education; hence, there is no reason for them to be in the program. If they are not in the program, they cannot be planning to enter higher education. The program is determined and controlled by the Ministry of Education, using the intermediate and final examinations as the controls. In recent years, and in some countries, these examinations have also been used to control the number of students eligible to enter higher education, through the simple expedient of raising or lowering the passing mark.

We can contrast this program in our own minds with our American college preparatory programs and find it a demanding one. Many American students, with current study habits, would not survive it. The specializations go farther than the standard college preparatory program, but, on the whole, no farther than Advanced Placement programs. The training is formal, rigid, thorough and allows a student to enter his professional field without further concern with general education, in sharp contrast to the American who expects to use his college program, at least in many instances, to help him determine what occupation he is going to enter.

There is no doubt that the European system carries its most favored students—those in the university preparatory program—farther than the American system carries the generality of its students. Nor on the other hand, is there any doubt that the European system includes a built-in limitation on access to higher education. The choice between the two must take these factors into account. Each serves its goals.

One of the most striking contrasts between the two systems lies in attitudes toward teachers and equipment. The European schools preparing for higher education are taught by teachers who in America would be considered qualified for college and university teaching. They are university graduates with the equivalent of at least an M.A. in a subject matter field. In general, they have had little pedagogical training. Pedagogical training is perhaps not considered important for these teachers because they teach by university methods, that is to say, they often lecture as a university professor would lecture and the student is held responsible for the material on the lecture. The textbook is often a reference book. Recitations are recitations on the material of the lecture, and are conducted in an established form with reference to a notebook which also has to be kept in an established form.

These are all rigorous methods and there is no doubt that they prepare students well for the rigor of European universities. The training of teachers, combined with the method of teaching, means that European teachers can bring a genuine richness to their classrooms that not all American teachers can bring. It also means that, in Europe, preparation for university becomes very much of a piece with university instruction. The training of American secondary-school teachers is not, on the average, as demanding as this.

However, once this contrast is taken from the European schools preparing for universities and carried to those which deal with technical training and teacher training, the balance shifts abruptly and the American secondary-school teacher is, on the whole, better prepared than his counterpart in those other forms of European schools. European teachers in the teacher training programs are themselves graduates of the teacher training programs. If they have had advanced work on the university level to prepare themselves for their teaching, it has been work in the field of pedagogy. They may have been permitted to sit in on lectures in other faculties, but their limitations are specific. In general, they cannot take advanced university degrees in subject matter fields. European teachers in technical fields are themselves technicians and have been trained in their own schools. Their advanced training is likely to consist of practical experience in industry or commerce. The concept of special pedagogical training for technical specialities is virtually unknown in Europe.

European school facilities are smaller than American, planned entirely in terms of classrooms, and have little flexibility. They are often old buildings, sometimes grossly inadequate. An important point of difference between European and American schools is in their libraries. European school libraries are, at best, study halls. My own habit of demanding to look at a school library wherever I go has led to a good many searches for the key. The door to the school library is often an entry to a dusty and ill-ventilated room, piled with books long disused. There is little for the student to read, even if he should browse among the shelves. However, we should not labor this comment too much. There are few European towns with a population of over 1,000 in which one needs to walk more than 100 yards to find a bookshop. Books are cheap and plentiful, and the titles are fascinating. A European child who is interested in his studies and who has even a small amount of pocket money can and usually does accumulate a good usable library of his own, for the entire intellectual environment supports this concept of book accumulation and book use as a private matter.

What has been said about libraries is also true, to a degree, with respect to laboratories, although this is now changing. European laboratories are usually an adjunct to a descriptive treatment of the sciences. The experiments are performed by the teachers, as demonstrations. The results these methods have achieved are such as to make Americans pause to wonder whether their emphasis on laboratory experiments is really worth while, but this is another topic outside of the scope of this article.

These points of difference—and they are many—add up to differences not only in pattern but, beneath those differences in pattern, differences in purpose. The purpose of European education can be fairly characterized as highly specific. Selections are made early and in terms of specific goals. The educational programs that the students enter lead only to those goals. These goals, like the schools which lead to them, are arranged in a hierarchy. At the head of the hierarchy are the universities, with their historical origins in the need to train the professional classes

that are required for a stable society—government officials, doctors, law-
yers, engineers, scholars and teachers (and these words are still often interchangeable in the European concept). The European society, evolv-
ing, has broadened its list of university professions, but the definitions
have extended only recently and, in reality, only slightly.

From this position in the hierarchy to the next is a long way down
in the European concept. This is signalized by the fact that the training
of the common school teacher is still conducted on a secondary level, or,
at most, on a level which does not go beyond the first year or two of
higher education. The distance between the top position and these secondary positions in the hierarchy leaves out the entire area of middle
professional skill, and leaves out, too, a tremendous range of professional
practice that we have long since accepted in America. Thus, social workers, librarians, accountants, dentists, nurses, and laboratory technicians
are trained in Europe in excellent schools, but are not accepted within
the university community. There are not alternative occupations for the
students who go through the university preparatory program, but are fed
from the other lines of European secondary schools or from those who
failed their final secondary examination, and their position in the hierarchy is determined accordingly.

Our goals, by contrast, are diverse. There are no limitations, at least
in theory, on any American student entering any American school. His
professional choice has not been made and it may well not be made until
some years later, perhaps in the middle of his college career, perhaps not
even until the end. He may train within what is acknowledged as higher
education in any number of specialties. And his specialized training,
when he has achieved it, is still no limitation on where he may go when
he gets out into professional life. It is thus no accident that five per cent
of the European age group finally enter universities, while thirty-five per
cent of Americans enter universities.

These differences in the attitudes towards specialization make differences in the expectations that are held for the students. It is entirely natural for European schools to have high expectations of their students in
terms of accomplishment. These expectations are already defined by the
professions which they plan to enter; because we do not have such sharp
definitions, we do not have such sharp expectations. This is not to excuse
the level of our expectations; they could well be higher and we could
well require more of our students. It does in some measure explain these
differences.

The fact that we do not have such sharp expectations leads to a
question which is, in a strict sense, beyond the scope of this article, but
which is so central that no one who is concerned with secondary education or with college entrance can possibly avoid it. It is the question of

whether we plan our programs in our secondary schools and our requirements for college entrance to draw from our students the maximum of intellectual achievement. More simply stated, it is whether our expectations are as high as they could be.

Whether or not we use the discussions in this article as a guide, the answer is clear enough. Our expectations are not as high as they could be or should be. We can expect more from our students, and the proof lies in the fact that we are now so often getting so much more than we expect.

A very large part of the difficulty now attending college entrance is caused by requirements which are set below the abilities of the students. It does not really matter whether these requirements are established within the secondary schools or by scores on College Board examinations or by the admissions offices of colleges or by the level of freshman courses. What does matter is that the requirements which now exist, set by all these agencies, are too low for the best of our students and, therefore, too low for all of our students. The problem is one of ceiling. Programs and requirements which do not challenge our best students act as dampers on achievements of students at all levels of ability. When the dampers are heavy enough, it becomes impossible to set a reasonable level of expectations.

In this jumble of requirements, the college programs are often to blame. They are often normed in terms of historical expectations. In other words, attuned to a college freshman class of a 500 verbal SAT when the class, in fact, has reached—as it has in so many colleges in the last three or four years—650. By being so normed, their internal standards are set too low and the college not only ignores superior ability and superior preparation, but also penalizes the student who has performed above the average by condemning him to a year of boredom.

These are problems of such importance that it is now clear that we must seek a direct dialogue between schools and colleges on the subjects of standards and requirements—that is to say, of expectations. It is now getting on towards the centennial of the last such dialogue, known in history as the Committee of Ten, held in 1889, so that we could hardly be accused of rushing matters if we were to undertake another.

Another point is worthy of comment. It is striking in Europe to realize the difference in position and public esteem held by the public and the private schools. Public schools in Europe occupy the senior position; private schools are, in many cases, for those who cannot succeed in public schools. There are a few exceptions to these, but they are exceptions made for individual schools. As we know, the reverse is true in America.

It is the private schools which conceive of themselves as having freedom of action, liberty to move, liberty to apply high standards.

Before leaving these discussions of contrasts to go to the more difficult task of summary, it is necessary to add some points on Russian education which are of special importance.

It has already been mentioned that a large number of students withdraw, or are withdrawn from the regular Russian 11-year school at about the equivalent of the American ninth or tenth grade. Those students who are left after these withdrawals are all fairly clearly oriented toward eventual entrance into university or equivalent programs. However, there is marked difference between the programs they follow and those that our students would follow in that work experience becomes an important part of their school life. Pupils spend as much as two days out of six in a week in employment. This means that when they finish secondary school, they have a skilled worker qualification as well as their secondary-school diploma. After secondary school, those who wish to go on to higher education must, in general, take employment and work a full two years before they can apply to higher education. Exceptions are made for the bright students, twenty per cent of the total graduating class, who may enter universities or other higher education institutions directly.

Russian higher education is very similar to American higher education in that university training, technical training, and teacher training are all recognized as higher education, unlike Western Europe. It is dissimilar in that the universities occupy a very privileged position. They are composed of the traditional university faculties, and they follow the European in teaching tradition. Most of the universities are teacher training institutions, in the sense that over sixty-five per cent of the output goes into secondary school or specialized teaching.

There are other differences, and these are significant. Russian higher institutions give their own entrance examinations, and manage to cut down on the multiple application problem by giving their examinations on pretty much the same dates throughout the Soviet Union. They also have three recognizably different levels of entrance for most institutions: the regular day program at the highest level, the evening program at a somewhat lower level, and, finally, a correspondence program, which is their general opportunity program.

The purposes of Russian education are another matter. It is clear that they are oriented toward work, toward duty to the state, and toward specialized skills. In this context, it is worth making a comment which is based on personal conclusions. It is the most striking contrast I found between the Russian educational system and the American. The American system of education is—as I think we would all agree—heavily committed to transmission of the culture and in the raising of cultural levels. By contrast, the Russian educational system concentrates heavily upon skills and upon factual knowledge. Transmission of the culture is an accepted task, but not a primary one. Transmission and advancement of the culture is in Russia primarily a government concern, and it is a concern which is expressed in innumerable ways—in the community centers which are called "workers' centers," in the great public libraries, in the subsidized book publications, in the relatively broad opportunities to go to the theatre, to see art exhibitions, to go to fairs and exhibits, and to participate directly in group cultural activities. It is a division of labor that enables the Russian schools to concentrate heavily upon academic materials and enables them to put a premium upon academic success as a path to individual self-sufficiency. Our premium on academic success is perhaps not so high. Our emphasis is on an individual ready to think and act for himself.

Our final point of contrast, I believe, includes the Russian in the European group, as contrasted with the American. Europeans who have been successful in their schooling, that is, those who have gone through the university preparatory line and have gone through the universities, take great pride in the rigorous tests to which they have been subjected. They seem to feel that successful academic performance in Europe represents a triumph of both mind and character over great obstacles. Their attachment to their institution, if they are university graduates, is often an intellectual attachment. It is perhaps a comradely attachment to a few friends. It is rarely an attachment to an institution as a social institution, rarely an attachment to a social group.

Our American attachments run almost the other way. We have pride in our association with our colleges and universities, but it is a pride of friendship and a pride of association to an institution which has molded our lives socially as well as intellectually. Americans, I think, have a many-sided experience in their higher education, perhaps broader, perhaps not so deep, as the European. This is to be borne in mind also in contrasting the secondary schools, for the secondary schools in the country have the tasks of preparing for their institutions with their characteristics.

These comments lead to a final comment which points to another series of contrasts. The American educational problem, as our system has developed, has always been a problem of how to achieve quality out of diversity. The European problem, I think, might almost be the same words turned around—the problem of how to achieve diversity out of quality. There is no particular reason to believe that these two characteristics are incompatible, but there is ample reason to acknowledge that they are difficult to achieve simultaneously. I believe that we have managed to achieve substantial quality within our patterns of diversity; I believe that the Europeans are beginning to achieve substantial diversity within their patterns of quality. But the problem on both sides of the Atlantic is the problem of how to reach a balance between these two.

TEACHING IN THE PEACE CORPS:
When the Right Hand Washes the Left

Peace Corps volunteers have made impressive contributions in many parts of the world, and their impact on the home front has recently begun to be felt. In his message to Congress espousing the Peace Corps idea, President Kennedy prophesied that Peace Corps volunteers "will return better able to assume the responsibilities of American citizenship and with great understanding of our global responsibilities." In the following selection David Schickele, a Swarthmore graduate, reviews his experience as a Peace Corps volunteer after returning from a twenty-month teaching term at the University of Nigeria. In living and working with people from another culture, Schickele found his sense of close identification with the Nigerian people to be an indispensable basis for a true cross-cultural understanding. His experience has helped him gain a greater empathy toward the Nigerian people. He sums up the value of the Peace Corps with the Ibo proverb that says, "When the right hand washes the left hand, the right hand becomes clean also."

David Schickele

" 'When the Right Hand Washes the Left,' " Swarthmore College Bulletin (*December 1964*). *Reprinted by special permission of the author and the* Swarthmore College Bulletin.

The favorite parlor sport during the Peace Corps training program was making up cocky answers to a question that was put to us 17 times a day by the professional and idle curious alike: Why did you join the Peace Corps? To the Peace Corps training official, who held the power of deciding our futures, we answered that we wanted to help make the world a better place in which to live; but to others we were perhaps more truthful in talking about poker debts or a feeling that the Bronx Zoo wasn't enough. We resented the question because we sensed it could be answered well only in retrospect. We had no idea exactly what we were getting into, and it was less painful to be facetious than to repeat the idealistic clichés to which the question was always a veiled invitation.

I am now what is known as an ex-Volunteer (there seems to be some diffidence about the word "veteran"), having spent 20 months teaching at the University of Nigeria at Nsukka in West Africa. And now I am ready to answer the question.

My life at Nsukka bore little resemblance to the publicized image of Peace Corps stoicism—the straw mat and kerosene lamp syndrome. The university, though 50 miles from anything that could be called a metropolis, was a large international community unto itself, full of Englishmen, Indians, Pakistani, Germans, Americans, and, of course, Nigerians. I lived in a single room in a student dormitory, a modern if treacherous building with running water at least four days a week and electricity when the weather was good. I ate primarily Western food in a cafeteria. I owned a little motorcyle and did my share of traveling and roughing it, but the bulk of my life was little different from university life in the States, with a few important exceptions.

In the first place, the university was only a year old when I arrived, and a spirit of improvisation was required at all times and in all areas, particularly the teaching of literature without books. The library was still pretty much a shell, and ordered books took a minimum of six weeks to arrive if one was lucky, and I never talked to anyone who was. The happier side of this frantic coin was that in the absence of organization many of us had practically unlimited freedom in what and how we were to teach, and we made up our courses as we went along according to what materials were available and our sense of what the students needed. This was a tricky freedom which I still blame, in my weaker moments, for my worst mistakes; but it allowed an organic approach to the pursuit of an idea with all its nooks and crannies, an approach long overdue for students trained in the unquestioning acceptance of rigid syllabi.

The longer I was there the more I became involved with a nucleus of students, and the weaker became the impulse to disappear over the weekend on my motorcycle in search of external adventure. My social and professional lives slowly fused into one and the same thing. I shared an office with another Volunteer, and we were there almost every evening from after supper until late at night, preparing classes and talking to students, who learned that we were always available for help in their work or just bulling around. . . . We sponsored poetry and short-story contests and founded a literary club which was the liveliest and most enjoyable organization I've ever belonged to, joyfully subject to the imperative of which all remote areas have the advantage: if you want to see a Chekhov play, you have to put it on yourself.

In some ways I was more alive intellectually at Nsukka than I was at Swarthmore, due in part to the fact that I worked much harder at Nsukka, I'm afraid, than I did at Swarthmore, and to the fact that one learns more from teaching than from studying. But principally it has to do with the kind of perspective necessary in the teaching of Western literature to a people of a different tradition, and the empathy and curiosity necessary in teaching African literature to Africans. It is always an intellectual experience to cross cultural boundaries.

At the most elementary level, it is a challenge to separate thought from mechanics in the work of students who are not writing in their native language. Take, for example, the following paragraph, written, I would emphasize, not by a university student, but by a cleaning man at the university in a special course:

TITLE:

I enjoy certain tasks in my work but others are not so enjoyable.

It sings a melody in my poor mind, when a friend came to me and said that: I enjoy certain tasks in my work, but others are not so enjoyable. I laughed and called him by his name, then I asked him what is the task in your work. He answered me and then added, for a period of five years, I have being seriously considering what to do to assist his self as an orphan, in this field of provision. That he should never play with the task of his work. But others who are not so enjoyable could not understand the bitterness to his orphanship. He said to those who are not so enjoyable that they have no bounding which hangs their thoughts in a dark room.

I regard this passage with joy, not to say a little awe, but beneath its exotic and largely unconscious poetic appeal there is a man trying to say something important, blown about in the wilderness of an unfamiliar language by the influences of the King James Version and the vernacular proverb. Where writing like this is concerned, it is impossible to be a Guardian of Good Grammar; one must try to confront the roots of language—the relationship between thought and word, with all the problems of extraneous influences and, in many cases, translation from a native tongue.

THEY SPOKE WHAT WAS
IN THEIR HEADS

At another level, the intellectual excitement came from a kind of freshness of thought and expression in minds that have not become trapped by scholastic conventions, or the fear of them. I remember times at Swarthmore when I kept a question or thought to myself because I feared it might be in some way intellectually out of line. But most of my Nsukka students had no idea what was in or out of line, what was a cliché and what was not, what critical attitudes were forbidden or encouraged (though I did my share, I confess, of forbidding and encouraging). They were not at all calculating, in a social sense, in their thought: They spoke what was in their heads, with the result that discussion had a lively, unadulterated, and personal quality which I found a relief from the more sophisticated but less spontaneously sincere manner of many young American intellectuals. It was also a little infuriating at times. I am, after all, a product of my own culture. But one has only to look at a 1908 *Phoenix* (the Swarthmore student newspaper) to realize how much sophistication is a thing of style and fashion, and how little any one fashion exhausts the possible ways in which the world can be confronted and apprehended.

In Nigeria, literature became the line of commerce between me and my students, as people, a common interest and prime mover in the coming together of white American and black African. Ours was a dialogue between equals, articulate representatives of two articulate and in many ways opposing heritages. Because literature deals more directly with life than other art forms, through it I began to know Nigeria as a country and my students as friends. An idealized case history might read something like this: A student brings me a story he has written, perhaps autobiographical, about life in his village. I harrumph my way through a number of formal criticisms, and start asking questions about customs in his village that have a bearing on the story. Soon we are exchanging childhood reminiscences or talking about girls over a bottle of beer. Eventually we travel together to his home, where I meet his family and live in his house. And then what began, perhaps, as a rather bookish interest in comparative culture becomes a real involvement in that culture, so that each new insight does not merely add to one's store of knowledge, but carries the power of giving pain or pleasure. If there is any lesson in this, it is simply that no real intellectual understanding can exist without a sense of identification at some deeper level. I think this is what the Peace Corps, when it is lucky, accomplishes.

This sense of identification is not a mysterious thing. Once at Nsukka, after struggling to explain the social and intellectual background of some classic Western literature, I began teaching a modern Nigerian novel, Achege's *No Longer At Ease.* I was struck by the concreteness of the first comments from the class: "That place where the Lagos taxi driver runs over the dog because he thinks it's good luck . . . it's really like that. . . ." It seems that the joy of simple recognition in art is more than an accidental attribute—not the recognition of universals, but of dogs and taxicabs. Before going to Africa I read another book by Achege, *Things Fall Apart*. I enjoyed it, and was glad to learn something about Ibo culture, but I thought it a mediocre work of art. I read the book again at the end of my stay in Nigeria and suddenly found it an exceptional work of art. It was no longer a cultural document, but a book about trees I had climbed and houses I had visited in. It is not that I now ignored artistic defects through sentimentality, but that my empathy revealed artistic virtues that had previously been hidden from me.

We in America know too much about the rest of the world. Subjected to a constant barrage of information from books, TV, photographers, we know how Eskimos catch bears and how people come of age in Samoa. We gather our images of the whole world around us and succumb to the illusion of being cosmopolitan. We study comparative literature and read books like *Zen and The Art of Archery* and think of ourselves as citizens of the world, when actually vast reading is simply the hallmark of our parochialism. No matter how many Yoga kicks we go on, we still interpret everything through the pattern of our own American existence and intellectual traditions, gleaning only disembodied ideas from other cultures.

If, as the critics have it, ideals are inseparable from their style of expression, it is equally true, in the cultural sense, that ideas are inseparable from the manner and place in which they are lived. This, to me, is the meaning of the Peace Corps as a new frontier. It is the call to go, not where man has never been before, but where he has lived differently, the call to experience firsthand the intricacies of a different culture, to understand from the inside rather than the outside, and to test the limits of one's own way of life against another in the same manner as the original pioneer tested the limits of his endurance against the elements. This is perhaps an impossible ideal, surely impossible in the narrow scope of two years; but it was an adventure, just the same. It was an adventure to realize, for instance, to what extent irony is an attribute, even a condition, of Western life and thought, and to live for nearly two years in a society in which irony, as a force, is practically nonexistent. But that is too complex a thing to get started on right now.

HUNDREDS OF 23-YEAR-OLD SPIES

Life at Nsukka was not always the easiest thing in the world, and the friendships I talk of so cavalierly were not the work of a day. Our group arrived at Nsukka shortly after the Peace Corps' first big publicity break, the famous Post Card Incident, which was still very much on Nigerian minds. We were always treated with a sense of natural friendliness and hospitality, but there was also quite a bit of understandable mistrust. Nigeria became a nation only in 1960, and the present university generation is one bred on the struggle for independence and the appropriate slogans and attitudes. I tended to feel guilty rather than defensive, except when the accusations were patently ridiculous, such as the idea that we were all master spies—hundreds of 23-year-old master spies—or when facts were purposefully ignored, as in the statement that the Peace Corps was run by the CIA. Amercia is a large, rich, powerful, feared, and envied nation; Nigeria is a new country naturally jealous of its independence and autonomy. All things considered, I am a little amazed at the openness and frankness of our reception.

There were other problems. Many Nigerians have an overdeveloped sense of status and found it hard to believe that we were paid practically nothing. Many reasoned that because we lived in the dormitories with the students instead of in big houses as the rest of the faculty, we must be second-raters, or misfits that America was fobbing off on them. But insofar as we made names for ourselves as good teachers, and made ourselves accessible as people (something that few of my friends had ever known a white man to do), our eventual acceptance into the community was assured. Shortly after our arrival a petition circulated among the students asking the administration to dismiss the Peace Corps. Months later, student grievances erupted into a riot that forced the school to close down for more than two weeks, but in the long list of grievances, the Peace Corps was not now mentioned.

I do not wish to imply that we "won them over"; indeed, I think they won us over in the final analysis. It's just that the intransigence of our preconceptions of ourselves and others gradually dissolved into a kind of affectionate confusion. Ideas often try to live a life of their own, independent of and separate from the people and objects with which they supposedly deal. In the intellect alone they are self-proliferating, like fungus under glass, without regard for what the weather is doing outside. But the kind of personal contact we had with Nigerians helped break up the false buttressing of formal thought, and when that happens, personal friction creates a warmth conducive to further understanding, and not a heat with which to light incendiary fires. A glass of beer can make the difference between fanatics and worthy opponents.

I was at first surprised by how little I felt the presence of any racial feeling in Nigeria. What little I did notice had a kind of second-hand quality, as if it were merely a principled identification with the American Negro, or a historical commitment. Though well-informed about civil rights events in the United States, most Nigerians I talked to showed little understanding of the state of mind of the American Negro as differentiated from themselves. Most Nigerians have had little contact with hardcore prejudice backed by social force. They have good reason to resent, sometimes to hate, the white man in Africa, but they have never been subjected, as a people, to the kind of daily and lifelong injustice that confronts the American Negro.

Racial feeling sometimes crops up in strange circumstances. A friend writes me, "Before Nsukka, the only whites I had ever known were reverend fathers in school who interpreted everything I did as a sure sign of fast-approaching eternal damnation. . . ." In Africa as in America all whites are, to a certain extent, guilty until proven innocent, but in a very short time we were joking about our respective colors with a freedom and levity which is not always possible in America. Color has its own pure power, too; and I soon felt ashamed of my chalky, pallid skin against the splendor of the African's.

Much has been written recently about the contradictory feelings of the Negro toward the white man—hating him, and yet buying facial creams to be more like him, and I think the same sort of contradictory relationship exists in Nigeria, but with a cultural rather than a racial basis. The African stands in a very delicate psychological position between Western industrial culture and his own. He is driven differently, the call to experience first hand the intricacies to a comparative evaluation and must build a society out of his decisions. America is not so much interested in changing as exporting its society; Nigeria is interested in change, and is of necessity much less parochial than ourselves in the sources of its inspiration.

THE ONLY THING THAT CUTS
A LITTLE ICE

"Africa caught between two worlds"—it is a cliché, but it is no joke. To the race problem it is at least possible to postulate an ideal resolution: racial equality and the elimination of intolerance. But in its cultural aspect—the struggle between African traditions and the heritage of the West—there is no indisputable resolution, not even in the mind. If I have learned anything from living in Nigeria, it is the unenviably complex and difficult position in which the young Nigerian finds himself; and if I have learned anything from the poems and stories written by my students, it is the incredible grace, honesty, and sometimes power with which many Nigerians are examining themselves, their past, and their future.

I don't know how friendship fits into all this, but somehow it does. My instincts revolt against the whole idea of having to prove, in some mechanistic or quantitative way, the value of the Peace Corps. If the aim is to help people, I understand that in the sense of the Ibo proverb which says that when the right hand washes the left hand, the right hand becomes clean also. E. M. Forster has said that "love is a great force in private life," but in public affairs, "it does not work. The fact is we can only love what we know personally, and we cannot know much. The only thing that cuts a little ice is affection, or the possibility of affection." I only know that when I am infuriated by some article in a Nigerian newspaper, I can summon up countless images of dusty cycle rides with Paul Okpokam, reading poetry with Glory Nwanodi, dancing and drinking palm wine with Gabriel Ogar, and it suddenly matters very much that I go beyond my annoyance to some kind of understanding. That my Nigerian friends trust me is no reason for them to trust Washington, or forgive Birmingham; but something is there which was not there before, and which the world is the better for having.

FACTORS ASSOCIATED WITH STUDENT ADJUSTMENT IN CROSS-CULTURAL CONTACT

With the expanding cross-cultural contacts between countries, it is of great importance to assess the influence of various factors on making these contacts yield the greatest possible learning to all. The following article is based on a paper presented by the author at the 1965 annual meeting of the American Educational Research Association in Chicago. In this article, the author tests the significance of four hypotheses as they affect the adjustment of a group of Middle Eastern students in certain California institutions of higher learning. The author is an associate professor of comparative and social foundations of education; he has had experiences as student and teacher in several cultures.

Kalil I. Gezi

California Journal of Educational Research, *16* (*May 1965*), *129–136*. *Reprinted by permission of the publisher.*

The increasing flow of international students to the United States has created new horizons for international understanding and cooperation on the one hand and new problems of attitude formation, interaction and adjustment in cross-cultural contacts on the other. These emerging problems have been the focus of a number of studies which have tended to probe the status of international students in the United States, their problems during their sojourn here, the effect of the sojourn on their attitudes and learning and their behavior, problems and readjustment upon return to their native lands (Smith, 1956).

From these studies, several factors associated with cross-cultural adjustment have emerged. It is the purpose of this article to examine four of these factors in relation to the adjustment of selected Middle Eastern students in the United States whose acculturation was the focus of a larger study by this writer (Gezi, 1960).

HYPOTHESES

Specifically, the purpose of this study is to test the following hypotheses: (1) International students who come to the United States with favorable or unfavorable attitudes toward this country tend, in the absence of a program of guided cultural contacts, to select certain positive or negative perceptions and/or interpret their perceptions in ways that foster their initial attitudes toward this country and influence their adjustment here; (2) The length of sojourn of international students in the United States is not in itself a factor in their adjustment, but their adjustment is affected by the type and quality of their sojourn experiences and interaction with Americans (Goldsen and others, 1956; Selltiz and others, 1956); (3) When the international student feels that Americans downgrade his homeland and hence threaten his self-esteem, he tends to become antagonistic toward Americans and to form unfavorable images of this country—all of which would make the student's adjustment more difficult (Morris, 1956; Lambert and Bressler, 1955); and (4) If college work is the main purpose of the sojourn of international students, academic success becomes a basis for the students' satisfaction with their sojourn and adjustment in their foreign milieu.

DESIGN OF THE STUDY

Procedure

In order to test the hypotheses mentioned above two open-end interview schedules were developed. The first consisted of five questions and was used with foreign student advisers and certain faculty members in the institutions where the majority of the students in the sample were studying, in order to elicit information regarding, among other things, the academic status and the adjustment problems of these students. The second interview schedule was composed of twenty questions and was used with each member of the Middle Eastern students' sample. The data derived from these questions related to the background of each interviewee, to his attitudes and images of the United States before arrival, upon arrival and during his sojourn, to his impressions of American education and culture, to his evaluation of the type and quality of the experiences he had in his American college or university and outside of it, and to his perceptions of the American view of his nation. The specific questions in the interview schedule which were directly related to the four factors being examined by this paper were: (1) What did you think of the United States before you came here? (2) Do you think that your interaction with Americans was generally meaningful or not meaningful to you? (3) How do you rank your country, and how do you think Americans rank your country according to the following criteria: standard of living, cultural standards and political standards? Check one of the following: highly advanced, slightly advanced, slightly backward, and highly backward; (4) What values and shortcomings do you personally find in studying in your American college or university?

Based on the students' responses to the first question, the students were divided into two groups: generally favorable and generally unfavorable to the United States before arrival here. This was done by rating the responses on the basis of the degree of over-all expressed liking or dislike of the United States first by the investigator and second by an independent rater. A high degree of agreement between the two raters was achieved. Where differences existed new ratings were made jointly by the raters leading to virtual agreement.

The responses from the second question were used to distinguish between the students who perceived their interaction with Americans to be generally meaningful and those who thought their contacts were generally not meaningful. The word "interaction" is used here to refer to the reciprocal contact between two or more persons and the influences which may be brought about as a result of such a contact.

The third question was used to discover what discrepancies, if any, existed between the students' self-given status to their countries and their perceptions of the American-ascribed status to their countries. The student's choice of each of the four gradations (highly advanced to highly backward), using Morris' (1956) three criteria (standard of living, cultural standards and political standards), was given a score. The highest score, four, was assigned to "highly advanced" and scores three, two and one to "slightly advanced," "slightly backward" and "highly backward" respectively. The discrepancy between the student's score for the subjective ranking and his score for the ascribed ranking of national status was the basis for placing each student into one of the following two categories: the first for those whose subjective status was higher than the ascribed status (or those who believed that Americans downgraded their native lands) and the second for those whose subjective status was lower than, or the same as the ascribed status (or those who believed that Americans did not downgrade their native lands). The terms "advanced" and "backward" were purposely not defined for the students because the investigator was interested in obtaining the students' subjective perceptions of how they ranked their countries and how they thought Americans would rank them, allowing the students to use these terms the way they understood them.

Each student's response to the fourth question and his response to another question concerning his adjustment problems were used as the first evidence of whether he was generally successful in college work or was beset by many academic problems. The second evidence of the student's scholastic status was obtained through interviews with faculty members and foreign student advisers who knew him well.

The dependent factor, to which all the previously-mentioned variables (pre-arrival favorableness, quality of interaction during the sojourn, national status and success in college work) are to be associated, is adjustment. Adjustment is defined, for the purposes of this study, as the expressed satisfaction of the Middle Eastern students with their sojourn in the United States. There were three separate ratings of the Middle Eastern students' satisfaction-dissatisfaction with their American sojourn. These ratings, however, were found to have had a high degree of agreement upon which a final satisfaction-dissatisfaction rating was made. The first rating of the general satisfaction of each student was based on the opinions of the student's advisers and teachers, the second rating was based on the opinions of his fellow students who knew him well and the third rating was based on an analysis of all the student's responses to the interview schedule.

In order to check the reliability of the investigator's interpretation of the protocols and hence his analysis of the students' satisfaction or dissatisfaction, an independent rater read the protocols and analyzed each subject's satisfaction or dissatisfaction. A high degree of agreement was found between the investigator's ratings and those of the independent rater.

After the satisfaction-dissatisfaction rating for each student was determined and convenient categories for each variable were established, contingency tables were drawn to associate each variable with the dependent factor, which was satisfaction or dissatisfaction. In order to discover whether any statistically significant associations existed between each variable and satisfaction-dissatisfaction, the chi square test was used with Yates' correction for continuity applied whenever frequencies smaller than ten were encountered.

Sample

The sample of this study consists of sixty-two Middle Eastern students who were studying at eleven California colleges and universities, with the majority of the students attending the University of California at Berkeley and Stanford University. The sample included students from

Iraq, Jordan, Kuwait, Lebanon, Libya, Sudan, the United Arab Republic and Yemen. The students ranged in age from nineteen to thirty-six years and were predominantly single male. Seventeen students were studying toward their Bachelor's degree, another seventeen were studying toward their Master's degree and twenty-eight were studying toward their Doctorate degree. The students' studies covered twenty-five fields. The students' sojourn in the United Sates varied from six months to twelve years, and the majority had to support themselves during their sojourn in this country.

FINDINGS

In this section, an attempt will be made to describe how the members of the sample responded to the four questions which were posed to them and to use the students' responses in testing the four hypotheses advanced earlier.

Pre-arrival Attitudes

An examination of the students' responses to the question, "What did you think of the United States before you came here?", indicated that fifty-one students formed generally favorable images of the United States before their arrival in this country whereas eleven students held generally unfavorable attitudes toward this country before they came here. Those who held favorable attitudes were aided in forming these attitudes principally by contacts with Americans in the Middle East, with native student returnees from the United States and by reading books and magazines. The students' favorable images of America included the freedom of the individual in this country, equality under the law, availability of opportunities, high standard of living, the value of hard work, industrial production and the hospitality of the American people. The students who came here with unfavorable attitudes toward this country testified that they had developed these attitudes from American movies, from stories in Mid-Eastern papers and from native student returnees from the United States. The unfavorable impressions focused on race prejudice, domination of machines over people in the United States, freedom of gangsters to operate, lack of family unity and preoccupation with materialism.

The students' pre-arrival attitudes were correlated with their satisfaction or dissatisfaction with the sojourn. Of the fifty-one students who had favorable attitudes toward the United States, forty-three showed satisfaction with their sojourn and eight showed dissatisfaction with it. On the other hand, of the eleven students who held pre-arrival unfavorable attitudes toward this country, only two showed satisfaction with their stay here, with the remaining nine showing dissatisfaction with it. The chi square test yielded significant differences ($p < .001$) on the satisfaction-dissatisfaction criterion between the favorable and the unfavorable students. This is consistent with the first hypothesis regarding the influence of the student's pre-arrival attitudes upon his subsequent sojourn in the host country.

Meaningfulness of Interaction

The association between duration of sojourn of an international student in the United States and his adjustment to its culture has been suggested by some studies. Passin (Cited by DuBois, 1956, pp. 88–89), for example, discovered in his study of Japanese students that "the longer the residence in the United States, the more balanced was the attitude toward this country; the shorter the stay, the more serious were adjustment difficulties here."

However, when the Middle Eastern students in the sample were divided in two groups—those who had a short sojourn of less than two years and those who had longer residence—the chi square test showed no significant differences between the two groups in terms of their satisfaction or dissatisfaction.

Furthermore, responses to the second question concerning the students' perceptions of their interaction with Americans revealed that forty-seven students thought highly of their contacts with Americans whereas fifteen students had negative impressions of such contacts. Of the students who perceived their interaction with Americans as meaningful, forty-two were satisfied with their sojourn and three were not. As for the students who felt that their interaction was not meaningful, only five were satisfied while the remaining twelve were dissatisfied. The results of the chi square test indicated significant differences ($p < .001$) in satisfaction with the sojourn between the students who thought their interaction with Americans was meaningful and the students who did not think so.

All of this seems to be consistent with the hypothesis that the duration of sojourn of an international student in a host country in itself does not seem to affect adjustment, but that the quality of the student's interaction with his hosts seems to do so.

National Status

Morris (1956) concluded from his study of foreign students that if the international student, who has a high degree of involvement with his nation, feels that Americans rate his country lower than his rating of his country, he would be inclined to have unfavorable attitudes toward the United States. His theory was that when "those in the minority feel that the majority are making comparisons unfavorable to them, they become more antagonistic. . . ." Lambert and Bressler (1955) concluded also from their study of Indian students in the United States that "visitors from low status countries develop their attitudes towards the United States not so much on the basis of their reactions to American life, but rather as an end product of a 'looking-glass' process based on their perceptions of the American image of their countries."

To find out the effect of the Middle Eastern students' perceptions of the American image of their countries upon the students' satisfaction or dissatisfaction with their sojourn, the students were asked first to rate their countries and second to rate their countries as they thought Americans would. The results indicated that thirty-eight students felt that their native lands were down-rated by Americans and twenty-four students did not feel that way. Of the first group, sixteen were dissatisfied with their sojourn whereas only one was dissatisfied in the second group. The significant differences between these two groups (p ⟨ .01) seemed to support the conclusions of Morris and of Lambert and Bressler.

Success in College Work

Based on the students' responses to the fourth question and the faculty evaluations of the students' academic work, the students were classified into two groups: those who had serious academic problems and those who had few or no academic problems. There were ten students who had serious academic problems, with the remaining fifty-two showing evidence of academic success. All of the ten academically troubled students showed dissatisfaction with their sojourn whereas among the successful students, forty-five were satisfied and only seven manifested dissatisfaction. The differences in satisfaction between the academically successful and those with serious problems in their studies were significant at the .001 level.

SUMMARY AND CONCLUSIONS

A group of sixty-two Middle Eastern students studying in eleven California colleges and universities during the 1958 summer session were interviewed in depth. Interviews were also held with members of the students' faculty advisers. Based on the data obtained from the interviews, the following conclusions may be drawn:

1. There is a significant association (p. ⟨ .001) between the students' pre-arrival attitudes toward the United States and their subsequent adjustment in this country.
2. Although the duration of the students' sojourn in this country was

not found to be significantly associated with their adjustment here, the meaningfulness of their interaction with Americans was found to be significantly associated (p. ⟨ .001) with their adjustment.

3. A significant association (p. ⟨ .01) was discovered between the students' perceptions of how Americans rated the students' homelands and their adjustment in the United States.

4. Success in college was found to be significantly associated (p ⟨ .001) with the students' adjustment here.

REFERENCES

1. Du Bois, Cora. *Foreign Students and Higher Education in the United States.* Washington, D.C.: American Council on Education, 1956.
2. Gezi, K. I. *The Acculturation of Middle Eastern Arab Students in Selected American Colleges and Universities.* Washington, D.C.: American Friends of the Middle East, 1960.
3. Goldsen, Rose K., Suchman, Edward A., and Williams, Robin M., Jr. "Factors Associated with the Development of Cross-Cultural Social Interaction." *The Journal of Social Issues.* 12:26–32; 1, 1956.
4. Lambert, Richard D., and Bressler, Marvin. "The Sensitive Area Complex: A Contribution to the Theory of Guided Culture Contact." *The American Journal of Sociology.* 60:583–592; May 1955.
5. Morris, Richard T. "National Status and Attitudes of Foreign Students." *The Journal of Social Issues.* 12:20–25; 1, 1956.
6. Newcomb, Theodore M. *Social Psychology.* New York: Dryden Press, 1950.
7. Selltiz, Claire, Hopson, Anna Lee, and Cook, Stuart W. "The Effects of Situational Factors on Personal Interaction Between Foreign Students and Americans." *The Journal of Social Issues.* 12:33–44; 1, 1956.
8. Smith, M. Brewster. "A Perspective for Further Research in Cross-Cultural Education." *The Journal of Social Issues.* 12: 56–68; 1, 1956.

PART TWO

ISSUES AND INNOVATIONS
IN TEACHING

4

CRUCIAL ISSUES

INTRODUCTION

In a democratic society such as ours, there is a basic belief that education is indispensable for the achievement of national goals. Since the individual has a greater latitude in decision-making in a free society than in a totalitarian system of government, he cannot make these decisions intelligently unless he is educated. Hence, teachers cannot escape the responsibility of helping their students deal intelligently with the problems confronting them in society. Teachers also need to know about the issues that face education, for the school, as a social institution, has its own problems, deriving not only from its unique structure but also from its position as an integral part of society.

The purpose of this chapter is to expose the student to a selection of vital issues in education which are most likely to concern him as a future educator. It is hoped that such an exposure will stimulate and challenge him to think intelligently about these issues. For this purpose, the following readings are presented: a selection by Virginia Franklin in which she relates the story of her plight as a school teacher in defending academic freedom in her school in Paradise, California; an article by Jack Culbertson which brings into focus the issue of religion in the schools, citing certain Supreme Court decisions on this issue; a reading by Thomas Pettigrew dealing with the crucial issue of school desegregation; a selection by the NEA Committee on School Finance raising some important questions and giving answers to certain support aspects of American education; an article by N. A. Fattu devoted to a review of research pertinent to the problem of evaluating teacher effectiveness; a reading by John Scanlon in which he describes vividly the power struggle between the AFT and the NEA to represent teachers; and a selection by Myers and Gezi in which they attempt to answer the vital question of whether teaching is a profession by analyzing education in the light of certain criteria.

PARADISE WON . . . OR LOST:
A Case of Academic Freedom

The following narration is a case in academic freedom in the schools. It is written by Mrs. Virginia Franklin—from 1955 until 1966, a social studies teacher in Paradise, California—adapted from her speeches before the NEA conventions on July 2, 1964, in Seattle, and July 1, 1965, in New York. She describes the attacks that were directed against her integrity and teaching ability by certain community members and her courageous fight to preserve academic freedom in her classroom. This case gained national attention when Life *magazine made it the subject of an eleven-page story in its April 26, 1963 issue, and when the* Teachers College Record *selected the Paradise controversy to be a case study in academic freedom in its May 1964 issue. In 1964, the California Assembly Subcommittee on Education conducted a hearing on this case and found, as did the Paradise Superintendent and school board, no substance to the charges leveled against Mrs. Franklin. One of the outcomes of the uproar in Paradise was the Unruh Act, which forbids the use of electronic recording equipment in California classrooms without the consent of the teacher and the principal.*

In 1966, Mrs. Franklin resigned from her teaching position at Paradise indicating that she no longer wanted to subject her faculty, administration and family to unwarranted attacks of the extremists in that area. The following year, five years after she had brought a damage suit against a Paradise woman and the American Legion 259, she was awarded a $16,500 judgment by Judge Bertram Janes, himself a Legionnaire, after a non-jury trial in Butte County Superior Court. During the trial, Mrs. Franklin's attorney painfully pointed out that she had applied for work in 62 schools and other institutions but had failed to get a job. However, later in 1967, she was selected by the San Rafael (California) Board of Education as a social studies teacher at San Rafael high school.

The right of teachers to preserve their academic freedom was perhaps best summed up by the judge when he said, "No one person, no one organization has any monopoly on patriotism, and it cannot be purchased, and certainly, our freedoms cannot be preserved, or patriotism purchased at the expense of individual liberties.

"One of those liberties to this case is the freedom of expression. It is my sincere opinion that on the one side here that liberty has been given full expression and upon the other side seriously abused. To the parties in this case there are, of course, material gains and material losses, but in my honest and sincere judgment, gentlemen, I feel that the real losers are the countless students who have lost the opportunity to be exposed to the type of teaching which these defendants condemn."

Virginia Franklin

> *Prepared especially for this volume.*

I have been teaching in the Paradise School District since 1955 and had received tenure at the end of the school term in 1958. Ours was a new school, and I had had the responsibility of developing the social studies program from the time we first housed our 9th- and 10th-grade students. I was given a great deal of autonomy and cooperation by my principal, who had been a social studies teacher himself. My first principal left in the spring of 1958 to take a job with David Lilienthal in Iran, and Mr. Glen Russell, our present principal, took charge of the administration. At all times I felt that I had complete support of the administration. We developed some outstanding programs, and I was encouraged to experiment with new materials and attempt some creative programs. We developed an active citizenship training class, and many students participated actively in politics. Suddenly, in 1961, a startling event rocked the community. An anonymous smear sheet wrapped around suckers was placed in children's Halloween trick-or-treat bags. This smear sheet attacked the Human Rights Conference sponsored by the American Friends Service Committee, a conference to which our students had gone in previous years. The sheet began with the following words:

> To Citizens of Paradise, California, on [sic] organized activity to weaken the souls and minds of our children.
> Virginia Franklin, Social Studies Teacher in Paradise High School, has been inviting our children to an Asilomar High School Human Rights Conference. . . .

This was not the first time that this conference had been questioned, but it was the first time such bizarre methods had been used to discredit it. Needless to say, our students attended the conference as planned.

We began to take more notice of our opposition as more dissident voices were raised in the community. A new church, headed by Carl McIntire's American Council of Christian Churches, was established in Paradise; its minister became a leading force in opposition to our schools. We realized that since the spring of 1961, our area had been deluged with anti-Communist speakers. During 1961, the area of Paradise, Chico, and Oroville in Butte County, a county whose total population is 92,000 persons, played host to such speakers as Dean Manion, Dan Smoot, Ronald Reagan, Robert Welch, Billy Hargis, and Rev. Brustadt of Scarsdale, New York. An impressive group of speakers for such a small area! At these meetings the speakers would make remarks such as these: "One teacher teaching 4 classes of 25 pupils can influence, day after day, 100 youths a year in a continuing brain-washing program." The claim was made that there was a Communist conspiracy to get one or more teachers into the school system who were not loyal Americans.

There began more intense letter-writing campaigns, especially letters to the editor which questioned the patriotism of the school people and me in particular. In the spring of 1962, parts of a test I had used in class were duplicated and distributed throughout the community as evidence of subversion in the schools. This particular test was used for showing various propaganda devices with emphasis upon half-truths.

Book lists were distributed attacking isolated passages from texts and it was suggested that authors were not 100 percent American. Youth study groups on anti-Communism were formed and a Minute Men's group was established. Some Paradise High School students were members.

In September of 1962, each new teacher in our district received an anonymous letter degrading the school system and casting doubts upon the teaching methods employed in our District. On September 14th, 1962, a letter to the editor of the Chico *Enterprise-Record* was printed from the American Legion's Americanism Committee of the Paradise Legion post which suggested to people that they not vote "Yes" on the coming bond elections. On September 18th, the bond issue lost.

On September 20th, the Paradise American Legion post held a public meeting to which I was not invited and about which I did not hear in advance, purporting to show documentary evidence of the fact that I was perhaps violating the school code which prohibits the teaching of subversion. On September 25th, the Legion appeared before the school board upon invitation from that body and presented its charges formally. When finally presented, the charges were unfounded and meaningless. One week later, the school people scheduled a meeting before the school board to answer the charges. The American Legion failed to represent itself at this meeting. The Board of Trustees and the public gave a standing vote of confidence to me and to our staff. For awhile we felt we had won a major victory.

However, attacks continued. Before I had completed an entire school day the school administration would be harrassed by telephone calls protesting the playing of a certain tape or the showing of a certain film. None of these materials were found to be questionable by the administration or by the legislative committee which subsequently investigated the charges made against our school.

As the attacks continued, I felt I had no other path open to me—all communication was virtually cut off—, and I filed a law suit for defamation of character against the Americanism Committee of the Paradise American Legion post and other individuals in the community who were siding in an effort to discredit me and the schools. This suit attracted national attention and brought the situation to the attention of *Life* magazine.

In April of 1963, three incumbents who had stood firmly by me had to run for re-election. They were opposed by a slate of three people who ran on a platform of economy, teaching the fundamentals, elimination of "Life Adjustment" classes, reducing adverse publicity that had highlighted the Legion hearings, and elimination of psychological testing. After a spirited campaign, the Board members were re-elected by a comfortable majority. Once more I felt that we had won a major victory. It was not to last long!

In the April 26th, 1963 issue of *Life,* the unrest in Paradise was depicted in an eleven-page spread. Of particular note were the startling pictures of the discovery of a hidden tape recorder. Although it is difficult for some people to believe, these pictures of the tape recording incident were not rigged and occurred as photographed by *Life.* I have always felt that *Life* magazine did a good job of pinpointing the opposition as uninformed and fearful people. Once more I felt that the entire story was rigged and unfair, but for the most part the *Life* article brought favorable publicity to the people of Paradise who had stood up to be counted. Unfortunately, Paradise citizens resented the publicity brought to the community and blamed me and the administration for this.

On October 8, 1963, our second bond issue failed by a 2 percent margin! Our victory had been short lived.

We tried again in February of 1964, and letters to the editor once more complained that no "Yes" votes would be forthcoming until the lawsuit was completed and until the public would become aware of the inept and inefficient administration. It was even suggested that we were also responsible for taking the Bible out of the schools. Isolated passages from the text of Eleanor Roosevelt's book, *Tomorrow Is Now,* were strung together in radio ads to show that Eleanor Roosevelt was aware of the fact that our public school system was failing to teach the students a respect for Americanism. Despite these tactics, we passed the bond issue. It was at this time that I entitled this speech, "We Won in Paradise."

One week following the passage of the bond issue, Paradise was visited by our Assembly Education Interim Committee on Academic Freedom, whose task it was to study the attacks upon the schools. The Paradise story had come to the attention of the speaker of the Assembly, Jesse Unruh, through the story in *Life* magazine. He had personally introduced the bill which now outlaws electronic recording equipment in a classroom without the teacher's and principal's permission. The bill had been passed without a dissenting vote. The issues in the Paradise story seemed to be clearly drawn, and the subcommittee on education decided to make its first investigation of threats to academic freedom in Paradise.

Once again the people of Paradise felt that we had been exonerated; once again we felt that it had been plainly shown that the charges against the school were stirring a controversy which had consumed hundreds of hours of our administrators' time, not to mention the school board's and my time. But this is not the end. The attacks continue because our opposition cannot face the reality that they might be misguided and mislead in making their groundless charges.

I quote from a letter to the editor which appeared in our local paper as late as May 27, 1964: "If the School Board and Mr. Tregarthen [our superintendent then [1]] insist on allowing Mrs. Franklin to ruin our schools and community by keeping us continually in the headlines, then I say get rid of her, the School Board and Mr. Tregarthen."

I think it is important to point out here that I truly believe our opponents are unaware of the fact that it is *they* who have brought about the controversy. As a result of the controversy, one of the most difficult tasks is to dispel the thinking of some individuals that where there is smoke there must be fire!

Although the story of such attacks appear to tell a grim story, it perhaps is more important that you find out what we did to combat the attacks. Our first line of defense was to inform the faculty, the school board, and the administration of the philosophy and nature of the attacks of the opposition. Our administrators and teachers had to evaluate their own philosophy, and we had to know what it was that we believed. The administrators of Paradise all developed and agreed upon a set of

---

[1] Mr. Tregarthen is now associate superintendent, Chico Unified School District—The Editors.

principles, stood fast upon it, and backed their teachers and their teachings. It was pointed out from the onset that this was not a problem of the high school or of the Social Studies Department alone, but a fight for the survival of all the concepts that we believed to be right.

During our long battle, we relied heavily upon certain resources: the attorney-general's office, the county counsel, the California Teachers Association (CTA), the NEA, Chico State College, and the county Department of Education.

With true concern that the public be informed, we brought our programs to the attention of the community; we organized speaker's panels and tried to clear up areas of dispute. While we did not receive support from the local daily newspaper in Chico, we did get excellent support from our weekly newspaper, the Paradise *Post*. Mrs. Kedma Utt, editor of the *Post*, was given the John Sweet Award from the CTA for outstanding editorials in support of the schools.

Our school board meetings which heard the charges of the opposition and the answers from the school personnel were carefully planned so that all facts and documentation would be made available. The school board went on record as reaffirming its confidence in the educational program and staff in our schools.

The northern section of CTA unanimously passed a strong resolution condemning the tactics of the American Legion post in Paradise. When my lawsuit was filed, the CTA and NEA came forth with financial aid and support. The Paradise Ministerial Association supported the schools throughout this entire conflict. In the midst of our greatest controversy during the time when the Legion was formally presenting its charges, I was awarded a Freedom's Foundation Medal from Valley Forge for outstanding teaching in the interpretation of Americanism. The issue was clouded by the fact that the Legion protested this action, and I have not as yet received my Medal. I have been told by the Foundation that I will receive it at the end of the litigation.

One of the most gratifying moments of the entire conflict came during the second public meeting, when a statement from our high school teachers was read. I should like to quote a part of it to you:

> For us to do our best as teachers, this freedom of discussion—this core of our democratic system—must be preserved in the classroom. We know that the pursuit of this democratic method will subject us to critical attacks from those persons who believe there is only *one* side to any issue—*theirs*.
>
> Such an attack has been made upon teachers in our school system. We, the undersigned, feel that this attack is, in reality, not an attack upon any individual teacher, but an attack upon those demo-

cratic principles to which we are dedicating our lives. Each of us is involved in this attack.

In the spring of 1965, two tax-override elections went down to defeat. During the first defeat, we were not aware of any organized opposition, so we did not know whom to answer nor what matters were at issue. During the second tax-override election, which occurred last May, we were opposed by a new committee called the "Academic Research Committee." Its members were drawn from those who had opposed the schools earlier and several newcomers to Paradise. None of the individuals involved were willing to participate in a League of Women Voters forum set up to give both sides of the issue according to a report given by the League.

The struggle for the schools continues. The persons in Paradise who are identified as the school supporters are people who cannot or do not devote as much time to the fight as do our opponents. Unfortunately, our greatest danger is that of losing workers to the school cause who claim it is someone elses' turn. In the meantime, the strength of the right-wing groups seems augmented by many full-time workers and newcomers to Paradise who have devoted themselves to the conservative cause.

RELIGION AND THE SCHOOLS:
Some Issues and Action Guides

After reading Chapter 1, the student should be familiar with the long history of conflict that has centered on religious practices in the public schools. Few other issues have brought about as much controversy as does the issue of religious practices in the public schools. The following article is based on a speech given by Jack A. Culbertson, Executive Director, University Council for Educational Administration at Ohio State University, before the Fifteenth Annual School Boards Association Conference, Wayne State University, January 17, 1964. In this selection the author brings up to date the issue of religion and the schools. He comments on the Abington v. Schempp *case, in which the Supreme Court gives its position on several issues pertaining to religious exercises and instruction. Culbertson admits that the answers he gives to certain questions in this article are based upon his interpretation of the* Abington v. Schempp *case, pointing out that men do disagree on the meaning of laws. With this in mind, the student is invited to argue for or against Culbertson's analysis and recommendations.*

Jack A. Culbertson

Theory Into Practice, 4 (*February 1965*), 33–39. *Reprinted by permission of the author and* Theory Into Practice.

School matters encompassing such fundamental concerns as worship and freedom involve century-long conflicting traditions that offer no easy resolution. They create sharp and sometimes irreconcilable differences between religious majorities and minorities and stir the deepest feelings about some of man's most cherished values.

We all remember the strong feelings and sharp differences reflected in the great storm that broke after the recent Supreme Court decision on the New York Regents Prayer case (*Engel v. Vitale*). However, such storms generated by religious practices in the schoool are not new. The following description of the aftermath of a school board decision more than a century ago illustrates the point:

> In Philadelphia, in 1844, a controversy over Bible reading in the public schools led to violence and bloodshed. The immediate cause of the controversy was a school board ruling to the effect that Bible reading in the schools could be, in the case of Catholic children, from the Douay version. Incensed by this action, a Protestant clergymen's association launched a campaign of inflammatory anti-Catholic propaganda. Tensions mounted in the weeks that followed, and finally erupted into open warfare. Before order was finally restored, at least twenty persons had been killed, and three times that number wounded. Entire blocks of homes belonging to Irish immigrants had been put to flames, in addition to three Catholic churches and a seminary.[1]

Although there is undoubtedly greater tolerance now among minority and majority groups than at the time of the Philadelphia incident, problems related to religion and the schools still remain. Recent court cases have once more thrust upon us problems related to the conduct of religious exercises and religious instruction in the school. In addition, new problems concerning the allocation of society's funds for financing public and nonpublic schools have arisen during the last three decades. I propose to discuss these two sets of problems.

School board members and superintendents will find the *Abington*

[1] Lloyd P. Jorgenson, "The Birth of a Tradition (Historical Origins of Non-Sectarian Schools)," *Phi Delta Kappan*, 4 (June 1963), 410.

v. Schempp case the best guide to follow when setting policy on religious exercises and instruction. This recent 117-page decision contains five separate opinions and gives the Court's most up-to-date positions on a number of the basic issues related to religious exercises and instruction in the schools. Of major significance for policy makers is the fact that the decision reflects a basic shift in the interpretation of constitutional theory. Many previous interpretations stressed the concept of the "wall of separation between church and state," but the *Abington v. Schempp* case sets forth the concept of "neutrality." This concept means that the state must be neutral in its attitude toward religion because of the Establishment and Free Exercise clauses of the First Amendment. Justice Clark, in the majority opinion, pointed to the danger of strict adherence to the concept of "separation of church and state," and Justice Stewart, the lone dissenter in the case, also argued against the separation concept.[2]

How can the schools be guided in their efforts to avoid the fearful and destructive elements inherent in the religious issue? Of major import is the test that the Supreme Court would apply in following a policy of neutrality toward religion. Justice Clark states it as follows:

> . . . what are the purpose and the primary effect of the enactment? If either is the advancement or inhibition of religion then the enactment exceeds the scope of legislative power as circumscribed by the Constitution. This is to say that to withstand the strictures of the Establishment Clause there must be a secular legislative purpose and a primary effect that neither advances nor inhibits religion.[3]

[2] Justice Stewart's argument follows:
The First Amendment declares that "Congress shall make no law respecting an establishment of religion, or prohibiting the free exercise thereof. . . ." It is, I think, a fallacious oversimplification to regard these two provisions as establishing a single constitutional standard of "separation of church and state," which can be mechanically applied in every case to delineate the required boundaries between government and religion. We err in the first place if we do not recognize, as a matter of history and as a matter of the imperatives of our free society, that religion and government must necessarily interact in countless ways. Secondly, the fact is that while in many contexts the Establishment Clause and the Free Exercise Clause fully complement each other, there are areas in which a doctrinaire reading of the Establishment Clause leads to irreconcilable conflict with the Free Exercise Clause.

A single obvious example should suffice to make the point. Spending federal funds to employ chaplains for the armed forces might be said to violate the Establishment Clause. Yet a lonely soldier stationed at some faraway outpost could surely complain that a government which did *not* provide him the opportunity for pastoral guidance was affirmatively prohibiting the free exercise of his religion. And such examples could readily be multiplied (374 U.S. 308–309).

[3] Justice Stewart, p. 222.

What then does this test mean for those responsible for making policy in regard to prayer, meditation, Bible reading, religious instruction, and related issues? I should like to provide some answers to these questions based upon *my* interpretation of the *Abington v. Schempp* case. I do this realizing that men disagree on the meaning of law and also on the interpretation of the facts to which law applies.

There will be differences in attorney generals' rulings and differences in the manner and speed with which states and school districts comply with the Supreme Court's ruling. In this regard, we should note that the rulings of state attorney generals are the effective guides for policy makers until and unless they are changed by the courts through litigation procedures. However, the *Abington v. Schempp* case appears to provide us with the most satisfactory base for determining future directions. Therefore, let us see how it can help answer some of the specific questions before us.

1. *Can Bible reading and prayer, when required by state law, be legally practiced in schools and school districts?* The answer to this question is very clear:

> In light of the history of the First Amendment and of our cases interpreting and applying its requirements, we hold that the practices at issue and the laws requiring them are unconstitutional under the Establishment Clause, as applied to the States through the Fourteenth Amendment.[4]

A more subtle question is whether or not the schools can have programs of Bible reading and prayer recitations on their own initiative when the state does not require them by law. Justice Clark found not only that the laws requiring religious exercises were unconstitutional, but that the "practices at issue" were also unconstitutional. This means that if the administrative machinery and policy of the school or school district are used to serve religious purposes, the neutrality principle is violated and those responsible for such practices would be open to litigation.

2. *Can a school schedule a period of silent prayer?* Since prayer is clearly a religious act, those responsible for instituting programs of silent prayer on a systematic basis would also be subject to litigation. However, periods of meditation which are set up to give students an opportunity for serious contemplation are permitted. Since our Constitution seeks to protect the freedom of individuals in regard to both religious belief *and* disbelief, meditation periods cannot be limited solely to religious contemplation. The states of Pennsylvania, New York, New Jersey, Vermont, and Massachusetts have recommended silent meditation as a way of obeying the laws of the land.

[4] Justice Stewart, p. 205.

3. *Are baccalaureate services in the schools a legal practice?* It is difficult to come to a clear-cut position on this question since the purpose and primary effect of these services may differ. The purpose of such services may range from an emphasis on devotion to an emphasis on objective religious instruction. If baccalaureate services are set up in a systematic fashion as a religious ceremony, the schools or school districts may be subject to litigation. Litigation might arise from those belonging to a religious sect not represented in the services or from religious disbelievers. However, the odds for prospective litigation in the case of baccalaureate services are not as great as in the case of required daily Bible reading, because such services are usually limited to a relatively small number in a given school year. Persons discriminated against would be less likely to take offense because of the infrequency of the practice. In addition, the recent *Chamberlain* case from Florida provides some support to those who would argue that baccalaureate ceremonies do not interfere substantially with the neutrality concept.

4. *Are special Christmas ceremonies permissible in the public schools?* In recent years, there have been increasing controversies concerning the manner in which Christmas is celebrated in the public schools. These controversies have arisen largely from the fact that certain religious aspects of Christmas reflected in "live" Nativity scenes and Creche ceremonies have been highlighted in some public schools. These religious ceremonies, which are within the Christian tradition, have offended members of minority groups, such as those in Jewish communities. The *Abington v. Schempp* decision has given support to those in minority groups. Those school districts that use religious ceremonies for devotional purposes within a particular religious tradition are subject to litigation. The Christmas period can be used to teach students about the meaning of ceremonies in different religions. Such practices as the singing of Christmas carols seem to fall within the more general tradition and are not likely to be challenged.

5. *Can the Bible be used as a historical and literary source, and can religion be studied in the public schools?* The opinions expressed in the *Abington v. Schempp* decision are very clear on these questions; the Justices (perhaps in part as a result of the great furor that was created by the Board of Regents case a few months earlier) seemed to go out of their way to emphasize the schools' role in religious instruction:

> . . . it might well be said that one's education is not complete without a study of comparative religion or the history of religion and its relationship to the advancement of civilization. It certainly may be said that the Bible is worthy of study for its literary and historic qualities. Nothing we have said here indicates that such study of the Bible

or of religion, when presented objectively as part of a secular program
of education, may not be effected consistently with the First Amendment.[5]

Although the principle may be clear, its actual application presents
problems. However, certain guides can be suggested. First, students
should be free to raise questions in school about religious matters, and
teachers should be free to respond to these questions. The purpose of
such interchange should be to promote instruction and not a particular
religion. Second, specific assignments for instructional purposes in Bib-
lical and religious literature may be made. Thus, an understanding of
poetry can be gained from studying selected passages in the Bible; or
light can be shed on early civilizations through a study of the record of
the Old Testament. Third, the *Abington v. Schempp* case does not interfere in any way with released time practices now carried on in many
parts of the country or with Bible classes that are held away from the
school premises.

Two different points of view in regard to religious instruction have
developed since the *Abington v. Schempp* decision. Some observers believe that the case actually encourages the schools to place a greater emphasis upon religious instruction. While accepting the illegality of religious exercises in the school, these persons call for a revision in the curriculum to include special courses in religious instruction. Thus, various
types of courses are being recommended for public schools; the state of
Florida, for example, has passed laws to permit the public schools to
teach courses in the Bible. Such developments could create problems for
school board members and superintendents. Is it possible to develop curricula, prepare teachers, and conduct instruction *about* religions without
engaging in indoctrination? The answer to this question may be found in
research and demonstration, not in pronouncements and speculation.

Others see in the decision a more limited role for the school in regard to religious instruction. These persons agree that religious questions
are basic to man's education, but they argue that the responsibility for
this instruction rests with the family and the church. The school, they believe, should concentrate on secular education and the inculcation of
democratic values; the churches, they maintain, will be stronger if they
take responsibility for religious instruction themselves and depend less
on the schools.

To summarize, concerning our first set of problems: prayer, Bible
reading, and religious exercises for devotional purposes in the schools are
unconstitutional. Since the opinions in the *Abington v. Schempp* case
represent a shift in thinking concerning the conduct of religious exer-

[5] Justice Stewart, p. 225.

cises, school boards will need to reassess their current practices and policies. The test of laws and policy is: does a particular practice advance or inhibit religion? If so, it is illegal. The intent of the *Abington v. Schempp* case is to encourage a posture of neutrality toward religion.

I would now like to turn to a second set of related problems. These concern the allocation of funds for financing public and nonpublic schools. Let us look briefly at some of the major forces that are generating new conditions, new problems, and new thinking.

First, we should note the very rapid growth of nonpublic schools during the last few decades. Between 1940 and 1960, Roman Catholic school enrollment jumped 210 per cent while public school enrollment rose 42 per cent—for every ten pupils in Roman Catholic schools in 1940, there were twenty-two in 1960; for every ten in the public schools in 1940, there were fourteen in 1960. To take another example, there were sixteen Jewish day schools in 1935; today there are approximately three hundred. These figures help explain why one out of every seven students of school age (K–12) is enrolled in nonpublic schools at the present time.

This growth in nonpublic school enrollment has been accompanied by an increase in the cost of education in both public and nonpublic schools. Some of the nonpublic schools have been harder hit than the public schools. For example, Roman Catholic parochial schools which enroll more than 90 per cent of all nonpublic school students, have found it necessary to employ a greater proportion of lay teachers. The present ratio of lay to religious teachers is about one to two and a half in the Roman Catholic schools. By 1970, some authorities estimate there will be at least as many lay as religious teachers in these schools. This means a radical increase in the cost of nonpublic education, for lay teachers command three to six times as much salary as teaching nuns. This substantial increase in cost has led to increases in class size, along with all of the problems associated with such changes. Because of the marked increase in both enrollments and costs, some nonpublic school educators feel they might be "priced out of the educational market." In fact, a number of nonpublic school systems have disbanded in recent years.

The economic duress experienced by those financing nonpublic school systems has not occurred in a vacuum; it has spilled over into the political arena at the local, state, and national levels. At the local level, for example, there is greater and greater uncertainty about whether or not those supporting nonpublic schools at increasingly high costs can and will continue to aid the public schools by voting for bond issues and related measures. The financing of nonpublic schools impinges upon state politics; proposals are now before state legislatures which, if enacted, will provide funds to nonpublic schools for such purposes as pupil transportation.

At the national level, proposals for general Federal aid to education have been before Congress for many years. However, expert observers do not expect the passage of *general* Federal aid for public schools in the immediate future. One of the basic reasons for the impasse is the fact that many of those interested in parochial schools, particularly Roman Catholic schools, have strongly opposed general Federal aid to the public schools. Further, they have maintained that proposals for massive general Federal aid should be extended to nonpublic schools.

At the same time, there is great and widespread apprehension about the possibility of general Federal aid for parochial schools. Such aid is seen as a threat to religious freedom, and its legality is questioned. The late President Kennedy argued that such aid was unconstitutional. Consequently, a deadlock of such proportions has developed that many observers believe that general Federal aid for public elementary and secondary schools is an unrealistic expectation. This deadlock comes at a time when opinion polls indicate that the majority of our people favor Federal aid to public schools.

Another force that is reshaping the thinking about the relationship of our public and nonpublic schools is the tendency, particularly during the last six or eight years, to see education as serving national as well as individual needs. The National Defense Education Act of 1958 was enacted to serve national purposes. More recently there has been widespread agreement that the extent and quality of our education is intimately related to continued economic growth, civil rights, and a thriving national economy. There is recognition that if we are to meet the challenges of outer space, of a growing and changing economy, of an elaborate defense system, and of related national needs, *all* students in society must be educated to the highest level of their abilities. Since the nonpublic school system educates a substantial proportion of our citizens, it can be argued that it is in the national interest to see that *both* the public and the nonpublic school systems achieve optimum performance— even if it means providing substantial financial support from the public treasury for both systems.

Because of the new economic, political, and social forces, the *status quo* is giving way to new financing patterns and to experimentation with untried modes of school support. The remainder of this paper will examine some of the emerging and potential patterns of support, particularly for the nonpublic schools.

One potential course of action discussed with increasing frequency is the provision of general Federal aid to both public and nonpublic schools. For example, Walter Lippman has argued that it is in the national interest to provide Federal aid for both public and nonpublic schools. While recognizing the risks in such a course of action, he maintains that there is a greater risk in impoverishing our public and nonpublic school systems through a lack of financial support, and that impoverishment is inevitable without massive Federal aid. Professor Wilber G. Katz, of the University of Wisconsin Law School, has argued that the "neutrality concept" affords legal justification for providing Federal aid to nonpublic schools, in part because these schools serve more than a religious purpose. Since they serve public purposes by providing general education to students which conforms to state standards, does not the state, Professor Katz asks, have a responsibility to support institutions serving the purposes of general education? [6]

Even though these views indicate some support for general aid to nonpublic schools, there seems to be much more support for the opposing position. Most leaders are deeply concerned about the fundamental risks that a free society would face in providing general aid to nonpublic schools. First, there is the risk of losing religious freedom, and this is of great concern to both public and nonpublic school leaders. Second, there is the risk that widespread, hostile relations among religious groups might develop, affecting the fabric of our democracy in deep and destructive fashion. Finally, there is the risk that our school system might break into many school systems, and that we would lose the tradition of pluralism *and* unity that are now present in society. Because of these risks, general Federal aid for nonpublic schools does not seem to be wise public policy.

While general Federal aid for all nonpublic schools seems clearly out of the question, it is just as evident that special kinds of support are emerging for nonpublic schools and their students. In addition, the public is indirectly sharing in financing parochial schools because these schools, especially the Catholic schools, are shifting current and prospective parochial school students into the public school.

This shifting process may gain favor, particularly in some of the larger urban communities. In 1963, some of the parochial schools in Cincinnati, Ohio, curtailed their lower grades, and Bishop Paul F. Leibold, Chairman of the Archdiocesan School Board there, announced that it might be necessary to drop the first four grades of all the church-operated schools in the Archdiocese. In 1964, more parochial classes were eliminated in Cincinnati. In recent years, lower grades have been curtailed in Kansas City, and St. Louis, Missouri; in Cleveland and Columbus, Ohio; in Spokane, Washington; in Clinton, Iowa; in St. Paul,

---

[6] Wilber G. Katz, "Religion, Education, and the Constitution," *Educational Administration Quarterly,* 1 (2), (Spring 1965.), 1–11.

Minnesota; and in Richmond, Virginia. Curtailment may take the form of eliminating grades or of having limited admission policies.

In those parochial school systems where the financial "breaking point" is being reached, many believe that curtailment policies are the only alternatives open. Some Roman Catholic school leaders are even considering the possible elimination of either the elementary school system or the secondary school system in certain localities. Substantial curtailment policies will create special and even severe problems for public school systems, if they are adopted hurriedly, particularly in large and medium-sized cities. A complicating factor is that the public school systems that are most heavily burdened financially are in the big cities, where the largest nonpublic school systems are also located. In Pittsburgh, for example, 47.6 per cent of the students are in nonpublic schools. In such cities as New York, Philadelphia, Detroit, St. Louis, and Chicago, approximately one-third of the school-age population is enrolled in the nonpublic schools. One out of three of all nonpublic schools are in the fifty largest cities whereas only one out of eight of the public schools are in these cities.[7]

Since parochial school authorities in general are still committed to providing a religiously oriented education for children throughout the formative years, they are likely to avoid radical curtailment policies as long as possible. This, along with the development of special governmental support, will likely lessen the need for sudden and marked adjustments in public school enrollments in the large majority of American communities.

Supplementing the curtailment policies are systematic efforts to enhance religious instruction by increasing and improving released time arrangements. Evidence for this is found in a Roman Catholic organization called Confraternity of Christian Doctrine (CCD).[8] This organization is devoting itself to improved religious instruction. It is seeking to achieve its goals through such measures as television, improved audio-visual aids, and improved textbooks. It has also been active in involving lay teachers and, reportedly, has more than 75,000 lay catechists teaching CCD courses. Some of these teachers have had 90 hours in schools of religion.

Plans call for building special schools near public schools for released time programs. Some of these buildings are already in use; in some places they are substitutes for parochial schools. About a dozen religious orders are now involved in this movement. This trend will require many

[7] "Nonpublic Schools in the 50 Largest Cities," *School Life*, **46** (July 1964), 14.

[8] "What Do Parochial Schools Accomplish?" *Phi Delta Kappan*, **45** (December 1963), 121–122.

public school systems throughout the country to take greater educational responsibility.

Another pattern of support for nonpublic schools is that of "shared time," defined by Harry L. Stearns as follows:

> The concept of shared time, quite different from the concept of released time, involves the division of a child's school time between public schools and church schools. The wall of separation will be very strong in that public schools will be totally supported by public funds. No religious instruction may be given in the public school buildings. Religious instruction must be supported by the church and carried on at church supported premises.[9]

According to a recent study conducted by the National Education Association, shared time, or "dual" enrollment arrangements as it has been called in Congressional hearings, exists in 183 communities in 25 different states throughout the country.[10] Industrial arts, vocational education, and home economics are the subjects most often provided to nonpublic school students in shared time arrangements, according to the NEA study. Music, physics, chemistry, and other nonreligious subjects which require expensive equipment are also popular offerings. The amount of shared time seems to vary in different communities from one time period for a given subject to one-half day or more.

The legality of shared time is still at issue in some circles. However, Leo Pfeffer, a leading constitutional lawyer, who has opposed general Federal aid to nonpublic schools on legal grounds, believes that shared time is constitutional. In addition, it has been declared legal by the courts of Wisconsin and Pennsylvania. Since the plan presents special administrative difficulties, further experimentation will be required to determine its general applicability. Some even believe that the difficulties in administering shared time programs are such that they will deter the widespread adoption of these programs. However, if Federal support for shared time arrangements in poverty-stricken areas is provided by Congress in line with President Johnson's recent recommendation, it can be predicted that the impetus will be sufficient to spur and speed its adoption.

Another pattern of support for nonpublic elementary and secondary schools is that of grants and loans. The National Defense Education Act of 1958 authorized 12 per cent of its Title III funds for loans to nonpublic elementary and secondary schools. These funds are to be used to reimburse manufacturers for materials and equipment necessary for the

[9] See "Shared Time," *Theory Into Practice,* 4 (February 1965), 15–17.

[10] "Shared Time Programs," *NEA Research Bulletin,* 42 (October 1964), 93.

study of sciences, mathematics, and foreign languages. In 1963, it was estimated that approximately two million dollars had been loaned to parochial schools. However, this is much less than the authorized 12 per cent. The Act also provides some assistance for testing students to improve counseling and guidance. During 1962, an estimated $212,000 in Federal funds was provided to parochial schools for testing purposes.

In the 1964 extension of the NDEA, grant and loan funds for nonpublic schools were considerably increased. Some of the changes included were: teachers from nonpublic schools may now attend institutes and receive stipends; the "forgiveness" features of loans made to students in teacher training programs are now extended to nonpublic school personnel training to be teachers; and loans may be made to students attending nonpublic business and technical schools. The new Economic Opportunity Act also provides aid to students in nonpublic schools.

Both Federal and state funds are also used to support nonpublic schools for needs related to, but in a sense auxiliary to, the educational process. Examples of Federal aid are found in the School Lunch Act, and the special milk and surplus commodities programs. In 1962–63, approximately fifteen million dollars went to nonpublic elementary and secondary schools under the School Lunch Act. There has been little interest in trying to eliminate such aid on constitutional grounds. It is also significant that in President Johnson's 1965 education message to Congress additional auxiliary aid for both public and nonpublic school children is recommended. In poverty-stricken areas, aid is recommended for such purposes as the following: mobile science laboratories, educational television systems, and special remedial or supplementary classes. The message also contains a recommendation that funds be provided to the various states for the purchase of textbooks and school library resources in both public and nonpublic school systems.

State aid to nonpublic schools for special services auxiliary to education are best represented in legislation to provide textbook and transportation to nonpublic schools. At the present time, for example, legislation to provide transportation for nonpublic school students is being sought in such states as Ohio and Pennsylvania. Much legal debate attends such efforts. No legislation relating to religion and the schools has produced such persistent church-state controversy and litigation as that of bus transportation and, to a lesser degree, textbook legislation.

The legal justification for providing textbooks and transportation centers on the so-called "child benefit theory," which holds that states may extend certain welfare aids to students attending nonpublic schools. Under this concept, textbooks and transportation are thought of as promoting general welfare rather than aiding education.

Many legal scholars have questioned the soundness of the child benefit theory. George La Noue, in recent years, has sought to give a more precise definition to the theory. He maintains that the child benefit theory, when properly qualified, is constitutional.[11]

Others question the child benefit theory, even with qualifications. These persons argue for new arrangements, such as taking the authorization for auxiliary aids completely out of the educational sphere and placing it under municipal authorities. This would mean that bus transportation could be legally provided to children in both public and nonpublic schools, but it would be handled by municipal authorities, not the school systems. The idea of transferring auxiliary services to municipal authorities is less feasible, because it demands substantial changes in current practices, although it may be more easily justified from a legal standpoint. Therefore, it seems likely that governmental support for such services will continue to be prevalent even though it will probably be accompanied by continued controversy.

To summarize, then, neither the *status quo* nor general aid to all public and nonpublic schools will be the pattern of support for the foreseeable future. In this period when public and nonpublic school systems are seen increasingly as interrelated parts of our national system of education, there is evidence of a continuing search for a middle ground. This search, which is shared by those at all levels of government, is apparently designed both to strengthen our educational institutions *and* to maintain our religious freedoms.

SCHOOL DESEGREGATION

Chief Justice Earl Warren, in writing the historic 1954 school desegregation decision, noted that segregation in the schools on the basis of race causes children to develop "a feeling of inferiority as to their status in the community that may affect their hearts and minds in a way unlikely ever to be undone." Despite this monumental decision, the school segregation picture has not been appreciably altered. The last decade has witnessed an intensive effort by many groups to make the public aware of the plight of the Negro and the need to extend his educational opportunities. The following paper deals with this vital problem. It was presented by Thomas F. Pettigrew—an educator in the field of social psychology and a recognized researcher on race—at the White House Conference on Education in July 1965. Pettigrew

[11] *See* "The Child Benefit Theory," *Theory Into Practice,* 4 (February 1965), 18–22. The qualifications that La Noue proposes appear on page 20.

*shows us that "the problem of racially separate schools is grow-
ing more, not less, complex as it evolves from de jure to de facto
segregation." He identifies five important issues in school desegregation and discusses their relevance to the extension of educational opportunities.*

Thomas F. Pettigrew

Contemporary Issues in American Education (*U.S. Office of Education Bulletin 1966, No. 3* [*Washington, D.C., 1965*]), 97–105.

I. INTRODUCTION

American public education finds itself today in the eye of a racial revolution. But it is a revolution with a difference, for it aims to join, not up-
root, the society it confronts. And public education is necessarily the
prime vehicle for this process of joining the mainstream—just as it was
for the assimilation of millions of immigrants at the turn of this century.

Thus, it is not surprising that the chief thrust of the Negro American
revolution throughout the nation has centered upon education. The reasons for this are numerous. Racially balanced schools are commonly
viewed by Negroes as the only form of public education which can adequately fulfill the American dream of equality for their children; they are
convinced that only integrated living begun in the earliest years can ever
eradicate racial bigotry. Furthermore, the United States Supreme Court's
1954 ruling against *de jure* school segregation bolstered these Negro attitudes. And, finally, the political realities of public education contributed
to the selection of this realm for special attention by the revolution.

For 350 years, Negro Americans have learned that separate facilities
for them almost always mean inferior facilities. Whether in the North or
South, hard political realities mitigate against predominantly Negro
schools receiving truly comparable instruction and facilities. Put force-
fully, racially balanced schools are needed to insure the necessary political leverage; many whites, unfortunately, reveal a strong interest in the
education of Negroes only when Negroes are found in the same schools
with sufficiently large numbgers of whites.

The basic question to be discussed at this session and to be answered in the events of the next few years concerns the response of public education to this revolutionary challenge. . . . Will public education
as an institution typically resist the demands for change? Will educators
and school boards so resent the picket lines and protest marches that

they will refuse to rise innovatively to the new challenge? Or will public education, following U.S. Commissioner of Education Francis Keppel's strong recommendation, seize the initiative and utilize this time of change and transition to achieve a new standard of educational excellence?

If these sound like "loaded" questions, then they befit the explosive nature of this panel's topic. All of us who care deeply about public education, of course, hope that the institution will respond positively to the times and come out of this difficult period stronger than ever before. Yet we also know of many communities, North and South, where the current response of education to the Negro American revolution is, to put it mildly, quite negative. The reasons for such reactions and the problems inherent in the central issue of school desegregation and racial balance are varied and complex. To open the panel's discussion on these concerns, this background paper briefly sketches out the problem and then raises five focal issues which often arise when school districts grapple with racial change.

II. THE PROBLEM

Without tracing the history of "Negro education," suffice it to say that the very need for the phrase "Negro education" signifies the long-term failure of American education to include the Negro American on fully equal terms. Even today, public education for Negroes, when compared with that for whites, remains in general "less available, less accessible, and especially less adequate." [1] In 1960, Negro college attendance was proportionately only about half that of whites; [2] the percentage of adult Negroes who had completed college was considerably less than half that of whites; and the percentage who had completed high school was precisely half that of whites.[3]

Worse, in some sectors of Negro America these nonwhite to white differences are actually widening. This is particularly the case with farm Negroes in the rural South—a segment that still comprises, despite heavy out-migration, over one-fifth of all Negroes in the United States. Thus, between 1950 and 1960, rural farm nonwhite to white differences in the completion of twelve or more years of formal education by the critical 25-

[1] Eunice Newton and E. H. West, "The progress of the Negro in elementary and secondary education," *Journal of Negro Education, 1963 Yearbook,* **32** (4), 465–484.

[2] H. H. Doddy, "The progress of the Negro in higher education, 1950–1960," *Journal of Negro Education, 1963 Yearbook,* **32** (4), 485–492.

[3] Metropolitan Life Insurance Company, "Nationwide rise in educational level," *Statistical Bulletin,* **44** (July 1963), 1–3.

to-29-year-old group widened in every one of the thirteen reporting southern states.[4]

Simply enumerating racial differences in years of schooling, of course, only begins to suggest the enormity of the educational hiatus now existing between Negro and white Americans. Sadly, the blunt truth is that "Negro education" is generally grossly inferior to "white education" in both the North and South; it typically involves less expenditure per child, less trained and experienced teachers, and less adequate facilities; and it often prepares Negro youth through both its explicit and implicit curricula to assume only low-skilled employment befitting "the Negro's place" as decreed by white supremacists. We can all think, of course, of notable exceptions to these harsh generalizations. But they spring to our minds because they are precisely that—notable exceptions. The most marked exceptions are found in truly integrated schools, where the concept of "Negro education" finally loses its meaning.

This situation would be alarming in any period of American history; but, it can only be described as desperate at this particular point in our national history. Apart from Negro American protests, automation and its attendant effects on the composition of the American labor force leave us no time for careful and deliberate solutions. Though there is considerable controversy as to whether automation does in fact decrease the size of the total labor force, there is complete agreement that it demands major occupational upgrading. The employment shifts are familiar: unskilled and even semi-skilled jobs are swiftly disappearing, while professional and technical jobs are rapidly expanding. Their serious educational deficiencies, together with employment discrimination, render Negro Americans especially vulnerable to these trends of automation. Already adult Negro rates of unemployment are roughly twice those of adult whites, and Negro youth rates of unemployment are almost twice those of white youth.

Nevertheless, Negro employment has been upgraded in recent years,

[4] J. D. Cowhig and C. L. Beale, "Relative socioeconomic status of southern whites and nonwhites, 1950 and 1960," *The Southwestern Social Science Quarterly*, 44 (September 1964), 113–124; and J. D. Cowhig and C. L. Beale, "Socioeconomic differences between white and nonwhite farm populations of the South," *Social Forces*, 42 (March 1964), 354–362. Note that the widening difference between nonwhite and white and educational attainment in the farm South is strictly relative; the actual attainments for both groups rose throughout the South between 1950 and 1960. For example, in North Carolina in 1950, only 18.6 per cent of the farm whites of 25-to-29-years-of-age had twelve or more years of school compared to a mere 6.5 per cent of the farm Negroes; but by 1960, the percentages were 44.1 and 18.1 respectively. Yet the racial difference had more than doubled from 1950 (12.1 per cent) to 1960 (26 per cent).

though the pace of this progress has hardly been breath-taking. Thus, at the rate of nonwhite gains from 1950 to 1960, nonwhites would not attain equal proportional representation in the nation among clerical workers until 1992, among skilled workers until 2005, among professionals until 2017, among sales workers until 2114, and among business managers and proprietors until 2730—eight centuries from now! [5]

Obviously, massive Negro educational advances are required for the equally massive Negro employment upgrading that must be accomplished in the next two decades. Indeed, the Negro American finds himself on a fast-paced treadmill. Significant educational gains will be necessary just for the Negro to keep up occupationally—much less progress—in this automated age. And there are indications that education may prove to be a major bottleneck to the Negro's needed gains in employment. Hence, major corporations, motivated by the equal employment imperatives of Title VII of the 1964 Civil Rights Act, are already seeking many more technically skilled Negro college graduates than are currently being produced by our educational system.

To be sure, public education can hardly be held solely responsible for the restricted numbers and quality of trained Negro Americans. Limited educational opportunities are only a part—though a critical part—of the complexly interwoven "vicious circle" that narrows the Negro's life chances at every turn—low income, high unemployment, poor health care, inadequate housing, ghetto living, broken family life, etc.

This point is relevant to two related claims that obscure the real issues undergirding educational considerations of race. Ignoring the Negro's typically lean environment, racists have made a recent resurgence with their claims of innate Negro inferiority. Thirty years of solid evidence, however, make it possible to state that these claims certainly have no scientific validity.[6] A related claim also attempts to relieve the public

---

[5] N. D. Glenn, "Some changes in the relative status of American nonwhites, 1940–1960," *Phylon,* **24** (Summer 1964), 109–122. These projected dates for the nation do not just reflect southern conditions. At the 1950 to 1960 rates of relative gains in metropolitan Boston, for instance, employed nonwhites would not achieve proportional representation among clerical and skilled workers until the late 1980's, among professionals until the early 1990's, and among business managers and sales workers until the 22nd and 23rd centuries respectively! T. F. Pettigrew, "Metropolitan Boston's race problem in perspective." In *Social Structure and Human Problems in the Boston Metropolitan Area* (Cambridge, Mass.: Joint Center for Urban Studies, 1965), pp. 33–51.

[6] T. F. Pettigrew, *A Profile of the Negro American* (Princeton, N.J.: D. Van Nostrand, 1964). It should be noted, too, that racist notions of the innate inferiority of Negro Americans are accepted today by far fewer white Americans than twenty years ago. Thus, 80 per cent of white Northerners and 59 per cent

schools of all responsibility for lowered Negro performance. It maintains that formal instruction is simply powerless to overcome the enormous deficits which many Negro children bring to the school situation— lowered motivation, poor speech patterns, broken family life, etc. This claim, too, is called into serious question as soon as one inspects the astonishing improvements in Negro performance made by truly imaginative school systems.

To say this is not to deny or minimize the real deficits from which many Negro children of impoverished backgrounds do in fact suffer. The job *is* difficult for any school system, and most of the problems are certainly not the making of the schools. But American public education has often been called on to tackle difficult problems that were not of its making. And it appears that, when approached with good faith, rich imagination, and full willingness to rise innovatively to the challenge, the nation's schools can meet this vital educational problem successfully.

The first order of business is the elimination of the *de jure* segregation of southern and border schools. The first eleven years after the 1954 Supreme Court ruling against *de jure* segregation of public schools have witnessed slow, but fundamental, alterations. By the fall of 1964, 43 per cent of biracial southern school districts had begun at least token desegregation programs that placed one out of every nine Negro southern school children in schools with white Southerners.[7]

A disproportionate share of this progress, however, has occurred in the border South. While 93 per cent of biracial school districts in the border South had desegregated, the figure for the ex-Confederate South was only 27 per cent; and while three out of every five border state Negro children attended biracial schools, only one in 47 did so in the ex-Confederate South. Yet there are unmistakable signs that this pace is quickening. The average annual number of newly-desegregated school districts in the South has recently increased three-fold, with the threatened cut-off of federal educational funds under Title VI of the 1964 Civil Rights Act proving to be an effective stimulant. Thus, if the first decade after the 1954 Supreme Court desegregation ruling can be described as a slow-paced era of judicial orders, then the second decade after the ruling promises to be a somewhat faster-paced Civil Rights Act era.[8]

of white Southerners in 1963 reported to survey interviewers that they believe the Negro to be as intelligent as the white, compared with only 50 per cent of white Northerners and 21 per cent of white Southerners in 1942. H. H. Hyman and P. B. Sheatsley, "Attitudes toward desegregation," *Scientific American*, 211 (July 1964), 16–23.

[7] *Southern School News*, 11 (December 1964), 1.

[8] T. F. Pettigrew, "Continuing barriers to desegregated education in the South," *Sociology of Education*, 38 (1965), 99–111.

Ironically, however, as *de jure* segregation of schools slowly recedes, *de facto* segregation is rapidly increasing. In literally every standard metropolitan area in the United States racial segregation of housing increased from 1940 to 1960.[9] Consequently, the ever-growing Negro ghettoes combine with the neighborhood school principle to establish an increasingly entrenched pattern of racially separate education throughout the urban North and South. The *de facto* segregation problem is particularly serious at the locally based elementary level. Even in Boston, where the nonwhite population in 1960 constituted only nine per cent, there are seventeen elementary and two junior high schools with 90 per cent or more Negro pupils.[10]

If anything, the shift from *de jure* to *de facto* school segregation complicates the issue further—though at least the shift frees the school system from virtually a legal mandate to discriminate. The judicial and legislative status of *de facto* segregated education is only now taking shape. Moreover, many southern cities are presently openly striving to emulate the northern *de facto* segregation pattern.[11] Indeed, the normal processes of urban development—continuing in-migration of Negroes to the central city and out-migration of whites to the suburbs—lead to much the same situation without conscious planning for such racially separate patterns. In short, the *de facto* school segregation controversy now raging in the North and West will soon erupt in the nominally "desegregated" cities of the South. . . .

In summary, the problem involves the need for a swift and massive expansion of educational opportunities for Negro Americans. The fact is, unless such an expansion occurs soon throughout the nation, educational deficiences will seriously impair the Negro American's ability to keep up with, much less gain on, the employment upgrading required by automation. Not all of this problem can be attributed to public education; much of it is a result of poverty, poor health, broken homes, and all the other special marks of oppression borne by Negro Americans. But much of the problem *is* attributable to separate and inferior schools in the North as well as the South. And the problem of racially separate schools is growing more, not less, complex as it evolves from *de jure* to *de facto*

[9] K. E. Taeuber, "Negro residential segregation, 1940 to 1960: Changing trends in the large cities of the United States." Unpublished paper read at the Annual Meetings of the American Sociological Association, 1962.

[10] Massachusetts State Advisory Committee to the U.S. Commission on Civil Rights, *Report on Racial Imbalance in the Boston Public Schools* (January 1965), p. 49.

[11] T. F. Pettigrew, "*De facto* segregation, southern style," *Integrated Education*, 1(5), (1963), 15–18; and Pettigrew, "Continuing barriers to desegregated education in the South."

segregation. Within this problem context, five focal issues worthy of panel attention can be identified.

III. FIVE FOCAL ISSUES

(1) *Political pressures.* The desegregating school system, and especially the school board, typically becomes the target of at least three distinct sets of political pressures: integrationist demands of committed Negro and white liberals; the fears of the less-committed, generally upper-status whites (who often mislabel themselves as "moderates" [12]); and the resistant demands of committed segregationists (who, depending upon regional euphemisms, may call themselves anything from the Citizens' Council to Parents and Taxpayers). Thus, the basic question here becomes: *How does a school system utilize these conflicting pressures to achieve racial desegregation and educational excellence?*

The precise answer to this query will vary, naturally, according to the particular community situation. But it should be possible to generate certain broadly applicable principles in this session's discussion. Toward that end, a number of relevant considerations can be proffered.

First, integrationist pressures are not likely to recede. In fact, it is highly probable that the Negro American revolution will expand further—in terms of size, intensity, and the scope of its demands.[13] This process has already posed a dilemma for school officials. On the one hand, refusal to deal with Negro demands for integrated education usually leads to community crisis. On the other hand, changes made in direct response to sharp Negro protest often act to encourage further Negro pressure and to intensify white fears and resistance. The not-so-easy-to-accomplish ideal is to stay ahead of the issue, thereby averting crisis and the necessity to meet eyeball-to-eyeball demands.

Second, white opinions on school desegregation have undergone extremely significant alterations throughout the country in recent years —far greater alterations than commonly recognized. Table 1 provides relevant data. Note the sharp shifts in both the North and South from 1942 to 1963, and the remarkable reversal in opinion toward token desegregation in the South from 1963 to 1965.

Finally, we should not overlook the vital "off-the-hook" functions that federal desegregation pressures often provide for local school systems. Federal court orders and threatened withdrawal of federal monies furnish many embattled school boards, North and South, with the publicly announced rationale they needed to desegregate. Indeed, one large

[12] T. F. Pettigrew, "The myth of the moderates," *Christian Century,* **78** (May 24, 1961), 649, 651.

[13] Pettigrew, *A Profile of the Negro American.*

Table 1   CHANGING WHITE ATTITUDES
TOWARD SCHOOL DESEGREGATION

*"Do you think white students and Negro students should go to
the same schools or to separate schools?"* [a]

	Percentage Answering "Same Schools"		
	1942	*1956*	*1963*
White Northerners	40	61	73
White Southerners	2	14	34
Total Whites	30	49	63

*"Would you, yourself, have any objection to sending your children
to a school where a few of the children are colored?"* [b]

	Percentage Answering "No, would not object"	
	1963	*1965*
White Northern Parents	87	91
White Southern Parents	38	62

". . . where half of the children are colored?"

White Northern Parents	56	65
White Southern Parents	17	27

". . . where more than half of the children are colored?"

White Northern Parents	31	37
White Southern Parents	6	16

[a] Studies conducted by National Opinion Research Center and report in H. H. Hyman and P. B. Sheatsley, "Attitudes toward Desegregation," *Scientific American,* **211** (July 1964), 16–23.

[b] Studies conducted by the American Institute of Public Opinion and reported in G. Gallup's press release of May 22, 1965.

northern city has allowed a *de facto* segregation school suit to remain in the federal courts long after it could have been dismissed, for the specific purpose of utilizing the suit as an "off-the-hook" excuse to carry forward its program of desegregation and educational upgrading. . . .

(2) *The focus of responsibility.* Mention of the effects of forces external to the local community introduces the next major question: *Where precisely is the focus of responsibility for expanding educational opportunities for Negro Americans?* This, too, is a difficult query, for it immediately involves us in such thorny issues as the limits of local school control, urban annexation, and the needed suburban contribution to inner city education.

The greatest strength of American public education—local school district autonomy and control—is also often its greatest weakness. Racial desegregation and massive compensatory education programs are examples of efforts that often need external support—political as well as economic. Recent federal legislation has certainly recognized this fact. Yet large outside aid complicates further an already complex and delicate relationship between federal, state, metropolitan area, and local district responsibility.

The focus of responsibility for racial issues, as with other educational issues, necessarily, then, becomes more involved. One point, however, is becoming increasingly clear: that is, urban desegregation and educational upgrading cannot long remain the sole responsibility of inner city school systems, even when bolstered by federal and state subsidies. In some cases, the central city is beginning to run out of white children in its public schools—as seen now in Washington, D.C. Central city enlargement through annexation, even when politically possible (as in Nashville, Tennessee and Richmond, Virginia), presents Negro leadership with a perplexing dilemma; for the same annexation process that brings white children into the school system dilutes Negro political power. Educators need not be surprised, then, if Negro leadership in their communities proves ambivalent at best in its attitudes toward annexation.

Suburban cooperation with central city desegregation and upgrading programs provides a more promising possibility than annexation. The so-called "white noose around the Negro's neck" must become a more positive force in racial change. But there are serious political and economic problems raised by such schemes, too; the urgent need for suburban involvement in inner city desegregation plans, however, commends this issue for special attention by the panel.

(3) *Problems of how to do it.* Much of the debate surrounding school desegregation has revolved around the practical nuts-and-bolts question: *How can racially balanced education actually be implemented?*

Again the precise answer must vary greatly with the particular community. But there is now a wide variety of devices from which a combination plan can be custom-styled for each school system. These devices include: (1) the district-wide redrawing of school lines to maximize racial balance (positive gerrymandering); (2) the pairing of predominantly white and Negro schools along the borders of the Negro ghetto (the Princeton Plan); (3) the alteration of "feeder" arrangements from elementary grades to junior highs and from junior highs to senior highs in order to maximize racial balance (the balanced feeder plan); (4) a priority for and careful placement of new and typically larger schools near but not within the ghetto (the rebuilding plan); (5) the conversion of more schools into district-wide specialized institutions (the differentiation of teaching functions); (6) the establishment of broad educational centers covering many levels and programs (campus parks); and (7) the subsidized transportation of students (bussing). Considerable controversy has resulted from the use of this final device; indeed, much of the public seems unaware of the significant amount of desegregation that can be achieved by the first six devices without resorting to subsidized transportation. Only in the largest metropolitan cities will extensive subsidized transportation be necessary to achieve significant desegregation.

Any combination plan adopted by a community could benefit from several additional features. First, as mentioned previously, any urban plan should ideally involve the cooperation of surburban school districts. Second, predominately white schools which, under the plan, would be receiving a sizable number of new Negro students should be bolstered with specialty courses of genuine appeal to white children and parents as well as Negro. . . .

These should include not just the latest in remedial techniques, but also classes in "prestige" subjects of obvious value that are not normally taught in public schools.

Third, the plan should include the racial balancing of teacher staffs as well as student bodies, for Negro children need models of authority and achievement with whom they can readily identify. Generally, the desegregation of teachers lags far behind the desegregation of pupils—especially in southern systems still shaking off the traditions of *de jure* segregation. For example, after a decade of pupil desegregation in the 133 elementary schools of St. Louis, only 19 had staffs during the 1964–65 year with at least 10 per cent of the minority race, 42 had less than 10 per cent of the minority race, and 72 had entirely Negro or white staffs.

A number of problems are involved here: the need for the upgrading of standards for many Negro teachers; the tendency to "cream-off" the conspicuously talented Negro teachers for predominantly white schools; and the operation of teacher seniority privileges. At least, a beginning can be made through the random assignment of all new teachers entering the system, though even this technique conflicts with seniority placements.

Fourth, it is a useful, if unfortunate, rule of thumb that those children who most need racially balanced education are the hardest to desegregate in any plan. For a variety of reasons, lower-status Negroes (who generally live deepest within the ghetto) and elementary school children (whose schools are traditionally most tied to the neighborhood) have the greatest need for racially balanced training.[14] This means that

[14] T. F. Pettigrew and Patricia Pajonis, "Social psychological considerations of racially-balanced schools," an appendix to *Because It Is Right—Educa-*

balance plans which look adequate in terms of gross numbers of children affected at the higher grade levels may be including only higher-status Negroes and not significantly reaching the critical early years. Careful checks by social class and grade level are thus in order. . . .

Mention of the difficulty of desegregating elementary schools raises one of the key issues to be discussed by the panel—*the concept of the neighborhood school.* Growing out of the "multiple communities" ideal of city planning at the turn of the century, the neighborhood school concept has assumed for many the aura of a sacrosanct shibboleth, a concept not to be questioned. Instead, we need considerable research, thinking, and open discussion on the subject. What are the real advantages of the neighborhood school? What are its disadvantages? How can it best be modified and blended with racial desegregation plans?

Finally, any implementation plan must be based on *a reasonable definition of just what constitutes meaningful "racial desegregation" and "racial balance."* Here there are at least two major alternatives to be compared in the session's discussion. One possibility is to peg the definition to the nonwhite percentage of the area's over-all school population; thus, if 12 per cent of a system's students are nonwhite, then ideally each school in the system would approach a nonwhite student composition of 12 per cent. There are at least two criticisms of this definition: it is often impractical in all but reasonably small areas; and it treats the individual school as a simple reflection of the community, rather than as an integumented institution with its own dynamics and requirements.

A second definition of a racially balanced school attempts to meet these criticisms with a relatively fixed, rather than variable, gauge. On the basis of several social psychological considerations (including the Gallup survey data shown in Table 1), the ideally balanced school is one whose student body includes from roughly 20 to 45 per cent nonwhites.[15] The disadvantage here is that uniracial schools must result in systems with fewer than 20 per cent or more than 45 per cent nonwhite children.

(4) *Racial balance and compensatory efforts.* Another focal issue boils down to the query: *How can a school system judiciously blend racial balance and massive compensatory training?*

The question arises because it is apparent that one without the other will not be enough. Merely balancing the schools without attention to the lower standards and achievement typically found in predominantly Negro schools is obviously fraught with serious difficulties.

Racial balance is one among many requirements of a first-rate public education in a multiracial society and world, but it alone does not guarantee educational excellence. Likewise, compensatory measures and the upgrading of standards in predominantly Negro schools are not enough either without also correcting the basic conditions which help to create the need for these compensatory measures in the first place. High on the list of factors contributing to the present situation, of course, are racial separation and discrimination. Thus, it makes no sense to correct past educational damage while allowing further damage to occur.

Granted then, the need for both, the session needs to discuss ideas for intermeshing the two processes.

(5) *Problems of the desegregated school and classroom.* A desegregated school does not guarantee an integrated environment, nor does it guarantee a good learning environment. Therefore, a final focal question becomes: *How can educators achieve interracial school and classroom environments which maximize intergroup acceptance and learning for all children?*

Social psychological research has specified the conditions toward which educators must strive. Desegregated situations achieve maximal intergroup acceptance when the groups are treated as complete equals, have common goals, do not directly compete against one another, and interact with the full support of authorities.[16] Moreover, desegregated situations provide an effective learning environment when they heighten the probability of success, reduce to a minimum both "social" and "failure threat," and exploit the social facilitation effect achieved by interracial acceptance.[17] Discussion by the panel and further research is needed, however, on the methods which educators might employ to achieve these desirable conditions.

In summary, five focal issues and an array of more detailed questions can be identified as relevant to the desegregation of America's public schools: political pressures, the focus of responsibility, problems of how to do it (including questions concerning the neighborhood school concept and a workable definition of "school desegregation" and "racial balance"), racial balance and compensatory efforts, and, finally, problems of the desegregated school and classroom.

If this session of the White House Conference on Education is to clarify effectively the critical problem of school desegregation, these five plus related issues must be dealt with forthrightly by all of us.

[16] G. W. Allport, *The Nature of Prejudice* (Reading, Mass.: Addison-Wesley Publishing Company, 1954), Chapter 16.

[17] I. Katz, "Review of evidence relating to effects of desegregation on the intellectual performance of Negroes," *American Psychologist,* **19** (June 1964), 381–399.

THE SUPPORT OF AMERICAN SCHOOLS:
Ten Questions on School Finance

Prospective and inservice teachers as well as lay citizens often raise questions about the methods and the adequacy of our school support system. The adequacy of school finance determines the degree to which a school district can attract highly qualified teachers, house its program adequately, and equip its schools with the needed aids for teaching and learning. In the following article an attempt is made to answer ten of the vital questions in the area of school support. Answers to these questions can help the reader to understand not only the methods by which the schools are financed by also who is paying for their support and what values are derived from spending public funds for this purpose.

NEA Committee on School Finance

"Ten Questions on School Finance," NEA Research Bulletin (*October 1965*), 86–89. *Reprinted by permission of NEA Research Division, NEA. Copyright* © *1965 by the National Education Association. All rights reserved.*

1. *Why should public funds support education even though many parents can afford to pay for the education of their own children?*
   Our society cannot function with an illiterate citizenry. Free public education has followed the extension of suffrage and the increasing needs of the economy and national security for highly skilled workers.
   Education is necessary for the exercise of citizenship, for an individual to be an efficient producer and consumer in a free enterprise economic system, for individual self-realization, for the civilization of man, for healthful living, for cultural and scientific progress, for national defense, for self-discipline in the use of freedom. Our society depends on these qualities.
   All society benefits when the individuals which comprise it are able to develop their talents and to use them constructively. This is the "social benefit" theory underlying public support of education.
   The traditional legal justification of free schooling is not a citizen's right to an education, although few would deny this right today. It is the obligation imposed upon young citizens for the good of society. Young

citizens are compelled to attend the public schools or to otherwise satisfy the states' minimum educational requirements with private schooling. Public funds have supported education beyond compulsory school-age limits because of the benefit all society gets from high levels of education.

While advantages accrue to the individual, the case for free public schools rests on the protection that the expenditure buys against an ignorant citizenry and the benefits the whole state gets from an educated citizenry.

2. *Who should determine how much money is spent on public education?*

The decisions on how much money will be spent on public education are reflected in the local school budget, but the total decision-making process involves all levels of government; all levels of the education profession speaking out on school needs; many individuals expressing opinions in financial elections and in the election of officials, in public hearings, and in contacts with public officials.

The federal government is an increasingly important source of school funds. Many aid programs stimulate matching state and local funds for specified programs. For example, the National Defense Education Act supplies funds to programs of special interest to national defense; and the availability of funds influences the decisions of state and local school governing bodies to direct more of their own funds to NDEA programs.

By determining the state aid for local school districts, the state legislature is important in setting the level of spending—the state can depress local support by permitting state funds to replace local funds, or it can stimulate local effort by providing financial incentives for local school districts to increase local efforts to support schools. In addition, many states restrict local taxing and borrowing powers. Unrealistic fiscal limits thwart local effort to support schools.

The local school authority is usually given the responsibility for the school budget. Most school systems start budgeting by determing how much was received and spent in the last fiscal period and how much will be available for next year. This retards the development of a quality school budget. Ideally a school board should decide what levels of education are needed irrespective of past offerings, and then determine the additional funds needed.

The professional staff has a primary responsibility for leadership in developing the school financial planning at all three governmental levels: federal, state, and local. And associations at all three levels—the National Education Association, the state education associations, and the local education associations—are actively working with citizens groups and public officials to present the financial needs of public education and to influence decisions on school support.

3. *How should the three levels of government share the cost of public education?*

All levels of government should share in financing the public schools. Today the federal government is almost as close to the people as the county courthouse in years gone by.

There are unique advantages to each tax system as a revenue agent for school support. The federal tax system, with heavy reliance on the progressive income tax, is the most responsive to economic growth, and is the least affected by fears of interstate and local competition for industry. State sales and excise taxes are a major source of state revenue for schools. In addition, state income taxes, severance taxes, and licenses and fees are also available for school support. Local revenues for schools, mainly property taxes, provide the means for local school authorities to support the type and quality of education the community wants and can afford. Local support, interest, and control of education are important in achieving quality.

Ways must be determined whereby the revenue of the federal and state governments can be brought into the local schools without destroying the advantages of local control. Much progress has been made in the techniques of combining state and local funds, but much needs to be done on the federal-state-local fiscal partnership.

4. *Is education an investment which pays dividends to society and to the individual?*

Money spent on education results in both consumption of goods and services and in the development of increased productive capacity of tomorrow's adults. Money spent on education has aspects of both consumption and production goods. It creates human wants and produces higher earning power. Hence it is an investment both in future consumption and in future earnings.

Investments in education pay tremendous returns in economic, social, and scientific progress both to individuals and to society.

Education is such a good investment that we should be putting a lot more money into it at all levels, nursery school through higher education and adult education both in general education and in training and retraining the experienced labor force.

5. *What is a state foundation program?*

The system by which the state takes into account local tax revenues for schools and apportions its grants-in-aid to the various districts is usually called the foundation program. State aid is apportioned to local school districts as general purpose and special purpose grants. General purpose grants are distributed without specification as to their use in financing the local program. Special purpose grants are designated only for the program or programs specified, such as driver education or libraries.

The foundation program describes the minimum program guaranteed in every district from local and state funds. The law usually sets a dollar amount per classroom, per pupil, or per teaching unit.

The minimum program can actually set the maximum provided throughout the state if state revenues are allowed to replace local effort. However, the foundation program can be designed to stimulate local effort. A few states have a program whereby additional state funds are granted to match additional local effort above the minimum program.

6. *Should we have equalization of tax resources and educational opportunity?*

All children should have equal educational opportunities regardless of where they might live in the state or the United States or how much taxable wealth exists in the districts which provide their schooling. Our human resources can be fully developed only when each child has the educational services he needs. Therefore, broad-based support should supplement local funds. State funds should be apportioned to local school districts to equalize the differences among the school districts in taxable wealth. Federal funds should equalize differences in the states' ability. Equalization has two dimensions: providing equal opportunities to the pupils and making more nearly equal the financial resources available to support the local school program.

7. *Why are school costs rising?*

Increasing *enrollments* are one factor in the increase in the total costs for schools. In addition, enrollments are increasing fastest at the secondary level where costs are highest. *Inflation* is another factor. The most important factor in cost increase in many school systems is *expansion of the school program* upward, downward, and outward to comprise a comprehensive system of education from nursery school through the fourteenth year for all youth, with emphasis on providing for individual differences.

8. *Does a higher level of school expenditure insure better quality of education?*

It is foolish to argue that a high expenditure insures quality education. Many conditions are associated with quality: good school organization, good administration, well-qualified teachers, good supporting staff, and high degree of interest in schools.

One research undertaking, Project TALENT, tested about one-half million high-school students in a sample of 19,000 high schools across the country in spring 1960. The school background factors that correlated best with test scores were starting salaries of teachers and average per-pupil expenditure. Almost all studies of cost-quality have concluded that a high educational expenditure is not the only ingredient of quality but it is a necessary one.

9. *Are school taxes too high?*

Many persons never relate their tax bill to the value of services received from government. To them, any tax is too high.

Over-reliance on one tax, the local property tax or a single state tax, for school support is conducive to attitudes that school taxes are too high. This is why the efforts of professional associations are directed to broadening the tax base for schools: at the local level to secure equalized property tax assessments, at the state level to secure both sales and income taxes for state school appropriations, and at the federal level to secure an increased share of broad-based federal revenues.

We have underinvested in education. High dropout rates and the young adults in the population who lack basic skills needed for employment are evidence of this underinvestment. We are at a high level of prosperity. We spent more in 1964 for all government services than in 1960, but we still spent more in the private sector of the economy than in the government sector. Despite a lower dollar gain, the government sector is advancing at a higher rate. Moreover, higher expenditures are needed for education to increase prosperity in the private sector.

10. *Why does the professional association work for increased taxes for schools?*

Professional associations are dedicated to advancing the welfare of pupils, teachers, and public education. This directs the efforts of the associations toward improvement of school organization, administration, curriculum and methods of teaching, preparation, recruitment, and retention of teachers and other school personnel, and toward an increase in the funds to pay for good schools.

No group has yet emerged to relieve the teaching profession of being the chief proponent of improvements in the school program and in the resources of schools to finance the salaries, materials, equipment, and buildings of a good school program. This role is uniquely lodged in the teaching profession.

RESEARCH ON TEACHER EVALUATION

How do you evaluate good teaching? This question has baffled administrators, teachers, students, and lay people as they strive to assess the quality of teachers. In view of the increasing em-

phasis on excellence in our schools, the problem of defining teacher effectiveness takes on an added measure of significance. In the following article Professor N. A. Fattu gives a concise and very helpful review of current research on teacher effectiveness. He stresses what research tells us about the meaning of effectiveness and the various approaches that have been used in its assessment. Among these approaches, he describes the characteristic studies with their emphasis upon such traits as "intelligence, knowledge of subject matter, scholarship, educational background, age and experience, professional knowledge, cultural background, socio-economic background, teaching attitude and interest, and voice and speech." He also reviews research on the measurement of teacher behavior and student growth because of their use as criteria of teaching quality. He sees the need for more research to determine experimentally the relationship between teacher effectiveness and the variables that may influence it. It may be challenging for the student to select his best teachers and try to apply the findings from the research reviewed here to analyze the factors which are closely associated with their superior performance.

N. A. Fattu

The National Elementary Principal (*November 1963*), 19–26. Reprinted by permission of the author and the publisher. Copyright © 1963, Department of Elementary School Principals, National Education Association. All rights reserved.

Studies on teacher effectiveness have been summarized and reviewed periodically since 1926. While empirical study of teacher effectiveness may be said to have begun about 1891, it was not until the period 1913–1917 that some momentum was attained. This momentum continued for almost twenty years. The advent of Gestalt psychology and the organismic point of view was reflected by a significant decrease in the number of studies based upon empirical data. Tomlinson has told the story of this movement in detail.[1]

Two major reviews of the literature on teacher effectiveness are

[1] L. R. Tomlinson, "Pioneer Studies in the Evaluation of Teaching," *Educational Research Bulletin,* 34 (March 1955), 63–71; L. R. Tomlinson, "Recent Studies in the Evaluation of Teaching," *Educational Research Bulletin,* 34 (October 1955), 172–186.

those by Domas and Tiedeman [2] and by Morsh and Wilder.[3] These summaries by no means list all of the publications on teacher effectiveness. They exclude the vast majority of the publications which were not empirical in some way. These two summaries cover the literature on quantitative studies up to 1952.

Other reviews and summaries that should be read by anyone seriously interested in further exploration of the field are the Mitzel and Gross review of the pupil growth criterion; [4] the series of reviews by Barr over a period of more than thirty years, of which only those in the period 1940–1958 are indicated here; [5] the annotated bibliography by Castetter and others; [6] the Leiderman and others summary of teacher behavior studies; [7] the Levin and others comments on the questions asked about, and the reasons for, unproductive studies; [8] the McCall,[9] Mitzel,[10] Remmers and others [11] studies; the American Educational Re-

[2] S. J. Domas and D. V. Tiedeman, "Teacher Competence: An Annotated Bibliography," *Journal of Experimental Education*, 19 (December 1950), 101–218.

[3] J. E. Morsh and E. W. Wilder, *Identifying the Effective Instructor: A Review of Quantitative Studies, 1900–1952*, Research Bulletin No. AFPTRC-TR-54-44 (San Antonio, Tex.: USAF Personnel and Training Center, 1954), 151 pp.

[4] H. E. Mitzel and C. F. Gross, *A Critical Review of the Development of Pupil Growth Criteria in Studies of Teacher Effectiveness*, Research Series No. 31 (New York: Office of Research and Evaluation, Division of Teacher Education, Board of Higher Education of the City of New York, 1956), 28 pp.

[5] A. S. Barr and R. E. Jones, "The Measurement and Prediction of Teaching Efficiency," *Review of Educational Research*, 28 (June 1958), 256–264.

[6] D. D. Castetter, L. S. Standlee, and N. A. Fattu, *Teacher Effectiveness: An Annotated Bibliography*. Bulletin of the Institute of Educational Research, Vol. 1, No. 1 (Bloomington, Ind.: Indiana University Press, 1954).

[7] G. F. Leiderman, T. L. Hilton, and H. Levin, "Studies of Teachers' Behavior: A Summary Report," *The Journal of Teacher Education*, 8 (December 1957), 433–437.

[8] H. Levin, T. L. Hilton, and G. F. Leiderman, "Studies of Teacher Behavior," *Journal of Experimental Education*, 26 (September 1957), 81–91.

[9] W. A. McCall, *Measurement of Teacher Merit*, Publication No. 284 (Raleigh, N.C.: State Superintendent of Public Instruction, 1952), 40 pp.

[10] H. E. Mitzel, "Teacher Effectiveness," *Encyclopedia of Educational Research*, Chester W. Harris (ed.) (3d ed.; New York: Crowell-Collier and Macmillan, 1960), pp. 1481–1485.

[11] H. H. Remmers, *et al.*, "Report of the Committee on the Criteria of Teacher Effectiveness," *Review of Educational Research*, 22 (June 1952), 238–263; H. H. Remmers, *et al.*, "Second Report of the Committee on Criteria of Teacher Effectiveness," *Journal of Educational Research*, 46 (May 1953), 641–658.

search Association's *Review of Educational Research* triennial summaries; the Ryans,[12] Tiedeman and Cogan,[13] and Watters[14] studies.

No one seriously interested in teacher evaluation can afford to neglect to read—diligently and frequently—the *Handbook of Research on Teaching*.[15] This book began in 1950 with the appointment of a Committee on the Criteria of Teacher Effectiveness by the American Educational Research Association. In 1956, the Committee, then called the Committee on Teacher Effectiveness, proposed the development of the handbook. In 1957, N. L. Gage, chairman of the Committee, was named editor. Most relevant to the present discussion are segments of Parts II, III, and IV in the *Handbook*. In Part II on *Methodologies in Research on Teaching*, the following chapters may be most useful to elementary school principals and supervisors: Chapter 6, "Measuring Classroom Behavior by Systematic Observation" by Donald Medley and Harold Mitzel; Chapter 7, "Rating Methods in Research on Teaching" by H. H. Remmers; Chapter 8, "Testing Cognitive Ability and Achievement" by Benjamin S. Bloom; and Chapter 9, "Measuring Noncognitive Variables in Research on Teaching" by G. C. Stern. In Part III, on *Major Variables and Areas of Research on Teaching*, Chapter 11, "The Teacher's Personality and Characteristics" by J. W. Getzels and P. S. Jackson is recommended. Part IV, *Research on Teaching Various Grade Levels and Subject Matters,* is addressed largely to high school and college people. Elementary school principals and supervisors would find Chapter 15, "Research on Teaching in the Nursery School" by Pauline Sears and Edith Dowley, and Chapter 16, "Research on Reading" by David Russell and Henry Fea, most useful.

Obviously, what research says about teacher effectiveness cannot be summarized in a few words. One who wishes to understand the findings should consult the sources indicated, especially the *Handbook of Research on Teaching*.

[12] D. G. Ryans, *Characteristics of Teachers* (Washington, D.C.: American Council on Education, 1960), 416 pp.; D. G. Ryans, "Prediction of Teacher Effectiveness," *Encyclopedia of Educational Research*, Chester W. Harris (ed.) (3d ed.; New York: Crowell-Collier and Macmillan, 1960), pp. 1486–1491.

[13] D. V. Tiedeman and M. Cogan, "New Horizons in Educational Research," *Phi Delta Kappan*, **39** (March 1958), 286–291.

[14] W. A. Watters, "Annotated Bibliography of Publications Related to Teacher Evaluation," *Journal of Experimental Education*, **22** (June 1954), 351–367.

[15] N. L. Gage (ed.), *Handbook of Research on Teaching*, A project of the American Educational Research Association, NEA (Skokie, Ill.: Rand McNally & Company, 1963), 1218 pp.

WHAT IS EFFECTIVENESS?

A difficult problem in the study of teacher effectiveness has been whether to assume that effectiveness is a statement about an attribute of the teacher in a particular teaching situation or to assume that it is a statement about the results that come out of a teaching situation.

It appears, as indicated by Barr, that most studies of teacher effectiveness are searching for a property of the teacher. As indicated by Remmers, the search has not been successful. But the assumption on which this search is based has not been tested. To do so would require a longitudinal study with repeated measurement of the same teacher on the same criteria under a wide range of teaching conditions. Such a study has not been conducted.

In examining the assumption that effectiveness is an attribute of the teacher, one should recognize that it lies along a continuum of assumptions. At one end is the assumption that effectiveness is determined almost wholly by the teacher, that it is one of his attributes, and that it depends very little on the variables within the situation. At the other end of the continuum is the assumption that effectiveness is almost wholly determined by the particular variables operating in the situation where teaching occurs.

One is free to choose his assumption anywhere along the continuum, but in choosing he implicitly makes a hypothesis about the adaptability of teachers to teaching situations. If he assumes that effectiveness depends on the particular variables operating in a situation in which a teacher teaches, he is saying that teachers simply react without close regard to the appropriateness of that behavior with respect to the variables in the situation. If a teacher happens to react properly for a particular set of conditions, then he is effective.

Or if one proceeds on the assumption that effectiveness is almost wholly attributable to the teacher, he claims that teachers are adaptive in their teaching behavior so that they react with a close regard to its appropriateness. He states that teachers are capable of fine discriminations in their environment and have available the responses appropriate to those discriminations.

Apparently a choice of one assumption or the other is not desirable, because the very act of choosing makes it necessary to exclude one of the assumptions. There is no reason to think that effectiveness depends entirely on variables operating in the situation or that it necessarily depends on the teacher. Perhaps both assumptions are valid, depending on differences among teachers. Some teachers are no doubt capable of producing desirable pupil behaviors in a wide variety of teaching situations.

The behavior they display, of course, depends on the situation, but this is not the point. The point is that their behavior is appropriate to that situation and that desirable pupil behaviors result because it is appropriate. These teachers do not have some sort of magical property called "effectiveness," but they are characterized by adaptability to teaching situations, or they have developed a high level of skill in dealing with the problems which arise in the course of their professional work.

There are other teachers who no doubt are capable of producing desirable pupil behaviors under more limited teaching conditions. These teachers are effective within the range of teaching situations for which their responses are appropriate.

Finally, there are no doubt teachers whose patterns of teaching behavior are so poorly developed that they can succeed in only a very few teaching situations or not at all.

In other words, effectiveness has several meanings, and no harm is done in using the term if one is clear as to which meaning is intended.

TEACHER CHARACTERISTICS

The purpose of teacher characteristics studies is to discover which traits or combinations of traits are closely enough associated with teacher competence to permit prediction of such competency. Among these traits are intelligence, knowledge of subject matter, scholarship, educational background, age and experience, professional knowledge, cultural background, socio-economic background, teaching attitude and interest, and voice and speech characteristics.

Intelligence and success

Whether or not intelligence is an important variable in the success of the instructor apparently depends upon the situation. In general, there appears to be only a slight relationship between intelligence and *rated* success of an instructor. Correlation coefficients for high school teachers tend to be somewhat higher and somewhat less variable than those reported for elementary teachers. For all practical purposes, however, this variable appears to be of little value as a *single* predictor of rated instructor competence.

This does not mean that teachers do not need to be intelligent. Rather, those who teach have been selected on the basis of intelligence, and within the range of scores characteristic of teachers, differences in intelligence have not been shown to be crucial. In more refined research where variables are more carefully controlled, intelligence test scores are more closely related to teacher performance.

Knowledge of subject matter and success

A common misconception is that knowledge of subject matter is a major factor in teaching performance. Except for occasional studies in mathematics, chemistry, and physics, research findings report little relationship. Again, whether or not knowledge of subject matter is related to instructor competence seems to be a function of the particular teaching situation and is generally a complex interaction rather than a simple variable.

Professional knowledge and success

It appears that a teacher's rated effectiveness at first increases rather rapidly with experience and then levels off at five years or beyond. The teacher may show little change in rated performance for the next 15 to 20 years, after which, as in most occupations, there tends to be a slow decline.

Cultural background and success

There is no substantial evidence that cultural background is significantly related to teaching effectiveness. Studies reviewed indicate the relation of Cooperative General Culture Test scores to instructor effectiveness is congruent with results reported for other subject-matter areas.

Socio-economic status and success

The relationship of socio-economic status (as measured by such devices as the Sims Socio-Economic Scales) to criteria of instructor effectiveness is low. The research suggests, however, that those from higher groups usually have greater probabilities of success in life than those less fortunate.

Sex and success

No particular differences have been shown when the relative effectiveness of men and women teachers has been compared. (See pp. 309–311 for Ryans' findings on this point.)

Marital status and success

Despite some prejudice to the contrary, there appears to be no evidence that married teachers are in any way inferior to single teachers.

Teaching aptitude and success

Results obtained from measures designed to predict teaching ability show great disparity. Data thus far available either fail to establish the existence of any specified aptitude for teaching with any degree of certainty or indicate the tests used were inappropriate to its measurement.

Teaching attitude and success

Attitude toward teachers and teaching as indicated by the Yeager Scale, which was devised for its measurement, seems to bear a small but positive relationship to teacher success measured in terms of pupil gains.

Job interest and success

In most of the studies reviewed, interest in teaching was measured by interest test scores which indicated similarity between the interests of teachers and the interests of persons undergoing the test. Correlations resulting from the use of several standard interest tests either cluster around zero or are so inconsistent as to render such tests of doubtful value as predictors of teaching success. The common factors that were found through factor analyses to underlie the reasons given for choosing the teaching profession are perhaps provocative of further research, but are based on too few cases to justify any clear-cut interpretation.

Voice-speech and success

On the basis of studies reviewed, it appears that the quality of the teacher's voice is not considered very important by school administrators, teachers, or students. In one study, however, certain speech factors were found to be correlated significantly with student gains and with effectiveness ratings of supervisors. The intercorrelations of the speech factors, however, were so high that general speech ability based on a single factor is probably as useful as a composite of judgments based on several speech factors.

Special abilities and success

Such instructor factors as empathy, professional maturity, general knowledge, mental ability, and social adjustment have been identified through factor analyses by various investigators. The statistical analyses so far reported, however, suffer from inadequacies of criteria, testing instruments, or number of cases.

Teacher failure

In most of the studies of unsuccessful teachers, it has been found that poor maintenance of discipline and lack of cooperation tend to be the chief causes of failure. Health, educational background, preparation, age, and knowledge of subject matter, on the other hand, appear to be relatively unimportant factors in terms of teacher failure.

The attempts made to identify characteristics of successful and unsuccessful instructors by making lists of traits based on opinion appear largely sterile in terms of usability for evaluation or selective purposes.

RYANS' STUDY OF TEACHER CHARACTERISTICS

Perhaps the most extensive study of teacher characteristics ever carried out is that by Ryans.[16] More than a hundred separate research projects were conducted. About 1,700 schools, involving 450 school systems and 6,000 teachers, took part.

Factor analyses of data revealed three patterns of teacher behavior: Pattern X_0—warm, understanding, friendly vs. aloof, egocentric, restricted teacher behavior. Pattern Y_0—responsible, businesslike, systematic vs. evading, unplanned, slipshod teacher behavior. Pattern Z_0—stimulating, imaginative, surgent vs. dull, routine teacher behavior.

Among elementary school teachers, X_0, Y_0, Z_0 patterns were positively correlated and each seemed to be correlated with pupil behavior in the teachers' classes. X_0, Y_0, Z_0 patterns for married elementary teachers tended to be higher than for single elementary teachers. Patterns did not vary significantly with Minnesota Multiphasic Personality Inventory scores or the Allport-Vernon-Lindzey Study of Values.

Other results were: (1) Educational views of secondary teachers appeared to be more traditional—those of elementary were more permissive; (2) Attitudes of elementary teachers toward pupils, administrators, fellow teachers, and non-administrative personnel were distinctly more favorable than were those of secondary teachers; (3) Male teachers, both at the elementary and secondary school levels, appeared substantially more stable emotionally than female; (4) Observer assessment of pupil behavior in the classroom did not seem to be related to teachers' attitudes; (5) Verbal understanding scores (on vocabulary and verbal analogy problems) of secondary teachers were significantly higher than those of elementary teachers.

Much of the study was devoted to determination of correlates of teacher classroom behavior. A 300 item multiple-choice and checklist self-report inventory of personal preferences, self-judgments, activities, and biographical data—called the Teacher Characteristics Schedule—was developed. Numerous item analyses were done using observer assessments and direct-response scales as criteria. Scoring keys were developed for a large number of teacher groups.

Comparing characteristics of teachers gave the following results:

1. Elementary school married teachers attained more favorable scores on these variables.

[16] D. G. Ryans, *Characteristics of Teachers.*

2. Teachers from large universities achieved higher scores on stimulating classroom behavior and child-centered views.

3. Teachers who had been outstanding students scored higher than other groups on most scales. The only exception dealt with emotional stability.

4. Teachers who claimed they entered teaching because they liked school and because of its social service usually scored higher on most of the characteristics. Teachers who entered the profession because they were advised to do so or because of favorable prospects for advancement generally scored lower.

5. Teachers who reported childhood activities as "reading to children" or "playing school," etc., had higher scores on "friendly, responsible, stimulating" classroom behavior, favorable attitudes toward pupils, and democratic classroom procedures than others.

6. Scores of the older teachers (age 55 and over) were not as favorable as those of younger teachers except on warm, understanding, friendly behavior and tradition-centered behavior. Trends for experience were like those for age.

7. At the elementary school level, men and women teachers differed in only four of the personal-social characteristics studied. Men were less responsible and businesslike in classroom behavior and more favorable toward democratic classroom practices, more inclined toward permissive, child-centered educational viewpoints, and more stable emotionally.

8. Teachers from larger schools and larger communities scored substantially higher than others on friendly, stimulating classroom behavior, favorable attitudes toward administrators, verbal understanding, and emotional stability. As a rule, teachers from smaller communities scored lower than those from large communities, except for teachers from the largest cities (1,000,000 and over) who scored about as low as teachers from very small communities.

Teachers were classified as "high" (at least a standard deviation above the mean) and "low" (at least a standard deviation below the mean) on characteristics. Results are summarized by Ryans as follows:

> There was a general tendency for high teachers to: be extremely generous in appraisals of behavior and motives of other persons; possess strong interest in reading and literary affairs; be interested in music, painting, and the arts in general; participate in social groups; enjoy pupil relationships; prefer nondirective (permissive) classroom procedures; manifest superior verbal intelligence; and be superior with respect to emotional adjustment. On the other hand, low teachers tended generally to: be restrictive and critical in their appraisals of other persons; prefer activities which did not involve close personal

contacts; express less favorable opinions of pupils; manifest less higher verbal intelligence; show less satisfactory emotional adjustment; and represent older age groups. (pp. 397–398).

The Teacher Characteristics Study was an impressive enterprise, but it is obvious that the author's cautions relative to conclusions are justified.

PERSONALITY PATTERNS

For many years, research on personality characteristics was conducted through opinion studies. On the whole, such studies failed to obtain anything more than agreement on a few general trait designations, such as "interested" and "sympathetic." These provided little insight or help; Guba and Getzels in 1955 commented, "Despite a large number of investigations, relatively little more is known now than in 1900." [17]

Recently, emphasis has shifted to greater use of psychological theory and carefully planned measurement devices. Cook and others developed the Minnesota Teacher Attitude Inventory. Studies by Gage and Cronbach (1955) [18] and Ryans (1960) [19] are recommended for reading. Chapter 11 of the *Handbook of Research on Teaching* summarizes a good deal of the literature.

Results obtained with personality tests of teachers have shown wide variation when correlated with other measures. However, until carefully controlled, well-designed studies employing adequate numbers of instructors have been made, the problem of determining the personality patterns of effective teachers must still remain unsolved.

ASSESSING TEACHER BEHAVIOR

Teacher behavior in the classroom obviously would seem to be the most useful source of data on teacher effectiveness, since it would appear to have an authentic on-the-job performance type of validity. Again, the problem is to obtain accurate and comprehensive measures. These measures usually consist of some kind of ranking or rating procedure.

[17] E. G. Guba and J. W. Getzels, "Personality and Teacher Effectiveness: A Problem in Theoretical Research," *The Journal of Educational Psychology*, **46** (October 1955), 330–344.

[18] N. L. Gage and L. J. Cronbach, "Conceptual and Methodological Problems in Interpersonal Perception," *Psychological Review*, **62** (1955), 411–422.

[19] D. G. Ryans, "Prediction of Teacher Effectiveness."

Rating devices

Rating scales are the most frequently used devices for assessing teacher behavior. In practice there is usually no clear delineation regarding what relevant behavior is. Rather, an attempt is made to use rating as a widespread net in the hope of catching some of the unsuspected variables. Rating scales and observation scales exhibit the characteristic features of common sense formulations—vagueness of definition, lack of specificity regarding the range of applicability, and absence of means of determining the invariant rather than the merely immediate and specific features.

In a sense, the use of rating scales to measure behavioral features tends to emphasize the subjectivity that characterizes broad definitions of behavior, interpretation or inference of goals from actions. Add the "natural" variability among raters, and the residue that is free of experimental error and errors of measurement becomes relatively small.

Surveys of appointment blanks and rating scales in use have failed to provide means for identifying the significant items to be used in setting up rating devices for teacher effectiveness. Frequently mentioned qualities on existing teacher appointment blanks are disciplinary ability, teaching ability, scholarship, and personality. There is no general agreement about what constitute the essential characteristics of a competent teacher. Similarly, items on rating scales tend to be subjective, undefined, and varied; there is little consistency as to what traits a supervisor might be expected to observe and evaluate. Chapter 7 of the *Handbook* contains a comprehensive summary of rating methods.

Administrative ratings   Over-all administrative opinion constitutes the most widely used single measure of teacher competence. Available studies have shown in general that teachers can be reliably rated by administrative and supervisory personnel (usually with correlations of .70 or above). For the most part, administrative ratings do not produce very high correlations with measures of student gain. Intercorrelations of rated traits or categories indicate that traits that are more objectively observable, or are more independent of opinion, tend to be less prone to logical error or halo effect than those traits that are more intangible and more subjectively estimated. Findings suggest that ratings made by a single person are apt to be contaminated by halo effects and that, in many such instances, a single rating of over-all effectiveness is useful only when based on a composite of a number of ratings of separate traits.

Peer ratings   Peer ratings are little used. For administrative purposes they are probably not very useful since teachers tend to have certain misgivings about expressing judgment on fellow teachers. As a rule, ranks probably give better results than ratings. Studies have shown substantial agreement between supervisors and fellow teachers in ratings assigned to teachers. As in the case of administrative ratings, substantial correlation is found among ratings given different traits by the same peer raters. In other words, halo effects influence peer ratings just as they do administrative ratings.

Student ratings When student ratings are compared with other measures of teacher effectiveness, varying results are found, depending in part upon the criteria employed. Considerable halo effect is usually noted when students rate their instructors on several traits. Results suggest that if the instructor favors the brighter students, he tends to be approved by them and a positive correlation between student ratings and grades results. If he teaches for the weaker students, he is not approved by the brighter students and a negative coefficient tends to be obtained. By and large, such factors as size of class, sex of students, age or maturity of students, and intelligence or mental age of students seem to have little bearing on student ratings. Research has been too sporadic and results too diverse to generalize about the influence of other factors on student ratings.

Self-ratings Instructors tend to overrate themselves. Self-ratings show negligible relationships with administrative ratings, student ratings, or measures of student gains. On the basis of the few available studies of self-ratings of instructors, the obvious, undisguised self-rating technique appears to offer little encouragment for evaluative or research purposes.

Systematic observation

Systematic observation techniques to determine differences in performance of effective and ineffective teachers were largely neglected until rather recently.[20] Most of the observations seem to depend upon the subjective judgment of the observer. In the case of planned observational recording, the reliability compares favorably with other methods of teacher evaluation. The most general criterion of validity of observation appears to be face validity. No single, specific, observable teacher act has been found whose frequency, or per cent of occurrence, is invariable and significantly correlated with student achievement. There seems to be a suggestion, however, that questions based on student interest and experience rather than on assigned subject matter, the extent to which

[20] D. M. Medley and H. E. Mitzel, "Measuring Classroom Behavior by Systematic Observation," *Handbook of Research on Teaching*, N. L. Gage (ed.) (Skokie, Ill.: Rand McNally & Company, 1963), pp. 247–328.

the instructor challenges students to support ideas, and the amount of spontaneous student discussion are related to student gains. Also, there seem to be no optimal time expenditures for particular class activities; a good teacher could apparently function successfully within a wide range of time distributions.

Critical incident technique

The critical incident technique described by Flanagan (1949) has been used in an attempt to describe teacher behavior. Observers and teachers reported anecdotal incidents in which they thought teachers were particularly effective or ineffective. Incidents were then classified in an attempt to isolate patterns. While many useful incidents were obtained, it has been difficult to put them into significant categories.

Other approaches

Students have been asked to describe their best and poorest teachers; parents and teachers have been asked to recall the behavior of teachers they remembered as being effective; leaders in education have been asked to describe what they regarded as effective and ineffective behavior. These approaches have not been rewarding. The time and effort could better be spent in more precise definition, observation, and analysis of the network of relationships among teacher behaviors, instructional goals, and pupil characteristics.

PUPIL GROWTH AND ACHIEVEMENT

Pupil growth and achievement in relation to teacher performance has been reviewed by Ackerman,[21] McCall,[22] Medley and Mitzel,[23] Mitzel and Gross,[24] Morsh and others,[25] Taylor,[26] and Webb and Bowers.[27] If the

[21] W. I. Ackerman, "Teacher Competence and Pupil Change," *Harvard Educational Review*, **24** (Fall 1954), 273–289.

[22] McCall.

[23] D. M. Medley and H. E. Mitzel, "Pupil Growth in Reading—An Index of Effective Teaching," *The Journal of Educational Psychology*, **48** (April 1957), 227–239.

[24] Mitzel and Gross.

[25] J. E. Morsh, G. G. Burgess, and P. N. Smith, "Student Achievement as a Measure of Instructor Effectiveness," *The Journal of Educational Psychology*, **47** (February 1956), 79–88.

[26] H. R. Taylor, "Teacher Influence on Class Achievement: A Study of the Relationship of Estimated Teaching Ability to Pupil Achievement in Arithmetic," *Genetic Psychology Monographs*, **7** (1930), 81–175.

[27] W. B. Webb and N. D. Bowers, *Student Performance as a Measure of Instructional Proficiency*. Research Project No. NM001077-01-06 (Washington,

purpose of teaching is to attain objectives by bringing about desired changes in pupils, the obvious measure of teacher effectiveness is the extent to which the teacher actually produces such changes. Unfortunately, some difficulties intrude upon this happy prospect: (1) It is difficult to measure pupil growth, and (2) it is difficult to determine precisely how much change can be attributed to a particular teacher. It is not surprising that the number of student gain studies is rather low. The great discrepancies in findings of the studies using student gains criteria emphasize the complexity of their relation to instructor performance.

The central difficulty is establishing sufficient experimental controls to show that certain changes in pupil behavior occur if, and only if, these changes are preceded by actions of a teacher.

To attain precise controls is probably impossible, although various statistical controls including matched groups, analysis of covariance, and various randomized and similar designs serve as approximations. A further difficulty in the matter of demonstrating that particular pupil behaviors are associated with actions of a particular teacher lies in the amount of confidence that can be placed in the criterion measure of pupil behavior. For instance: the immediate goal of a teacher may be to get the pupils to perform long division problems of a given level of difficulty. If the pupils learn to do such problems, one has some confidence that the teacher has achieved the goal; but if at a later time the pupils have difficulty in learning to do more difficult problems in division, or have difficulty in learning to use division in algebra, or can't use division to solve elementary science problems, confidence in the criterion is not as firm.

At this point, an interesting paradox appears. As one moves from the more immediate and more convenient criteria for assessing pupil achievement to those that are more distant but more valid, the pupil behavior attributable to a given teacher becomes increasingly confounded with the effect produced by other teachers. Thus, as one's confidence in the criteria of effectiveness increases, the likelihood of being able to attribute it to any one teacher correspondingly decreases. A reason for this is not hard to see. The more distant criteria depend on the transfer of learning. Transfer depends both on initial learning and on what is done later. One of the criteria for how well a fourth-grade teacher teaches arithmetic depends on how well his students learn fifth-grade arithmetic, while one of the criteria of how well a fifth-grade teacher teaches arithmetic is the extent to which he can create situations to which the pupils coming from the fourth grade can transfer their knowledge. The fourth-

D.C.: U.S. Naval School of Aviation Medicine, 1957), 7 pp.; "The Utilization of Student Learning as a Criterion of Instructor Effectiveness," *Journal of Educational Research*, **51** (September 1957), 17–23.

grade and fifth-grade teachers here become interacting units, and to which of them the arithmetic behavior at the end of the fifth grade is to be attributed is a very interesting problem in logical and statistical analysis.

The problem of inter-teacher influence is further complicated by the other influences that shape pupil growth: home, community, clubs, communication media, books, magazines, and libraries, to name a few. Considering the theoretical importance of pupil gain criteria for the assessment of teacher effectiveness, it is surprising that so few studies have used this measure. Barr's 1948 summary lists only 19 investigations that could possibly be said to use student gain as a criterion. In 1956, Mitzel and Gross found only 20 studies which had used student gain as a criterion. These studies exhibited conflicting results.

The criterion has been used most effectively by Morsh, Burgess, and Smith (1956). However, it should be indicated that the objectives of concern were strictly limited to subject-matter achievement in an Air Force technical specialty school. Mastery involved simply rote learning rather than cultivation of higher mental processes. In this restricted case, clear demonstration of pupil gains in relation to teacher activity was possible.

THE ADMINISTRATOR
AND TEACHER EFFECTIVENESS RESEARCH

So far we have considered only the point of view of researchers. When talking about teacher effectiveness, it is equally important to consider the concerns of teachers and administrators.

Within the arena of practical affairs, concern about teacher effectiveness is frequent. By virtue of local control, it is the responsibility of school officials to obtain an estimate of teacher effectiveness in order that decisions on retention, promotion, salary, or helping teachers to improve may be made.

School officials cannot make a decision as to how well a particular teacher performs without defining, however loosely, the teacher's job. When the job is loosely defined, school officials may base their evaluations on how well they like the teacher; or the number of complaints or commendations received about the teacher from parents; or the extent to which the teacher disrupts or facilitates smooth operation of school machinery.

At a slightly more organized level, administrative officials may work with the school board, the teachers, and the community in attempting to determine what the functions of a teacher in the local schools should be.

Decisions of such groups may range from so rigidly specifying the functions and activities that little autonomy is left to the teacher, to stating functions so vaguely that virtually all is left to the judgment of the teacher. Whatever the position of the group, the definitions refer to teacher function only within a limited geographical area.

Under local control, teacher function is free to vary from school system to school system. The job of the teacher thus varies with its location. Given that the functions a teacher should perform are well defined within a particular school system, one must consider the further complication that while first-grade teachers and senior high school teachers perform the same general functions, their specific responsibilities are quite different. Thus the teacher's job also varies with the grade.

Because most administrators are responsible to a local board of education, they can assess teacher performance by reference to locally defined functions. Generally speaking, all evaluations can be categorized as either formal or informal. Within this context, three techniques for local appraisal of teacher performance are typically used—ratings, observations, or student gains measured by standardized tests.

Ratings may consist of an over-all estimate of teacher effectiveness or of separate evaluations of specific teacher behaviors or traits. Self-ratings may be used, or ratings may be determined by the teacher's peers, by students, or by administrative personnel.

Ratings may involve ranking per cent of efficiency, indication of the level of a trait, forced choice, or any of the devices indicated in the *Handbook of Research on Teaching*.

Observation of teachers in the classroom may be used by local school officials; in practice, this technique is seldom the only one used for judgments of teacher effectiveness, and it is rarely used in an objective, scientific fashion.

Student gain, as measured by standardized tests, may be used appropriately to evaluate teacher effectiveness only if extensive controls and adjustments are made to recognize and compensate for factors other than teacher influence.

From the standpoint of the local school administrator, the extent to which any or all of these procedures are used depends on how much and what kind of evidence is desired in making decisions about local school personnel.

If one wants only to make a decision, ratings may be sufficient. If one wants to provide for in-service training and upgrading, ratings are not sufficient. It then becomes necessary to search for more explicit connections between attainment of objectives, teacher behaviors, characteristics and education. The process of joint inquiry, involving both the teachers and administrators, has much to recommend it. Administrators and teachers can help each other clarify their thinking and knowledge, and in the process both gain something in professional fulfillment.

STRIKES, SANCTIONS, AND THE SCHOOLS

In the following reading educator John Scanlon describes the important similarities and differences between the New York teachers' strike, which was backed by the AFT, and the Utah teachers' sanctions, which were supported by the NEA. He presents a vivid picture of the AFT-NEA power struggle to represent teachers and raises some important questions relating to the implications and use of strikes and sanctions in the schools and the future effect of teacher militancy in education.

John Scanlon

Saturday Review (*October 19, 1963*), 51–55, 70–74. *Reprinted by permission of the author and* Saturday Review.

"Up until now teachers have always been too complaisant, too docile, too willing to let themselves be put upon. I personally welcome the new show of vigor and muscle which has now become apparent in many parts of our profession. But I would also counsel the use of wisdom and foresight—and the careful exercise of responsibility—as we work out together new ways of rebuilding school systems which have lost their former excellence."

The speaker was Calvin E. Gross, superintendent of the New York City public schools, and his remarks were addressed to delegates attending the 47th annual convention of the American Federation of Teachers (AFL-CIO) in New York on August 19. But Calvin Gross's words had significance far beyond the confines of the Hotel Americana ballroom in which they were delivered, far beyond the boundaries of the world's largest school system, which he heads, and far beyond the ranks of the American Federation of Teachers. In a very real sense, Calvin Gross was speaking to all members of the teaching profession, to his fellow school superintendents, and to members of school boards throughout the country. And in his words there also was a message for parents and for the people who support the U.S. public schools with their tax dollars.

What Mr. Gross was saying, in essence, was that teachers are on the march—for higher salaries, for better working conditions, for improvements in the schools, and for a voice in determining school policy. And, like the Negroes who recently marched on Washington to dramatize their determination to win a redress of their grievances, the teachers are not in a mood to tolerate official indifference or delay. They believe that the time for patience has long since passed.

The new militancy of American teachers was dramatically illustrated on two widely separated fronts this past summer. In Utah, members of the Utah Education Association, an affiliate of the National Education Association, threatened a state-wide shutdown of the public schools when the state legislature passed a school appropriation bill providing less money than the Association had recommended. In New York City, members of the United Federation of Teachers, an affiliate of the AFT, voted to strike—in defiance of state law and a court order—when their demands for salary increases and other benefits were not met by the board of education. In neither case did the threatened closing of schools actually take place, but in both cases the teachers were convinced that they had won a victory by a show of force—or, in Calvin Gross's words, a show of muscle.

Although there is not room here to present a detailed account of the conflicts in Utah and New York, it might be instructive to examine some of the similarities between the two, and also some of the important differences, because such an examination throws into sharp relief the basic elements of an AFT-NEA power struggle which has profound implications for the future of public education in the United States. Briefly, the elements of this struggle are these:

1. To an increasing number of teachers, it appears that the best way of getting what they want is by joining a union and bargaining collectively with their employers, relying on the political and economic strength of organized labor, and, as a last resort, the ultimate weapon of any union—the strike—to enforce their demands. This attitude is reflected in the dramatic growth of the American Federation of Teachers, which has more than doubled its membership since the end of World War II. Although is is still only a tiny organization (82,000 members, as compared to the NEA's 860,000) the AFT has the power of the entire AFL-CIO behind it, and is actually stronger than the NEA in several of the nation's largest cities, including New York, Chicago, and Detroit.

2. The NEA, in recognition of the new militancy among teachers and in response to the threat posed by the rapid growth of the AFT, has become much more aggressive during the past few years. It has launched a special Urban Project whose primary aim is to strengthen the structure of NEA affiliates in large urban centers. It has strongly urged its local associations to engage in "professional negotiations" with their school

boards, and to develop written agreements based on these negotiations. (Many such agreements already exist, in varying degrees of precision and formality.) And finally, the NEA has come up with its own version of labor's ultimate weapon, which it calls "sanctions." The NEA has said that "sanctions" can take various forms, but in their most drastic form they involve (a) withholding of teacher contracts and (b) advising other members of the NEA not to take teaching positions in the affected school system. It is clear, therefore, that in this form their net effect is the same as that of strikes—classrooms without teachers.

The increasing militancy of teachers, and the power struggle between the AFT and the NEA, have caused considerable uneasiness on the part of school superintendents and school board members throughout the country. The American Association of School Administrators, which enrolls most of the nation's school superintendents, (and which is a powerful affiliate of the NEA) takes a dim view of teacher unions and even frowns on the NEA's official policy regarding "sanctions." In a recently published booklet entitled *Roles, Responsibilities, Relationships of the School Board, Superintendent, and Staff*, the association specifically mentions "strikes, demagogic appeals, threats, withheld services, and sanctions or threatened sanctions by teachers" as actions "not likely to lead to lasting and satisfying resolution of disagreements." The booklet was issued in the latter part of June, after the Utah teachers had already voted to withhold their services in the fall, and about a week before the NEA convention in Detroit, where the NEA executive board officially declined the request of the Utah teachers for national sanctions against Utah. The National Association of School Boards is wary of the whole idea of professional negotiations and collective bargaining, because it sees in these procedures a potential threat to the authority of local boards of education. It is flatly opposed to "strikes, sanctions, boycotts, mandated arbitration or mediation."

It is against this background that the nature and significance of the Utah and New York disputes must be examined in order to be fully understood.

Utah is a state of 85,000 square miles and about 1,000,000 population. Its public schools enroll about 265,000 students, and the teaching staff numbers about 10,500, of whom about 96 per cent belong to the Utah Education Association. There are forty local school districts that vary in size from a few square miles to more than 7,000 square miles, and in pupil population from 200 to 48,000. About 65 per cent of the total state school enrollment is concentrated in eight school districts located in the urban area stretching from Provo to Ogden, at the foot of the towering Wasatch Range, where most of Utah's population is concentrated. Education is defined by the state constitution as a state responsibility, but provision is made for direct control by locally elected boards of education. Approximately 61 per cent of the total state school bill is financed by out of state revenues, and only about 39 per cent by locally imposed property taxes. This over-all ratio does not apply uniformly to all districts in the state, but by and large educational finance in Utah is a state concern.

Historically the citizens of Utah have been proud of the effort they have put forth to support their schools. But despite high expenditures *per taxpayer,* Utah has usually ranked below the national average in expenditures per pupil and in teacher salaries. In the school year of 1947–48 Utah reached the national average in current expenditures per pupil because of a special school bill enacted by the legislature but since then Utah's relative position in this respect has been declining. The decline has been most pronounced since 1961, when the legislature made only a token increase in school appropriations. In the 1962–63 school year according to estimates by the National Education Association, Utah's current expenditures per pupil were $354, which was about 22 per cent below the national average of $432. There has been a similar decline in Utah's relative standing with respect to teacher salaries. It should be emphasized, however, that Utah's relative decline in the national standings on these two measures of school support is *not* an indication of public indifference to the needs of education. In 1961, according to NEA estimates, Utah stood fourth among the states in *per capita* expenditures of state and local governments for local schools. Also, Utah ranked first among the states in the proportion of total public expenditures, state and local, devoted to public education. One of the principal reasons why Utah generally ranks below the U.S. average in expenditures per pupil and in teacher salaries despite higher per capita expenditures on education is that Utahns have large families. In 1962, according to the NEA estimates, the school-age population of Utah (5 to 17) was 28.2 per cent of the total resident population of the state. In this respect Utah was tied for third place among all the states.

In preparation for the 1963 session of the Utah state legislature, a state-wise organization known as the Cooperating Agencies for Public Schools (CAPS) drew up a legislative proposal calling for a $24.7 million increase in the annual level of school expenditures. CAPS was composed of representatives from the Utah Education Association, the Utah Society of Superintendents, the Utah School Boards Association, the Utah Congress of Parents and Teachers, and the State Department of Education. Its proposal, which would have meant an increase of $100 in Utah's current expenditure per pupil, was designed to bring the Utah figure up to the average of the seven surrounding mountain states—

Arizona, Idaho, Colorado, Nevada, New Mexico, Montana and Wyoming. The estimated gap was based on figures developed by the Utah Education Association. The UEA estimate immediately ran into trouble, because it was considerably higher than the estimates of other Utah organizations. The Utah Foundation, a taxpayer group, had estimated the gap at $75 per pupil, and the Utah Legislative Council had set it at $77. (The state estimates of the National Education Association placed the gap at $78.)

CAPS recommended that 42 per cent of its proposed $24.7 million increase in school funds be devoted to raising teacher salaries (which would have meant increases ranging from $800 to $1000 per teacher), that 28 per cent be spent for more adequate staffing, and 30 per cent for additional teaching supplies, equipment, and maintenance. (The amount CAPS recommended for more adequate staffing included funds for hiring enough new teachers to eliminate half-day sessions and establish a state-wide kindergarten program. These measures would have required additional classrooms and would have necessitated a substantial increase in school construction expenditures. Consequently, CAPS also recommended a $7.7 million increase in state support for local building funds, but this was not a major issue in the Utah school controversy.)

The CAPS program was laid before the appropriate committees in both houses of the Utah legislature, and was publicized throughout the state by way of billboards, newspaper advertisements, radio and TV programs, brochures and information kits, a series of "grass roots" meetings sponsored by the Utah School Boards Association, and a state-wide "Lights On for Education" night at every schoolhouse in the state under the sponsorship of PTA units. The UEA also did a considerable amount of lobbying with legislators. However, the CAPS bill never got out of committee, and was not debated on the floor of either house of the legislature. Instead, each house came up with its own school bill. Governor George D. Clyde, in his budget message to the legislature, had recommended an increase of $8.7 million in school operation and maintenance funds, which the UEA had called "inadequate and totally unacceptable." The Senate brought out a bill with an increase of a little more than $13 million, and the House figure was $9.9 million. A compromise, which the governor approved and eventually signed into law, provided for an increase of $11.6 million in school funds for each year of the 1963–65 biennium. Under the terms of the bill, Utah teachers will receive an average salary increase of about $700 per year. (The actual increases will range from $300 to more than $1000 per teacher, varying according to district, experience, and other factors.) Under the CAPS proposal, the average salary increase would have been about $900 per year.

Members of the Utah Education Association met in Salt Lake City on

March 16, while the legislature was still in session, to decide what to do. It was a cold morning, following a bad snowstorm, but more than 80 per cent of the membership turned out. By individual ballot, they voted 7,788 to 189 (a margin of forty to one) to discontinue contract discussions for the 1963–64 school year until the school finance issue was "satisfactorily resolved." They also adopted a resolution requesting the National Education Association "to inform its members of the Utah situation and to urge them to refrain from seeking employment and entering into verbal or written agreement with a Utah board of education" until the issue was settled.

The NEA gave immediate national publicity to the Utah situation and, according to Executive Secretary William G. Carr, "allocated expert legal assistance and substantial funds to help make UEA objectives clear to the citizens of Utah." The NEA also advised its members that if contracts were offered for jobs in Utah, they "might be for positions in which Utah teachers expect to remain."

The UEA, maintaining that the CAPS proposal had not received a fair hearing in the legislature, demanded that the governor call the legislature back into special session to reconsider the school finance bill. The governor refused. He pointed out that the $11.6 million increase voted by the legislature was the largest of its kind ever granted in Utah, and he argued that it would be inappropriate for him to ask the legislature to reconsider a matter it had already considered and acted upon. When the UEA demanded that he include school finance on the agenda for a special session of the legislature necessitated by his veto of a state building bill, the governor refused again. This time, however, he announced that he would appoint a blue-ribbon citizens' committee to make "a thorough study and factual analysis" of Utah's school finance problem. He said he was convinced that "we do not have sufficient basic data, objectively collected and analyzed, on which to base final jugment" on the school finance question, and that the study "should give us a sound basis on which to build our future programs." He emphasized that he was not promising to call a special session of the legislature when the committee's findings became available. "On the other hand," he added, "I am giving Utah citizens my full assurance that I shall do whatever my best judgment indicates in the light of the facts developed by the committee. Obviously, this could include the summoning of a special session of the Legislature." He said the study should be completed within a year, and sooner if possible, but that in any event the report should be submitted in ample time so that it could be studied and analyzed, and any needed legislation carefully prepared, before the next session of the legislature. The governor made his announcement on May 27. It was interpreted to mean that the action the legislature had already taken would be final for the 1963–64 school year, but that if the study committee's findings warranted, the governor would call a special session in sufficient time for action to be taken for the 1964–65 school year. The UEA demanded that it participate equally in naming the members of the committee, that the committee start work on June 15 and be given an August 15 deadline, that the committee be charged with determining whether a special session was necessary, that if the committee so recommended the governor call the session not later than January 1964, and that the session "be allowed to consider the recommendations of the committee without further executive instructions."

The governor hit the ceiling. He replied that he would not abdicate the responsibilty of naming the committee members, and that he could not and would not allow the committee to make decisions that legally were his alone to make.

By now, the relations between Governor Clyde and John C. Evans, Jr., executive secretary of the UEA, were anything but cordial. The governor resented the pressure the UEA was applying, and made it clear that neither he nor the legislature could be intimidated. Evans and his colleagues, on the other hand, felt that the governor was being obstinate. An impasse had developed, and it persisted through the end of the school year and well into the summer. The UEA had asked the NEA to invoke national sanctions against Utah, and this raised a very real question whether the schools would reopen in September. In response to the UEA's request for national sanctions, the NEA sent a fact-finding team from its Commission on Professional Rights and Responsibilities into Utah to study the controversy. Members of the team found Governor Clyde adamant. He told them that the issue had ceased to be school finance and had become a question of "whether the state shall remain sovereign or be dictated to by an organized group."

The Utah School Boards Association, caught squarely in the middle of the controversy, now parted company with the Utah Education Association on the matter of sanctions. W. Dean Belnap, president of the USBA, said in July that while his group still supported the original CAPS proposal, "we have a divergence of feeling regarding the nature of the pressure which should be brought to bear on the governor and the legislature in the solution of financial problems in Utah. We cannot think compatibly with the strong sanctions they (the teachers) have taken." The National School Boards Association, at its annual convention, went on record in support of its Utah affiliate.

When the NEA convention opened in Detroit on June 30, the Utah controversy was the principal topic of conversation among delegates, and it also was one of the most important items on the convention agenda, because it appeared that the NEA's policy on "sanctions," adopted the year before, was about to face its first real test. (At the 1962 convention in Denver, the NEA's delegate assembly had passed a resolution calling for the use of sanctions "as a means for preventing unethical or arbitrary policies or practices that have a deleterious effect on the welfare of the schools," and asking affiliated state associations "to cooperate in developing guidelines which would define, organize, and definitely specify procedural steps for invoking sanctions by the teaching profession." During the ensuing year, the staff of the NEA's Commission on Professional Rights and Responsibilities, working with representatives of the state associations, had framed a tentative set of guidelines, but many of the delegates arrived in Detroit without a clear understanding of the precise nature of sanctions or the procedural steps for invoking them. They did know, however, that the teachers of Utah had voted to withhold their contracts and to ask the NEA to invoke sanctions.)

The NEA convention opened on Sunday, June 30, and the following morning reporters covering the event where invited to a press conference at which the Utah controversy was to be discussed by Mr. Evans, executive secretary of the UEA, and William G. Carr, executive secretary of the NEA. At the conference, the reporters were given three press releases. The first, issued by the UEA, reminded the reporters that the UEA had asked the NEA to invoke sanctions against Utah, and then went on to express cautious optimism regarding Governor Clyde's study committee. "The Utah Education Association hails this first step toward solving the Utah school crisis," the release said. "If the views and interests of Utah teachers are given due consideration, the Governor's school study committee may be able to effect a settlement of the controversy." To most of the reporters, this was the first inkling that the UEA's attitude had softened. The second release, issued by the Executive Committee of the NEA, said that "vigorous efforts" were being made "by the responsible parties" to resolve the impasse, and that "pending the outcome of these efforts, the National Education Association withholds judgment concerning the application of national sanctions." The UEA had received its answer on the first business day of the convention, before there had been any discussion of the Utah controversy on the convention floor. The third press release, issued by the UEA, said:

> The President and Executive Secretary of the Utah Education Association agree that no useful purpose would be served by imposing national sanctions against the State of Utah while current negotiations for settlement are in progress.
>
> However, the NEA Executive Committee will be asked to impose national sanctions immediately if present negotiations fail to result in a satisfactory resolution of the Utah school controversy.

In response to a question at the press conference, Mr. Evans offered another piece of news: "If the makeup of the Governor's study committee is favorable, and if it is properly charged, then the trustees of UEA will recommend that teachers sign new contracts."

Unaware of what was transpiring at the press conference, the representative assembly of the Department of Classroom Teachers, which embraces most of the NEA membership, was in session at the Cobo Hall Arena, principal meeting hall of the convention. When the reporters arrived at the Arena, the Utah controversy was under discussion. It was immediately apparent that the rank and file of the NEA membership were in a much more militant mood than the NEA executive committee or the officers of the Utah Education Association. Brushing aside the plea of its representative on the NEA's Commission on Professional Rights and Responsibilities, who had urged "no rash acts or resolutions" until the NEA's fact-finding team in Utah made its report, the Department of Classrooom Teachers passed by an overwhelming vote a resolution which had grown stronger with each amendment. In its final form it called on the NEA "to do everything possible to assist the teachers of Utah," asked "all local associations to urge their members not to apply for teaching positions in Utah until such time as this condition no longer exists," and called on the NEA "to establish a fund for financial assistance to the teachers of Utah in the event of needs resulting from their efforts to improve the educational program of the state." The Utah delegation got to its feet and applauded vigorously, and a reporter at the press table leaned over to Mrs. Marie L. Caylor, editor of the American Federation of Teachers' publications, and whispered: "This sounds like an AFT convention." Mrs. Caylor smiled appreciatively. (At their annual dinner a few nights later, the classroom teachers took up a collection and raised $3,115 for the Utah fund.)

The Department of Classroom Teachers also passed strongly worded resolutions on professional negotiations and sanctions. The former asserted that "local professional associations *have* the professional right and *should have* the mandatory legal right" to negotiate with boards of education in the determination of policies affecting professional services of teachers," that "local board policies and/or state laws should authorize a means of appeal through designated educational channels to appropriate educational agencies when agreement cannot be reached;" it commended state and local associations that have developed written procedures for professional negotiations, and it urged teachers in states not now recognizing or accepting the idea of professional negotiations "to press for legislation to legalize such procedures." The resolution on sanctions asserted that "the profession must establish and enforce sanctions to protect the right and responsibilities of its members and to insure a con-

sistent and favorable learning climate," and, among other things, urged
the NEA "to continue to give leadership in refining guidelines for the establishment and enforcement of such professional sanctions."

Although the Department of Classroom Teachers embraces more
than 90 per cent of the NEA membership, it does not speak for the entire NEA. The resolution on Utah which the full representative assembly
of the NEA subsequently adopted in Detroit was considerably milder
than the one adopted by the classroom teachers, and said nothing about
urging teachers not to accept positions in Utah. However, it did authorize
a loan fund (later set at $500,000) for the financial assistance of the Utah
Education Association, to be used in the event of failure to resolve the
impasse. The decision of the full Representative Assembly not to vote
sanctions against Utah was generally interpreted as a victory for the
NEA's Executive Committee.

The Utah delegates returned home from Detroit with mixed feelings. They had received enthusiastic support from the Department of
Classroom Teachers, but their request for national sanctions had been
turned down and this weakened their bargaining position with the governor. During the summer, a special effort to mediate the impasse was
made. Dr. O. Preston Robinson, general manager and editor of the
Deseret *News and Telegram,* finally brought the adversaries together
after what one observer described as "many, many hours of painstaking
and sometimes frustrating behind-the-scenes negotiations." Also involved
in these negotiations (which received very little publicity) was Dr. Carr,
the NEA executive secretary.

On August 3, the UEA met again in special session, this time in
Provo, and voted 4,586 to 1,148 to resume contract negotiations for the
new school year. One of the factors in the decision was an agreement
that the UEA would participate in recommending citizens for appointment to the governor's study committee. On August 9 the governor instructed the committee to prepare, in addition to its final report, an interim report, "early enough so that if this report should indicate to me
that emergency action is needed, such action could be taken before the
start of the 1964–65 school year."

Strictly speaking, the UEA vote ended the state-wide impasse and returned negotiations to the local level. In some instances, however, especially in Salt Lake City and the suburban Granite district, where the
teachers were particularly militant, the negotiations were touch and go
for a while and it appeared that the state impasse had become a local
impasse. UEA locals in these districts eventually won additional recognition from the boards of education. The boards recognized the right of
teachers to join (or not to join) professional associations, accepted the
right of these organizations to represent their members in negotiations

with the board, and set up joint committees of teachers and board members to study "problems of mutual concern" and to make recommendations to the boards. The boards did not agree to be bound by these recommendations.

The concensus among Utah observers who followed the controversy but were not involved on either side is that most teachers were relieved that the impasse was resolved, particularly since they received their largest salary increase in many years. But, as one observer pointed out, the large negative vote at Provo indicated quite clearly that a significant minority was not happy with the settlement. "The controversy could rise again in the spring," he told *SR*, "if the study committee should recommend something less than the teachers will accept or if the governor should choose not to follow the committee's recommendations." Another Utahn went further in his comments to *SR*. "My personal opinion," he said, "is that the militants in the UEA were motivated by a single desire —to show their power to the state by delaying the start of school by a month, a week, or even by only a day. They controlled the UEA power structure and were not defeated until the entire membership was given a chance to vote on acceptance of the governor's proposal. Quiescent now, they are hopefully waiting an unsatisfactory report by the governor's study committee."

Although the Utah controversy ended a month before the schools were scheduled to reopen, the situation in New York City was different. As one wag put it: "The United Federation of Teachers stood eyeball to eyeball with the Board of Education all through the summer, and at the eleventh hour it was the mayor who blinked."

This description of the New York City controversy may have been somewhat irreverent, but it wasn't completely inaccurate. The New York teachers held out in defiance of state law and a court injunction, until the afternoon of the day before the schools were scheduled to reopen. Then they accepted, with jubilant cries of "We won!" settlement terms which clearly indicated that they had not surrendered.

In their negotiations for a two-year contract, they had demanded salary increases totalling $9 million for the 1963–64 school year, and another increase of $20 million for 1964–65. They had also demanded smaller classes, "total improvement" in New York City's "difficult" schools, additional remedial and other services in all schools, additional teacher time during the school day for lesson preparation, and improvements in the machinery for handling teacher grievances. The Board of Education had flatly refused to grant any salary increase for 1963–64, on the ground that the New York teachers had won a $750 increase last year (largest in the history of New York City) and on the further ground that "drastic" cuts in its budget had forced the board to cut back or eliminate desperately-needed school improvements which, in the board's view, had priority over salary increases. "Faced with this critical situation," said Board Chairman Max J. Rubin in a radio-television address on July 31, "the Board was and is convinced that for this year, weighing the direct educational needs of the children against further salary increases, we have no right to divert funds from these urgent educational needs in order to provide for higher salaries." The Board did agree, however, to set aside 25 per cent of whatever increase in school funds it might obtain next year and apply this to salary increases for 1964–65. "We can only deal in percentages," Mr. Rubin pointed out, "because we do not know now how much money will be appropriated by the City and the State to the school system." With respect to the union's other major demands, the Board took the position that many of them involved educational policy or administrative discretion, and that while it was willing to *discuss* them with the union it was not prepared to *negotiate* them in the collective bargaining sense, because this would be an abdication of its legal authority to operate the schools. The union insisted, on the other hand, that "anything that relates to working conditions in the broad sense is negotiable."

The 47th annual convention of the American Federation of Teachers was held in New York at the height of the school controversy, and it was evident throughout the proceedings that the AFT was not only proud of its New York local, but willing to back it to the hilt. AFT President Carl J. Megel announced that AFT membership had increased by more than 11,000 in the preceding year, and he said that most of the increase had occurred in New York, where the UFT now claims more than 20,000 members out of a total teaching force of 43,000. (The NEA has less than 1,500 members in New York.) Harry Van Arsdale, president of the New York Central Labor Council, brought greetings from the New York City labor unions and added: "We're very proud of the UFT and Charles Cogen. They have helped us with many of our problems, and you can be sure we are going to help them with theirs." He also reminded the delegates that Mayor Wagner has often described New York as "a good union town," and he said he hoped the mayor would appear at the convention "so we can hear it from him again." (The mayor was invited to address the opening session of the convention, and his name was listed on the program, but official business required his presence elsewhere.)

Raymond R. Corbett, president of the New York State AFL-CIO, also was a speaker at the opening session. He denounced the state's Condon-Wadlin law, which prohibits strikes by public employees as "a repressive, discriminatory and punitive measure," and pledged that the State AFL-CIO "will not rest until this infamous piece of legislation is scrapped from our statute books." He also had harsh words for what he called "the perennial shadow-boxing between city hall and Albany" over school finance. "It has sometimes served as a diverting and diversionary circus which the people regarded with indulgence, disdain, and indifference," he said. "But suddenly it has ceased to be amusing and may become a deadly serious matter if labor's just and hallowed 'no contract, no work' principle is put into effect on September 9."

Bearing a message from the national headquarters of the AFL-CIO was Nicholas Zonarich of the AFL-CIO's powerful Industrial Union Department, headed by Walter Reuther. The IUD, which has more than six million members and is spearheading the AFL-CIO's vigorous efforts to organize the nation's "white collar" workers, has been actively assisting the American Federation of Teachers in its organizing drive, and has been especially helpful to the United Federation of Teachers in New York. (The IUD sees in the "white collar" workers the new frontier in union organization because their number is growing rapidly with the advance of technology and because up until recently they had not received as much attention from union organizers as have "blue collar" workers, whose number in the total labor force has been dwindling.) Mr. Zonarich also had words of praise for Mr. Cogen and the UFT. He said the New York teachers had given inspiration to the teachers in Gary, Boston, Philadelphia, and other cities, and he pledged the IUD's "full support" to the UFT in its dispute with the New York City Board of Education.

At the closing session, the AFT delegates passed a resolution strongly supporting the UFT, and voted to send copies to Governor Rockefeller, Mayor Wagner, and United States Senator Jacob K. Javits of New York. (Senator Javits, in an address to the delegates on the preceding evening, had expressed sympathy with the aims of the New York teachers and had applauded their militancy "wholeheartedly," but he also had reminded them that "a state law remains on the books which makes strike action by government employees illegal and therefore not part of (the) democratic process." He said he therefore favored mediation of the New York dispute.) The delegates also voted to strengthen and clarify the AFT's policy regarding strikes. The previous policy, embodied in a resolution adopted at the 1952 convention, was open to the interpretation that the AFT opposed strikes by its local affiliates. This had caused some consternation among UFT members during and after the one-day strike of 1962. The new policy, adopted at the request of the New York local, says that the AFT recognizes "the right of locals to strike under certain circumstances," and will "urge the AFL-CIO and affiliated international unions to support such strikes when they occur."

(The new policy is also ambiguous, because it does not spell out the meaning of "certain circumstances," but it apparently was satisfactory to the UFT and to the other locals represented at the convention. In response to a question from the floor, the AFT's general counsel emphasized that the AFT does not claim, and in fact "disdains," the right to strike against the federal government or any of its departments or agencies. This, it was explained, is because all federal employees are required to sign a "no strike" agreement as a condition of employment. The Condon-Wadlin law does not require such pledges by New York state employees, but it does impose severe penalties on those who actually strike. The law was not enforced against UFT members after their one-day strike in 1962, but the New York Board of Education left no doubt in anyone's mind that the law would be enforced in the event of a strike this year. In fact, amendments passed after last year's UFT strike now make enforcement of the law mandatory.)

The New York deadlock persisted throughout the summer and into September, with the union giving every indication that it was prepared to carry out its threat to close the schools. At the last minute the mayor appointed a mediation committee to settle the dispute. The action was taken on Friday, September 6, a few hours after the union, at a general membership meeting, had voted 5,219 to 758 to reject the Board's final offer and to strike, as scheduled, on the following Monday morning, the opening day of school. The meeting was held at an outdoor stadium in a driving rain, and the large turnout surprised many observers because on the preceding night the union's delegate assembly had turned down the Board's offer by a vote of 1,500 to 17, in defiance of a court order restraining the union and its members from proceeding with their plans for a strike. Charles Cogen, president of the union, had announced that he and other leaders of the union would conduct the strike from jail, if necessary, and the relatively large turnout for the membership meeting was interpreted by union officials as an indication that the members were solidly behind their leaders.

The men the Mayor named to the mediation committee were Theodore W. Kheel, a labor lawyer and impartial chairman of New York City's transit industry; Frank E. Karelsen, a lawyer and vice president of the executive committee of the Public Education Association, an influential citizens' group active in school affairs; and former United States District Judge Simon H. Rifkind, a member of New York City's board of higher education. (It is worth noting at this point that two weeks earlier, in an interview during the AFT convention, Mr. Cogen said that "as a last resort" the union might be willing to submit the dispute to mediation by a group of distinguished citizens acceptable to the union and the Board of Education and, when pressed further, he mentioned Messrs.

Kheel, Karelsen, and Rifkind as examples of the type of men he had in mind. The point is made here not because it raises any question about the impartiality of the mediators, but because it supports a view held by some observers that the union's basic strategy was to go to the brink with the Board of Education and then, when the pressure for a settlement became intolerable, rely on the mayor to intervene. The Board was bargaining *after* its budget had been fixed, so that there was a limit to what it could offer. The union realized this, and there are reasons to believe that this was a factor in the UFT's unblinking militancy. As Fred Hechinger, education editor of the New York *Times,* observed a week after the settlement: "The temptation is to keep saying 'No' until the politicians, anxious not to invoke anti-strike laws, rush in the mediating Marines at the last minute to offer more than the board did—not because the board hates teachers but because it has no money of its own." It is not unreasonable to assume that the union this year may have remembered what happened last year, when, after its one-day strike, Mayor Wagner and Governor Rockefeller "found" an extra $13 million for salary increases.)

The delicate task of the mediators was to arrive at a compromise that would avert the threatened strike without undermining the Board's authority, and to persuade the union and the Board to accept the terms within less than seventy-two hours. At 4:30 Sunday afternoon, after nearly two days of almost continuous mediation, Mr. Rifkind, speaking for the Mayor's committeee, announced at a news conference: "Gentlemen, the marathon is over." The compromise proposed by the mediators received the unanimous approval of the Board of Education, and the union ratified it that night by a vote of 5,265 to 181.

Under the terms of the contract, New York teachers will receive more than $24 million in salary increases over the next two years, which is about twice the amount the Board of Education had offered. The increases will average about $580 per teacher, and most of that will come in the second year. But there will be a token increase effective in April, and this was regarded as a key factor in the settlement, because it inabled the union to claim it had won a salary increase "now," without increasing the Board's budget. (The April increase will not require any "new money," because the total amount is so small that the Board can pay it by reshuffling items in its current $600 million budget.) The maximum salary next year will be $11,025 as compared to the present $10,445.

In addition to the salary increases, the agreement provides for many of the other things the union had sought, and it also gives the union the right to participate in the determination of school policy. UFT officials will meet once a month with Superintendent Gross to discuss problems of mutual concern, and chapter chairmen of the union will hold similar meetings with school principals. How this arrangement will work out remains to be seen, but Mr. Gross, whom the union came to respect as a tough but fair bargainer, has left little doubt about his attitude toward these discussions. He welcomes them, and he sees in them an opportunity to bring the teachers into the continuing search for solutions to the massive problems confronting the New York City schools. In a radio interview on September 15, a week after the impasse had ended, he revealed that it was he, and not the union leaders, who had put forth the idea of holding monthly consultations with union representatives. During the course of the negotiations, he said, "it became quite clear to me that there are genuine aspirations for professional contributions to the school system—the kind of contributions the teachers make in any professional organization worth its salt, to any school system that wants to get somewhere, and I welcome this." He made it clear, however, that neither he nor the Board of Education is abdicating any responsibility under the new arrangement. "The Board of Education will continue to run the schools," he said, "and I work for the Board of Education."

The New York contract also includes the same "no-strike" clause that was written into the 1962 agreement at the insistence of the Board of Education. The UFT had demanded its deletion.

What conclusions can be drawn from the Utah and New York controversies? What implications for the future seem to emerge from them, and from the power struggle being waged between the NEA and the AFT? How will the power struggle, and the new militancy of teachers, affect the nation's schools?

These are large questions, and there are no easy answers, but at the risk of over-simplification it is possible to set down a few impressions one gets from studying the two conflicts:

1. There is little doubt that teachers are increasingly conscious of their growing power, whether it flows from membership in a professional association or a labor union, and that they are prepared to exercise it to obtain what they regard as legitimate goals. (A woman teacher in Utah expressed it this way: "How can teachers prove that they can act with power until they actually have used power? Until then we have only a phantom power." The union view was summed up succinctly by Raymond R. Corbett, president of the New York State AFL-CIO, in his address at the opening session of the AFT convention: "We are traditionally and philosophically committed to the principle that all employees must be permitted to band together to bring balanced strength to the collective bargaining table. We believe that collective bargaining turns into collective begging if the basic right to strike granted to every free worker is taken away from him.")

2. Professional negotiations and collective bargaining have the same

basic aim—written agreements between teacher organizations and school boards regarding salaries and other matters of mutual concern (including some degree of participation in the determination of school policy, which up until recently has been regarded as the sole province of the school board). But there is an important distinction between negotiating with a school board and negotiating with an employer in private industry. The essence of this distinction is that the school board is a *public* body and the teachers are *public* employees, and the *public* interest should be paramount—whether the discussions are called "collective bargaining" or "professional negotiations." (It is undoubtedly true that "professional negotiations" are by nature more polite than collective bargaining procedures. NEA negotiators usually regard the superintendent as a professional colleague, since most superintendents belong to the NEA. The AFT, on the other hand, does not admit superintendents to membership because they have the authority to hire and fire. This fact, in the AFT view, makes the superintendent an agent of management and therefore somewhat of an adversary at the bargaining table. However, there do not appear to be any compelling reasons why, in both types of negotiating procedures, a mutually satisfactory agreement cannot be reached by teachers and school boards if both sides negotiate in good faith.)

3. Sanctions have the same net effect as strikes. Or, to put it another way, when teachers vote to withhold their contracts and to urge other teachers not to man their positions, the result is the same as when teachers vote to strike and throw up a picket line to keep other teachers out of the classroom. Here there was a distinction between the Utah and New York controversies, because the action of the Utah teachers did not constitute a threat to violate the law and the action of the New York teachers did, but one cannot escape the conclusion that in both instances the school children would have been the ultimate losers if the threat had been carried out. (William G. Carr, executive secretary of the NEA, expressed some concern about the public's reaction to sanctions in his remarks to the NEA convention. He warned the delegates that the effectiveness of sanctions would be impaired if they were invoked for "trivial and transitory reasons.")

4. The power struggle between the NEA and the AFT will continue, and it will be waged with greatest intensity in the large cities, where the NEA is admittedly weak and the AFT has the benefit of a traditional urban sympathy with the aims of organized labor. It is in the urban areas, therefore, where teacher militancy is likely to be most pronounced and where school boards already burdened by a whole host of problems peculiar to big-city school districts are likely to find themselves with the additional headaches that professional negotiations or collective bargaining involve. (In New York, in addition to the threat of a teacher strike, the Board also had to contend with a threatened boycott of the

schools by Negro parents protesting *de facto* segregation. This, too, was called off before it materialized, but Superintendent Gross was kept busy during the summer dashing from one kind of bargaining conference to another.)

To sum up, teachers are making it increasingly clear that they want a voice in school affairs and that they are willing to fight for their rights, if necessary. This means that stubborn school boards will find it increasingly difficult to run the schools by unilateral action, and that ignoring the legitimate demands of teachers will increasingly involve some peril. But the new power the teachers are coming to exercise also carries with it grave responsibilities. Superintendent Gross left with the American Federation of Teachers another admonition which applies with equal force to teachers everywhere: "You are now a power in American education, and you are obliged to use your capacities to build, and not to destroy."

IS TEACHING A PROFESSION?

Horace Mann believed: "All the high hopes which I entertain for a more glorious future for the human race are built upon the elevation of the teacher's profession and the enlargement of the teacher's usefulness." Is teaching really a profession?

Myers and Gezi probe this question in the following selection. In an attempt to define "profession," they trace the several criteria by which scholars have tried to distinguish between professions and "non-professions," synthesizing these criteria into a list of four. They examine teaching under the light of each of these criteria, and in this process an evaluation is made of the effectiveness of two major teacher organizations and of the Code of Ethics drafted by the NEA.

The authors stress that "the most important outcome of gaining professional status is that American children are assured of receiving a high quality education from their teachers."

James E. Myers
Kalil I. Gezi

Prepared especially for this volume.

One of the frequent questions posed in educational discussions is whether teaching is truly a profession. But before one can attempt to answer this question, he must determine the meaning of the word "profession."

WHAT IS A PROFESSION?

The difficulty in defining "profession" stems from several sources. First, continual change over the years has brought changes in the character and the function of many professions, thus an appropriate definition of a profession at a given time may not be suitable at another time. Second, the word profession has been used by the public synonymously with the words "occupation" and "vocation." Hence, there are references to the acting profession, the mortuary profession, the laundry profession, and the barbering profession. The problem is compounded by references to the professional athlete, the professional soldier, the professional photographer, the professional gambler, and even to the "oldest profession of all." Third, since there is a distinct advantage to being known as a profession, several groups have so labeled themselves even though they may not have met the criteria of such established professions as medicine and law. Fourth, there appears to be various degrees of professionalism and, hence, the question in some cases may not simply be whether or not a group constitutes a profession, but rather what extent of professionalism has it attained. A group may be recognized as a full-fledged profession, while another might be known as semiprofessional, and yet a third group may be seen as an emerging profession that has not yet met all the criteria of an established profession. Finally, there is no single acceptable definition of a profession.

However, even though the word "profession" is difficult to define, several notable attempts have been made to identify its criteria.

CRITERIA OF A PROFESSION

Abraham Flexner set forth in 1915 one of the earliest definitive statements regarding the criteria of a profession. According to Flexner, a profession (1) is based on intellectual activity, (2) requires from its members the possession of a considerable amount of knowledge and learning, (3) has definite and practical purposes, (4) has certain techniques which can be communicated, (5) has an effective self-organization, (6) is motivated by a desire to work for the welfare of society.[1]

Carr-Saunders, in 1928 and 1933, described the characteristics of a profession. His list included: (1) intellectual competence, (2) a pro-

[1] Abraham Flexner, "Is Social Work a Profession?" in *Proceedings of the National Conference of Charities and Correction* (Chicago: Hildmann Printing Company, 1915), pp. 576–590.

longed period of specialized training, (3) the formation of a professional organization.[2]

The NEA, in 1948, suggested that a profession "(1) involves activities essentially intellectual, (2) commands a body of specialized knowledge, (3) requires extended professional preparation, (4) demands continuous inservice growth, (5) affords a life career and permanent membership, (6) sets up its own standards, (7) exalts service above personal gain, (8) has a strong, closely knit professional organization." [3]

Myron Lieberman, in 1956, advanced the following eight characteristics which he thought must be present to some degree in all recognized professions: "(1) a unique, definite, and essential service, (2) an emphasis upon intellectual techniques in performing its service, (3) a long period of specialized training, (4) a broad range of autonomy for both the individual practitioners and the occupational group as a whole, (5) an acceptance by the practitioners of broad personal responsibility for judgments made and acts performed within the scope of professional autonomy, (6) an emphasis upon the service to be rendered, rather than the economic gain to the practitioners, as the basis for the organization and performance of the social service delegated to the occupational group, (7) a comprehensive self-governing organization of practitioners, (8) a code of ethics which has been clarified and interpreted at ambiguous and doubtful points by concrete cases." [4]

Becker pursued what he termed a "radically sociological view" by identifying professions as those occupations which have gained and maintained "that honorific title." He distinguished between the symbolic dimension of a profession, which is the image commonly conceived by the public, and the reality dimension, which is the actual practice of the members of a profession. Futhermore, he maintained that the practice of most professions has failed in varying degrees to match their symbols.[5]

There have been other attempts to delineate the characteristics of a profession, but an objective examination of the criteria found in the lit-

[2] A. M. Carr-Saunders, *Professions: Their Organization and Place in Society* (Oxford: Clarendon Press, 1928); and A. M. Carr-Saunders and P. A. Wilson, *The Professions* (Oxford: Clarendon Press, 1933).

[3] National Education Association, Division of Field Service, "The Yardstick of a Profession," *Institutes on Professional and Public Relations, 1938–1947* (Washington, D.C.: The Association, 1948), p. 8.

[4] Myron Lieberman, *Education as a Profession* (Englewood Cliffs, N.J.: Prentice-Hall, 1956), pp. 2–6.

[5] Howard Becker, "The Nature of a Profession," in *Education for the Professions*, Sixty-first Yearbook of the National Society for the Study of Education, Part II, Nelson B. Henry (ed.) (Chicago: University of Chicago Press, 1962), pp. 27–46.

erature can be synthesized into the following three. A profession exhibits: (1) an intellectual competency based on specialized knowledge that requires a prolonged period of preparation, (2) a strong organization which has a clearly defined and enforceable code of ethics, (3) a high degree of autonomy for the group as well as for each of its members, (4) an emphasis upon service above economic gain.

Now that the common characteristics of a profession have been identified, let us examine teaching to determine whether it meets these four criteria.

IS TEACHING A PROFESSION?

1. *Does teaching involve intellectual competency based on specialized knowledge?* Effective teaching presupposes, among other things, a body of specialized knowledge which deals with learnings from the disciplines of history, sociology, anthropology, psychology, philosophy, and the various other fields of general education as well as professional education.

An important question may be raised here as to whether all teachers do indeed possess a specialized knowledge and intellectual competency. This question leads us into the area of teacher preparation.

The NEA Research Division Survey of 1.5 million public school teachers in 1961 revealed that 14.6 percent of these teachers had less than four years of college preparation,[6] and even though this proportion decreased to 7 percent in 1966,[7] it is shocking to realize that there are still many teachers in American classrooms who have not had an adequate training. From these statistics, it is obvious that there are still many teachers in our classrooms who have not had an adequate period of specialized training. But, if the growing emphasis upon teacher certification continues, there would be an increasing number of teacher candidates who complete the bachelor's or the master's degrees. This growing emphasis upon certification is reflected in the following statistics. In 1947–1948, 40 percent of the teachers completed less than four years of college education with the percentage decreasing in 1953–1954, to 20 percent,[8] and shrinking even more in 1966, to 7 percent. Equally impressive is the increasing number of states enforcing the bachelor's degree requirement for elementary and high school teachers. While in 1950, 21 states enforced degree requirements for elementary

---

[6] National Education Association, "Teachers in Public Schools," *NEA Research Bulletin,* **41** (February 1963), 23–26.

[7] National Education Association, "Characteristics of Teachers: 1956, 1961, 1966," *NEA Research Bulletin,* **45** (October 1967), 87–89.

[8] A. Huggett and T. Stinnett, *Professional Problems of Teachers* (New York: Crowell-Collier and Macmillan, 1956), p. 438.

teachers, and 42 states enforced degree requirements for secondary school teachers, in 1964, 45 states and the District of Columbia required the bachelor's degree for their elementary teaching certificates and 48 states and Puerto Rico required a bachelor's degree for the secondary teaching credential. In the same year, Arizona, California, and the District of Columbia had a five-year requirement for the secondary credential, and, furthermore, it is expected that as the general level of education rises, more states will require a fifth year of college preparation for their teaching credentials. But even though more states today are requiring increased college preparation for teachers, many states still allow persons with inadequate preparation to teach by granting them provisional credentials.

2. *Do teachers have a strong organization and a clearly defined and enforceable code of ethics?* An attempt will be made here to determine whether teaching can meet this second criterion of a profession. Of the several organizations of teachers, our discussion will be centered on two major associations: the NEA and the AFT, each of which represents a different approach to organizing teachers in the United States.

NATIONAL EDUCATION ASSOCIATION

The National Education Association was established in 1857 in order "to elevate the character and advance the interests of the profession of teaching and to promote the cause of popular education in the United States." [9] Although the association was originally called the National Teachers Association, its name was changed in 1870 to the National Education Association (NEA). It is by far the largest organization of teachers in the United States with 1,028,456 regular members in 1967. As shown in the organizational chart presented here, the NEA had, as of August 1967, 8264 local and 59 state affiliates. The NEA's executive secretary, who is appointed by the Board of Trustees for a four-year term, appoints in turn the members serving divisions, commissions, and committees.

The NEA has been increasingly successful as an information gathering and disseminating body for education. Its publications, research, and inservice programs have made very important contributions to education. The NEA membership consists of classroom teachers, school administrators, college professors and administrators, and specialists in school, colleges, and educational agencies.

The comprehensive nature of NEA's membership may be viewed as a source of strength because it allows the various persons involved in the

[9] National Education Association, *NEA Handbook for Local, State, and National Associations* (Washington, D.C.: The Association, 1967), p. 18.

educational endeavor to work together. However, this fact has also been viewed by some educators as a source of weakness. To place under the umbrella of the NEA all of these people who have different educational interests has not contributed to making the organization closely knit. The many departments, committees, and commissions of the NEA often work autonomously, thus causing a degree of overlap in their approaches and efforts. Furthermore, the AFT contends that the NEA membership of administrators and teachers presents a conflict of interest between employers and employees.

The NEA may also be criticized for the weakness of its local organizations, which indeed have often been less than effective. Nor has the NEA been as influential as one would expect from an organization of its many years of existence and its size in matters related to salaries, working conditions, fringe benefits, and professional negotiations with school boards.

THE AMERICAN FEDERATION OF TEACHERS

The American Federation of Teachers (AFT) was organized and affiliated with the American Federation of Labor in 1916. The AFT membership, 144,534 as of August 1967, is distributed over approximately 450 locals in the United States and the Canal Zone. The AFT has grown mostly in urban areas and some of its most powerful locals are in metropolitan centers, such as New York, Chicago, Los Angeles, and Seattle, where labor unions are generally influential.

The governing body of the AFT is its convention, to which each local sends its delegates. The Executive Council, as shown in the accompanying table of organization, consists of a full-time president elected every two years and sixteen vice-presidents who are full-time teachers.

The AFT differs from the NEA in that the former is affiliated with labor and includes only classroom teachers in its membership, advocates the use of collective bargaining—and as a last resort, the use of the strike—and puts a high priority on the improvement of teacher salaries and fringe benefits.

The affiliation of the AFT with organized labor is seen by the AFT as a source of strength because "labor affiliation gives the American Federation of Teachers the support of the fifteen-million members in the AFL-CIO." [10] This affiliation, however, is construed by some educators as an undesirable association with blue collar workers which impedes the development of education as a profession.

The AFT's restriction of membership to classroom teachers is viewed

[10] American Federation of Teachers, *Questions and Answers about AFofT* (Chicago: American Federation of Teachers, n.d.), p. 5.

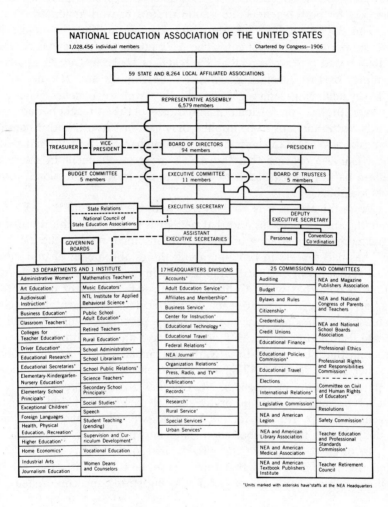

NATIONAL EDUCATION ASSOCIATION OF THE UNITED STATES
1,028,456 individual members   Chartered by Congress—1906

59 STATE AND 8,264 LOCAL AFFILIATED ASSOCIATIONS

REPRESENTATIVE ASSEMBLY
6,579 members

TREASURER   VICE-PRESIDENT   BOARD OF DIRECTORS 94 members   PRESIDENT

BUDGET COMMITTEE 5 members   EXECUTIVE COMMITTEE 11 members   BOARD OF TRUSTEES 5 members

EXECUTIVE SECRETARY   DEPUTY EXECUTIVE SECRETARY

State Relations
National Council of State Education Associations

GOVERNING BOARDS

ASSISTANT EXECUTIVE SECRETARIES   Personnel   Convention Coordination

33 DEPARTMENTS AND 1 INSTITUTE		17 HEADQUARTERS DIVISIONS	25 COMMISSIONS AND COMMITTEES	
Administrative Women*	Mathematics Teachers*	Accounts*	Auditing	NEA and Magazine Publishers Association
Art Education*	Music Educators*	Adult Education Service*	Budget	
Audiovisual Instruction*	NTL Institute for Applied Behavioral Science *	Affiliates and Membership*	Bylaws and Rules	NEA and National Congress of Parents and Teachers
Business Education*	Public School Adult Education*	Business Service*	Citizenship*	
Classroom Teachers*		Center for Instruction*	Credentials	NEA and National School Boards Association
Colleges for Teacher Education*	Retired Teachers	Educational Technology *	Credit Unions	
Driver Education*	Rural Education*	Educational Travel	Educational Finance	Professional Ethics
Educational Research*	School Administrators*	Federal Relations*	Educational Policies Commission*	
Educational Secretaries*	School Librarians*	NEA Journal*		Professional Rights and Responsibilities Commission*
Elementary-Kindergarten-Nursery Education*	School Public Relations*	Organization Relations*	Educational Travel	
Elementary School Principals*	Science Teachers*	Press, Radio, and TV*	Elections	Committee on Civil and Human Rights of Educators*
Exceptional Children*	Secondary School Principals*	Publications*	International Relations*	
Foreign Languages	Social Studies*	Records*	Legislative Commission*	Resolutions
Health, Physical Education, Recreation*	Speech	Research*	NEA and American Legion	Safety Commission*
Higher Education*	Student Teaching * (pending)	Rural Service*	NEA and American Library Association	Teacher Education and Professional Standards Commission*
Home Economics*	Supervision and Curriculum Development*	Special Services *		
Industrial Arts	Vocational Education	Urban Services*	NEA and American Medical Association	
Journalism Education	Women Deans and Counselors		NEA and American Textbook Publishers Institute	Teacher Retirement Council

*Units marked with asterisks have staffs at the NEA Headquarters

Organization chart of the National Education Association, August 1967. Used by permission of The Association.

with mixed feelings. The AFT argues that by doing so it removes the inevitable domination of the employers in determining the destiny of their employees. Other educators argue that in order to improve education there must be an educational organization which would provide the opportunity for both teachers and administrators to work together.

The AFT's methods of improving teacher welfare have also had their supporters and opponents. The AFT points to the New York strikes of 1963 [11] and of 1967 as well as the teachers' strike in Detroit in 1967 as examples of the benefits of collective bargaining and the use of the strike in achieving salary gains and other welfare benefits. The NEA, however, prefers "professional negotiations" between teachers and school boards, with sanctions to be applied only as a last resort, and it considers the strike as a blow to the image of the teacher as a professional person. The NEA also charges that the AFT's great involvement in salary and welfare battles has caused it to do less to aid in the professional growth of its members.

From the above, it is obvious that both the NEA and the AFT have strengths and weaknesses and that neither is as strong as the professional organizations in medicine and law. For instance, neither the NEA nor AFT has had success in bringing about the establishment of uniform national standards of certification and accreditation of teachers. It is interesting to note that while California requires five years of college training for the lowest regular teaching certificate for elementary teachers, Nebraska requires only one year of college preparation for the same certificate. Furthermore, the AFT does not have an accrediting agency, and although the NEA created the National Council for the Accreditation of Teacher Education (NCATE) in 1952, to enforce professional standards in the preparation of teachers, NCATE has not been recognized by all teacher training institutions or by state departments of education, and has faced sharp criticism for not being answerable to the institutions it evaluated and for the shortcomings of its process of evaluation.

In order to maximize the effectiveness of the NEA and the AFT, Lieberman has suggested that they merge, and if this is done, the new organization can lay a better claim to being strong and comprehensive.[12]

CODE OF ETHICS

Besides having a strong and a comprehensive organization, a profession must also have a clearly-defined and enforceable code of ethics. In this section the NEA code of ethics will be introduced and examined.

[11] See Scanlon's artice in this chapter for the details of this strike.
[12] Myron Lieberman, *The Future of Public Education* (Chicago: University of Chicago Press, 1960), pp. 230–236.

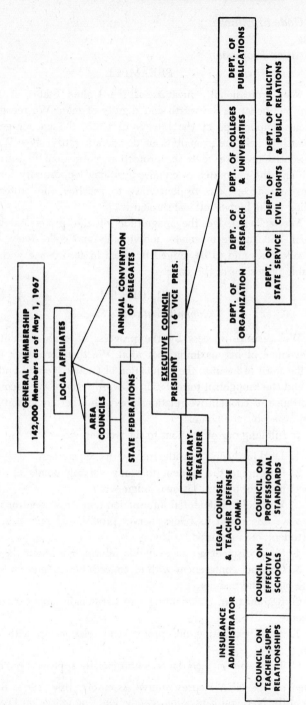

Table of organization of the AFT from American Federation of Teachers,
Constitution of the AFT (*Washington, D.C.: AFT, n.d.*), p. 24.

The Code of Ethics
of the
Education Profession [13]

PREAMBLE

We, professional educators of the United States of America, affirm our belief in the worth and dignity of man. We recognize the supreme importance of the pursuit of truth, the encouragement of scholarship, and the promotion of democratic citizenship. We regard as essential to these goals the protection of freedom to learn and to teach and the guarantee of equal educational opportunity for all. We affirm and accept our responsibility to practice our profession according to the highest ethical standards.

We acknowledge the magnitude of the profession we have chosen, and engage ourselves, individually and collectively, to judge our colleagues and to be judged by them in accordance with the applicable provisions of this code.

PRINCIPLE I

Commitment to the Student

We measure success by the progress of each student toward achievement of his maximum potential. We therefore work to stimulate the spirit of inquiry, the acquisition of knowledge and understanding, and the thoughtful formulation of worthy goals. We recognize the importance of cooperative relationships with other community institutions, especially the home.

In fulfilling our obligations to the student, we—

1. Deal justly and considerately with each student.

2. Encourage the student to study varying points of view and respect his right to form his own judgment.

3. Withhold confidential information about a student or his home unless we deem that its release serves professional purposes, benefits the student, or is required by law.

4. Make discreet use of available information about the student.

5. Conduct conferences with or concerning students in an appropriate place and manner.

6. Refrain from commenting unprofessionally about a student or his home.

7. Avoid exploiting our professional relationship with any student.

8. Tutor only in accordance with officially approved policies.

[13] Adopted by the NEA Representative Assembly, July, 1963. Reprinted by permission of the National Education Association, Committee on Professional Ethics.

9. Inform appropriate individuals and agencies of the student's educational needs and assist in providing an understanding of his educational experiences.

10. Seek constantly to improve learning facilities and opportunities.

PRINCIPLE II

Commitment to the Community

We believe that patiotism in its highest form requires dedication to the principles of our democratic heritage. We share with all other citizens the responsibility for the development of sound public policy. As educators, we are particularly accountable for participating in the development of educational programs and policies and for interpreting them to the public.

In fulfilling our obligations to the community, we—

1. Share the responsibility for improving the educational opportunities for all.

2. Recognize that each educational institution may have a person authorized to interpret its official policies.

3. Acknowledge the right and responsibility of the public to participate in the formulation of educational policy.

4. Evaluate through appropriate professional procedures conditions within a district or institution of learning, make known serious deficiencies, and take any action deemed necessary and proper.

5. Use educational facilities for intended purposes consistent with applicable policy, law, and regulation.

6. Assume full political and citizenship responsibilities, but refrain from exploiting the institutional privileges of our professional positions to promote political candidates or partisan activities.

7. Protect the educational program against undesirable infringement.

PRINCIPLE III

Commitment to the Profession

We believe that the quality of the services of the education profession directly influences the future of the nation and its citizens. We therefore exert every effort to raise educational standards, to improve our service, to promote a climate in which the exercise of professional judgment is encouraged, and to achieve conditions which attract persons worthy of the trust to careers in education. Aware of the value of united effort, we contribute actively to the support, planning, and programs of our professional organizations.

In fulfilling our obligations to the profession, we—

1. Recognize that a profession must accept responsibility for the conduct of its members and understand that our own conduct may be regarded as representative.

2. Participate and conduct ourselves in a responsible manner in the development and implementation of policies affecting education.

3. Cooperate in the selective recruitment of prospective teachers and in the orientation of student teachers, interns, and those colleagues new to their positions.

4. Accord just and equitable treatment to all members of the profession in the exercise of their professional rights and responsibilities, and support them when unjustly accused or mistreated.

5. Refrain from assigning professional duties to non-professional personnel when such assignment is not in the best interest of the student.

6. Provide, upon request, a statement of specific reason for administrative recommendations that lead to the denial of increments, significant changes in employment, or termination of employment.

7. Refrain from exerting undue influence based on the authority of our positions in the determination of professional decisions by colleagues.

8. Keep the trust under which confidential information is exchanged.

9. Make appropriate use of time granted for professional purposes.

10. Interpret and use the writings of others and the findings of educational research with intellectual honesty.

11. Maintain our integrity when dissenting by basing our public criticism of education on valid assumptions as established by careful evaluation of facts or hypotheses.

12. Represent honestly our professional qualifications and identify ourselves only with reputable educational institutions.

13. Respond accurately to requests for evaluations of colleagues seeking professional positions.

14. Provide applicants seeking information about a position with an honest description of the assignment, the conditions of work, and related matters.

PRINCIPLE IV

Commitment to Professional Employment Practices

We regard the employment agreement as a solemn pledge to be executed both in spirit and in fact in a manner consistent with the highest ideals of professional service. Sound professional personnel relationships with governing boards are built upon personal integrity, dignity, and mutual respect.

In fulfilling our obligations to professional employment practices, we—

1. Apply for or offer a position on the basis of professional and legal qualifications.

2. Apply for a specific position only when it is known to be vacant and refrain from such practices as underbidding or commenting adversely about other candidates.

3. Fill no vacancy except where the terms, conditions, policies, and practices permit the exercise of our professional judgment and skill, and where a climate conducive to professional service exists.

4. Adhere to the conditions of a contract or to the terms of an appointment until either has been terminated legally or by mutual consent.

5. Give prompt notice of any change in availability of service, in status of applications, or in change of position.

6. Conduct professional business through the recognized educational and professional channels.

7. Accept no gratuities or gifts of significance that might influence our judgment in the exercise of our professional duties.

8. Engage in no outside employment that will impair the effectiveness of our professional service and permit no commercial exploitation of our professional position.

Criticisms of the Code

The value of a code of ethics to a professional group is that it is the group's means of establishing and regulating acceptable standards for its members. An effective code must be clear, realistic, and enforceable.

Is this Code clear? Unfortunately, it has many vague phrases. For instance, principle II, number 7, states: "Protect the educational program against undesirable infringement." What is meant by "undesirable infringement"? What constitutes desirable infringement? Who decides when an infringement is desirable, the school board, the school administrator, the teachers, the pupils, or the community? The Code does not define "undesirable infringement."

Another example of vagueness can be seen in principle III, number 12, which states: "Represent honestly our professional qualifications and identify ourselves only with reputable educational institutions." There is no definition of a reputable institution in the Code. Assuming that such a definition is found, who will then be entrusted to determine the degree of reputability of each institution, and how will reputability be determined?

Is the Code realistic? Consider principle IV, number 2, which states "apply for a specific position only when it is know to be vacant. . . ." When a teacher in Chicago applies for a position in the Los Angeles school district, with no intention of displacing someone else, would his act be held by the Code to be unethical? Indeed, it is not realistic to expect all vacancies to be known to all teachers.

Again, principle IV, number 3, states: "Fill no vacancy except where the terms, conditions, policies, and practices permit the exercise of our professional judgment and skill, and where a climate conducive to professional service exists." Is it realistic to expect all teachers to abandon the children in a district where such a climate does not exist? Also, would we call a teacher unethical if he accepts a position in such a district in order to bring about a change in its professional climate?

These examples lead to the conclusion that there are certain unrealistic expectations in the Code.

Is the Code enforceable? No, because since the first code was written in 1929 up to the present, no machinery has been established to enforce it. The practice of "moonlighting" is a good example of the inability to implement the code. Principle IV, number 8, urges teachers not to engage in outside employment which would impair the effectiveness of their professional service, yet in 1965, one-fourth of all teachers held a job in addition to teaching without losing their teaching position.

Why is the Code not enforced? There are several reasons for the lack of enforcement. First, the Code grew out of the NEA's Committee on Professional Ethics, and hence teachers who do not belong to the NEA have no obligation to conform to it. Second, the Code, as pointed out earlier, incorporates many vague terms and sets forth unrealistic expectations regarding teachers and administrators which would make it very difficult to enforce. Third, the legal question of enforcing a voluntary code of ethics has not been settled.

It is important to remember that a code of ethics which is not enforced has little value in regulating and promoting acceptable standards of behavior among the members of a professional group.

AUTONOMY

Good defines autonomy as "the freedom to act without external controls." [14] In using this definition, we must observe that it is highly inconceivable that there is a profession which has complete freedom from external control. Nevertheless, the various professions do have differing degrees of autonomy. Viewed in this context, teaching does not have the same degree of autonomy that medicine and law enjoy, for the major decisions in education are made by lay people. Historically, education has been a state function. State legislators, not educators, are entrusted with making laws for education in their states. These laws are interpreted and specific regulations are developed by the lay-dominated state

[14] Carter V. Good (ed.), *Dictionary of Education* (2d ed.; New York: McGraw-Hill, 1959), p. 51.

boards of education for the operation of the schools. The administration of these regulations is then relegated to the local boards of education, which are usually made up of lay people.

While the public is and should be concerned about education, there are many educational decisions which ought to be dealt with by the educational practitioner, because of his training and expertise, and not by the public. For example, decisions related to the entry into, and expulsion from, teaching, which are handled by lay boards, should be made by the teachers themselves.

IS SERVICE ABOVE PERSONAL GAIN IN TEACHING?

Historically, teaching has been guided by service to society, and those who select teaching as a career do so not because it will lead them to wealth but because of their interest in working with children and their desire to help young people grow. However, putting service to society above personal gain should not be used by any community to justify low teacher salaries and poor fringe benefits.

A LOOK AHEAD

From the previous discussion it is clear that education meets only some of the criteria of a profession and perhaps can best be described as an "emerging" profession. But will education become a profession in the future? On the basis of the available evidence, education appears to be moving toward full professional status. In the near future it is likely that teacher organizations will become more powerful because they will not only show impressive gains in membership but will also draw greater participation from the grass roots level. Furthermore, it is expected that the NEA and the AFT will find more areas of agreement in their goals and activities, which could make a merger between them a possibility. A strong organization can establish and maintain effective and uniform standards of accreditation and certification, obtain acceptance of a single code of ethics and find the machinery to enforce it, bring about a greater public recognition of the role teachers should play in making educational decisions, and initiate a united effort to achieve the goals of education.

When all prospective educators are required to meet high standards of preparation to enter education, and when practitioners are required to maintain high levels of achievement on the job, then the public will fully recognize education as a profession. It is through this public recognition that autonomy for practitioners will be gained.

Undoubtedly, professionalization will bring with it social and economic rewards to educators, but the most important outcome of gaining professional status is that American children are assured of receiving a high quality education from their teachers.

5

PROMISING IDEAS
AND PRACTICES

INTRODUCTION

*The rate of change in American society is so dramatically rapid
that before many people adjust to certain developments, new
changes emerge requiring other adjustments. Since the school
mirrors our innovative society, it is subjected to continuous pressures for innovations. "In the past ten years," according to Francis Keppel, former U.S. Commissioner of Education, "more time,
talent, and money than ever before in history have been invested
in pushing outward the frontiers of educational knowledge, and
in the next decade or two we may expect even more significant
developments." Some of these pressures have come from technology, the knowledge explosion, the population growth, and
this country's expanding world commitment. Most innovations in
education can be traced to university and college researchers,
projects sponsored by the government and private foundations,
and by creative teachers and administrators.*

*Innovations in education have taken many forms. For ex-
ample, several—such as teaching machines and educational television—have stemmed from the use of technological advances in
the classroom; others—such as team teaching, nongradedness,
and new curriculums—have relied upon the expanding frontiers
of knowledge in the humanities, the physical, social, and behavioral sciences, and education; others—demonstrated by such organizations as the Peace Corps—were prompted by the greater
involvement of the United States in world affairs.*

*The articles included in this chapter have been selected in
order to familiarize the reader with some of these innovations.
Dwight Allen describes some of the major innovations in education today. Frank Brown explores three methods of providing for
individualized learning in the schools. Ernest Hilgard defines co-*

operative teaching and discusses its organization. Wilbur Schramm's article deals with some major questions relating to the use of television as a classroom tool. Gezi and Myers explore the meaning of creativity, some approaches which might foster creative growth in students, and the impact of contemporary American culture on creativity.

The material presented in this chapter should expose the student to various innovations in education and stimulate him to become an innovator in his classroom. Educators should transmit a fixed body of knowledge, but above all they should help the student develop the understanding, skills, attitudes, and feelings which would equip him to function as an effective participant in the process of change.

INNOVATIONS IN ELEMENTARY AND SECONDARY EDUCATION

What are the major innovations in public schools today? The answer to this question is the primary concern of educator Dwight W. Allen in the following selection, a paper prepared by Allen for use at the White House Conference on Education in July 1965. He describes three kinds of educational innovations, summarizes the major "expedient" characteristics of the current educational scene, and offers some helpful suggestions for further school innovations. The author is recognized for his work in flexible scheduling and micro-teaching.

Dwight W. Allen

Contemporary Issues in American Education (*U.S. Office of Education Bulletin 1966, No. 3* [*Washington, D.C.: 1965*]), *125–131.*

If we were to have a national suggestion box labeled "elementary and secondary education," the chances are that it would be filled to overflowing. Some of the ideas finding their way into the box would be old proposals cast in a slightly new light. Others would be fresh and unique. Many would be trivial, some important. Some would support each other. Still others might be in conflict. The suggestion box symbolizes our dedication to innovation, a distinctly American characteristic for accepting new ideas from wherever they may come.

THE PROCESS OF INNOVATION

Innovation in education is not a one-step process with a termination point. It is a continuous evolutionary process of identifying alternatives, examining and testing them, and making alternatives into new forms.

The range of alternatives to be considered for improving education is wider today than ever—"new" proposals abound. Of greater significance are the methods used for assessing their worth.

Three kinds of educational innovations may be identified:

1. *Those consisting of genuinely new ideas and approaches to existing problems.* A new perspective often presents new alternatives. Limitations are often no more than a lack of imagination. For example, it is assumed that students should be under constant supervision while they are at school; yet when school is dismissed they often are on their own for several hours, particularly as they reach high school age. New proposals for individual study suggest that students should be given the opportunity to demonstrate their ability to accept increased responsibility as one of the major goals of learning.

2. *Those made up of new technologies which offer possibilities heretofore not feasible.* One example is the use of computers to give us new information on which to base more sophisticated decisions.

3. *Those arising from new needs and demands on the educational system* due to social change, merging scholarly insights, cultural invention, altered perspective on scientific and technological developments. No longer, for example, can we prepare students for jobs and responsibilities that are clearly understood, well defined, and stable. Nor can we assume that many people will spend all or most of their lifetimes in the same place.

Educationally innovative efforts today are too often isolated and fragmented. We need comprehensive frameworks within which they can be studied.

How can we examine the context of innovation? How can responsible educators and educational policy makers make valid decisions regarding individual innovations and systems of innovation? We must begin with the goals of education and examine proposed curriculum changes, new processes and alternative structures for the probable effects on these goals. The goals, themselves, must be subjected to scrutiny for they may have unintended results. For example, an increased emphasis on science and mathematics as a worthwhile educational goal may have unanticipated results in weakening the humanities curriculum unless the structure of education is changed to accommodate the new curriculum goals.

We will attempt to identify some of the elements in the uneasy balance of expedients that characterizes the current educational program. Not enough is known to propose solutions. Examining alternatives is therefore much more important. It is hoped that the following issues will provide a substantive basis for discussion.

NEW GOALS

Significant new goals for elementary and secondary education are emerging in this decade. For example: higher education for a greater proportion of the population; occupational choices in the national as well as in the individual interest; and commitment to an international community.

In the past, the goals of education have too often been stated as pious hopes and in vague generalities. In the past, goals have been like New Year's resolutions. This is no longer adequate. We are beginning to learn that goals must be tied specifically and realistically to what students shall be expected to think, to feel, and to do.

NATIONAL CURRICULUMS

Should the curriculum be locally or nationally determined? This debate often blocks any innovation at either level. Some skills, for example, in reading, writing, arithmetic, and social studies have long been common to almost all school programs in the United States. Other aspects of the curriculum belong uniquely to a local situation. For example, a school district near a mountain wildlife refuge may conduct an open-air laboratory, using the unique local resources to study ecology, provide the stimulus for creative writing activities, or engage in the study of geological formations. To deny an individual school district the right to develop its unique aspect of the curriculum would be as foolish as to deny the nation the right to be served by those agencies which are alone powerful enough to cope with national problems. The argument should shift to one of which parts of the curriculum can better be developed on a national scale, and which at a state and local level.

For some subjects a properly devised national curriculum could provide a program flexible enough to meet the educational needs of a wide variety of students. Because of a concentration of effort, these national curricula can be more effective than most locally devised programs. Local programs lack resources to build the individualized programs they seek to provide. It is unrealistic to think that a group of teachers, however dedicated and competent, spurred on by curriculum consultants, can, at a series of meetings at four in the afternoon, devise a curriculum as powerful as a national effort on which specialists in learning theory, academicians, teachers, administrators, professors of educational methodology, and others, as well as the most competent teachers, are available to spend years of concentrated study.

INSTRUCTIONAL SYSTEMS

In early times the teacher was the instructional system. With the invention of the motion picture projector, teachers, it was predicted, would be turned into little more than projector operators. These dire predictions of the obsolescence of the teacher, never realized, continue apace as new technologies roll off the assembly lines: programmed learning, video tape, and computer-based learning systems. Partisan enthusiasts (not necessarily those developing the technology) foretell the day when the teacher will be replaced by machine. Any teacher who can be replaced by a machine should be.

The teacher does not perform a single function called "teaching," rather he is in turn: lecturer, counselor, evaluator, questioner, stimulator, encourager, coach, listener, arbitrator, friend, critic, interpreter, helper, and judge, among others. No teacher can perform each of these functions equally well. Some may be better performed by the new technologies. The organization of learning as we now know it places undue emphasis on certain of these tasks at the expense of others. It is unlikely that each of these tasks should occupy the same time or that they are equally significant. Nevertheless, we are unable to agree on their relative importance or to determine the balance required for each student. The availability of machines only highlights the long present need for the development of more precise instructional systems. The problem is to render unto the machine those things which are the machine's, and to direct to the teacher those that are truly human.

PERSONNEL CONSIDERATIONS

Education is the concern of the entire society; education is not confined to formal institutions. Personnel of quality are in short supply in all segments of society's endeavors. How important it is to use the competences of all to the best advantage.

Society recognizes that the home is where the child gets his initial education. It is from this base of initial family training that all formal education proceeds. New proposals for an earlier beginning point for formal education for some children underline the importance of this initial education.

This is but one way in which education becomes the direct responsibility of the community at large. This responsibility continues throughout the fabric of community life. Industries train their workers to perform specific tasks. Mass media seek to cultivate audiences both shaping and reflecting educational values. As our society becomes more complex, there is need for higher levels of education in both the formal and informal structures. There is also need for more coordination between formal and informal education. More precise definitions are needed. Parents need to know what schools are teaching, and schools need to know the assumptions they can make. As instructional systems become more comprehensive, general policy makers will have less ability to monitor the specific instructional procedures; new criteria for evaluation will need to be developed, and new bases for collaboration worked out.

The most competent teachers should be called upon to perform only responsibilities at the highest level. Tasks that can be performed with a lower level of training and competence should be assigned to other staff members. The tacit assumption has been made in the past that all teachers are interchangeable parts.

Once a concept of teacher specialization is introduced, a number of alternatives become available. The beginning teacher is not required to assume full professional responsibilities immediately upon completion of formal training. At present, the beginning teacher frequently gets the most difficult and complicated assignment and the most difficult students to teach. Teachers tend to promote themselves away from responsibilities for difficult teaching situations as they gain staff seniority. If levels of responsibility could be identified so that senior teachers would have genuinely different tasks to perform, this trend might be reversed.

Team teaching and cooperative teaching offer alternatives which create interesting challenges for senior teachers and provide for systematic assistance from less highly trained members of the instructional staff. We can no longer afford the meaningless luxury of having highly trained personnel performing tasks irrelevant to their training at the expense of having less competent personnel performing tasks requiring the highest level of skill.

THE SEQUENCE OF EDUCATIONAL OFFERINGS

Focusing attention on the individual progress of the child is important, yet organizing students by arbitrary grade level destroys many opportunities to deal with the unique combination of skills and accomplishments of any one individual. A non-graded approach overcomes much of this difficulty. No completely non-graded programs have yet been established at either elementary or secondary level, due partially at least to the difficulty in identifying concepts which must be taught sequentially as compared with those which are independent of other experiences.

Assumptions about sequence are not always valid. Physics is a 12th-grade course not because it depends upon 11th-grade science concepts, but only because 11th-grade mathematics is used in the problem sets which accompany physics. Some topics in physics obviously depend upon relatively advanced mathematical notions; most elementary topics do not. Geometry, traditionally a 10th-grade high school subject, has been successfully taught at various elementary levels. Questions of sequence are still relevant; just because you *can* offer a subject earlier or later in the curriculum sequence for any or all students does not mean you *should*. Some blurring of sequences has already taken place. Algebra is offered at an earlier age; reading is now commonly taught in the senior high school.

Sequence within subjects is inconsistent. Our goals almost always talk of "building and maintaining" skills in the various subjects. Yet, especially at the high school level, we often have a "stop-and-go" curriculum. In mathematics, for example, non-college students rarely study any mathematics after the nineth grade. There is no *educational* reason for this lapse; but present *organizational* alternatives demand that a subject be taught five hours per week or not at all. If curriculum sequences are to be more educationally valid, students must have the opportunity to study in each major curriculum area each year, though for substantially differing times and in different arrangements, depending upon their interests and abilities.

INDIVIDUAL STUDENT ATTENTION

Individual attention diminishes through the elementary grades, reaches a low point during senior high school and college undergraduate years, and comes back to a level approximating the kindergarten degree of attention when a candidate reaches the final work for his doctorate. The assumptions which underlie this policy call for identification of the appropriate advisory relationship for teachers. These should be based upon educational considerations rather than organizational or administrative *de facto* relationships.

TIME

In the early development of education in our country the assumption was appropriately made that *more* education was needed. Yet *more*, in and of itself, is an inadequate basis for making intelligent decisions regarding educational offerings.

New conceptions of time are challenging the long established assumptions which have permeated elementary and secondary education. We now tend to organize school programs into rather arbitrary segments such as the school year, semester, course, and period. Too often we begin with units of time and then turn our attention to what will be placed within those units. It is appropriate to ask whether any such arbitrary time units should be identified at all. We should also ask whether all content at all levels should be taught to all pupils within a rigid, hardened time framework. Time can be easily adjusted to purposes if we think of it as a variable resource instead of a preordained absolute.

Other time facets should also be considered. The optimum length for a school day and a school year needs analysis. Different standards of open and closed campuses and set school hours could be developed. Schools might be opened for longer periods of time, but students, depending upon their experience, might not be required to come and go at set times.

FLEXIBLE SCHEDULING

To avoid limits on the curriculum because of time restrictions, new organizational concepts are being tried. Flexible scheduling has received considerable attention. It allows for different combinations of teachers and students, provides for new dimensions in the development of individualized instruction, and encourages different levels of student responsibility in independent study. Greater variation in class size and period length is made possible. Instruction in large groups can be presented as appropriate; small groups of students can gather with a teacher for discussion; and individual students can practice or pursue ideas on their own with teachers available to help when needed. Length of class time, class size, sequence of studies, and the organization of instruction can differ for each subject and for each student. The impact of flexible scheduling has been primarily at the secondary level. Elementary schools are currently examining flexible scheduling alternatives: scheduling resource centers, instituting individual study time, and developing cooperative staff arrangements.

SELF-CONTAINED SCHOOL DAY

Our objective is to create a school day which provides a variety of learning experiences for pupils, contact with a wealth of ideas and materials, and a significant amount of personal encouragement from the teachers. By eliminating the assumption that homework is a necessary and desirable part of the educational system, thereby bringing individual work within the context of the school day, a closer monitoring of learning becomes possible. The discouragement of learning something wrong and having to relearn it can be avoided, and socioeconomic differences which make it more difficult for certain groups of students to accomplish homework become less important. Students are no longer left to their own resources to understand a hastily explained assignment. Teachers are no longer limited to assigning individual work that requires only those resources which can be counted upon to be available at home. Perhaps the establishment of resource centers for individual and independent study at school and the provision of time within the school day for their use will eliminate homework entirely as an obsolete educational notion.

FACILITIES

Facilities are an integral part of present innovation. Issues here are permanence, adaptability, and aesthetics. The goal is maximum adaptability of facilities with minimum financial outlay. Often a combination of highly specialized facilities will provide for more educational adaptability than will multi-use facilities. Facility limitations discourage innovation. Current innovations call for facilities for individual study, teacher offices, open laboratories, and sites for different kinds of student research. Planning is also necessary so that facilities may serve diverse community activities, summer school, adult education, and extended school days. Since programs will continue to change, we should plan facilities which will not freeze current programs in concrete and mortar.

Schools need to be planned which will accommodate new technologies. The role of programmed learning is not yet determined. In some instances, programmed learning has assumed the full burden of instruction in given course materials; in other instances it has been used to supplement teaching; and it has also been used as a remedial device. Similar experiments with computer-based learning will come soon.

FINANCE

The sources and amounts of financial support for the schools is not a concern for this panel. Of importance here is the expenditure of available resources. The emphasis has long been on annual "per pupil cost," how much money it costs to keep one pupil in school for one year. The description of a "learning unit cost" would be more educationally relevant. A "learning unit" would be defined in terms of *specific perfor-*

mance. For example, "level one in reading" would include a specified level of performance in reading skills such as vocabulary recognition, reading speed, and comprehension. Research would indicate the financial resources needed to obtain that level of performance for students of different ability levels and educational experience. This cost would vary with alternative technological devices and under different instructional situations. Learning units would be independent of time. Some districts would elect to concentrate "level one in reading" into 15 months of instruction; other districts, perhaps with different circumstances, might elect to take double that time for most students. The time would also differ widely for individual students within each situation. The advantage of thinking of "learning unit cost" rather than annual "per pupil cost" is that it focuses on the level of learning, not the maintenance of children in school. Communities can make conscious decisions about the intensity of learning units they wish to support. This will provide a more direct basis for evaluation of needed financial equalization as a district can point to experience with student and community factors influencing comparative "learning unit cost."

CONCLUSIONS

Innovation in elementary and secondary education is not the property of any one group. School systems must have the freedom to innovate. State departments of education must develop legal and operational structures which encourage alternatives. Legislative bodies must make funds available for research and experimentation. Communities must place more premium on exploration of new ideas and procedures. Teachers, administrators, educational innovators at all levels must be given the right to be wrong.

The following structure is suggested for discussion:

1. *Advanced research centers.* These centers would be analogous to the advanced research centers of a number of industrial complexes where study is not limited to the immediate practicability of ideas. Research staff would have a free run to investigate new ideas. Such research facilities need not be exclusively "laboratory oriented" but would include experimental schools providing real student and teacher populations available for the testing of innovations.

2. *Experimental application centers.* Innovative programs could be tested. Curriculum areas, school organization, staff use, time variables, administrative structures and other wide-ranging studies would be appropriate for such experimental investigations. These activities would be supported as specific areas of inquiry, but without consideration of prac-

tical restraints or economic considerations. The difference between the experimental application laboratories and the advanced research laboratories would be that the advanced research laboratories would not limit their staff to particular areas of inquiry whereas the experimental application laboratories would have a specific focus.

3. *Developmental centers.* These groups would be responsible for taking procedures and programs from the experimental centers and making economic determinations of feasibility, considering the training of staff for their use, and developing models of implementation.

4. *Dissemination centers.* Dissemination facilities would systematically provide for familiarization and adoption of innovation on a widespread basis.

Our part in the course of educational innovation offers exciting possibilities for responsible action. The contribution of each citizen is necessary if we are to continue in a democratic environment where freedom to grow is a major value. We are a part of the changing times, and we must learn to live with it, to direct it, and to gain from it. America has pioneered frontiers in mass education that have contributed substantially to the growth and maturation of our democracy. The emphasis has been on the education of all the children of all the people. But even as the physical frontiers have pushed into new dimensions, our educational frontier must be raised to an ever higher base of quality in education. The search for quality will demand approaches, techniques and systems as different from the tools of mass education as the ether of space differs from the rails of iron that bound together a new Nation.

A NEW DESIGN
FOR INDIVIDUAL LEARNING

B. Frank Brown, the author of the following article, has distinguished himself not only by advocating change but also by putting his ideas into practice. He is the author of The Nongraded High School *and a member of the White House Panel for Research and Educational Development. As the principal of Melbourne High School, Melbourne, Florida, he has become known nationally for making his high school nongraded and for emphasizing individual learning by providing students with opportunities to advance commensurate with their own abilities. The Melbourne innovations resulted in an increase in its student entrance into college from 40 percent to 70 percent and a decrease in the number of its dropouts to the low rate of 4 percent. In*

this article Brown makes a strong appeal for innovation in the
organization and curriculum of the school. He centers his atten-
tion on three important areas of innovation aimed at achieving
individualized learning: nongradedness, intellectual inquiry, and
independent study.

B. Frank Brown

Journal of Secondary Education (*October 1962*), 368–375. *Reprinted*
by permission of the Journal of Secondary Education.

What is one to say to the putative child in the fully automated school of
the future who says to his classmate, "The only way you can get any attention around here is to bend your IBM card"?

If he does bend the card, the child will be punished for non-
conformity. He will be given a new card which has been punched with
an extra hole. He doesn't go to see the principal. There may not even be
a principal. The school's administrator might well be an IBM program-
mer. In an era in which individuals may be replaced by machines—in
fact are being replaced—the challenge to the schools is incredible. We
are faced with the job of educating more students than ever before and
doing it better and more quickly. School administrators can profit universally from a bit of wisdom in *Alice in Wonderland* to the effect that,
"You have to keep running just to keep up."

The complex matrix of automation and cybernation will bring the
need for gainfully employed individuals down dramatically. As cybernation expands its domain both blue collar workers and displaced service
workers must learn new skills not likely to be cybernated in the future.
The provocation for a new kind of flexible education is enormous.

While man is reaching new pinnacles in science and technology,
education is still pedestrian. The first school was started nearly 2400
years ago and the educational enterprise has made little progress since.
In an era of rapid and swiftening change, a pedestrian school system will
have about as much impact as a feather falling on velvet.

Education has failed to match the challenges of this century. There
has been too much housekeeping in administration. The routine of running the school—the pure cussedness of the place—has had priority. The
image of administrivia reflects "window shade" and "chalkboard" men
rather than dynamic leaders. We must be done with organization jug-
gling. The accordion plat is pretty well stretched—we can't stretch it any
more. We must stop running the schools as in the era when "fall out"
meant nothing more ominous than losing one's place in the ranks.

THE NEED FOR IMAGINATIVE ORGANIZATION
AND PROCESSES

We have innovated cautiously, taking baby steps where giant steps are indicated. Instead of experimenting boldly with promising new orthodoxies, our innovations have been introduced with trepidation and caution. The bravery with which schools introduce new heresies can be compared to the quavering whistle of a man taking a short cut through a cemetery at midnight in the dark of the moon. Experimentation must become so much a part of the educational enterprise that as soon as a school has a good thing going, it must begin planning to make it obsolete. We cannot start out to be experimental and then let our new and exciting programs become fixed. When we do this, we cease being experimental and become hardened to the experiment. We must take care that promising new heresies do not become dull new orthodoxies. We must get used to being on the cutting edge. To paraphrase Browning: "A man's reach must exceed his grasp or what's a heaven for?" And a youngster's scope must exceed his skills, or what is an education for?

Where does the conventional principal fit into this scheme of things? We can be sure only that if we kow-tow to present adequacies, we are lost. Conventional administration is being swept from the educational scene as the period of blandness and calm comes to an end. Multi-varied action is required, and it is suggested that this action be hung on three prongs of concern. These are non-gradedness, intellectual inquiry, and independent study.

THE NON-GRADED INNOVATION

I would like to focus on intellectual development. If it is fashionable to have a slim waistline, can it not also become fashionable to be bright? Along with the new emphasis upon physical education, driver education got into the schools with relative ease. It is my hope that intellectual education will not have to wait too long outside the school yard.

The big obstacle to a new kind of intellectual Gulf Stream is the graded lockstep, the most pernicious pedagogical device ever invented. The idea of grouping children chronologically into grades is medieval. It was first conceived in a gymnasium in the Middle Ages. The graded plan was introduced in this country in 1848. Overnight the innovation caught fire and in no time the schools of America moved from no system at all to nothing but system. In all fairness it should be stated that the plan of dividing the learning process into 12 areas, called grades, was admirably suited to the 19th century; but the graded school is simply not relevant to 1962. In the age of space, the most important thing to be achieved pedagogically is freedom of the imagination. Grades have been a promissory note of the education field for a century and it is high time that the bank called them in. If administrators weren't so conventional, graded schools would long ago have gone up in a mushroom cloud.

A hundred years after the grade was invented, we are still grouping all youngsters in the first grade when they are six years of age. This is educational nonsense, and about as effective as grouping children by the length of their legs. As an organization, the grade has reduced the school to a genteel middle-browism. The administrator has become a caretaker. There is so much housekeeping in the administration of graded schools that the principal's job is largely concerned with bells, and schedules, and lockers, and ledgers. Learning has been so incidental that we have never even developed a theory of instruction. In graded schools we march boys and girls towards diplomas in lockstep conformity while their abilities and ambitions are shaped and colored as differently as pebbles on a beach. The idea that all 10th grade students are the same and should read the same books and study the same materials is educational nonsense. Some youngsters must be allowed to escape forward to enjoy the excitement of self-propelled and self-reliant learning. Those who fall behind must have work geared to their academic pace. The grade is too inflexible for this kind of learning. It is immobile and sticky like the "tar baby."

Perhaps it is too much to ask that a school stimulate the imagination and creativity of every student. All I am asking is that the schools not make children less creative by making them all read the same books, hear the same lectures, and do the same homework just because they are the same age. It has lately become apparent that the slowest student in the school, as well as the brightest, is capable of things that we have never dreamed he could do. Both slow and fast are slowed down because they are prisoners of each other in lockstep education. Until one breaks up grades, he does not realize how futile it is to be teaching a group of youngsters the same material merely because they happen to be the same age.

Learning is a many-splintered thing. The educational enterprise should have multiple paths. Instead we have been saying, "Here—take a card—take any card—take this card," and with a stacked deck we have been sending students down a single path. Non-grading is highly desirable for the bright students. For the dull ones it is essential. The way to treat the slow is the same as we treat the fast. If we treat one properly, then we treat the other properly. We should not educate them together merely because they were born in the same 365 day period.

There is nothing difficult or even new about ungrading. Athletics and Band have long been non-graded. In the effort to have a bigger band or a better football team, the grade lockstep was broken in these areas years ago. By contrast, academic subjects which are less passionate matters have remained frozen to the grade. The result is that schools are now suffering from an academic arteriosclerosis—a sort of intellectual hardening of the arteries. Yet if the IBM machines which group youngsters mixed some up, or if the textbooks got mixed up and pupils took English 12 before English 11, it wouldn't make a great deal of difference in académia.

Let me illustrate how rigid subject placement deters learning with the case of a 3rd grade teacher whose classroom I visited recently. A very excellent elementary school teacher was bursting with pride as she demonstrated the skill of her youngsters in dealing with arithmetic problems, particularly in the area of short division. Pridefully concluding the lesson, the teacher, bubbling with enthusiasm, said, "You know, I believe that they are ready for long division." "Why don't you try it?" I asked. "Oh," said the teacher, "that doesn't come until the 5th grade." By the same token many 9th graders are capable of doing 12th grade work but the system requires that they first finish grades 9, 10, and 11 in chronological order.

The schools today must not only be on the cutting edge of curriculum change, they must keep cutting and not let the blade get dull. As educators we should relinquish our role as hucksters of tradition and become warriors of the imagination. It was Einstein who gave us the viable notion that imagination is more important than knowledge, and freedom of the imagination is the most important thing to be achieved pedagogically. In America we have the peculiar notion that a thing is good merely because we have been doing it for a long time. This is reflected in the schools which are both the inheritors and prisoners of a lengthy tradition. Our curriculum was largely developed in the 19th century and much of it has a "built-in" obsolescence. Grades should long ago have been retired on a pension. I am not asking that we be slam-bang up-to-date, only that we come up to 1946. We have tried to open young minds with the two-edged can openers of "drill" and "grill." The school's emphasis should be placed upon the student rather than upon the subjects to be studied. The school will then adapt itself to the students' rate of learning rather than the placement of subjects in the curriculum.

The question frequently arises as to how quickly a school can reorganize away from the graded concept. For the iconoclast who is willing to drive all the sacred cows out of the barnyard at one fell swoop, the new organization can be planned in the summer and instituted in the fall. For the less venturesome I suggest the "spin out" approach. This is a technique whereby you introduce a new practice alongside an old and the cataclysm of the new spins out the old. With the "spin out" approach the school simply ungrades its top students and its bottom students. Superior youngsters are always ready to move and the slower group will welcome a breathing spell in which subject matter is geared to their rate of learning. Once introduced, the viability of non-gradedness will spin out of existence the system of grades.

We are educating young people who will have active lives of from 60 to 70 years and most of it in the 21st century. To meet this challenge, the goal of the school then is to come out with individuals who are adaptable. If we fail in this goal our society will be too rigid to deal with the future. Yet we cling tenaciously and securely to the graded school organization which is like an ice tray guaranteed to freeze into rigidity anything that is put into it.

INTELLECTUAL INQUIRY

In this era of surging culture not only the organization but also the process of education must change. We have weaved the secondary school curriculum with looms of finite size. Our efforts have concentrated upon infinitesimal problems, such as how we can get the grocery store out of arithmetic. Our concentration must be expanded to the broad universe of intellectual inquiry. This is a majestic ideal and a surprisingly new one. The schools should cease giving the impression that the body of learning is a closed group of facts. Education must surpass the outlook that knowledge is something that can be dealt with and solved like an algebra problem.

If education is to become the big instrument of change in this epoch of rapidly expanding intellectual horizons, a new dimension—the cultivation of inquiring minds—must be added. The school and all in it must oppose the out-moded system of the teacher providing authoritative answers to questions. Teachers must cease the endless routine of asking questions to which they have pat answers. To garner motivation we must marshal some significant questions. In too many classrooms questions are no more than an exchange between the teacher and the student. The process implies that learning can be transacted like dry goods across a counter. The teacher who keeps his mouth shut for 10 minutes may be doing his best teaching! The classroom performance which has been structured around a feed-back of passive citation of facts must move toward a problem-solving atmosphere.

The new high value then is on inquiry. This is a shift in intent. What is inquiry? In its simplest form inquiry is curiosity linked to action. It means new and deeper perceptions for the individual. In its ultimate form, it leads to the development of traits of imagination and creativity and eventually to new discoveries for science and the humanities. Pressures of conformity have educated students away from the process of asking questions. Perhaps the greatest offense to original research and individual study is the encyclopedia, and yet this is the best stocked item in the school libraries. This medium reports factually on assimilated data. As an instrument of research even for young children, it is a straw in the wind. To the marriage of the child and his mind it is a dubious dowry. Students throughout the length and breadth of the land copy and paraphrase from encyclopedias hour after monotonous hour. In the face of complete inadequacy, the encyclopedia remains the chief source of information in most schools. For remedy, it is suggested that the encyclopedias be taken off the library shelves before school opens in September. About mid-semester they may be slipped quietly back into place—one volume at a time. In the meantime students will have been weaned away from compendious types of data and will have discovered other and more original sources of information.

Students must be taught to analyze important and erudite monographs weighted with conflicting opinion. They must be rigorously exposed to interpretive study. They must learn that there are always more questions than there are answers, but they also must learn that quest for questions and for answers is exciting, vital, and worthy of a life's dedication. I am not interested in bringing the level of the schools up to *Life Magazine*. We must set our sights high and if we fail, fail honorably.

The encyclopedia is only one of a number of highly muscled ways of operating which must be overcome. Another large obstacle to intellectual inquiry is the lack of imaginative textbooks and materials. Current printed materials are oriented to the jawbone of the teacher rather than the mind of the student. New and thought-provoking materials designed to stimulate the mind must be devised if we are to reach our goal.

In an exotic new world of creativity the role of the teacher must change. Our present conception of the teacher's function is epitomized in 18th century poetry which says, about the schoolmaster—

> *And still they gazed*
> *And still their wonder grew*
> *That one small head*
> *Could carry all he knew.*

No longer can one small head carry all that a student must learn. The build-up of knowledge is staggering. With knowledge being doubled every decade, we must abandon the fruitless task of trying to cover facts and shift the emphasis to the development of traits of curiosity, intellectual inquiry, and intuitive thinking.

When we speak of discarding the teaching of facts, we are talking about something which is just a cut above football, mother, and the United States Marines. The methodology of teaching facts is counted by many people as among the first ten American blessings. In the past our subject matter has dealt only with candidly honest subjects. We must now reckon also with approximations and we must face the stark fact that the techniques of instruction in America's schools reflect an appalling lack of creativity. The dogmas of the quiet past are inadequate for the stormy present.

The best definition of the teacher is still in the dialogues of Socrates where the teacher acts in the function of a midwife. Schools are made for learning—not teaching. The teacher's job then changes from one of imparting knowledge to one in which he delivers learning. The role of a teacher shifts from a dispenser of knowledge to a remover of road blocks. The teacher moves to the sidelines and becomes a catalyst. The era calls for a ground swell in this direction. We are moving then from the shibboleth of memorized learning towards intellectual inquiry.

EDUCATION BY APPOINTMENT

We come then to our third innovation—Education by Appointment. This may well be the most promising new heresy of them all. Unconventional space arrangements must be made in the school, allowing students to work in solitude with an increasing degree of independence. In this arrangement students see teachers on a consultative basis, by appointment. In the reduction of classroom contact hours, the school's image becomes multi-dimensional. Students receiving their education by appointment assume a larger share of responsibility for their learning, giving thrust to the idea of research and individual work in the high school.

Since the stern demands of our era can best be met through training individuals in research and independent study, schools should plan an increasing amount of small spaces for larger numbers of students to enter into these activities. The only rigid space in the school plant of tomorrow should be the individual carrels for students. The rest of the physical plant should consist of flexible and malleable spaces.

As modern business has dealt with the characteristics of the "organization man," the school must now deal with the "organization student." To do this, the entire educational process must turn on the idea of independent study. Make independent study interesting and attractive so that each child will no longer be afflicted with groupism. Once introduced in a school, the process of Education by Appointment acts like a cataclysm as it spins out the old organization of groupiness and togetherness.

We must also revise the lost art of heuristics. Heuristics is derived from the Greek word *heuriskein* meaning "to discover." We need a Pandora's box full of heuristic questions for students in independent study.

Benjamin Franklin, through independent study, learned a great deal about science, something about the style of prose, and six foreign languages. So will school students in independent study, behaving elegantly, recognize elegance when it occurs. The intention of independent study does not imply a great emphasis upon programmed learning. The student needs, as Franklin did, open-ended rather than Skinnerian education.

Universally, teachers have smugly drawn the lines around what Johnny can learn. It is when Johnny moves outside the lines that the teacher feels uncomfortable. He gets the uneasy feeling that he may have thrown the baby out with the bath water. The result has been a tendency in the self-contained classroom to keep the lines tightly drawn. In independent study there must be no lines. Most students will acquire greater knowledge in some areas than that possessed by the teacher.

Each individual is a unique event and the rubric of the learning process must be redesigned for the individual. In the self-contained classroom the individual has been *e pluribus unum* or just one among many to the teacher. About the only place that the individual is worse off than in the self-contained classroom is in the mind of the anthropologist where he is about as significant as a gene.

By way of summary I would like to emphasize that the process of education and its direction must now be viewed in the setting of an exotic new world. We can no longer get by with variations of the old theme. The thrust which has been in the direction of education for an epoch of stability must be re-phased to education for an era of rapid and swiftening change. The schools which in the past have neither accommodated nor consented to change must now reverse the process. As educators we must develop a strategy for change. We must build a program on a dimension with an open end. Consequently—

1. We must move from the self-contained classroom to the self-contained school.

2. We must move from optimum grade placement to variable grade placement.

3. We must move from grouping of children towards grouping of teachers.

4. We must move from groupiness for all to solitude for many.

5. We must move from the self-contained classroom to independent study.

6. And, finally, with blandness gone from the educational enterprise, we must move from education in the mass to education by appointment.

COOPERATIVE TEACHING:
Definitions and Organizational Analysis

In the previous article Brown pointed to the discontent with the self-contained classroom. In this selection educator Judson T. Shaplin focuses attention on the discontent with the self-contained teacher. Shaplin, one of the leading researchers in the area of cooperative teaching, believes that the issue of team organization is no less important than statements of aims or objectives in education. "When we talk of team organization," Shaplin states, "we are talking about the basic conditions of work for the teacher, about the human organization for the accomplishment of objectives and goals, about the basic ways in which teacher and pupils will work together." The author distinguishes between team teaching and cooperative teaching and brings the student up-to-date on the terminology and the organization involved in cooperative teaching.

Judson T. Shaplin

The National Elementary Principal (*January 1965*), *14–20. Reprinted by permission of* The National Elementary Principal. *Copyright* © *1965, Department of Elementary School Principals, National Education Association. All rights reserved.*

My assignment in this article is to define and to describe the components of cooperative teaching, including team teaching. I will also attempt to make an organizational analysis of team teaching and to make comparisons with other types of school organization, both past and present. Finally, I will comment upon the future potential of team organization.

COOPERATIVE TEACHING

In this generation in American education, there appears to be a widespread increase in the amount of cooperative or collaborative activity among teachers, particularly of activity directly connected with classroom teaching. In the preceding generation, there had been a professional focus upon influencing teacher behavior through group activities: study committees, curriculum committees and workshops, in-service programs, etc. This approach persists, but with the added phenomenon of increased interaction between teachers at the classroom level. Though this collaboration and cooperation takes many diverse forms, there appear to be certain persistent themes, all of which reflect a deep discontent with the standard organization of the school on the basis of the self-contained teacher and the self-contained classroom.

One persistent theme is the desire of teachers to spend more time teaching those subjects or in those areas in which they are more interested, more highly specialized, or more talented. This leads to an *exchange of functions* between teachers; for example, one teacher may teach all of the arithmetic in two classes, the other might handle social studies.

A second theme is the desire of teachers to achieve greater flexibility in the grouping of pupils, at the same time maintaining economy of teaching time. This leads to the *exchange of pupils* between teachers; for example, the combining of the gifted students of two classes into a group taught by one teacher, while the other teacher handles the rest of the children, or similar arrangements for handling reading groups.

A third theme is that of *efficiency of instruction* by *combining classes* for certain purposes. If two teachers are planning the same acitivity with pupils—and there is no apparent disadvantage in doing this in a larger group—why not combine the classes, releasing one of the teachers for other work? There may be a further advantage if one of the teachers has a greater talent for doing this particular task.

A fourth theme is a consequence of the first three. If teachers exchange teaching functions or pupils or combine classes, then there is a need for *joint planning and evaluation*. Two or more teachers are now teaching the same children, not entirely separate groups, and the teachers must plan the program together, develop a schedule, and share their evaluations of pupil progress within the areas of collaboration. As we examine this kind of cooperation or collaboration between teachers, we find every degree of organization from informal permissive cooperation, often ephemeral in time, to carefully defined formal organizations, the latter often labeled *team teaching*. Robert H. Anderson has recommended that the generic term *cooperative teaching* be applied to all these forms of cooperation and collaboration among teachers, including team teaching.[1]

TEAM TEACHING OR TEAM ORGANIZATION

Elsewhere, I have given the following definition of team teaching: *"Team Teaching is a type of instructional organization, involving teach-*

[1] Robert H. Anderson, "An Overview of Team Teaching," *Team Teaching at the Elementary School Level—Report of an Invitational Workshop Sponsored by The Perkins and Will Partnership, Architects,* May 1964, pp. 10–11.

*ing personnel and the students assigned to them, in which two or more
teachers are given responsibility, working together, for all or a significant
part of the instruction of the same group of students."* [2] This definition
was based on the common characteristics displayed by projects which
called themselves team teaching and was intended as an inclusive, general statement. The wording of the definition was intended to carry
rather specific meanings: that the team is an organization with formal,
legitimate status; that certain responsibilities are delegated to the team,
particularly the responsibility for the scheduling, grouping, and instruction of a shared group of students; that a team implies a close working
arrangement between two or more professional teachers in planning, instruction, and evaluation; and that the relationship with the students is a
sustained one, affecting a substantial portion of the students' programs.
The definition does not require specialization in teaching function, the
hierarchical ordering of team personnel, the improvement of supervisory
arrangements in teaching, the utilization of nonprofessional aides for
teachers, or the expanded use of mechanical aids to teachers, though all
these were noted as directions which many teams have taken.

A number of definitions of team teaching have now appeared in
print, offering some disagreement with the definition given here. Goodlad has suggested that team teaching is characterized by three things: 1)
a hierarchy of personnel, 2) differential staff functions, and 3) flexible
kinds of grouping.[3] Anderson agrees that a hierarchical structuring of
personnel is essential and adds that a minimum of three or more teachers
is required to develop a team with sufficient maneuverability to make a
difference.[4] Bair and Woodward also question whether two teachers,
working together, can be called a team.[5] They prefer a description of
team teaching given by Dean and Witherspoon which stresses "the essential spirit of cooperative planning, constant collaboration, close unity,
unrestrained communication, and sincere sharing," rather than details of
structure and organization.[6] Singer, affirming a size of two or more

[2] Judson T. Shaplin and Henry F. Olds, Jr. (eds.), *Team Teaching* (New
York: Harper & Row, Publishers, 1964), p. 15.

[3] John I. Goodlad, *Planning and Organizing for Teaching*, National Education Association, Project on the Instructional Program of the Public Schools
(Washington, D.C.: The Association, 1963), pp. 81–82.

[4] Anderson, pp. 14, 76.

[5] Medill Bair and Richard G. Woodward, *Team Teaching in Action*
(Boston: Houghton Mifflin Company, 1964), p. 24.

[6] Stuart E. Dean and Clinnette F. Witherspoon, *Team Teaching in the
Elementary School*, U.S. Department of Health, Education, and Welfare, Office
of Education, Education Brief No. 38 (Washington, D.C.: Government Printing Office, January 1962), p. 4.

teachers, includes in his definition that the team must take advantage of the special competencies of the team members.[7]

Perhaps the resolution of these difficulties of definition and description comes with Paul Woodring's comment that team teaching is a misnomer because "the teaching, at any given moment, is done by an individual rather than by a team." [8] He suggests that team teaching might more appropriately be called "team organization and planning." I would shorten this to *team organization,* since planning is implied in the term organization. This renaming of *team teaching* to *team organization* fits my earlier attempt to develop a theoretical rationale for team teaching based upon sociological and administrative theory and the effort by Olds to develop a taxonomy for the description of team teaching.[9]

THE TEAM AS A SMALL GROUP

Team organization involves the formation of small working groups, organized on a formal basis, for the accomplishment of certain goals. From a sociological view, teams are *secondary* or *instrumental* groups, in contrast to *primary* groups. In secondary groups, the emphasis is upon task orientation, and evaluation is based upon principles of universalism and achievement; whereas *primary* groups emphasize localism, friendship, kinship, and other personal factors. Viewed as a social system, following Getzels and Thelen, the *nomothetic* dimension, or rational organization of human behavior toward certain desired goals, is stressed in a working team.[10] Careful attention is given to the definition of goals and to the creation of positions and roles appropriate for reaching the goals. For a variety of reasons, it is possible for such a working group to change into a primary group with stress upon the affective needs of the individuals in the group, particularly if the goals are unclear or the related roles poorly defined.

Since teams in teaching are usually composed of a relatively small number of individuals, from two to six in most situations, they have ca-

---

[7] Ira J. Singer, "What Team Teaching Really Is," David W. Beggs, III (ed.), *Team Teaching—Bold New Venture* (Indianapolis: Unified College Press, 1964), p. 16.

[8] Paul Woodring, "Reform Movements from the Point of View of Psychological Theory," *Theories of Learning and Instruction,* Sixty-third Yearbook, Part I, National Society for the Study of Education (Chicago: University of Chicago Press, 1964), p. 292.

[9] Shaplin and Olds, Chapters 3 and 4.

[10] J. W. Getzels and H. A. Thelen, "The Classroom as a Unique Social System," *The Dynamics of Instructional Groups,* Fifty-ninth Yearbook, Part II, National Society for the Study of Education (Chicago: University of Chicago Press, 1960), pp. 53–82.

pability for the accomplishment of only a small number of limited goals. One of the major confusions in the team teaching movement has been the tendency to claim all-embracing objectives and goals, on a grandiose scale, phrased in the most general terms. The goals of a team must be consistent with its size and capability. Given the multiplicity of goals available in American education, goals which are often conflicting, we can see that team organizations will vary significantly in their choice among these goals, with important effects, then, upon the structural variables chosen for the organization of the team.

It should be recognized, also, that there are almost infinite possibilities for the structural organization of small working groups in teaching. Olds has made a start in the analysis of the structural variables which can be chosen in developing a team organization.[11] The team, as a small group, is located structurally within a larger context, including such factors as gradedness, departmentalization, and available financial resources, all of which place limitations upon the team. The amount of autonomy given to the team for the control of pupil and teacher assignments of time, tasks, and space locations may vary enormously, and the same restriction applies to the delegation of responsibility for curriculum decisions. Teams may also be organized on differing principles of authority structure, some emphasizing a hierarchical system of authority based on either decision making processes or on substantive specialization and others maintaining equalitarian or collegial principles. Other important variables are the type and extent of procedural and substantive coordination built into the team organization.

Viewed in this context of the team as a small, goal-oriented, working group, the basic question confronting school administrators is "What problems can be approached through team organization?" not "Shall I *do* team teaching?" The selection of reasonable objectives and goals comes first, in the context of unsolved problems. We should proceed then to an analysis of the goals which have been stated for team teaching, remembering always that we are faced with a choice among possible goals and that no one system of team organization can encompass *all* of the goals discussed here.

Following Talcott Parsons, I have divided my discussion into two sets of functions and goals, the *managerial* and the *technical*, with the full realization that managerial and technical functions and goals are closely interrelated.[12] In the discussion, I will also relate cooperative

[11] Shaplin and Olds, Chapter 4, "A Taxonomy for Team Teaching."

[12] Talcott Parsons, "Some Ingredients of a General Theory of Formal Organization," Andrew W. Halpin (ed.), *Administrative Theory in Education* (Chicago: Midwest Administrative Center, University of Chicago, 1958), pp. 40–72. (For an extended discussion, see Shaplin and Olds, pp. 71–98.)

teaching and team organization to other organizational plans, past and present.

The managerial functions we will consider here are of two types: first, those decisions regarding what educational services will be offered, what groupings of pupils will be made, and what the disposition of the teaching force will be with respect to pupil groups; and second, the decisions concerning what resources in the form of personnel, classrooms, books, and materials will be provided.

In most team organizations, there is a transfer of managerial functions from the principal and central staff to the team, particularly with respect to the grouping and scheduling of pupils and the assignment of teachers in accordance with their special interests and talents. This often leads to new divisions of labor, increased specialization, and a different distribution of authority. Exercise of these managerial functions requires skill and time on the part of team members. There are enormous increases in the amount of time required for planning, communication, coordination, and evaluation which may lead to a reduction in teaching time and productivity in dysfunctional teams.

Claims for enormously increased flexibility of pupil grouping and teacher assignments in teams are often greatly exaggerated. The basic restraints are the amount of school time, the number of pupils, and the number of teachers. These factors usually remain unchanged in team organization as compared with ordinary school arrangements, with the consequence that choice of one grouping arrangement within a team limits all subsequent choices. Rigorous priorities among choices are required, with a full knowledge of the consequences as compared with those inherent in possible alternative strategies.

In most of the major reorganization plans of the past, administrative control of pupil and teacher assignments was retained externally from the teacher group, and the teachers did not function in a team organization as here defined. In the platoon school or Gary Plan, developed by Wirt in 1900, teacher and pupil assignments were made by the administration. The same condition applied in the Winnetka and Dalton Plans developed in the 1920's, though the teachers were much more involved in applying the standards which moved the pupils on to new groups. The present Dual Progress Plan follows a pattern similar to these early plans. One exception is the Cooperative Group Plan developed by James F. Hosic in the early 1930's, which had a short life in the New York City schools and adjacent areas.[13] If this plan were in existence today, it

[13] J. F. Hosic, *The Cooperative Group Plan: Working Principles for the*

would be called team teaching and would be outstanding in terms of its goals and detailed plans. The delegation of these managerial functions to the teaching force is a relatively *new* and *distinctive* aspect of team organization, with this one abortive predecessor, and has not been a persistent theme in American education. I believe this new theme is emerging because despite persistent shortages, our corps of teachers is now trained to the highest educational level in our history, and we can foresee a more effective use of this talent.

Let us now turn to the second type of management functions, called by Parsons the *procurement* function, in which our concern is with decisions affecting personnel and material resources available for teaching. Here team organization is used by the administration to create more attractive careers within teaching, to recruit subprofessional technical and clerical personnel to relieve teachers from these duties, and to create units of sufficient size to allow the economical allocation of technical aids to teaching. The implications for learning by the children are more remote.

The creation of specialist posts within teaching and of a hierarchy of authority and responsibility within the teaching ranks accompanied by suitable rewards *might* make it possible for elementary and secondary school teaching to attract a higher proportion of able college graduates, particularly men, into long-term careers. The incentives offered in team organization, especially in hierarchical teams, differ from other schemes such as merit salary schedules in that increased rewards come with higher rank and position based on greater responsibility and specialization. A number of Eastern projects—particularly those involving the entire elementary school as in Lexington, Massachusetts, and Greenwich, Connecticut—have the creation of rank and position careers as important objectives.

Teams have also been used as a vehicle for attaching secretarial, clerical, and technical personnel to the schools on an economical basis, opening up a large reservoir of skilled labor for schools and relieving teachers of subprofessional duties. It is difficult to attach such personnel to individual teachers in an efficient, workable way; a team of some size—four or five members—is required to absorb an aide into a working, supervised situation without loss of teaching time or extra expense. Team organization is thus furthering the utilization of teacher aides started in Bay City, Michigan, and Fairfield, Connecticut, in the 1950's. A similar argument can be developed in regard to the use of audiovisual equipment and other technical aids to teaching. The difficulties of reaching individual classrooms with suitable equipment and materials can be

Organization of Elementary Schools (New York: Bureau of Publications, Teachers College, Columbia University, 1929).

overcome if a team is of sufficient size to command its own resources and provide economical utilization.

Technical functions include the development of the curriculum, the organization of instruction, the specific methods of teaching, and the assessment of the needs and progress of the students. In this area, the team teaching movement has created few new functions and goals. Rather, it has proposed new ways of organizing for the promotion of long persistent aims in American education: particularly the aims of greater specialization in teaching, the promotion of continuous individual progress in students, the coordination of various elements of the curriculum, and the flexible grouping of students in terms of interest, ability, and common purposes.

Team organizations thus have close kinship with past and present innovations which have had the same purpose of breaking the lockstep pattern of the graded, self-contained classroom school. Some teams share the interest in continuous individual pupil progress so notable in the Pueblo, the Winnetka, the Dalton plans, the more recent Dual Progress Plan, and the nongraded school movement. Others share the objective of specialized teaching prominent in the Gary Plan, the Dalton Plan, the "cultural electives" sector of the Dual Progress Plan, and the movement toward departmental organization. Still others share the values of the Core Curriculum movement, stressing the interrelationships between the subjects. Team organization then becomes a way of organizing for the accomplishment of some combination of these objectives.

Perhaps the greatest innovation in technical functions promoted by team organization is in the area of supervision—supervision from within the teaching force rather than from the administration or a special supervisory staff. Within some hierarchical teams—particularly those involving beginning teachers, interns, and apprentices—it is possible to vary teaching loads in accord with the teachers' energy, ability, and experience and to provide immediate, on-the-job evaluation and help.

It should be clear from this analysis that team organization per se is of necessity incompatible with only one form of school organization—the self-contained, single teacher classroom—and with any instructional plan dependent upon that organization. Team organization can be adapted to further the objectives of most other forms of organization and instructional plans. Teams can be formed within departments or can be used to achieve a degree of departmentalization in the absence of departments. A nongraded school can be organized on the basis of teams, as can the Dual Progress Plan.

THE FUTURE OF COOPERATIVE TEACHING
AND TEAM ORGANIZATION

What, then, is the future of cooperative teaching? Are we faced with a fad, fed on the educational discontents of the present generation, or can we anticipate a long-range reorganization of the schools?

With respect to cooperative teaching as described in the first pages of this article, I am confident that we are engaged in a long-range trend destined to increase. The discontent with the rigidities of the graded school is endemic. I predict a continued and gradual increase in cooperative teaching, including all the elements of pupil exchange, exchange of teacher functions, combined classes, and joint planning and evaluation, much of it on an informal permissive basis stimulated by the needs of the teachers themselves. Cooperative teaching is already characteristic of the organization of nursery schools and kindergartens; it is common in college instruction, particularly in the sciences, the languages, and in general education or common studies programs; and it is increasingly common at all levels of the elementary and secondary schools.

With respect to team organization in the more formal sense developed here, the road ahead is still rocky and tortuous. Sand and Thompson in a recent review make the following statement:

> These reviewers believe that the subject of this book—team teaching—is a relatively trivial issue when compared with the more fundamental problems of decision-making, establishing priorities for the school, selecting content, providing a balanced program, educating all youth including those not college bound, and improving the quality of learning experiences.[14]

I obviously do not believe that the issue is *trivial* relative to any statement of aims or objectives. When we talk of team organization, we are talking about the basic conditions of work for teachers, about the human organization for the accomplishment of objectives and goals, about the basic ways in which teacher and pupils will work together. Analysis of these issues cannot be trivial in any context, yet there are distinguished educators who state this view.

Sand and Thompson go on to place a very narrow interpretation upon team teaching, quite at odds with the positions taken in the book they were reviewing: "Specifically, it [team teaching] relates to horizontal organization, a system for dividing a given student population into

[14] Ole Sand and Margery Thompson, Review of *Team Teaching*, Judson T. Shaplin and Henry F. Olds, Jr. (eds.), *Harvard Educational Review*, **34** (Fall 1964), 601–602.

instructional groups and allocating these students to teachers." This statement, of course, discards the richness of potential for organization in teams, which I have tried to convey in this article, and indicates a growing tendency to narrow and sharpen the definition of team teaching in order to give it a definite structure and place. Both Anderson and Goodlad, previously cited, show this tendency in their insistence upon hierarchical structure and role differentiation. If this tendency is accepted, and the hierarchical, specialized team becomes *the* model for team teaching, I predict that the movement will fall of its own weight, as did Hosic's Cooperative Group Plan and other highly specific and detailed plans in the past.

The issue here is fundamental: Are we talking about basic principles of human organization into small working groups adapted in personnel and resources to the tasks they undertake, or are we talking about a standardized approach of a highly structured, prescribed team organization? I envision a flexible development of team organization, comparable to the complex and variable small-group organizations characteristic of business and industry. Viewed in this way, I think team organization is viable—it offers no specific answer but is a way of marshaling resources to tackle problems.

The most difficult problem facing the team teaching movement today is that of the clarification of goals. In the early stages of the movement, the tendency has been to claim that team teaching is the answer to the most general and all-encompassing problems: the teacher shortage, the improvement of instruction, the flexible grouping of pupils, and the proper utilization of teacher talent. As the bandwagon developed, schools have gone into team teaching for the sake of being in. Much of team teaching is organization for the sake of organization, with a mystical belief and confidence that team organization per se will solve problems, however undefined the problems may be. I am not sure that the movement has settled down to a more rational and sane course. In the present trajectory, it will become increasingly difficult to justify team teaching in terms of the learning by students.

Another ominous sign is the relative detachment of the team teaching movement from the various curriculum reform groups.[15] Team teaching organization is only rarely being used as a vehicle for the introduction of national curriculum reform programs or, if it is, this is not being reported. Characteristically, curriculum reform in teams is proceeding on a local basis, with enormous waste of energy. I doubt that the

[15] Judson T. Shaplin, "Team Teaching and the Curriculum," *Proceedings of the Annual Conference of the Educational Records Bureau*, October 1964.

present pace, requiring herculean efforts by teachers, can be sustained on a long-term basis. We need to build the connections between team organization and curriculum reforms for their mutual benefit.

The concept of a hierarchical structure among teachers, based on team organization, is perhaps the hardest for the teaching profession to accept. Notions of autonomy in the classroom and equality among teachers are widespread and strongly held, and hierarchical team organization is often viewed as threatening. This situation is complicated by the fact that the talents required in a hierarchical vision as well as in substantive fields, are often not yet fully developed in the teachers who hold the leadership posts, though these talents may be developing under the stimulus of the team.

In balance, I think that the future of team organization may be brighter than my pessimistic statements would indicate. The curriculum reform movement at the elementary school level is just gathering strength, and we still have a chance to use team organization for the implementation of the reforms. In addition, the overwhelming problems of educating the culturally deprived almost demand team organization, and a broad new front for team organization, with more specific aims and objectives, is opening. Team organization will have further chances to prove its worth.

TEACHING MACHINES AND CREATIVITY

Do teaching machines aid or stifle creative thinking? Ernest Hilgard, a distinguished professor of psychology and education, demonstrates in the following article the compatibility of programed learning with creativity. He cites the advantages of programed materials to the student and the teacher, discussing the role of the latter in understanding and utilizing technological advances in the classroom. Hilgard contends that teaching machines will not be a substitute for the good teacher. Indeed, as Skinner has said, "Any teacher who can be replaced by a machine should be." Hilgard terminates his essay by outlining what he believes teachers can do to help their pupils develop problem-solving abilities. It would be interesting for the reader to apply these suggestions in developing his lesson plans or to check, through his observations of teachers, the extent to which these suggestions have been used in fostering creativity.

Ernest R. Hilgard

Stanford Today (*Autumn 1963*), Series 1, No. 6. Reprinted with permission of the publisher. Copyright © 1963 by the Board of Trustees of Leland Stanford Junior University.

While the use of technological devices in education in the form of audio-visual aids (slides, motion pictures, electromagnetic tape, closed-circuit TV) is familiar, programmed learning is something essentially new, and a brief characterization of it may be in order for those who are unfamiliar with it. By a program is meant an orderly presentation of some subject-matter to be mastered, in the form of small steps, usually called "frames" because they were originally intended to be exposed in the "windows" of a teaching machine. Programmed books are now very common, without any machinery other than a piece of cardboard to cover the answers, but the term "frame" has persisted for the single item. At first each frame calls for a very easy answer, one that is suggested or prompted by the way in which the frame is worded. The student writes down his answer, then uncovers the correct response for comparison before proceeding to the next frame. He thus knows that he is learning, as he moves from frame to frame. New knowledge is gradually grafted upon earlier knowledge, until quite complex subject matter is mastered in this small-step manner. Various complexities are introduced; for example, a program that moves straight ahead from the easier to the more difficult, without any detours, has come to be called a *linear* program, while one that allows for alternative routes is called a *branching* program. By the use of modern computers many refinements are introduced, permitting the learner to ask questions of the machine, to call for other examples when he is confused, and so on. The main point is that this is not like the usual workbook, which tends to test or examine something previously learned, but it is a self-contained device for teaching. The rate at which the program unfolds is determined by the learner; a successful program is such that a learner going through it but a single time, at his own rate, is expected to have at least 90 per cent of his answers correct.

Programs are now available for the teaching of many college-level subjects (as well as subjects beginning with kindergarten). It is quite natural that the first expressed attitude of a college or university professor at the thought of using a teaching machine is one of alarm, if not of horror; the device seems to be the very worst form of mechanistic pedantry. However, it turns out that the program does not replace the teacher, but can hopefully free the teacher from routine exposition, and give time for doing the things that only a teacher can do. It differs from the mass-media methods in that it is essentially an individual method; it permits many of the advantages of the tutor, without the expense—usually un-bearable—that tutorial teaching involves.

Without going into the technical details, programmed learning has some of the following advantages that appeal to investigators interested in the psychology of learning:

1. Programmed learning recognizes *individual differences* by begin-ning where the learner is and by permitting him to proceed at his own pace. It is possible that programmed learning may succeed in reducing individual differences because of these features.

2. Programmed learning requires that the learner be *active*. Learn-ing by doing is an old educational adage, and it is still a good one. The teaching machine (or program in book form) fights the tendency for the student to be passive and inattentive by requiring his participation if the lesson is to move.

3. Programmed learning provides immediate *knowledge of results*. Whether because it provides reinforcement, reward, or cognitive feed-back (to use some of the ways in which experts talk about these mat-ters), there is abundant testimony that an instantaneous report of results is important in learning. It favors learning the right thing; it prevents re-peating and fixating the wrong answers.

4. Programmed learning emphasizes the *organized nature of knowl-edge* because it requires continuity between the easier (earlier) concepts and the harder (later) ones. Again, all learning theories have some place for meaningfulness, for understandable relationships, for assimilating the new to the familiar. The program builder cannot be totally arbitrary about content: he has to make one step fit the next and provide the hint or cue for the next. He has to examine the subject matter very carefully in order to find out what has to be known before something else can be learned, and he eliminates side issues that do not lead to cumulative learning.

5. Programmed learning provides *spaced review* in order to guaran-tee the high order of success that has become a standard requirement of good programs. Review with applications, if properly arranged, permits a high order of learning on the first run through the program.

6. Programmed learning reduces anxiety because the learner is not threatened by the task: he *knows he is learning* what is required, and gains the satisfaction that this knowledge brings. Lest this may seem to be a trivial observation, we need only to be reminded of the number of

students who have been so frustrated by lectures and examinations that they have never had the satisfaction of coming up to expectations; we have no way of knowing what price we have had to pay for this accumulated frustration.

There are many ways in which programmed learning can be fitted in with other kinds of teaching, just as lectures are supplemented by library work, projects, term papers, personal consultation, and laboratory exercises. It is not necessarily a matter of going over completely to programmed learning in order to take advantage of what it has to offer.

Universities in general (and Stanford is no exception) are unusually slow in adopting new technological aids to instruction. They rely heavily upon the time-honored lecture, accompanied with a minimum use of the blackboard. The other familiar technical aid is the laboratory, but this is often routine and dull, and tells little of what scientific research is really like. Grade schools and high schools have tended to pick up technological aids more quickly. They are ordinarily better equipped with motion picture projectors and teaching films than their college counterparts; anyone who has lectured about at leading colleges and universities can attest to the amount of fumbling that goes on if he wishes to show lantern slides or a sound film in some classroom other than the public auditorium. What applies to motion pictures applies also to closed-circuit television and the teaching machine. It is paradoxical that Stanford, a leader in electronics, computers, communication research, and the psychology of learning, should be one of the laggards in using the new knowledge for its own purposes of instruction. The individual instructor, even if willing, is baffled by new devices, and universities are surprisingly lacking in techniques of innovation by which those unfamiliar with new developments can learn about them and can find out about the steps that would be necessary to make use of them. This is less true in matters of research: somehow we find out about such aids as giant computers and how to use them. An important purpose of a university is to teach; it is strange that we do not take more seriously the kinds of aid that would make instruction increasingly effective.

Let me turn now to the teacher's role in the midst of the new technology. If through new technical devices, such as audiovisual aids and programmed learning, we free the teacher from routine instruction, from imparting information and questioning about facts and computations, then the teacher can face up to the essential tasks of inspiring, stimulating, and encouraging students to bring out the best they have to offer.

Following a distinction made by Professor Jerome Bruner of Harvard, teaching can go on in either the *expository* or the *hypothetical* mode. In the expository mode firm knowledge is communicated; it may be difficult, and the interrelationships intricate, so that skilled teaching is involved. Yet it is in this mode that good presentations via televised programs or motion pictures or a well-constructed program can serve very well. In fact, the "canned" presentation has the advantage that a great deal of time and effort can go into its preparation, ancillary materials (such as demonstrations of experiments, animated diagrams, maps, scenes from historical movies, etc.) can be woven into the presentation in a manner that the ordinary lecturer cannot afford in either time or expense. Some complete courses on film are proving very successful at the secondary school level, and they are beginning to be used at the college level as well. In the hypothetical mode learning is more of an adventure into the realm of possibility rather than established fact, how to attack a problem, to judge between alternatives, how to discover and invent. It is my contention that the highest success in teaching is in this mode, no matter how skillful and esthetically satisfying some expository teaching may be.

Another closely related distinction frequently made by psychologists is that between *convergent* and *divergent* thinking. Convergent thinking addresses itself to the logical problem of centering upon the correct solution of a problem; you may "beat around the bush" for a while, but in the end, you pluck the intended fruit. A standard mathematical proof is of this kind; the end-product of quantitative analysis in chemistry is of this kind. Divergent thinking, by contrast, is concerned with novelty, with the creation of products that are useful or beautiful, with original solutions; the end-products of this process are multiple, not single. It is not easy to train for good clear convergent thinking, but it is even more difficult to train for divergent, original, creative thinking. Here the skilled teacher has the advantage over technological aids, although not all teachers take full advantage of the opportunities that are open to them. The program-makers are not blind to the need for divergent thinking and they are at work on the programs encouraging such thinking. For example, it is possible to teach flexible thinking through programming by insisting on a second and different solution to a problem after one solution has been achieved. This is similar to what a good teacher does as one way of encouraging original thought; the superiority of the teacher in doing this cannot be assumed but must be shown to be superior to what the programmers can achieve.

Let me indicate some of the things that an able and alert teacher can do to help the student to become a problem-solver and a creator.

1. Problem-solving and creativity are open to those who have prepared themselves through knowledge and skill for such creation. Hence the teacher has obligations in exposition and training. It is important to note, however, that the complexities of modern knowledge are such that the student should not be asked to store in his head all the facts that he needs to think about complex problems. The teacher's role is to help him *to discover what facts he needs and to search them out for himself*. The formal program (in the teaching machine sense) is not usually designed with this in mind. Thus the dictionary habit, the encyclopedia habit, and the library-catalog habit are fully as important as memorized facts. Content becomes obsolete very quickly; knowing how to keep abreast never becomes obsolete.

2. While many kinds of problems can be solved through application of the appropriate computational formulas, the teacher's task is to make the student *alert to problems,* and to help him to learn *general aspects of problem-solving* that go beyond specific content. The puzzle-form (where there is one right answer to discover) classifies as convergent thinking, and can be taught readily by teaching-machine methods; but the full nature of problem-solving is harder to teach. Really good problem solvers, and among these I include research scientists, are able to see a problem where others do not see one, or are able to clarify a problem so that an attack upon it becomes manageable in the midst of a situation so complex that others are merely baffled.

3. In order to tolerate the frustrations along the way, prior to the thrill and excitement of discovery or creation, a student has to develop *confidence in his own capacities as a creative person*. There is no way short of engaging in inquiry and in creation, and receiving the rewards that come through creative efforts, for this confidence to be achieved. The teacher helps by acknowledging and celebrating *small* achievements, so that the larger ones can come in due time. The reverse of this is to belittle, to criticize adversely, to dig back in history to show that someone else did the same job earlier, to compare unfavorable with the work of a master. We are not all Galileos or Michelangelos or Shakespeares, yet each, in his own way, can find some satisfaction in creation. Maybe the first product will be a limerick instead of a sonnet, a carving in soap instead of in marble, a short computational procedure instead of a new proof, a cigar-box violin instead of one modeled after Stradivarius. Whatever the product, if it is one's own, it contributes to the picture of oneself as potentially original and creative. The lives of very distinguished men often show a *saga* from early youth of parental expectation of something out of the ordinary, creating a sense of destiny for great achievement; if this is present, the task of the teacher is easier, but when

it is not present the teacher can help to supply it. The teacher as model, as father-figure, as enthusiastic supporter and granter of hope, can never be replaced by a machine.

4. Finally, life is not lived in a sedentary world; while we value the work of the monk in his cell and the philosopher alone in his meditation (and perhaps modern life makes too little room for solitude and contemplation), there are values in learning to do intellectual work in interchange with others, sharing experiences and insights, trying ideas out on others, seeking and accepting their suggestions and criticisms. *The communication and interchange of ideas* is therefore part of what needs to be learned, even when education is conceived purely intellectually. Again it takes a skilled teacher to stimulate and guide group thinking. Beyond this, for effective social and community life we need those who learn to live with diversity, who can seek the compromises between factions that permit a common life to go on, who see individual behavior in terms of its consequences for others, who develop a sense of responsibility. There is no way to learn these aspects of the educated person but to participate responsibly in group processes. To leave these matters solely to the extracurricular life is to evade an important aspect of the educational process. Again the role of the teacher is evident.

By relieving the teacher of much that is routine, the technological aids to learning, including programmed learning, open the oppportunity for the teacher to devote more time to those aspects of education where the role of the teacher is paramount. Then the art of teaching will remain where it belongs, in the teacher as a person.

EDUCATIONAL TELEVISION AND CLASSROOM LEARNING

Does the use of educational television really improve classroom learning? Wilbur Schramm, communication research expert, deals with this issue by describing what research tells us about learning from instructional television. He raises six questions which are frequently asked about this medium and backs his responses to them by evidence from communication research. He then evaluates the major strengths and weaknesses of television as a teaching device and poses provocative questions, such as: Can television become a substitute for the teacher, and what is the place of television in a team teaching situation?

Wilbur Schramm

Educational Television: The Next Ten Years (*Stanford, Calif.: The Institute for Communication Research, 1962*), *pp. 61–71. Reprinted by permission of the author. Bibliographical citations have been eliminated here.*

THE CHIEF QUESTIONS

Beyond the basic problems of learning and attitudes, several questions are asked oftener than others about instructional television. Among these are:

1. *Is there any kind of student who profits more than other kinds from instructional television?* A bright student learns more than a slow student, a motivated student more than an unmotivated one, in almost any learning situation. But given equally bright, or equally motivated students, is there any level of ability or motivation at which learning by television is markedly superior or inferior?

On these problems the data are muddy. Here, for example, is at least a partial tabulation of the studies of mental ability as related to instructional television:

> *Fritz*, 1952. Military subjects at Fort Monmouth. Divided radio electronics students into high and low aptitude groups. Some of each group were taught by TV. Found no significant difference in scores of TV and non-TV groups when equated for ability.
> *Kanner, et al.*, 1954. Split both TV and non-TV groups of basic trainees at Camp Gordon into high and low aptitude groups. N.s.d. in high group, but 10 of 17 tests in low group favored TV; other 7 tests n.s.d.
> *Williams*, 1954. Taught four groups of students at University of Toronto by TV, radio, lecture and reading assignments, respectively. TV higher than lecture in high and low ability groups, but equal in average group.
> *Kumata*, 1958. Michigan State University students. Unable to reproduce Kanner's finding of superiority of TV instruction for low ability students.
> *Seibert*, 1958. Purdue University students in English composition. Found that low ability TV students compared less favorably with control group than did high ability TV students.
> *Seibert*, 1958. Purdue University students in freshman mathematics.

No important interactions between mental ability and method of instruction.

Macomber and Siegel, 1960. Miami University students in educational psychology, economics, physiology, zoology, and government. Breaking both TV and control groups by quartiles on mental ability, they found 1 significant difference out of 4 in top quartile —this in favor of TV group. In bottom quartile, found 2 significant differences out of 4 in favor of TV, 1 in favor of control. Breaking the groups by halves on mental ability, they found no significant differences out of 10 in the upper, 2 significant differences out of 10 in the lower half. Both these were in favor of the control group.

When the research evidence is as unclear as this, observations by experienced teachers may be as valuable as a research study. But these observations, too, are far from unanimous. Milwaukee teachers voted nearly five to one that TV was better for the fast than the slow learners. Anaheim teachers and principals, asked which ability group benefits most from televised instruction, responded as follows:

	Teachers (Percent)	Principals (Percent)
Fast learners	17	0
Average learners	28	38
Slow learners	31	25
No difference	24	38

A group of 226 North Carolina teachers were asked whether ITV or classroom instruction was better for the different ability groups, and responded thus:

	TV Better (Percent)	No Difference (Percent)	Non-TV Better (Percent)
Superior students	93	2	5
Average students	79	8	13
Slow learners	73	9	18

It may well be, as some recent and unpublished research suggests, that both the brightest and the slowest students may derive some differential benefit from televised teaching—the former, because they learn rapidly anyway, and television can theoretically offer tham a great number and variety of responses to learn; the latter, because television concentrates their attention as the classroom often does not. But it must be admitted that we do not yet understand the relation of mental ability to differential learning from television.

It is the general feeling of most persons who have taught or done research in connection with instructional television that motivation is closely related to the results they have obtained. Erickson and Chausow, for example, though lack of motivation probably explained the lower results of students who were assigned to television sections, just as high motivation explained the very good results obtained in teaching home students by television. But the results have been equivocal in cases where the motivation has been measured and controlled. For example, when Mullin motivated some eleventh-graders (but not others) by offering a monetary reward for a high examination score, he found that the motivated students learned more than the others from a televised program on education, and concluded that the classroom was probably a better place than the TV room for unmotivated students. This seems to make sense, in that the classroom teacher may well be better able to take care of individual problems and thus raise motivation. But when Dreher and Beatty measured need-achievement in their TV and classroom students, they could find no significant difference in the amount of learning by television or classroom groups among the high or the low achievers.

No significant results have yet turned up in the literature to suggest that any other common personality traits make for greater or less learning from televised instruction as compared to classroom teaching.

2. *Does size of class make any difference in learning from instructional television?* Students generally prefer to be in small rather than in large classes, but no differential effect of class size on learning from ITV has been reported in cases where viewing conditions were equally satisfactory. Penn State varied the size of television classes between 19 and 120 students without producing differential results in learning.

3. *Does televised teaching make any difference in retention of subject matter over a long period?* One study of military training found that television students remembered more of the subject matter one month later. Another military study and five civilian studies found no significant differences.

4. *Is there a novelty effect in the reported results?* It may be taken for granted that there is. In some cases, it can be isolated. For example, an early military study (1952) found that trainees preferred to study from, and learned more from, lessons which they thought were kinescopes (television recordings) than from films—even though the "films" were identical to, or poorer in quality than, the kinescopes. Several years

later (1955), the finding could not be repeated. It was assumed, therefore, that the novelty effect of television teaching had worn off.

A number of the studies in school systems and colleges, however, have records of three or more years of experimentation with instructional television, during which time their students have in many cases taken a number of courses by television. Yet there seems to be no downward curve of achievement in these studies. Many observers feel that the growth in skill at using television counterbalances the loss of novelty effect.

It must be remembered, also, that the novelty effect is not always favorable. Many college students have not welcomed the opportunity to study by television when they have first been offered it. Many students have been made self-conscious and resistant, rather than achievement-minded, when researchers have paid more attention to them.

Although we cannot rule out the novelty or the Hawthorne effect, still there is little evidence to indicate that these might be giving us, over-all, spuriously high scores from ITV classes.

5. *Are we measuring the "intangibles"?* The more "intangible" they are, the less likely it is that they are being measured. Yet the question is important, and must be faced seriously.

The intangible qualities which people most often talk about in connection with supposed lacks in televised teaching are those related to social interaction. It is contended that instructional television substitutes for direct personal contacts, for the give and take of discussion and recital, a passive relationship of the student to a televised image. Students of television now tend to believe that the viewer is much less passive than formerly thought, but the rest of the statement is manifestly true: television cuts down on interaction within the classroom. What effect does it have? In the San Francisco study there is evidence that students in television classes knew fewer of their classmates than students in non-televised classes. In the lower grades, where pupils are together all day, and television absorbs only a minor part of the time, this result would not be expected. There is no evidence to indicate that reduced interaction in the classroom has any harmful effect on children's personalities, or on their social skills, although this is conceivable. Milwaukee teachers rejected overwhelmingly the suggestion that the TV classroom is "cold, or lacking in human warmth."

The other set of "intangibles" most often mentioned are those related to individual differences. It is contended that one of the functions of education is to help a child solve some of his own problems. These may be solved either by personal counseling by the teacher or another official, or by skills and insight derived from the classroom. The skills may be measured, but the outcomes are not. Therefore, an important set of outcomes may not be represented in ordinary measurements of learning. These contentions are manifestly true, and to the extent that television makes it harder for the student to get individual counseling or to assemble his learning around his personal needs, then there may indeed be some intangible loss. The question is whether, in a well-planned learning experience, of which television is a part, there need be any less opportunity for a student to solve his personal problems.

The research has so far been unable to locate any other intangible losses resulting from instruction by television. There has been some attempt to find out whether televised teaching—because it presents an "authority" rather than inviting democratic discussion—might develop authoritarian personalities in students. Carpenter and Greenhill found no evidence to confirm this. The same researchers, however, found that a group of students taught by the discussion group method scored higher on a test of problem-solving than did a comparable group taught by television. In general, however, television students have held their own in tests of critical thinking, problem-solving, and other non-rote aspects of learning.

6. *What do we know about the relation of forms of televised teaching to learning?* There is a great deal of research on the forms of effective teaching from film,[1] and much of this is undoubtedly applicable. The amount of such research concerning television is growing. However, the net result so far is to reinforce the belief that good teaching is much the same on television or films or the lecture platform.

A student who wants to learn can learn from a great variety of experiences. Williams assigned parallel groups to television, radio, and classroom teaching, and still another group to read in the library and attend no classes at all. All these groups learned, although the television group learned a little more. Stuit and others compared a variety of ways of studying political science: TV lecture, TV discussion, small and large group discussion, and lecture. There was little difference in learning. Brandon compared the same individuals communicating the same material in the form of a lecture, an interview, and a panel discussion, and found no significant differences.

One trend in the literature is toward simplicity of treatment. Although Klapper found that students liked TV-teaching better with a number of visuals than when it was straight lecture, Carpenter and

---

[1] For example, see M. A. May and A. A. Lumsdaine, *Learning from Film* (New Haven, Conn.: Yale University Press, 1958); also, C. A. Hoban and Van Ormer, *Instructional Film Research, 1918–1950,* Report SDC 269-7-19 (Port Washington, N.Y.: Special Devices Center, 1950).

Greenhill found that lecture and blackboard alone made for more learning than lecture plus charts, plus models, plus training films, plus visiting speakers, plus dramatizations, and so forth. A replication of this experiment in another class, however, resulted in no significant difference, which is itself a useful finding. The implication is that complexity of presentation, and a great variety of visual cues, may distract a student from the main principles of the presentation. This was tested by Kumata who presented two advertisements, one with visuals in color projected on a large screen, the other with black and white visuals projected on a television-size screen. He found that subjects remembered more details from the colored version, but remembered *principles* better from the black and white version.

One of the rules held to by television professionals seems not to apply to teaching by television. This is "eye-contact," meaning that the speaker looks the viewer directly in the eye. Westley and Mobius found this made no difference in learning.

WHAT WE KNOW AND MOST NEED TO KNOW
ABOUT LEARNING FROM INSTRUCTIONAL TELEVISION

On the basis of this information, what can we say about the process of learning from instructional television?

We can say confidently that students learn from it, and that they learn fast and efficiently. But of that we have been fairly certain for some time. The further step we have now taken has put us in position to say something about the conditions under which a student learns *more* from television, and something about *what* he learns from television.

But before turning to those matters, let us consider for a moment the central fact that apparently about as much learning takes place in a television class as in a nontelevision class. In a sense, this is a remarkable discovery. As Hoban says, there is every reason to expect that there should be *less* learning in a television class. There is an absence of the intellectual give and take believed to characterize some of the most effective teaching. There is little opportunity to adjust to individual differences, rates, and needs. The student can't so readily feed back his responses, or signal his lack of understanding, or clear things up with a question. There is indeed good reason to expect that conditions would make for a less favorable outcome and a less well-informed student.

However, we have seen that 86 percent of 393 experimental comparisons in life situations have resulted in as much or more learning in a television, as compared to a conventional, classroom. Why should this be? Is it something in the quality of the teaching, or something in the nature of the process?

One of the significant things about the literature of instructional television is the repeated observation that teachers who are going on television feel the need to put many additional hours into preparation. Some of these teachers are given an entire term free of teaching, or put on special appointment for the summer term, in order to get ready for teaching a television class. Ordinarily, when one teaches a television class, he teaches nothing else: one class. And when a teacher is putting one of his courses on television, a great effort is made with lesson plans, student guide, workbook, visuals, and so forth.

Remember that these teachers are not teaching their television courses for the first time. In many cases, they have taught the subject for years, in the classroom. They have taught it along with half a dozen other subjects. They have never before insisted on a free term to prepare, or trial films to see themselves teach, or a schedule reduced to one course; nor have they made such efforts with outlines and materials. Indeed, they have never had the opportunity to indulge in such relative luxuries.

Regardless of whether the class is televised on open circuit or closed circuit, it puts the teacher's classroom on *open* circuit. The teaching is on the screen for all the teacher's colleagues to watch. The sanctum of the classroom is opened to critical eyes. And therefore, we are getting better prepared and more skillful teaching on television, and this is doubtless overcoming some of the disadvantages which result from lack of classroom interaction.

But let us look further at those disadvantages. What are the great weaknesses of television? It doesn't stop to answer questions. It doesn't readily permit class discussion. It can't very efficiently conduct drill. It doesn't adjust very well to individual differences. It tends to encourage a passive form of learning rather than an active seeking.

It also has great strengths. It is very good at bringing demonstrations to the classroom: it lets everyone look through a microscope at the same time, gives all the medical students a good view of surgery, handles films and other changes from straight classroom presentation with a minimum of transitional difficulty. It lets a school or a college share its *best* teachers, rather than rationing them. It provides a change of pace, often a lift, for the classroom. It brings a sense of timeliness to classes where that helps. It concentrates attention.

These advantages are not small. They help to explain why television has not done so badly in the classroom as many observers expected it would. More important, they help us to understand why certain subject-matter areas have been taught more effectively than others. We could predict, for example, that courses which gain from great demonstrations (as science does) would gain from television. One would expect science to gain more from television treatment than, for example, philosophy, which depends largely on clear verbalization. One could predict that subjects like reading, writing, and spelling would not gain much from being televised, because mastery of those skills depends so largely on individual practice. We could predict that social studies, which gain from timely demonstration, would gain more from television than a course in history.

Clearly there is an interaction between characteristics of subject matter and characteristics of the student and the school at a given grade level.

In grade school, television is still fresh and interesting to children. As a teaching device, it is accepted as simply another instrument from which they can learn—like the textbook, the film projector, the language laboratory, and the blackboard. They have never gotten used to any kind of instruction that does not include television. They take to it naturally, and seldom think about alternative ways they might be learning.

Things are different when television comes to high school or college students. In general, they are less favorable to education anyway. Education has lost its edge. Many of them are unwilling learners. Furthermore, they have become accustomed to a different kind of teaching. They are used to asking a question when they feel the need to ask one. They have learned to enjoy, many of them, the classroom interaction. In college, many of the students are extremely serious about career goals, and personal contact with a professor is something they feel they are paying for. They tend to regard a television screen as a place to look for entertainment, not a place to study with a professor.

In addition to this, students at the higher levels typically are aware of unfavorable faculty attitudes toward television. The college teacher, in particular, is threatened by the idea of having his classroom opened up to critical eyes. He sometimes regards colleagues who are successful on television as showmen, rather than scholars. These attitudes are communicated to students, and it is not surprising that motivation at the higher levels has sometimes been less than in the early grades or in the case of home students.

There is a difference that is still more important between the meaning of television to the lower grades and to the higher ones and college.

In grade school, television is typically thought of as only a part of the learning experience, and efforts are taken to integrate it, just as the textbook, the film, the blackboard, the class drill, are integrated. The teacher is with the child five hours a day, and only half an hour or so of that is given over to television teaching. Therefore, the lesson is carefully built around the television experience. Care is taken to motivate the children to want to learn from television, and to ask the teacher the questions they cannot ask television directly. The program is thus prepared for, and followed up, and is accompanied by other learning experiences (such as drill and discussion) which television cannot so readily accomplish.

In other words, it is usually the classroom teacher, rather than the television teacher, who is in command of the situation. The TV teacher is a valued ally and helper. But a teaching team is in operation, the different roles are meshed, and the student still has a teacher of his own to give him personal attention and help him progress in his own best way.

Colleges are much less likely to integrate a television course into a broader course. Whereas in grade school television is usually thought of as a resource, and the classroom teacher is still in command, in college television takes over, and the television teacher is in command. In both high school and college, the administrations are more likely to put a good teacher on the screen and let him give a lecture course.

It is interesting to us that no college has yet used this concept in what seems to be one of its most exciting applications. Recall the pattern of an English university like Oxford or Cambridge. These universities typically offer a limited series of lectures each year, voluntary to students, and supposedly given by the greatest authorities who care to expose their ideas in this way. Some of the students go to a number of lecture series; some go to almost none. The chief activity of the student is to prepare for a continuing series of intensive tutorial sessions with teachers, to work in laboratories, and to read for a challenging set of examinations. This pattern is one to which television seems almost ideally suited. Why not put the best lectures on television, on a voluntary basis? This would require fewer lectures, and better ones. It would leave more time for individual study and guidance. It would put the emphasis where it seems it ought to be: on active learning by the student.

So far as we know, television has never been employed in that way by an American university, and in many ways it seems an opportunity lost. If the colleges are not going to integrate their television teaching into such a learning plan as the grade schools use, then this voluntary lecture plan seems one of the most promising ways to use it.

One of the keys to understanding the pattern which we have been describing in this paper is the extent to which instructional television is perceived as different and as a threat. It was much more often so perceived when it was very new, and it is more often so perceived now in college than in the grades. The schools which have used it for a few years now tend to take it in stride. They realize that it can do certain things very well and other things not well at all. The attitude studies referred to in the preceding pages are full of teachers' criticisms of the way they themselves were using television. The chief mistake they admit to is the same one, from school to school: not enough "follow-up time." Not enough time to answer the questions, to add the necessary drill and relate the television material to other material, and otherwise integrate it into the package. When there is a "team" in charge of the teaching, when the classroom teacher is centrally concerned with the total learning experience, then this kind of problem usually gets solved. Television comes to seem no more different than other aids to good learning. Television is not in command as it typically is in college-televised teaching. It can be much used or little used, as works best. It can be leaned on heavily for science, and hardly at all for spelling or arithmetic. It is not threatening; it is a friend and aider.

The concept of a teaching team and an arsenal of resources is about to be strengthened by the availability of self-teaching programs and devices. These will aid the teacher in drill and practice, as television aids him by contributing expert lecturing and skillful demonstrations. They will complement television where it is weakest, and leave the teacher freer to take care of individual learning problems, and to help the student combine the various resources open to him.

Neither these self-teaching devices nor television will put the classroom teacher out of business. Indeed, our observation is that the classroom teacher, who wondered if she might be obsolescent when the television teacher appeared, is now really more important than ever. We are encouraged in this belief by reading this statement in the report of the Philadelphia Public Schools:

> The classroom teacher has emerged as a key entity of the 'teacher team.' Excellent TV lessons are enhanced by skillful handling of pupil questions, lesson extension and application. Pupil learnings and attitudes are determined by the skill, enthusiasm and attitudes of the classroom teacher. TV will not supplant teachers: rather it creates the need for more good teachers.

To the researcher, as well as the educator, this has an implication: that he would do well to shift his sights from the uniqueness of television to the totality of the learning behavior and process. We have no intention of giving advice to educational administrators, but perhaps may be permitted to say a few words to researchers.

It is still of great importance to clear up, if we can, the interaction of television learning with different levels of ability. It is also clearly of importance to find out more about the "intangibles" which may be differentially learned or not learned from television and which are not measured by the usual end-of-term test. And there are a number of questions of what goes on the screen or on the sound track which need to be cleared up.

CREATIVITY: *Its Meaning and Development*

In its zeal to transmit a standardized culture, the American school has rewarded student conformity and discouraged non-conformity. The tyranny of the clock and the unrelenting adherence to classroom routine have hampered creative teachers and students from pursuing innovative ideas and practices. The previous selections in this chapter have dealt with innovations in education. Since the primary force which underlies innovation is creativity, the following article by Gezi and Myers is presented. In it, the authors discuss the meaning of creativity, characteristics of the creative individual, the relationship of creativity to intelligence and achievement, and the various cultural factors which suppress its development.

Kalil I. Gezi
James E. Myers

Prepared especially for this volume.

Although there have been some sporadic efforts in the past to study creativity, it is only recently that this subject has become the focus of considerable research interest. Researchers continue to struggle with the problems of defining creativity, identifying and measuring it, and determining the best ways in which it can be fostered in the schools.

WHAT IS CREATIVITY?

Researchers have not agreed on a single definition that adequately covers all the dimensions of creativity. Carl Rogers, a prominent American psychologist, perceives the creative process as "the emergence in action of a novel relational product, growing out of the uniqueness of the individual on the one hand, and the materials, events, people, or circumstances of his life on the other." [1]

E. Paul Torrance, a leading researcher and writer in the field of creativity, describes creative thinking as "the process of sensing difficulties, problems, gaps in information, missing elements, making guesses or for-

[1] Carl Rogers, "Toward a Theory of Creativity," *Creativity and Its Cultivation,* Harold H. Anderson (ed.) (New York: Harper & Row, Publishers, 1959), p. 71.

mulating hypotheses about these deficiencies; testing these guesses and possibly revising and retesting them; and finally in communicating the results." [2]

John C. Flanagan, of both the American Institute for Research and the University of Pittsburgh, asserts that "creativity is shown by evoking something new into being. The emphasis here is on the newness and lack of previous existence of the idea or product." [3]

Donald MacKinnon, Director of the Institute of Personality Assessment and Research at Berkeley, sees creativity as "process extended in time and characterized by originality, adaptiveness, and realization." [4]

J. P. Guilford, a pioneering authority on creativity in education, thinks that creative thinking appears "to depend upon the ability to do divergent-productive thinking and to affect transfer of information." Divergent-production, according to Guilford, is manifested in fluency in producing information, flexibility, elaboration, and redefinition. [5]

Many other definitions of creativity can be seen in the current research in the field. For instance, Rhodes categorized about fifty definitions into what he called the four P's of creativity: person, process, press (interaction between individuals and their environment), and product. [6]

Frank Barron, of the Institute of Personality Assessment and Research at the University of California at Berkeley, has developed twelve hypotheses characteristic of creative people. They are as follows: [7]

> 1. Creative people are more observant, and they value accurate observation, truth-telling to themselves, more.
>
> 2. They often tell or express only part truths, but vividly, and the part they express is the generally unrecognized—they point to the usually unobserved.

[2] E. Paul Torrance, *Rewarding Creative Behavior* (Englewood Cliffs, N.J.: Prentice-Hall, 1965), p. 8.

[3] John C. Flanagan, "The Definition and Measurement of Ingenuity," *The Second (1957) University of Utah Research Conference on the Identification of Creative Scientific Talent,* Calvin W. Taylor (ed.) (Salt Lake City: University of Utah Press, 1958), p. 111.

[4] Donald W. MacKinnon, "The Nature and Nurture of Creative Talent," *American Psychologist,* 17(7) (July 1962), 485.

[5] J. P. Guilford, "Creative Thinking and Problem Solving," *California Teachers Association Journal,* 60(1) (January 1964), 8–10.

[6] M. Rhodes, "An Analysis of Creativity," *Phi Delta Kappan,* 42(7) (April 1961), 305–310.

[7] Frank Barron, "The Needs for Order and for Disorder as Motives in Creative Activity," *Scientific Creativity: Its Recognition and Development,* C. W. Taylor and F. Barron (eds.) (New York: John Wiley & Sons, 1963), p. 159. Reprinted by permission of the publisher.

3. They see things as others do, but as others do not.

4. They are thus independent in their cognition and also value clearer cognition, so that they will suffer great personal pains to testify correctly.

5. They are motivated to both this value and this talent (independent, sharp observation) for self-preservation reasons (the ego instincts at work).

6. They are born with greater brain capacity—more ability to hold a lot of ideas in their head at once, and to compare more ideas with one another, hence to make a richer synthesis.

7. In addition to unusual endowment in terms of the ego instincts, they have much sexual drive as well (both pregenital and genital) because they are by constitution more vigorous organisms and more sensitive (nervous).

8. Their universe is thus naturally more complex, and in addition they usually have more complex lives, leading them to prefer much tension on the interest of the pleasure they obtain upon its discharge.

9. Hence, they also have more apprehensions of unconscious motives, fantasy life, etc. They note or observe their impulses more and allow them expression in the interest of truth.

10. Creative people have exceptionally strong egos. The self is strongest when it can go far back regressively and return to a high degree of rationality. The creative person is both more primitive and more cultured, more destructive and more constructive, crazier and saner, than the average person.

11. When the distinction between subject (self) and object is most secure, this distinction can with most security be allowed to disappear for a time. This is based on true sympathy with the not-self or with the opposite of the things which comprise defensive self-definition. The strong ego realizes that it is secure in the knowledge that it can correct itself.

12. The objective freedom of the organism is at a maximum when this capacity exists, and creative potential is directly a function of objective freedom.

From the foregoing remarks on the meaning of creativity, and the characteristics of the creative individual, it is evident that creativity can be viewed as a process of arriving at new solutions for problems, or new methods of dealing with problems, leading to new products. There seems to be two levels of newness. The first is when the product is new to the individual himself, such as in the case of a child or an adult discovering something for the first time, but which is not new to his culture. The second level, which is higher, is when the product is new to the whole culture.

RELATIONSHIP OF CREATIVITY
TO INTELLIGENCE AND ACHIEVEMENT

It appears from research that a certain level of intelligence is necessary for creativity. This level, according to Torrance, Roe, Getzels and Jackson, and C. Taylor, seems to be between IQ scores of 115–120. However, beyond this level intelligence does not seem to make much difference in creativity. Thus, intelligence *per se*, as measured by IQ tests, is not a sufficient criterion of creativity. A person may be creative without being particularly intelligent, and he can be highly intelligent although not creative.

Research demonstrates that there is a relationship between creativity and achievement. Getzels and Jackson found that the achievement of creative students as well as students with high IQ's was superior to the achievement of the school population as a whole.[8] Yamamoto found that high creativity students were significantly better in achievement than low creativity students.[9]

IDENTIFICATION AND MEASUREMENT
OF CREATIVITY

The creative potential is complex, involving a spectrum of abilities. It is this fact that has made the identification and measurement of creativity difficult.

Attempts to measure creativity have ranged from case studies of inventors to the more recent tests of creative thinking. Some of the well-known tests of creativity include Flanagan's Ingenuity Test, Guilford's A-C (sparkplug) Test of Creative Ability, Burkhart's Divergent Questions Test, Fredericksen's Formulating Hypotheses Test, Mednick's Remote Association Test, and the Torrance Tests of Creative Thinking.

Unlike the traditional tests of intelligence, most creativity tests attempt to measure one or more of the following: fluency flexibility, originality, elaboration, redefinition, and sensitivity to problems.

But even though many of these tests suffer from inadequate or incomplete statistical procedures, they represent important steps in the process of evaluating creativity.

[8] J. W. Getzels and P. W. Jackson, "The Highly Intelligent and Highly Creative Adolescent: A Summary of Some Research Findings," *The Third (1959) University of Utah Research Conference on the Identification of Creative Scientific Talent*, Calvin W. Taylor (ed.) (Salt Lake City: University of Utah Press, 1959).

[9] Kaoru Yamamoto, "Validation of Tests of Creative Thinking: A Review of Some Studies," *Exceptional Children*, 31 (February 1965), 281–290.

In order to give the student an illustration of a creativity test, the Torrance Tests of Creative Thinking will be described briefly. These tests contain tasks which can be divided into the following three major categories: non-verbal tasks, verbal tasks using non-verbal stimuli, and verbal tasks using verbal stimuli.

I. *Non-verbal tasks* include:
   a. *Picture construction.* With a piece of paper, and a piece of glued colored paper in the form of an egg or a curved jelly bean, the student is asked to draw an original picture and give it a title.
   b. *Picture completion.* As shown in the accompanying figure, the student is asked to complete certain figures.

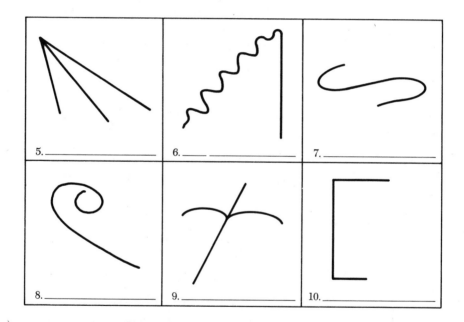

Picture completion. Adapted from "Thinking Creativity with Pictures," Booklet B, Torrance Test of Creative Thinking *by E. Paul Torrance (Princeton, N.J.: Personnel Press). Copyright © 1966. Reprinted by permission of the publisher.*

   c. *Circles or lines.* The student is given ten minutes to make as many original pictures as he can from a number of circles or lines.
      All non-verbal tests are scored for fluency, flexibility, originality, and elaboration.
II. *Verbal tasks using non-verbal stimuli* include:
   a. *The ask and guess.* A picture is provided the student and he is

asked to ask questions, guess about causes and consequences related to the picture.

b. *Product improvement.* A student is asked to show how to improve a toy nurse kit, a friction fire truck, a stuffed toy monkey.

III. *Verbal tasks using verbal stimuli* include:

a. *Unusual uses.* Student is requested to describe unusual uses for tin cans or books.

All verbal tests are scored for elaboration, flexibility, and originality. [10]

CULTURAL INHIBITORS TO CREATIVITY

It is paradoxical that the cohesiveness of society is based upon cultural norms that demand certain degrees of conformity, and yet at the same time its progress is dependent to a large measure upon the nonconforming behavior of its creative members. Clearly, conforming behavior is the antithesis of creative behavior, for conformity binds the individual to what is expected of him, whereas the creative potential is maximized when the individual is free to explore novel ways of perceiving and behaving.

Pressures adversely affecting creativity can come from peer group, family, various community agencies, mass media of communication, and schools.

The influence of the peer group on the individual has been demonstrated by many studies. The conforming members of the group are usually rewarded, while the member with different ideas and modes of behavior is likely to be rejected.

The family, perhaps more than any other institution in society, is responsible for the socialization of the child. Children are expected to conform to their family's norms and values.

Community agencies, such as churches, youth clubs, and civic organizations, strive not only to foster allegiance in their members to the traditions and values of their culture, but also to their own unique beliefs.

The explosive growth of the mass media of communications in the United States has had a marked influence on standardizing our behavior. Newspapers, magazines, radio, television, movies, and other mass media have persuaded us to conform to prescribed ways of not only consuming but also thinking.

The school has the dual function of at the same time transmitting the cultural heritage and changing and improving culture, but the Amer-

[10] E. Paul Torrance, *Torrance Tests of Creative Thinking* (Princeton, N.J.: Personnel Press, n.d.).

ican school has historically emphasized the transmission function. In its zeal to transmit a standardized culture, student conformity has been encouraged and rewarded, while student nonconformity has been discouraged and penalized.

Many practices in American classrooms bear witness to the stifling of creativity. Jules Henry, a prominent anthropologist, speaks of the "witch-hunt" syndrome in some of our elementary schools. Some teachers unconsciously place barriers against creativity by encouraging students to partake of a witch's brew. "In this witch's brew," Henry writes, "*destructive criticism* of others is the toad's horns; *docility* the body of the worm; *feelings of vulnerability* the chicken heart; *fear of internal (intragroup) hostility* the snake's fang; *confession of evil deeds* the locust's leg; and *boredom and emptiness* the dead man's eye." [11] If a student is subjected to criticism from others, rewarded for being docile, made to feel vulnerable, threatened by intragroup hostility, encouraged to confess his evil deeds and is bored, he is unlikely to be creative. In fact, research shows that the highly creative student tends to be unduly penalized in the school because curriculum and evaluation place a heavy emphasis on memory and other traditional tasks.[12]

Torrance cites the following factors as inhibitors to creative growth: [13]

1. *Success-orientation.* American culture places a heavier emphasis upon prescribed ways of success than it does on adequate motivation for experimentation and acceptance of failure.

2. *Sanctions against questioning and exploration.* Curiosity and free inquiry "are often brutally squelched" in the schools.

3. *Sex-role conditioning.* Creative efforts by boys or girls are inhibited because the activities undertaken may be perceived to belong to the opposite sex.

4. *Being different is equated with abnormality.* Individuals who behave and think differently from the accepted norms are often penalized because of their "abnormalities."

5. *Work-play dichotomy.* American culture fosters the notion that play is fun and work is serious business. Creative activities in the classroom are often seen by some teachers as play and students are admon-

[11] Jules Henry, "Attitude Organization in Elementary School Classrooms," *The American Journal of Orthopsychiatry,* **27** (January 1957), 117–133.

[12] For example, see Joseph Bentley, "Creativity and Academic Achievement," *The Journal of Educational Research,* **59** (February 6, 1966), 269–272.

[13] E. Paul Torrance, "Education and Creativity," *Creativity: Progress and Potential,* Calvin Taylor (ed.) (New York: McGraw-Hill, 1964), pp. 49–128.

ished to "get busy" with their school work, thereby, curtailing these activities.

It is not implied in this discussion that in order to be creative. pressures for conformity must cease to exist, for without some conformity, cultural cohesion could not be maintained in a society. What is implied is that there should be a proper balance between the forces for conformity and the freedom to act as an individual. Indeed, there is a great potential for nurturing creative behavior in our culture. American democracy has thrived on the encouragement of independent thinking and the freedom of choice. The continuous flow of immigrants to this country has assured the existence of a certain degree of diversity in values, thought, and behavior. Besides, the American free enterprise system has spent millions of dollars on research and experimentation rewarding creative ideas. Furthermore, research has become an integral part of an increasing number of universities, colleges, and school districts, and experimentation has also been encouraged by funds from governmental and private foundations sources.

DEVELOPING CREATIVITY
IN STUDENTS AND TEACHERS

Creative potential is not possessed solely by the gifted students, but is widely distributed among the school population. The school in American culture has the responsibility of providing an environment conducive to the development of creativity.

What can the teacher do to aid the creative growth of the student? Based on our school experiences, the following suggestions have been found to be helpful:

1. The teacher must value creativity if he is to encourage it among his students. It would be helpful for the teacher himself to be creative in the classroom, thereby encouraging the students to be independent thinkers.

2. Establishing a classroom environment supportive of creativity is another important factor. The teacher must provide an abundance of educational materials that evoke curiosity; use a variety of approaches and ideas; encourage students to work independently on classroom projects; and should not allow the tyranny of the clock and classroom routine to hamper creative activities.

3. Instead of an overemphasis on a correct method or solution, the teacher should strive to present different ideas and to help his students see things from varying perspectives. The students should be motivated

to accept diversity and ambiguity and to seek different ways of solving problems.

4. The teacher and his students should continuously analyze and evaluate the process and the products of the creative act. Such evaluation can help them develop a concept of what is creative and may spur them to creative work.

5. The teacher should help the student develop an adequate self-concept, for without such support the student may not have enough confidence to be explorative and take the risk of uncertain solutions.

6. The teacher must grant his students the freedom to explore, investigate, think, feel, and express themselves in the classroom.

7. Creative behavior in the classroom should be rewarded by the teacher and the students. Reward will reinforce the value of creativity.

While most researchers have emphasized the encouragement of creativity in students, few have focused on the development of creativity among teachers. Teacher education programs and inservice training for teachers should help them learn how to be creative in their classrooms, for the same cultural pressures that adversely effect creativity in children can also hamper its expression in teachers. Under the name of efficiency, many schools impose a rigid routine on the teacher which leaves him little opportunity for creative instruction.

The importance of encouraging creativity is perhaps best summed up by Toynbee:

> To give a fair chance to potential creativity is a matter of life and death for any society. This is all-important, because the outstanding creative ability of a fairly small percentage of the population is mankind's ultimate capital asset, and the only one with which Man has been endowed. . . . If society fails to make the most of this one human asset, or if, worse still, it perversely sets itself to stifle it, Man is throwing away his birthright of being the Lord of creation and is condemning himself to be, instead the least effective species on the face of this planet.[14]

[14] Arnold Toynbee, "Has America Neglected Her Creative Minority?" *The Utah Alumnus*, **34** (February 1962), 10.

6

PROGRESSIVE EDUCATION: AN APPRAISAL

INTRODUCTION

In the previous two chapters the student was introduced to some of the major problems and innovations in education. In this chapter a single theme is explored in some depth. Of all the educational movements that have engaged the attention and energy of educators and the public in this century, few have generated as much controversy as progressive education. It has caused heated debates throughout the country and drawn sharp outbursts from the average citizen to a President of the United States. President Eisenhower, in 1959, condemned progressive education by writing, "Educators, parents and students must be continuously stirred up by the defects in our educational system. They must be induced to abandon the educational path that, rather blindly, they have been following as a result of John Dewey's teaching." [1]

The uproar among educators regarding progressive education was equally vigorous and sometimes even more emotional. Writing about the fears some people hold of progressivism, Lawrence Cremin, an authority on the progressive education movement in the United States, tells a tale about John Dewey, who, in the image of Abou Ben Adhem, "awakes one night with a new vision of the American school: the vision is progressive education. Over the years, with the help of a dedicated group of crafty professional lieutenants at Teachers College, Columbia University, he is able to foist the vision on an unsuspecting American people." [2] *The story terminates with an appeal to exorcise "this devil" from our schools and return to the good ways of the past.*

[1] *Life* (March 16, 1959), p. 104.
[2] Lawrence Cremin, *The Transformation of the School: Progressivism in American Education, 1876–1957* (New York: Vintage Books, 1964), p. viii.

Max Rafferty, State Superintendent of Public Instruction in California, voices some of the fears held by a segment of American educators toward progressive education. He writes that when progressive education began to infiltrate the school, "the mastery of the basic skills began insensibly to erode, knowledge of the great cultures and contributions of past civilizations started to slip and slide, reverence for the heroes of our nations past faded and withered under the burning glare of pragmatism." [3]

Underlying the controversy over progressive education are two important questions: What are the goals of the school, and what are the best ways in which the school can achieve these goals? The progressives and the traditionalists give different answers to these questions.

Some traditionalists, such as Adler, Hutchins, and Maritain, have held that the major goal of education is the development of the intellect, and the best way of achieving this goal is by exposing the students to the great classics of our heritage. Other traditionalists, such as Bagley and Bestor, believe that the primary purpose of education is to prepare the child to live a responsible and worthy adult life by transmitting to him through the school curriculum the time-tested basic essentials of knowledge, such as the three R's.

The traditionalists also believe that the universal values upon which education is based are unchanging: What has been found to be Good and True in the past will be Good and True today and in the future. They emphasized the importance of the subject matter to be learned.

The progressives, on the other hand, have stressed that education should develop critical thinking so that the individual can continuously reorganize his experiences in order to solve his problems. Values are continuously changing, they argue, and what was of value in education and society in the past may no longer be so in the present or in the years to come. The goals of education are best accomplished by stimulating the students' interest in learning, helping them learn by experiencing, and developing their ability to use the scientific method as a means of solving problems. The progressives also emphasized the importance of the learner in a democratic setting.

Progressive education must be considered as part of a wider

---

[3] Max Rafferty, *What They Are Doing to Your Children* (New York: New American Library, 1964), p. 19.

*progressive movement that pervaded American society as a re-
sponse to the emerging urban-industrial conditions during the
second half of the nineteenth century. The Progressive Education Association was organized in 1919, and its leaders became
the spokesmen for the progressive education movement. In 1955,
the Progressive Education Association ceased to exist, with its
supporters feeling that it had achieved its goals and its critics
claiming that it had failed.*

*The question often asked is whether progressive education is
dead. Even though the Association is disbanded, the questions
raised by Dewey, Counts, Kilpatrick, Bode, Childs, and other
progressives, the methods they proposed, and the insights they
offered are applicable to present day education.*

*Thus, the controversy over progressive education is very
much alive today. It is unfortunate, however, that many educators and laymen do not know the meaning of progressive education, its philosophical bases, its contributions, and its present
status in American education. These concerns underlie the rationale for this chapter. It opens with one of Dewey's classic essays describing his basic educational beliefs. This is followed by
an amplification of the principle concerns of progressive education
as John Childs saw them in the 1930s. The next two articles are
written by two critics of progressive education, Bagley in the
1930s and Rafferty in the 1960s. The last two articles, by Cremin
and Bruner, respectively, provide scholarly analyses of the historical development of progressive education and a perceptive
discussion of Dewey's views as they apply to the present and the
future in education.*

MY PEDAGOGIC CREED

*John Dewey (1859–1952), public school teacher, professor, phi-
losopher, and social reformer, is considered to be the greatest
American philosopher in this century. His books, articles,
speeches, and experimental work at the Laboratory School of the
University of Chicago have had a profound influence on American and world education. Dewey taught at the universities of
Michigan, Minnesota, Chicago, and at Teachers College, Columbia University. He was a prolific writer, and among his notable
books are* Experience and Education, Democracy and Education, The School and Society, *and* How We Think. *He cham-
pioned pragmatism (experimentalism), upon which progressive*

education was largely based. Dewey wrote the following essay in 1897, the second year of his work at the Laboratory School. It was first published in The School Journal *and was reprinted in the same year in a pamphlet. This statement is a very significant one, not only due to the wide circulation it has received but also because in it Dewey spelled out succinctly his basic educational beliefs, which changed little over the years. For instance, Dewey asserts one of his major beliefs in this article when he says, "Education must be conceived as a continuing reconstruction of experience; that the process and the goal of education are one and the same thing." After studying "My Pedagogic Creed," the student will find it valuable to read the selection by Bruner in which he examines this statement by Dewey in the light of present educational practices.*

John Dewey

The School Journal, 54 (1897), 77–80.

ARTICLE ONE—WHAT EDUCATION IS

I believe that all education proceeds by the participation of the individual in the social consciousness of the race. This process begins unconsciously almost at birth, and is continually shaping the individual's powers, saturating his consciousness, forming his habits, training his ideas, and arousing his feelings and emotions. Through this unconscious education the individual gradually comes to share in the intellectual and moral resources which humanity has succeeded in getting together. He becomes an inheritor of the funded capital of civilization. The most formal and technical education in the world cannot safely depart from this general process. It can only organize it or differentiate it in some particular direction.

The only true education comes through the stimulation of the child's powers by the demands of the social situations in which he finds himself. Through these demands he is stimulated to act as a member of a unity, to emerge from his original narrowness of action and feeling, and to conceive of himself from the standpoint of the welfare of the group to which he belongs. Through the responses which others make to his own activities he comes to know what these mean in social terms. The value which they have is reflected back into them. For instance, through the response which is made to the child's instinctive babblings the child comes to know what those babblings mean; they are transformed into articulate language, and thus the child is introduced into the consolidated wealth of ideas and emotions which are now summed up in language.

This educational process has two sides—one psychological and one sociological—and neither can be subordinated to the other, or neglected, without evil results following. Of these two sides, the psychological is the basis. The child's own instincts and powers furnish the material and give the starting point for all education. Save as the efforts of the educator connect with some activity which the child is carrying on of his own initiative independent of the educator, education becomes reduced to a pressure from without. It may, indeed, give certain external results, but cannot truly be called educative. Without insight into the psychological structure and activities of the individual, the educative process will, therefore, be haphazard and arbitrary. If it chances to coincide with the child's activity it will get a leverage; if it does not, it will result in friction, or disintegration, or arrest of the child-nature.

Knowledge of social conditions, of the present state of civilization, is necessary in order properly to interpret the child's powers. The child has his own instincts and tendencies, but we do not know what these mean until we can translate them into their social equivalents. We must be able to carry them back into a social past and see them as the inheritance of previous race activities. We must also be able to project them into the future to see what their outcome and end will be. In the illustration just used, it is the ability to see in the child's babblings the promise and potency of a future social intercourse and conversation which enables one to deal in the proper way with that instinct.

The psychological and social sides are organically related, and that education cannot be regarded as a compromise between the two, or a superimposition of one upon the other. We are told the psychological definition of education is barren and formal—that it gives us only the idea of a development of all the mental powers without giving us any idea of the use to which these powers are put. On the other hand, it is urged that the social definition of education, as getting adjusted to civilization, makes of it a forced and external process, and results in subordinating the freedom of the individual to a preconceived social and political status.

Each of these objections is true when urged against one side isolated from the other. In order to know what a power really is we must know what its end, use, or function is, and this we cannot know save as we conceive of the individual as active in social relationships. But, on the other hand, the only possible adjustment which we can give to the child under existing conditions is that which arises through putting him in complete possession of all his powers. With the advent of democracy and modern industrial conditions, it is impossible to foretell definitely just what civilization will be twenty years from now. Hence it is impossible to prepare the child for any precise set of conditions. To prepare him for the future life means to give him command of himself; it means so to train him that he will have the full and ready use of all his capacities; that his eye and ear and hand may be tools ready to command, that his judgment may be capable of grasping the conditions under which it has to work, and the executive forces be trained to act economically and efficiently. It is impossible to reach this sort of adjustment save as constant regard is had to the individual's own powers, tastes, and interests—that is, as education is continually converted into psychological terms.

In sum, I believe that the individual who is to be educated is a social individual, and that society is an organic union of individuals. If we eliminate the social factor from the child we are left only with an abstraction; if we eliminate the individual factor from society, we are left only with an inert and lifeless mass. Education, therefore, must begin with a psychological insight into the child's capacities, interests, and habits. It must be controlled at every point by reference to these same considerations. These powers, interests, and habits must be continually interpreted—we must know what they mean. They must be translated into terms of their social equivalents—into terms of what they are capable of in the way of social service.

ARTICLE TWO—WHAT THE SCHOOL IS

I believe that the school is primarily a social institution. Education being a social process, the school is simply that form of community life in which all those agencies are concentrated that will be most effective in bringing the child to share in the inherited resources of the race, and to use his own powers for social ends.

Education, therefore, is a process of living and not a preparation for future living.

The school must represent life, life as real and vital to the child as that which he carries on in the home, in the neighborhood, or on the playground.

That education which does not occur through forms of life, forms that are worth living for their own sake, is always a poor substitute for the genuine reality, and tends to cramp and to deaden.

The school, as an institution, should simplify existing social life; should reduce it, as it were, to an embryonic form. Existing life is so complex that the child cannot be brought into contact with it without either confusion or distraction; he is either overwhelmed by the multiplicity of activities which are going on, so that he loses his own power of orderly reaction, or he is so stimulated by these various activities that his powers are prematurely called into play and he becomes either unduly specialized or else disintegrated.

As such simplified social life, the school should grow gradually out of the home life; it should take up and continue the activities with which the child is already familiar in the home.

It should exhibit these activities to the child, and reproduce them in such ways that the child will gradually learn the meaning of them, and be capable of playing his own part in relation to them.

This is a psychological necessity, because it is the only way of securing continuity in the child's growth, the only way of giving a background of past experience to the new ideas given in school.

It is also a social necessity because the home is the form of social life in which the child has been nurtured and in connection with which he has had his moral training. It is the business of the school to deepen and extend his sense of the values bound up in his home life.

Much of present education fails because it neglects this fundamental principle of the school as a form of community life. It conceives the school as a place where certain information is to be given, where certain lessons are to be learned, or where certain habits are to be formed. The value of these is conceived as lying largely in the remote future; the child must do these things for the sake of something else he is to do; they are mere preparations. As a result they do not become a part of the life experience of the child and so are not truly educative.

The moral education centers upon this conception of the school as a mode of social life, that the best and deepest moral training is precisely that which one gets through having to enter into proper relations with others in a unity of work and thought. The present educational systems, so far as they destroy or neglect this unity, render it difficult or impossible to get any genuine, regular moral training.

The child should be stimulated and controlled in his work through the life of the community.

Under existing conditions far too much of the stimulus and control proceeds from the teacher, because of neglect of the idea of the school as a form of social life.

The teacher's place and work in the school is to be interpreted from this same basis. The teacher is not in the school to impose certain ideas or to form certain habits in the child, but is there as a member of the community to select the influences which shall affect the child and to assist him in properly responding to these influences.

The discipline of the school should proceed from the life of the school as a whole and not directly from the teacher.

The teacher's business is simply to determine, on the basis of larger experience and riper wisdom, how the discipline of life shall come to the child.

All questions of the grading of the child and his promotion should be determined by reference to the same standard. Examinations are of use only so far as they test the child's fitness for social life and reveal the place in which he can be of the most service and where he can receive the most help.

I believe that the social life of the child is the basis of concentration, or correlation, in all his training or growth. The social life gives the unconscious unity and the background of all his efforts and of all his attainments.

The subject matter of the school curriculum should mark a gradual differentiation out of the primitive unconscious unity of social life.

We violate the child's nature and render difficult the best ethical results by introducing the child too abruptly to a number of special studies, of reading, writing, geography, etc., out of relation to this social life.

The true center of correlation on the school subjects is not science, nor literature, nor history, nor geography, but the child's own social activities.

Education cannot be unified in the study of science, or so-called nature study, because apart from human activity, nature itself is not a unity; nature in itself is a number of diverse objects in space and time, and to attempt to make it the center of work by itself is to introduce a principle of radiation rather than one of concentration.

Literature is the reflex expression and interpretation of social experience; hence it must follow upon and not precede such experience. It, therefore, cannot be made the basis, although it may be made the summary of unification.

Once more, history is of educative value insofar as it presents phases of social life and growth. It must be controlled by reference to social life. When taken simply as history it is thrown into the distant past and becomes dead and inert. Taken as the record of man's social life and progress it becomes full of meaning. I believe, however, that it cannot be so taken excepting as the child is also introduced directly into social life.

The primary basis of education is in the child's powers at work along the same general constructive lines as those which have brought civilization into being.

The only way to make the child conscious of his social heritage is to enable him to perform those fundamental types of activity which make civilization what it is.

In the so-called expressive or constructive activities is the center of correlation.

This gives the standard for the place of cooking, sewing, manual training, etc., in the school.

They are not special studies which are to be introduced over and above a lot of others in the way of relaxation or relief, or as additional accomplishments. I believe rather that they represent, as types, fundamental forms of social activity; and that it is possible and desirable that the child's introduction into the more formal subjects of the curriculum be through the medium of these constructive activities.

The study of science is educational insofar as it brings out the materials and processes which make social life what it is.

One of the greatest difficulties in the present teaching of science is that the material is presented in purely objective form, or is treated as a new peculiar kind of experience which the child can add to that which he has already had. In reality, science is of value because it gives the ability to interpret and control the experience already had. It should be introduced, not as so much new subject matter, but as showing the factors already involved in previous experience and as furnishing tools by which that experience can be more easily and effectively regulated.

At present we lose much of the value of literature and language studies because of our elimination of the social element. Language is almost always treated in the books of pedagogy simply as the expression of thought. It is true that language is a logical instrument, but it is fundamentally and primarily a social instrument. Language is the device for communication; it is the tool through which one individual comes to share the ideas and feelings of others. When treated simply as a way of getting individual information, or as a means of showing off what one has learned, it loses its social motive and end.

There is, therefore, no succession of studies in the ideal school curriculum. If education is life, all life has, from the outset, a scientific aspect, an aspect of art and culture, and an aspect of communication. It cannot, therefore, be true that the proper studies for one grade are mere reading and writing, and that at a later grade, reading, or literature, or science, may be introduced. The progress is not in the succession of studies, but in the development of new attitudes towards, and new interests in, experience.

Education must be conceived as a continuing reconstruction of experience; the process and the goal of education are one and the same thing.

To set up any end outside of education, as furnishing its goal and standard, is to deprive the educational process of much of its meaning, and tends to make us rely upon false and external stimuli in dealing with the child.

ARTICLE FOUR—THE NATURE OF METHOD

I believe that the question of method is ultimately reducible to the question of the order of development of the child's powers and interests. The law for presenting and treating material is the law implicit within the child's own nature. Because this is so I believe the following statements are of supreme importance as determining the spirit in which education is carried on.

The active side precedes the passive in the development of the child nature; expression comes before conscious impression; the muscular development precedes the sensory; movements come before conscious sensations; I believe that consciousness is essentially motor or impulsive; that conscious states tend to project themselves in action.

The neglect of this principle is the cause of a large part of the waste of time and strength in school work. The child is thrown into a passive, receptive, or absorbing attitude. The conditions are such that he is not permitted to follow the law of his nature; the result is friction and waste.

Ideas also result from action and devolve for the sake of the better control of action. What we term reason is primarily the law of order or effective action. To attempt to develop the reasoning powers, the powers of judgment, without reference to the selection and arrangement of means in action, is the fundamental fallacy in our present methods of dealing with this matter. As a result we present the child with arbitrary symbols. Symbols are a necessity in mental development, but they have their place as tools for economizing effort; presented by themselves they are a mass of meaningless and arbitrary ideas imposed from without.

The image is the great instrument of instruction. What a child gets out of any subject presented to him is simply the images which he himself forms with regard to it.

If nine-tenths of the energy at present directed towards making the child learn certain things were spent in seeing to it that the child was forming proper images, the work of instruction would be indefinitely facilitated.

Much of the time and attention now given to the preparation and presentation of lessons might be more wisely and profitably expended in training the child's power of imagery and in seeing to it that he was continually forming definite, vivid and growing images of the various subjects with which he comes in contact in his experience.

Interests are the signs and symptoms of growing power. I believe that they represent dawning capacities. Accordingly the constant and careful observation of interests is of the utmost importance for the educator.

These interests are to be observed as showing the state of development which the child has reached.

They prophesy the stage upon which he is about to enter.

Only through the continual and sympathetic observation of childhood's interests can the adult enter into the child's life and see what it is ready for, and upon what material it could work most readily and fruitfully.

These interests are neither to be humored nor repressed. To repress interest is to substitute the adult for the child, and so to weaken intellectual curiosity and alertness, to suppress initiative, and to deaden interest. To humor the interests is to substitute the transient for the permanent. The interest is always the sign of some power below; the important thing is to discover this power. To humor the interest is to fail to penetrate below the surface, and its sure result is to substitute caprice and whim for genuine interest.

The emotions are the reflex of actions.

To endeavor to stimulate or arouse the emotions apart from their corresponding activities is to introduce an unhealthy and morbid state of mind.

If we can only secure right habits of action and thought, with reference to the good, the true, and the beautiful, the emotions will for the most part take care of themselves.

Next to deadness and dullness, formalism and routine, our education is threatened with no greater evil than sentimentalism.

This sentimentalism is the necessary result of the attempt to divorce feeling from action.

ARTICLE FIVE—THE SCHOOL AND SOCIAL PROGRESS

I believe that education is the fundamental method of social progress and reform.

All reforms which rest simply upon the enactment of law, or the threatening of certain penalties, or upon changes in mechanical or outward arrangements, are transitory and futile.

Education is a regulation of the process of coming to share in the social consciousness; and the adjustment of individual activity on the basis of this social consciousness is the only sure method of social reconstruction.

This conception has due regard for both the individualistic and socialistic ideals. It is duly individual because it recognizes the formation of a certain character as the only genuine basis of right living. It is socialistic because it recognizes that this right character is not to be formed by merely individual precept, example, or exhortation, but rather by the influence of a certain form of institutional or community life upon the individual, and that the social organism through the school, as its organ, may determine ethical results.

In the ideal school we have the reconciliation of the individualistic and the institutional ideals.

The community's duty to education is, therefore, its paramount moral duty. By law and punishment, by social agitation and discussion, society can regulate and form itself in a more or less haphazard and chance way. But through education society can formulate its own purposes, can organize its own means and resources, and thus shape itself with definiteness and economy in the direction in which it wishes to move.

When society once recognizes the possibilities in this direction, and the obligations which these possibilities impose, it is impossible to conceive of the resources of time, attention, and money which will be put at the disposal of the educator.

It is the business of everyone interested in education to insist upon the school as the primary and most effective interest of social progress and reform in order that society may be awakened to realize what the school stands for, and aroused to the necessity of endowing the educator with sufficient equipment properly to perform his task.

Education thus conceived marks the most perfect and intimate union of science and art conceivable in human experience.

The art of thus giving shape to human powers and adapting them to social service is the supreme art; one calling into its service the best of artists; no insight, sympathy, tact, executive power, is too great for such service.

With the growth of psychological service, giving added insight into individual structure and laws of growth; and with growth of social science, adding to our knowledge of the right organization of individuals, all scientific resources can be utilized for the purposes of education.

When science and art thus join hands the most commanding motive for human action will be reached, the most genuine springs of human conduct aroused, and the best service that human nature is capable of guaranteed.

The teacher is engaged, not simply in the training of individuals, but in the formation of the proper social life.

Every teacher should realize the dignity of his calling; he is a social servant set apart for the maintenance of proper social order and the securing of the right social growth.

In this way the teacher always is the prophet of the true God and the usherer in of the true kingdom of God.

WHITHER PROGRESSIVE EDUCATION?

John Childs, emeritus professor of education at Teachers College, Columbia University, studied under Dewey and later collaborated with him. Childs provided leadership in applying pragmatic ideas to education and made one of the clearest and most important restatements of the progressive philosophy in his book, Education and Morals. *He advocated that the school, using the experimental method, should become the agent for social reform. Among Childs' other writings are:* American Pragmatism in Education, *two chapters with Dewey in* The Educational Frontier, *which was edited by Kilpatrick, and many articles. In the following essay, Childs offers six important emphases for progressive education which, he said, and perhaps prophetically so, would endure even should the Progressive Education Association disband. He also criticizes the Association for its failure to develop an adequate social philosophy for America's industrial society.*

John L. Childs

Progressive Education (*December 1936*), 583–589. *Reprinted by permission of the John Dewey Society and* The Education Digest.

Progressive education owes much to individuals. For several decades some of our ablest minds have actively shared in the development of its philosophy and methods. Under their leadership progressive education has become an important movement which exerts influence in the world of art, recreation, religion, science, and politics, as well as in the field of education. To a remarkable extent, its fundamental conceptions have also been incorporated into a working American philosophy of life. So inextricably are the ideas of these leaders woven into the warp and woof of progressive education that it is difficult, if not impossible, to think of one without the other.

In its fundamentals, however, progressive education is not the sheer invention of a few eminent figures. Its deeper source lies in cultural developments—intellectual and practical—which called for a reconstructed world outlook and a modified educational practice. The individuals who pioneered progressive education discerned that the consequences and the implications of these cultural changes called for a new life orientation, and also perceived that a reconstructed educational procedure would provide an effectual agency for making this new outlook prevail in the experience of the ordinary person. The response which has accompanied their effort is a tribute to the accuracy of their analysis.

To the degree that we comprehend the deeper cultural roots of this new intellectual and moral orientation we shall be confident about the future of progressive education. This regardless of what may be the ultimate fate of the particular educational devices with which it is now associated. It would be surprising if further experimentation did not discover educational techniques better suited to the new points of view than those now available. These new outlooks, moreover, were not created by the Progressive Education Association. Today it does not hold, nor does it desire to hold, any monopoly of them. Important as has been its service in gaining popular support for them, these attitudes and ideas will not disappear should the Progressive Education Association cease to exist.

Within the limits of this article, it will be possible only to summarize some of the more important of these new emphases which I believe will endure so long as men retain faith in intelligence and in the democratic way of life. The general knowledge of the readers of this Journal can supply the material necessary to give concrete educational meaning to this bare skeletal outline.

1. *A functional conception of mind.* In its primary form, behavior is viewed as the interaction of a sentient, active, human organism with the objects in the natural and social environment. It is typically undertaken in order to attain more satisfactory adjustment and it is, therefore, intrinsically goal-seeking—purposive—in nature. Mind is developed through this active process of adjustment. Responses which facilitate the functioning of the organism get built into habits which become effectual components of the organized human personality. Thus mind is not considered to be a metaphysical, or psychical, substance inserted in the human body which develops primarily by a process of unfolding from within. Mind is a type of behavior—behavior which, because of knowledge of events and their connections, is able to turn anticipated eventual outcomes into directive stimuli in present experience. The traditional notion of a mind-body dualism is thus supplanted by the conception of a

human organism which, through association with others in the organized life of the community, becomes progressively aware of the meanings involved in its own activities.

2. *An empirical interpretation of values and morals.* The view of the good as that which corresponds to the fixed moral structure of "reality" is replaced by a conception of the good as that which satisfies the needs of flesh and blood human beings in their concrete relations with one another and with their natural environment. That is considered good which sustains and expands human activity. Activity, as stated above, is always *in* and *of* the environment, and is relative to that environment. Success and failure—satisfaction and dissatisfaction—in these ordinary interactions, which in their myriad forms constitute human experience, contribute the final criteria by which the good is measured.

Ethical behavior does not signify habitual obedience to fixed moral codes: it signifies the capacity to respond intelligently in actual life situations. In harmony with the conception of social democracy, that behavior is judged most ethical which, in terms of actual resources and limitations found within the situation, best promotes the greatest good of the greatest number. Ethical ideals, moral values, and all regulative principles grow from within this process of actual experience which is the ultimate test of both truth and value. Norms for human conduct have no other sanction than that which experience itself contributes.

3. *Experimental naturalism.* Nature is not viewed as a mere phenomenal order created by some underlying principle, or spirit, which is more real and rational than the product of its activity: it is the totality of actual conditions, vastly extended in time and space, in which our lives are set. In so far as explanations are to be intelligible, and not fanciful, they must be made in terms of what is going on within this context of natural events. Truths, scientific laws, and ethical principles are in the nature of statements about observed behaviors and inferred connections and correlations of these natural affairs. In short, all knowledge is *of* these concrete events and is not more ultimate than the behaviors it describes.

Experience discloses that nature is a process. "It is a scene of incessant beginnings and endings" in which unique, individualized events emerge. No analysis, no matter how far it is carried, can legitimately eliminate these qualitatively unique occurrences. Individuality is therefore considered to be an "irreducible trait" of all existence. In the process of interaction, which is nature, novel events emerge. These later events are in no sense less real than those which preceded them. Each occurrence is to be taken at full face value for whatever traits it exhibits in its behavior. The nature of a thing is found in what it does, not in some alleged underlying substance from which it is supposed to be made.

Human society and human personality are emergents within this natural process. Although mind is a late development in the evolutionary series, it is none-the-less real. The appearance of mind, however, does not justify the inference that it is necessarily the product of conditions which *purposed* its development. Nature is the context in which human personality emerged, and the structures of man, therefore, must necessarily have a certain congruence with its essential conditions. But this obvious fact does not warrant the conclusion that all of nature is friendly to man. Experience discloses the opposite to be the case. Forces which are hostile to his welfare seem to be as characteristic as those which support his activities. In this complex of favoring and thwarting events, in which our lives are vitally implicated, intelligent control is a necessity.

The meaning of culture is found in this effort to create an environment more favorable and meaningful for human beings. The deepest purpose of education arises from the necessity of nurturing human beings who understand this cultural inheritance, and who also are equipped with the initiative and intelligence to conserve and further extend this equipment of meanings and controls upon which human welfare depends.

4. *The activity principle.* The foregoing conceptions have their implications for our view of the educative process. Mind—the effectual capacity to make creative adjustments—is a necessity, not a luxury, in a world in which novelty occurs, and in which satisfactory experience is dependent upon foresight and control. This mind, moreover, is not an original gift; it is achieved through an educative experience. Freedom for the individual is a function of the development of this type of responsible initiative, in which behavior is informed by understanding, and is controlled by anticipated outcomes. In other words, freedom is the correlative of a behavior which can transform conditions into constructive means for the achievement of human purposes. Thus real freedom is synonymous with capacity to make effectual response and to learn progressively from experience.

It follows that neither freedom nor responsibility can be given to the young. Both alike must be learned through active experience which provides opportunity for the carrying out of complete acts in which planning, constructing, testing, judging are all included. It is the business of the school to arrange for such complete meaningful experiences. In affirming that this activity principle is the real "minimum essential" in the education of the young, progressive education has made a fundamental contribution. This, notwithstanding the ill-considered educational programs of extremists, who have confused freedom with mere relaxation of external controls, and growth with indulgence of momentary impulse.

5. *Educational provision for individuality.* Individuality, a trait of

all existence, is particularly exhibited at the social level of behavior. Human beings differ both in their natural endowments and in the habits, capacities, and interests they acquire through experience. The ultimate locus of the good, moreover, is in these concrete human individuals. The democratic conception justly holds, therefore, that individual human beings are the ultimate objects of ethical consideration, and that all institutions, moral codes, and religious and educational organizations are means for realizing the good-life for individuals. Hence they are to be judged strictly by their fitness to further this supreme end.

Education to be moral must make its primary purpose the *growth* of persons, not the mere molding of them to the requirements of established, or projected, institutions. To care adequately for this growth of persons, individuality must be prized and cultivated, not levelled out through the imposition of standardized behaviors. No more serious mistake can be made, however, than to suppose that individuality denotes mere difference and eccentricity, and is to be developed by freeing the child from the materials of the culture. It is only by participation in the culture that he becomes significantly human. The problem of education is to cherish individual uniqueness while at the same time providing for the progressive mastery of the resources of the culture.

Responding to the democratic ideal, progressive education has given it further extension by demanding that respect for personality be interpreted to include respect for the child, and by also affirming that no conception of respect for personality which does not include respect for the mind of the individual is adequate. Unfortunately this has led, at times, to an undue fear of adult imposition, and to the assertion of the dangerous half-truth that the purpose of education is "to teach the child to think, not what to think"—as though process and product can thus be torn apart. The importance of the above principle, nevertheless, cannot be denied by anyone who has experienced the deeper meaning of democracy. By broadening the conception of respect for personality to include both respect for childhood and for the integrity of individual mind, progressive education has made an important contribution not only to the work of the school, but to the whole ethical insight of mankind.

6. *The whole individual.* As a consequence of its rejection of the mind-body dualism, progressive education has advocated a conception of the educative process which assumes responsibility for the total learnings which grow out of any significant activity. In line with the best psychological insight, it has stressed that information, skills, attitudes, emotional sets, and dispositions are all acquired in one and the same process. It has urged that education—particularly that which deals with the young in the years when the very style of life is in process of formation—should assume responsibility for emotional and moral as well as intellectual re-

sults. Its conception has increasingly been accepted and is accomplishing a revolutionary transformation in the field of character education.

Viewing character, as it does, as capacity to make effectual response to one's environment, and as that which is nurtured by all of the direct and indirect influences which operate in the experience of the individual, progressive education has also sought to correlate the work of the school with other community agencies. Following genuine educational leads it has gradually come to see that education in its broadest meaning involves conscious control of institutional practices in terms of the educative consequences which they produce. It has affirmed that the nurture of wholesome human individuals requires the maintenance of a social environment which reinforces in the pattern of its ordinary, practical activities the esthetic, artistic, ethical, intellectual, and social attitudes which it desires to have the school nurture in the young. This has culminated in its interpretation of education as the whole community consciously planning and continuously reconstructing its activities so as to increase both their human meaning and the possibility of further control over subsequent experience.

Obviously the foregoing constitutes a very inadequate statement of the principles of progressive education. But even this brief summary is sufficient to suggest the fundamental character of the reconstruction in philosophy and education which the progressive movement represents. I do not agree with those who assert that these are mere commonplace views, too general in scope to carry any definite meaning for educational activity. In view of the supernatural, magical, intuitive, and authoritarian elements which pervade our traditional approach to human nature, morals, and education, it is clear that the empirical attitudes and procedures of progressive education mark a profound departure. To be sure, not all who guide their educational activities by these conceptions are conscious of their wider implications, and often they are associated with older outlooks and practices with which they are in conflict. But, after all discounts are made, the fact remains that already an important group of teachers and parents now guide their educational work by these ideas. Until this present vigorous minority, however, has grown into a dominant majority, it will be premature to dismiss as mere truisms the conceptions involved in this new orientation.

In the face of reactionary obscurantist movements which are sweeping whole nations, he is, indeed, complacent who assumes that this whole-hearted empirical approach is now so deeply rooted that it requires no further conscious cultivation. Even under the most favorable circumstances, several generations will be required before this new world outlook and its associated experimental attitudes and methods become axiomatic in American culture. The importance of a progressive educational movement which holds as one of its main objectives the communication and elaboration of this new orientation can scarcely be overestimated.

But there is a real difference between making this a central objective of the Progressive Education Association and in permitting it to become the exclusive objective. If these admirable philosophical, psychological, and ethical principles are to avoid the fatal weakness of barren formalism, they must be given concrete meaning in terms of developing social conditions. For example, it is not enough to affirm the importance of faith in intelligence and the value of critical inquiry. It may also be legitimately asked that those who proclaim the worth of these processes should champion them in the concrete, not stopping short of stating plainly the actual institutions, practices, and special interest groups which now limit and oppose the exercise of these critical functions.

Again, it is not enough to assert that in a world in which change and novelty are ultimate traits we should support a continuous criticism and reconstruction of institutions in order that they may be progressively adapted to changing conditions. The demand for a bill of particulars cannot be safely ignored. Confronted with our present discordant civilization, what does the Progressive Education Association consider to be the fundamental sources of the present disorder, and what kind of economic, political, and ideological changes are now necessary?

Search, inquiry, and discussion are, indeed, valuable activities. But suppose as the result of prolonged historical and social analysis certain ethical and social conclusions are reached. As progressive educators, what do we do with these conclusions? Are we under obligation to continue our inquiry, discussion, and educational activity as though we had not reached them? If not, how do they enter into our educational work?

To be more concrete: suppose our study of industrial society has led to the conviction that power production has built an interdependent world in which both laissez-faire economic individualism and narrow nationalism are surviving anachronisms; or, suppose that we discover that power production could produce a relative abundance, and that today we are denied that abundance because of adherence to an anarchistic privately owned and controlled property system; or, suppose that we learn, after repeated trials and failures, that efficient social planning —the deliberate social control of our collective affairs in terms of the consequences they produce in the lives of individuals—is incompatible with the maintenance of the competitive private-profit system, in what manner, then, does the progressive educator take account of these conclusions? Surely if his research and criticism are to be viewed with respect either by himself or by others, the progressive educator will have to find some means of incorporating his findings into his educational program. A process of inquiry and criticism which is ever starting anew, which is uneasy and evasive in the presence of a specific result, cannot be taken seriously indefinitely.

Finally, along with others, progressive education has affirmed that the deepest moral meaning in American life is found in the conception of social democracy. As we have already seen, it has even given important new interpretations to what respect for human personality involves. Confronted with a society in which the purposes of millions are disregarded —even the opportunity to engage in remunerative, socially useful labor being denied them; with a society in which the majority live in chronic insecurity; with a society in which a small privileged class legally controls many of the major means of livelihood; and with a world-society in which competition for markets and raw materials is increasingly organized on a militant national scale so that its economic practices breed war, despite all humanitarian desires to the contrary—confronted with a society of this sort, what concrete implications does the progressive educator find in his democratic purpose?

To judge by its official pronouncements, the Progressive Education Association has not as yet found it possible to make statements about the present situation other than those of the most general sort. These statements are considered to lack definite meaning because they can be construed by almost any special interest group to serve its own purposes. The following is taken from the statement of one of the most representative of the Progressive Education Association commissions. It was developed in a conference called in order to formulate the social philosophy of the Commission.

> Some philosophy of society and of life inheres in every educational program. This may be a generous philosophy, clarified by the knowledge and wisdom of the race, or it may be a petty or provincial philosophy, reflecting the narrow interests of some group or class.
>
> An adequate philosophy for the American school can be extracted from elements of the American tradition. The great points of reference are to be found in such documents as the Declaration of Independence, the Constitution, and the primary writings of the great contributors to American life.
>
> As a nation, we include among the basic purposes of government as distinguished from the exercise of power for its own sake, the establishment of justice and the promotion of the general welfare. As a nation we adhere to the ideal of government by the people as against

government by prescriptive rights. We believe in political procedures that provide for proposal, discussion, acceptance, and adoption. Implicit in these procedures, and possessing values in themselves, are freedom of speech, religious toleration, freedom of the press and freedom of assembly.

As a people we believe in the dignity and worth of the individual. That the individual is not to be bent to purposes alien to humanity, is a doctrine imbedded in the tradition, the thought, and the striving of the Western World. This basic faith in the individual must be continuously reinterpreted and reimplemented in the social world on the basis of a realistic knowledge of the movement of ideas and interests at work in contemporary society. The schools face this problem: how are we to contribute to a social order which in the individual will provide opportunity, promote growth, and develop character, which in turn will sustain and elevate the social order?

We suffer notably from an underlying lack of social integration. It is of critical importance that our economic life, political practices, religious beliefs, cultural interests, social relationships, and individual motivation be synthesized in a comprehensive and unified purpose. To attain this objective there must be: (1) with the individual, an understanding of the nature of existing maladjustments and problems, and a realization of the necessity of an integration of his own individual thought and aspiration and (2) with society, a continuous and comprehensive reformulation and reconstruction of social organization, endeavor and ideal.

In the midst of what some of its most eminent leaders have called "a crisis in culture," why is the Progressive Education Association willing to issue statements so general as this? Does it believe that a more definite statement of the implications of industrial conditions and trends is contrary to the principles of progressive education? Does it fear that a meaningful statement of the actual characteristics of modern society would necessarily encourage a program of indoctrination in the school? If so, how valid is this fear? In the natural sciences, we do not consider the expression of definite findings to be hostile to the spirit of true educational inquiry. Moreover, the social forces which operate to inhibit the process of searching objective inquiry, and which are unwilling to let pupils reach their own conclusions after thorough study, are not, for the most part, those who favor social reconstruction. Few of the latter group will be found among the advocates of loyalty oaths. It is critically important that we do everything possible to maintain the freedom of the schools, but we should remember that the center of opposition to the exercise of academic freedom now resides in the economic sphere. For the most part, the present leaders of repressive movements are those who desire to preserve the status quo. A pronouncement of social purpose which studiously avoids all mention of actual economic conditions and forces which are hostile to genuine freedom and democracy unconsciously reveals the actual control which these vested interests exert. Under certain conditions, "silence is not neutrality, but consent."

Certain groups offer a very different explanation of the failure of the Progressive Education Association to contribute adequate social leadership at the present time. According to their analysis, its supporters are so largely drawn from the favored upper-middle class—the constituency of the private schools—that it cannot speak plainly about the present situation. They assert that it is bound by the bias of the class it represents.

Whatever may be the causes which have kept the Association from developing a democratic philosophy for industrial society, sufficiently concrete to give American education necessary guidance, its friends will hope they may be speedily overcome. The evidence accumulates that the task of educational reconstruction and that of social reconstruction are bound together. The agency which is to lead in the former must have an adequate philosophy for the latter.

PROGRESSIVE EDUCATION IS TOO SOFT

William Chandler Bagley (1874–1946) was one of the most prominent "essentialists" in American education. He was Dean of the School of Education at the University of Illinois, and later became Professor of Education at Teachers College, Columbia University. It is interesting to note that Bagley, one of the leading opponents of progressive education, was on the same faculty with such influential proponents of progressivism as Kilpatrick, Rugg, Childs, Counts, and Dewey. Bagley was not an extreme conservative, but he was opposed to extreme positions in education, and the progressive movement represented a radical departure to him. He believed that essentialism, the teaching of those basic subjects necessary for the perpetuation of democracy, must replace progressivism in the schools if the United States and its democratic tradition should hope to repel the threat of totalitarianism. In Atlantic City, in February, 1938, Bagley presented a paper which served as a platform for a group of educators who called their organization The Essentialist Committee for the Advancement of American Education. In addition to authoring several important books in education, Bagley was the editor of School and Society *and* Educational Administration and Supervision. *In the following article, Bagley attacks progressive education and states the advantages and the necessity of essentialism to American education.*

William C. Bagley

Education (*October 1939*), 75–81. *Reprinted by permission of the publishers, The Bobbs-Merrill Company, Inc.*

In the minds of some people there is an implication of newness, or freshness, about the term Progressive Education which is scarcely justified. Take, for example, the emphasis on child-freedom. This has appeared repeatedly in the history of educational theory; in practice, it long antedated that form of organized and directed education which we know as the school. The school is very distinctly a product of civilization, but child-freedom, most people are likely to admit, is one of the most striking features of primitive, untutored, uncivilized societies. Other tenets now characteristic of present-day Progressivism have cropped out frequently in the development of organized education in civilized societies, some examples being: (1) emphasis upon present or current problems as centers of learning; (2) stressing of the immediate and the local; (3) disparagement of the past and the remote; (4) belittling of sequence and system; (5) enthronement of individual interests, purposes, and desires.

There is evidence to support the statement that the Progressive movement is at least two hundred and eighty years old. In Barnard's *American Journal of Education* for March, 1859, there appeared an article translated from the German of Karl von Raumer entitled "The Progressives of the Seventeenth Century." Doctrines of the 17th-century Progressives as set forth by Raumer included many of the points of emphasis cited in the preceding paragraph.

PASSING "ON SCHEDULE"

The Progressives today, in many school systems at least, are showing a tendency to abandon rigorous standards of scholastic achievement as a condition of promotion from grade to grade, and the passing of all pupils "on schedule." This policy, which found a strong initial support thirty years ago in the studies of "retardation and elimination," has of late been given even a wider appeal by the teachings of mental hygiene regarding the possible effects of failure in disintegrating personality. The

problem is extremely complicated, but the movement has already resulted in at least one very important change. Instead of having "over-
age" pupils piling up in the intermediate grades, we now have "over-
graded" pupils handicapped in the work of the junior and senior high
schools by their lack of thorough training in the so-called fundamentals.

The Progressives today are largely responsible for the wide vogue of
the "activity movement." This is an outgrowth of the so-called "project
method" which in its turn was an effort to find, or to encourage the
learner to find, problems of vital purposes in the solution of which desirable learnings could be effected. The activity movement and the resulting "activity programs" and "activity curricula," like the project method,
have an important place—a central function in the primary school, and a
very useful supplementary function on all educational levels. The tendency to make them a substitute for systematic and sequential learning
and to go even further and regard activity as a sufficient end in itself
irrespective of whether or not anything is learned through the activity is
another matter. It is, however, a fascinating proposal. As one enthusiastic
activist said, "Let us not use activities as pegs on which to hang subject-
matter." If the schools only provide an abundance of "rich experiences"
for the learner, it seems, other things will miraculously take care of
themselves. This is not at all absurd if one accepts the premises; it is a
thoroughly consistent result of the theory of incidental learning carried
to its logical conclusion.

DISCREDITING EXACT STUDIES

The Progressives today tend to discredit the exact and exacting studies. Most fortunately for their purposes there appeared just at the turn
of the century the report of the first careful psychological experiments
testing the validity of the theory of mental discipline. These really classic
experiments of Thorndike and Woodworth were followed by a long series of similar investigations that aimed to determine how far learnings acquired in one subject were, or could be, applied in other situations. The results in general indicated that such a "transfer" was far from
inevitable and in some cases either quite negative or so slight as to bring
the whole theory into question.

The proponents of the universal high school and of other educational movements that were impeded by the requirement of subjects inherently difficult to the average mind were not slow to capitalize these
experimental findings. As is natural under conditions of this sort, the evidence was generalized to a far greater extent than the experiments war-
ranted, and with far-reaching results in school practice. Although the absolute number enrolled in Latin classes has increased, only a small pro-

portion of pupils graduating from the high schools during the past ten years have even been exposed to Latin. Increasing proportions, too, are quite innocent of any training in elementary mathematics beyond the increasingly ineffective modicum of arithmetic acquired in the elementary schools. But the important fact is that there has been a growing practice of discouraging even competent learners from undertaking the studies that are exact though exacting; hence the upward expansion of mass-education, while sincerely a democratic movement, is not guarding itself against the potentially most fatal pitfall of democracy. It has deliberately adopted the easy policy of leveling-down rather than facing resolutely the difficult task of leveling-up—and upon the possibility of leveling-up the future of democracy indisputably depends.

STRESSING OF "SOCIAL STUDIES"

The Progressives today choose to place an increasingly heavy emphasis upon the "social studies." While the exact and exacting studies were in effect being discredited, the primrose path of least resistance was opened even wider in the field known as the social studies. The argument here is plausible and appealing. "Education for citizenship" is a ringing slogan with limitless potentialities, especially in an age when high-sounding shibboleths, easily formulated, can masquerade as fundamental premises and postulates wrought through the agony of hard thinking.

But obviously the social sciences, so-called, are not in the same class with the natural sciences. Their generalizations permit trustworthy predictions only in a few cases and then only in a slight degree. When the human element enters, uncertainty enters—else the world could have anticipated and adjusted itself to Hitler and Mussolini and Stalin and the military oligarchy of Japan and would not be standing dazed and impotent as it stands today. And while to expect an educational pabulum of social studies in the lower schools essentially to overcome this inherent limitation of the social sciences is an alluring prospect, it is to expect nothing less than a miracle. It is, indeed, just as sensible as would be a brave and desperate effort to incite immature minds to square the circle.

PLANS FOR NEW SOCIETY

The Progressives today believe that the lower schools should be used to establish a new social order. The proposal definitely and deliberately to indoctrinate immature learners in the interest of a specific social order and one that involves wide departures from that which prevails in our country is to be questioned. With the growing ineffectiveness of the lower schools in failing to lay adequate foundations in fundamental and established learnings of unquestioned permanence and value, such efforts would necessarily be superficial in the last degree. It would be an extreme case of building what may be characterized for the sake of argument as a perfectly splendid edifice on shifting sands—in this case, quicksands would be the more appropriate metaphor. And here we might well study certain people that have actually achieved a social order which is pointed to by our idealists as exemplifying in many ways the realization of their dreams. Reference is made, of course, to such countries as Sweden, Denmark, Norway, and New Zealand. An outstanding fact of fundamental significance is that these countries have *not* achieved these laudable results by emasculating their educational systems. Their people indeed would stand aghast at the very suggestion.

VAGARIES IN CURRICULUM CHANGE

The Progressives today are behind a "curriculum-revision" movement which certainly has numerous vagaries. The various reform proposals just discussed have culminated in the general movement known as curriculum-revision which has dominated the lower schools for nearly twenty years. A primary emphasis has been the alleged need of building the programs of instruction around the local community. As long ago as 1933 more than 30,000 different curricula were on file in the curriculum-laboratory of Teachers College, Columbia University. Most of these have been prepared during the preceding decade by committees of teachers in local school systems throughout the country. Sometimes the committees were personally directed by a "curriculum-expert"; in practically all cases a rapidly developing theory evolved by these specialists guided the work. Insofar as we can learn, this theory has never explicitly recognized that the state or the nation has a stake in the content of school instruction. The need of common elements in the basic culture of all citizens, especially in a democracy, has in effect been denied. Furthermore, with the American people the most mobile in the world, with stability of residence over the period of schoool attendance the exception and not the rule in many sections of the country, and with a significantly higher average of school failure among pupils whose parents move from place to place than among those who remain in the same community, the curriculum theorists have been totally insensitive to the need of a certain measure of uniformity in school requirements and in the grade-placement of crucial topics. In addition to all this, the clear tendency of the curriculum-revision movement has been to minimize basic learnings, to magnify the superficial, to belittle sequence and system, and otherwise to aggravate the weakness and ineffectiveness of the lower schools.

OPPOSITION OF ESSENTIALISTS

Opposed to the program of the Progressives are the Essentialists, a group that met at Atlantic City on February 26, 1938, and adopted the name The Essentialist Committee for the Advancement of American Education.[1] The Essentialists believe that a primary function of American education is to safeguard and strengthen the ideals of American democracy, with especial emphasis upon freedom of speech, freedom of the press, freedom of assembly, and freedom of religion. After recent changes in Europe, it is clear enough that whenever any one of these is permitted to collapse, the whole democratic structure will topple like a house of cards.

The Essentialists are sure that if our Democratic society is to meet the competition or conflict with totalitarian states, there must be democratic discipline that will give strength and solidarity to the democratic purpose and ideal. If the theory of democracy finds no place for discipline, then before long the theory will have only historical significance. French education, much closer to the danger, has recognized this imperative need. Still unswerving in fidelity to the ideals of democracy, and still giving its first emphasis to clarity of thought and independence in individual thinking as the time-honored objectives of French education, it recognizes no less the fundamental importance of social solidarity in the defense of solidarity.[2]

Progressive educational theory long since dropped the term "discipline" from its vocabulary. Today its most vocal and influential spokesmen enthrone the right even of the immature learner to choose what he shall learn. They condemn as "authoritarian" all learning tasks that are imposed by the teacher. They deny any value in the systematic and sequential mastery of the lessons that the race has learned at so great a cost. They condone and rationalize the refusal of the learner to attack a task that does not interest him. In effect they open wide the lines of least resistance and least effort. Obedience they stigmatize as a sign of weakness. All this they advocate in magic names of "democracy" and "freedom."

[1] Besides the writer, other members of the committee are: Dr. M. Demiashkevich; Dr. Walter H. Ryle; Dr. M. L. Shane; Mr. F. Alden Shaw, Chairman and Organizer; Dr. Louis Shores; Dr. Guy M. Whipple.

[2] See the concluding paragraphs of C. Bougle, "The French Conception of 'Culture Generale,'" a series of lectures at Teachers College, Columbia University, April 1938.

ESSENTIALISTS ON DEMOCRACY

The Essentialists stand for a literate electorate. That such a literate electorate is absolutely indispensable not only to its welfare but to its very survival is clearly demonstrated by the sorry fate that so speedily overtook every unschooled and illiterate democracy founded as a result of the war that was "to make the world safe for democracy." And literacy in this sense means, of course, far more than the mere ability to translate printed letters into spoken words; it means the development and expansion of ideas; it means the basis for intelligent understanding and for the collective thought and judgment which are the essence of democratic institutions. These needs are so fundamental to an effective democracy that it would be folly to leave them to the whim or caprice of either learner or teacher.

The Essentialists recognize, then, the right of the immature learner to guidance and direction when these are needed either for his individual welfare or for the welfare and progress of the democratic group. The responsibility of the mature for the instruction and control of the immature is the biological meaning of the extended period of human immaturity and necessary dependence. It took the human race untold ages to recognize this responsibility. It is literally true that until this recognition dawned man remained a savage. Primitive societies, as numerous students have observed (and their testimony seems to be unanimous), pamper and indulge their young. Freedom of children from control, guidance, and discipline is with them a rule so nearly universal that its only brief but significant exception during the nearly universal savage ceremonies marking the adolescent onset of maturity is regarded as the first faint beginning of consciously directed human education.

The essentialists are certain that an effective democracy demands a community of culture. Educationally this means that each generation be placed in possession of a common core of ideas, meanings, understandings, and ideals representing the most precious elements of the human heritage.

ESSENTIALS OF ESSENTIALISTS

There can be little question as to the essentials. It is by no means a mere accident that the arts of recording, computing, and measuring have been among the first concerns of organized education. They are basic social arts. Every civilized society has been founded upon these arts, and when these arts have been lost, civilization has invariably and inevitably collapsed. Egypt, Asia Minor, and Mesopotamia are strewn with the ruins of civilizations that forgot how to read and write. Contemporary civilization, for the first time in history has attempted to insure its continuance by making these arts insofar as possible the prerogative of all.

Nor is it at all accidental that a knowledge of the world that lies beyond one's immediate experience has been among the recognized essentials of universal education, and that at least a speaking acquaintance with man's past and especially with the story of one's country was early provided for in the program of the universal school. Widening the space horizon and extending the time perspective are essential if the citizen is to be protected from the fallacies of the local and the immediate.

Investigation, invention, and creative art have added to the heritage and the list of recognized essentials has been extended and will be further extended. Health instruction and the inculcation of health practices are now basic phases of the work of the lower schools. The elements of natural science have their place. Neither the fine arts nor the industrial arts are neglected.

TEACHER RESPONSIBILITY

The Essentialists would have the teachers responsible for a systematic program of studies and activities to develop the recognized essentials. Informal learning through experiences initiated by the learners is important, and abundant opportunities should be provided for such experiences throughout the range of organized education. Beyond the primary grades, however, where as we have said it may well predominate, informal learning should be regarded as supplementary rather than central.

The Essentialists appreciate the fact that failure in school is unpleasant and that the repetition of a grade is costly and often not very effective. On the other hand, the lack of a stimulus that will keep the learner to his task is a serious injustice both to him and to the democratic group which, we repeat, has a fundamental stake in his effective education. Too severe a stigma has undoubtedly been placed upon school failure by implying that it is symptomatic of permanent weakness. By no means is this always the case. No less a genius than Pasteur did so poorly in his first year at the Higher Normal School of Paris that he had to go home for further preparation. One of the outstanding scientists of the present century had a hard time in meeting the requirements of the secondary school, failing, it is said, in the most elementary work of the field in which he later became world-famous. The list could be extended almost indefinitely.

ATTITUDE TOWARD FAILURES

Obviously not all learners can progress at the same rate. Some will go very, very slowly. Others will have trouble in getting started but will progress rapidly when they overcome the initial handicaps. Let us not stigmatize failure as we have done in the past. On the other hand, if education abandons rigorous standards and consequently provides no effective stimulus to the effort that learning requires, many persons will pass through twelve years of schooling only to find themselves in a world in which ignorance and lack of fundamental training are increasingly heavy handicaps. This in an all too literal sense is to throw the baby out with the bath.

The Essentialists are positive that a clear and primary duty of organized education at the present time is to recognize the fundamental character of the changes that are already taking place, and to search diligently for means of counteracting their dangers. Let us repeat that an educational theory to meet these needs must be strong, virile, and positive, not feeble, effeminate, and vague. The theories that have increasingly dominated American education during the past generation are at basis distinctly of the latter type. The Essentialists have recognized and still recognize the contributions of real value that these theories have made to educational practice. They believe, however, that these positive elements can be preserved in an educational theory which finds its basis in the necessary dependence of the immature upon the mature for guidance, instruction, and discipline. This dependence is inherent in human nature. "What has been ordained among the prehistoric protozoa," said Huxley, "cannot be altered by act of Parliament"—nor, we may add, by the wishful thinking of educational theorists, however sincere their motives. "Authoritarianism" is an ugly word. But when those who detest it carry their laudable rebellion against certain of its implications so far as to reject the authority of plain facts, their arguments, while well adapted perhaps to the generation of heat, become lamentably lacking in light.

EDUCATION IN DEPTH

On January 7, 1963, Max Rafferty began a four-year term as California's State Superintendent of Public Instruction. During a hard-fought campaign, Rafferty loudly denounced throughout the entire state "life-adjustment" education, "undisciplined" schools, and any type of education that aimed at developing the "total-child." Consistently presenting himself as a foe of the pro-

gressive education which he believed had California schools and educators in its grip, he promised to scrap such terms and practices as "language arts" and "social studies" (history should be taught as history, geography as geography, and civics as civics). He referred to his emphasis on subject matter as the "conservative revolution in education" and sometimes as "education for survival." Rafferty's victory was all the more significant when one considers that the major teacher organizations in California (the California Teachers Association, the American Federation of Teachers, and the Affiliated Teacher Organizations of Los Angeles), the California State Board of Education, and even the school board in La Canada, California, where Rafferty was a school superintendent prior to his election, publicly supported his opponent. Rafferty gained the support of various conservative organizations in California and, although not a Bircher himself, received the backing of many of the members of the John Birch Society. Out of nearly five million votes cast, Rafferty overwhelmed his opponent by 232,000 votes. In 1966, he was re-elected for a second four-year term by another landslide. Max Rafferty has written numerous articles for professional journals in education; he is the author of Suffer Little Children *and* What They Are Doing to Your Children *and the co-author of* Practices and Trends in School Administration. *In the following excerpt Rafferty describes the "education in depth" revolution and wages a blistering attack on progressive education.*

Max Rafferty

Excerpt from What They Are Doing to Your Children (New York: New American Library, 1964), pp. 90–96. Copyright © 1964 by Max Rafferty. Published by arrangement with the New American Library, Inc., New York.

What is the real nature of this revolution? What is the new philosophy that we in the west are recommending to the nation in the place of outworn, exploded progressive education?

Californians are calling it "education in depth." And as is usual in such matters, it's easier to tell what it isn't than what it is.

It is not, for instance, a return to the dear, dead past. It believes in the "three R's," right enough, but only as a springboard for vastly more complex subject matter. It doesn't want a curriculum that harks back to the turn of the century, when a reading and speaking knowledge of

Greek and Latin was required to get into Harvard and when a sterile and stereotyped classicism was the major goal of the learning process. It doesn't approve, either, of the often brutal "hickory-stick" discipline of the old days.

Education in depth does not believe that the children belong to the schools, but rather that they belong to the parents. These parents pay the teachers to provide expert information, to teach the skills that a child must learn if he is to become a well-rounded, successful adult, and above all to open the multiplicity of doors to which only education has the key. It is not the job of the school to amuse the child, to condition him psychologically, to feed and clothe him, or indeed to do anything except teach him. This, heaven knows, is a big enough task in itself to preclude virtually everything else.

Education in depth calls a spade a spade. History is taught as history, geography as geography, and civics as civics. It is not all caught up together, and blended, and watered down, and broadened, and prechewed until it comes out as something labeled "social studies," or worse yet, "social living." The theory behind this is simple: while it is perfectly true that a knowledge of geography will help in the study of history, it does not follow that therefore the two should be combined and taught as a single subject. This would be just as ridiculous as to claim that because a knowledge of algebra will help in the study of physics, the two should be combined and taught as a single subject labeled "quantitative studies" or "quantitative living."

Education in depth holds that there is a tremendous accumulation of knowledge added to each generation by the thinkers and doers of that period and that one of the principal functions of the schools is to transmit this cultural heritage to the citizens of tomorrow. This means that a reasonable amount of material must be committed to memory and that there is nothing wrong with this. In addition, memorizing phrases and lines from famous works of poetry and prose should be encouraged as a means of perpetuating our literary birthright.

A new philosophy means a new curriculum. Subjects like "ninth-grade orientation" and "student leadership" and "senior problems" should come out. Subjects like "world geography" and "modern economics" should go in. On the elementary level, the units on "the home and the community" can safely be turned out to pasture in favor of some on "great American heroes" and "the Bill of Rights." In junior high school, the repetitive, boring courses in "general math" and "general science" could well be telescoped into single seventh-grade subjects, with specific foreign languages, biology, and algebra taught in the eighth grade for those fitted to tackle them. The new mathematics, geared to the Space Age, is already appearing on the scene. It should be welcomed, its weaknesses analyzed and eliminated, and its strengths acknowledged.

Education in depth stands for the equal dignity and status of each subject, whether it be art or auto mechanics, history or homemaking, mathematics or metal shop. If it is in the school curriculum, placed there by the people through their own locally elected representatives, then it deserves to be accorded exactly the same respect as any other subject. Furthermore, it deserves to be taught by a teacher who is prepared to teach it, who honors its importance in the overall picture—yes, and who loves it for its own sake. If a subject is not worth this kind of treatment, take it out of the school altogether. But don't set up first- and second-class citizens among our teachers, based on the imagined superiority of one subject or group of subjects over another.

The same advice, however, does not apply to reading materials. Here a very definite priority listing should be made. Children today do not have nearly the time for reading that their parents did, especially at home. A dozen stimuli, unknown to an older generation of Americans, compete for the attention of the boys and girls. Therefore it behooves the schools to assign literary materials carefully chosen from the great children's classics and to see that this basic food of the mind is carefully ingested and digested before the less tried and tested items of current and popular taste are placed before the pupil. After the child has trudged the Scottish hills with David Balfour and plumbed the ocean's depths with Captain Nemo, there will be ample time for him to explore the space lanes with Flash Gordon. First things first.

Education in depth demands from the teacher a knowledge of subject matter in excess of what has been demanded during the past twenty years or more. The English teacher is going to be expected to know English grammar backwards and forwards, and no nonsense about teaching "toastmastership" or "how to be popular in a mixed group." The history instructor will be expected to be able to distinguish between the Guelfs and the Ghibellines on the one hand, and between Benjamin Harrison and William Henry Harrison on the other. The physical-education teacher is seeing the time rapidly drawing to a close when he can toss a few basketballs or volleyballs to a swarm of boys and tell them to choose up sides and get some games going. The elementary instructor is going to have to tighten up and bear down. No more pupil papers handed back with grades of A but containing misspelled words and faulty constructions that haven't even been circled.

Education in depth stresses the value and importance of competition in the schools. Such competition should not be excessive or unreasonable, but it should exist. Life itself is competition, and the sooner the child learns to compete, the better for him and for his country. Within the range of the child's own ability potential, good work should be praised and rewarded, bad work criticized and labeled unacceptable. Subject-matter report cards graded *A-B-C-D-F* or a reasonable facsimile thereof are a must. Parent-teacher conferences are fine, but they cannot and should not take the place of report cards. The latter constitute a sort of semiannual day of reckoning, a summing up of assets and liabilities that is invaluable training for later life.

Speaking of a day of reckoning, we are going to have to have one for the elementary reading and "social-studies" books, and in the near future. The new philosophy cannot coexist with Dick and Jane, and Tom and Susan, and their ilk. The namby-pamby, nonexistent plots; the one-dimensional and insipid characters; the painfully successful attempts to remove anything exciting or adventurous or *glamorous* from the contents—all these things will have to be changed. Before the great publishing houses can expect to sell their wares in California at least, they are going to have to get us some books with real meat in them, books with sparkle and zing, books that are worth reading. After all, children don't learn to read in order to please the teacher or gratify their parents. They learn to read because they become sufficiently interested in what they are reading to want to tackle page two because of what happened on page one. I submit that for far too long we haven't supplied them with books that would cause anyone to want to turn the pages.

There is another fault to find with the school books, however, other than general lack of interest. There are downright inaccuracies and misrepresentations in all too many cases. For instance, one complaint against publishers lies in the way they treat our racial minorities, picturing the Negro either as a barefooted plantation hand or an Olympic athlete, and our Mexican neighbors invariably wearing sandals and serapes. If there is one vital area of weakness in our entire educational structure that deserves to be singled out and taken vigorously in hand, it is the textbook situation.

Let us sum up the differences between progressive education and education in depth, always remembering that we do not intend to throw the baby out along with the bath water. Progressivism had some good points. Few things are all black or all white. The problem-solving approach fathered by Dewey was sound. It should be retained. So should the willingness on the part of the instructor to give reasons to the children for the many things he must ask them to do every day. Basically, however, the differences are these:

1. Progressive education teaches that there are no positive and eternal values. Education in depth maintains that there are and that the main purpose of education is to seek out these lasting truths, to identify them, and to explore them to the greater benefit of the individual and the nation.

2. Progressive education stresses "life adjustment" and "group ac-

ceptance" as the primary goals of the instructional program. Education in depth holds that the teaching of organized, disciplined, and systematic subject matter is the principal objective of the schools.

3. Progressive education downgrades the role of the individual and glorifies the importance of the group. Education in depth intends to regard the individual as the be-all and the end-all of the educative process.

4. Progressive education feels that the curriculum should depend upon the interests and needs of the group. Education in depth wants a curriculum to provide for the individual the tools and skills he needs to be a cultured, productive, patriotic American citizen.

5. Progressive education believes that memorization is stultifying and a waste of time. Education in depth teaches that committing important names, places, events, dates, and passages of poetry and prose to memory is a necessary part of instruction.

6. Progressive education advocates "experiencing" learning through as many sense avenues as practicable. Education in depth thinks this is a pronounced waste of time and regards reading and recitative discussion as still the most effective and economical method of instruction.

7. Progressive education holds that the pupil should be encouraged to compete only with himself, or rather with his own previous best efforts. Education in depth believes that the very survival of our country and the success of the individual in later life depends upon how well he is taught to hold his own in a highly competitive world.

8. Progressive education, as interpreted by several of its high priests, has doubts about the American free-enterprise system and has advocated various form of collectivism. Education in depth teaches the facts about our country's phenomenal growth and development and reminds its pupils that our economic system has made us the envy and the wonder of the whole world.

The issue is clearly drawn. The difference is as great as that between day and night. Public opinion all over the United States is lining up on one side or the other. No greater or more significant decision will be made by our people in this century.

In California, the determination has already been reached. But we have no monopoly on truth; there is room in education in depth for all.

WHAT HAPPENED TO PROGRESSIVE EDUCATION?

It is appropriate that the following article be included in a chapter dealing with an appraisal of the progressive education move-

ment in the United States. In the previous articles the student was introduced to some of the ideas of the proponents and the critics of progressive education, but in this selection the student learns about the history of the progressive education movement itself. Lawrence A. Cremin—in order to answer the question: What happened to progressive education?—explores the origins of the movement, who sponsored it, what it contributed, why it declined, and what its current status is today. Few scholars are as eminently qualified as Cremin to write on progressive education. He is an educator and an acknowledged authority on the history of the progressive education movement, and has contributed many scholarly articles and several books pertaining to this subject, notably, The Transformation of the School: Progressivism in American Education, 1876–1957, *and* The Genius of American Education, *both of which received wide critical acclaim. A historian as well as an educator, Cremin was president of the History of Education Society and of the National Society of College Teachers of Education.*

Lawrence A. Cremin

Teachers College Record (*October 1959*), 23–29. *Reprinted by permission of the author and the publisher. This article has been subsequently incorporated in the author's book* The Transformation of the School: Progressivism in American Education, 1876–1957 (*New York: Vintage Books, 1964*).

The death of the Progressive Education Association in 1955, and the passing of its journal, *Progressive Education*, two years later, marked the end of an era in American pedagogy. Yet one would hardly have realized it from the pitifully small group of mourners at both funerals. Somehow a movement which had for half a century enlisted the enthusiasm, the loyalty, the imagination, and the energy of large segments of the American public and the teaching profession became, in the decade following World War II, anathema, immortalized only in jokes which begin, "There was this mixed-up youngster who went to this ultra-progressive school"; in cartoons like H. T. Webster's classic drawing in the "Life's Darkest Moment" series picturing the day little Mary got a D in blocks and sand piles; in comedies like *Auntie Mame* with its utterly delightful caricature of a Freud-oriented Greenwich Village private school of the 1920's; in feature articles like the one in *The New York Times* several months ago describing a retired professor who had realized his lifelong ambition to be an animal trainer with a circus, and who was using progressive education (learned, by the way, at Teachers College) on his Ringling Brothers lions; in vitriolic attacks on John Dewey, mostly by people who have never read him (I might say he is too often defended by people who haven't read him either); and in the rhetoric and jargon of professional educators.

What was this progressive education movement which in two generations worked a transforming influence on American education? When did it begin? Who sponsored it? What were its contributions? What happened to it? And what remains of it today? Is it quite as dead as its critics believe, or are the reports of its demise, in Mark Twain's classic remark, very much exaggerated?

There is currently afoot a simple story of the rise of progressive education—one that has fed mercilessly on the fears of anxious parents and the hostilities of suspicious conservatives. In it John Dewey, somewhat like Abou ben Adhem, awakes one morning with a new vision of the American school; the vision is progressive education. Over the years, with the assistance of a dedicated group of crafty professional lieutenants at Teachers College, he is able to foist the vision on an unsuspecting American people. The story usually ends with a plea for exorcising this devil from our midst and returning to the ways of the fathers. This kind of morality play has always been an important brand of American political rhetoric, used by reformers and conservatives alike. The point is never to confuse it with history!

When did the progressive education movement actually begin? A recent publication of the National Education Association entitled *Ten Criticisms of Progressive Education,* repeats an often-made assertion: Progressive education refers to a reform movement in education; the term was first used in founding the Progressive Education Association in 1919. The NEA cites as its source the *Dictionary of Education,* edited by Carter V. Good.

The assertion is nonsense—but commonly accepted nonsense. John Dewey once said that the progressive education movement began during the 1870's with the work of Francis W. Parker in Quincy, Massachusetts; indeed, he called Parker the "father of progressive education." And while I would submit that Quincy was only *one* beginning—one tributary among several—Dewey is entirely correct with respect to time. The term *progressive education* appeared sporadically in the newspapers and magazines of the 1880's, sometimes referring to manual training, sometimes to new pedagogical techniques of the sort Parker pioneered in developing. By the nineties, it had become a commonly used expression in the professional literature and in the broader press. Indeed, there is reference not only to progressive education but also to *progressive teach-*

ers, progressive schools, and *progressive techniques;* the reformist literature was filled with the vision of a new kind of education.

Why, then, this common error that the movement began in 1919, and the term *progressive education* with it? The answer of course is that this is what the founders of the Progressive Education Association believed, and wanted us to believe. "The movement began with us," they said; "hence we *are* the movement. Join us; we will lead the way!" We know how common this sort of thing is among reform organizations; it's fine for recruiting. In the case of the Progressive Education Association the propaganda simply worked extraordinarily well.

To understand when the movement began is to have the key to the question, What was it? The popular notion, I'm afraid, is that progressive education represented the effort to remove all restrictions on children, to allow them to behave as they please—after the fashion of the *New Yorker* cartoon in which the children ask the teacher, "Do we have to do what we want to do today?" This, too, while providing good sport for every humorist worth his salt, is a bit of historical whimsy.

The word *progressive* provides the clue to what it really was: merely the educational phase of the larger progressive movement in American political and social life. This larger movement represented a vast reformist, humanitarian effort to apply the premise of American life—the ideal of government by, of, and for the people—to the new and puzzling urban-industrial civilization that was coming into being at the turn of the century. Progressive education began as progressivism in education: a many-sided effort to use the schools to improve the lives of individuals. In the minds of the progressives this meant several things.

First, it meant broadening the program and function of the school to include a direct concern for health, vocation, and the quality of family and community life.

Second, it meant applying in the classroom the pedagogical principles derived from new scientific research in psychology and the social sciences.

Third, it meant tailoring instruction more and more to the different kinds and classes of children who were being brought within the purview of the school. In a sense, the revolution Horace Mann had sparked a generation before—the revolution inherent in the idea that everyone ought to be educated—had created both the problem and the opportunity of the progressives. For if everyone was to attend school, the progressives contended, not only the methods but the very *meaning* of education would have to change. It was all very well for some educators to say, in effect, "We know what good education is; take it or leave it"—in much the same fashion that Henry Ford told customers they could have their cars in any color they wished so long as it was black. What happened was that youngsters in droves deserted the schools, as irrelevant to the world of here and now.

Fourth, progressivism in education implied the faith that everyone could participate in building a new culture, a popular culture, one in which all could share not only in the benefits of the new sciences but in the pursuit of the arts as well. Jane Addams, that noble lady who founded Hull House and led its efforts for fully forty years, once remarked, "We have learned to say that the good must be extended to all of society before it can be held secure by any one person or any one class; but we have not yet learned to add to that statement, that unless all men and all classes contribute to a good, we cannot even be sure that it is worth having." Here was the spiritual nub of progressive education, and it simply negates contemporary nonsense about the movement being narrowly practical and nothing more.

A final point concerning what progressive education was: given these more general commitments, progressive education from the very beginning meant very different things to different people. To the social settlement workers, for instance, it meant transforming the school into a community center which would provide what they called "social education." To the National Association of Manufacturers it meant vocational training, pure and simple. To agrarian reformers it meant a new sort of "education for country life" which would give youngsters a sense of the joys and possibilities of farm life—and, incidentally, keep them from moving to the city. To the General Education Board, a foundation which distributed millions of Rockefeller dollars to educational programs in the South, progressive education meant demonstration farms and an increasing war against hookworm, using the schools as medical aid stations.

Nowhere is this diversity more vividly documented than in a book published in 1915 by John Dewey and his daughter Evelyn called *Schools of To-Morrow*. To leaf through the volume is to discover that progressive education embraced Marietta Johnson's very Rousseauan school at Fairhope, Alabama; Patty Smith Hill's *avant garde* kindergarten at Teachers College; the neighborhood-oriented program of P.S. 26 in Indianapolis; and William Wirt's Work-Study-Play Plan in Gary, Indiana. In a final chapter, Dewey argues that all these add up to a new kind of education, one appropriate to a democratic society, one that, by equipping all people to live intelligently and sensitively in the new industrial society, can help make that society a better and richer one to live in. This is what Dewey meant by "adjusting" education to society: to bring the resources of the school to bear in building a better society.

It is patent nonsense—indeed, an intellectual perversion—to contend that by adjustment he meant educating people to go along with the social conditions which surrounded them.

Let us move on to the question of who sponsored progressive education. Again, there is currently a bit of whimsy—this one popularized by Mr. Bestor and the Council for Basic Education—to the effect that the educationists, octopuslike, reached for power under the aegis of the progressive education movement, and that in doing so, they committed the ancient sin of pride in assuming that the school could do everything. Now the fact is that the rise of progressive education *did* coincide with the development of a new, self-conscious educational profession, and that the profession *did* have a significant part in formulating and advancing the cause of progressive education. But nothing could be further from the truth than the assertion that the profession put something over on the public. If anything, the records reveal that time and again, in local situations, the profession dragged its feet while the public demanded change. Indeed, if we look closely at the groups pressing for reform, we soon discover that some of the most distinguished figures of the large progressive movement were enthusiastic sponsors of progressive education.

President Theodore Roosevelt, for example, was an eloquent spokesman on behalf of vocational education and domestic science; President Woodrow Wilson paid glowing tribute to Seaman Knapp's efforts in the realm of agricultural education. I have already alluded to the support of Jane Addams; it is not widely known that she actually served a term on the Chicago Board of Education, appointed, by the way, by a progressive mayor in 1905. Jacob Riis, the New York journalist who did so much in the cause of slum clearance, wrote in *The Battle with the Slum:*

> Do you see how the whole battle with the slum is fought out in and around the public school? . . . The kindergarten, manual training, and the cooking school, all experiments in their day, cried out as fads by some, have brought common sense in their train. When it rules the public school in our cities . . . we can put off our armor; the battle with the slum will be over.

Many other distinguished persons could be cited: Henry Wallace and Walter Hines Page from the world of journalism; Charles W. Eliot, William James, Charles Van Hise, and Wesley Clair Mitchell to choose merely a few from the academic world. My point is not that the profession had nothing to do with progressive education—this is an approach which has been defensively argued by some educationists who have now climbed down off the band wagon and would like to wash their hands of the whole business; it is rather to argue that the movement enjoyed widespread public support from its infancy on. To argue otherwise does simple violence to the facts.

All these remarks, of course, indicate that the ideas of the progressive education movement had matured and that a great deal of experiment had already taken place in both public and private schools before the Progressive Education Association came into existence. Nevertheless, the founding of the Association in 1919 marked a turning point in the movement. The organization was started by a small group of private school people on the fringes of the cause. It soon broadened, however, and became a spearhead of reform. Its membership climbed steadily, passing 5,000 in 1927 and reaching a peak of 10,500 in 1938. It inaugurated a quarterly, *Progressive Education,* which served as a forum for the exchange of new ideas and a clearing house for educational innovations of every conceivable kind. It held conferences, summer institutes, and workshops galore; it sponsored studies and carried on experiments; it published useful materials; it gave the progressive education movement shape and entity. During the heyday of the Association, in the 1930's, educational reform made tremendous headway in school systems across the nation; and I think we can say that at the beginning of World War II, progressive education enjoyed a substantial measure of acceptance in many quarters, particularly among intellectuals and other influential segments of the middle class.

Why, then, the cartoons and the spoofs? Why the public withdrawal? Why the loss of favor? Why the steady decline after 1945 and the collapse a decade later? I would suggest five reasons.

First, distortion. As frequently happens with social movements, success brought schism in the ranks. The movement developed factions; and within some factions there arose cults, cliques, and fanatics. During the 1930's, for example, one wing of the movement combined the doctrines of liberty and self-expression into a highly individualistic—and sometimes anarchic—pedagogy which held that schools in which children are encouraged freely to develop their uniquely creative potentialities are the best guarantee of a larger society devoted to human worth and excellence. A second group, following the leadership of George S. Counts, sought to tie progressive education much more closely to specific programs of political reform, contending that educators could lead in the building of a new social order. A third group, typified perhaps by Elsie Ripley Clapp, saw the crux of progressive education in school activities directed to the social and economic regeneration of local communities. A fourth group, exemplified by Eugene Randolph Smith—one of the early presidents of the PEA—concentrated on reorganizing and enlivening the traditional school studies. And finally, there were those who, like Dewey himself, continued to regard progressive education as the pedagogical expression of the larger philosophy of Experimentalism, with its emphasis on scientific method, naturalism, and social planning. The movement became strife-ridden, given to bandwagon behavior, dominated by the ideological feuding of minorities. The strife made headlines, and within these headlines lie the seeds of many current caricatures.

Second, I would cite the negativism inherent in this and in all social reform movements. Like many protestors against injustice, the early progressives knew better what they were against than what they were for. And when one gets a true picture of the inequities of American schools during the quarter-century before World War I, one realizes they had much to be against. The physical and pedagogical conditions in many schools were indescribably bad, an effrontery to the mildest humanitarian sentiments. I recall a survey by a New York journalist in the 1890's for a series of magazine articles on the schools. He went to thirty cities, and what he discovered was shocking. He found public apathy and political corruption; he found a terribly provincial curriculum being taught by appallingly incompetent hacks. One teacher in Baltimore told him, "I used to teach in high school, but I had an attack of nerves and my doctor recommended a rest. So now I teach in the primary grades." A New York City principal, asked why the children weren't allowed to turn their heads, replied, "Why should they look behind them when the teacher is out there in front of them?" A Chicago teacher, rushing her children through a memory lesson, commanded, "Don't stop to think; tell me what you know." Yes, difficult as it is to believe, the schools *were* that bad.

Like any protest movement, progressive education developed slogans and war cries to stir the faithful to action. Shibboleths like "the whole child" or "according to nature" or "creative self-expression" served as powerful battering-rams against the old pedagogical order, but in classroom practice they weren't very good guides to positive action. At least the generation which invented them had an idea of what they meant. The generation which followed adopted them as a collection of ready-made clichés, clichés which weren't very helpful when the public began to raise searching questions about the schools.

Third, and again this is a common phenomenon of social reform, the movement became the victim of its own success. Much of what it preached was simply incorporated into the schools at large. Once the schools did change, though, progressives too often found themselves wedded to specific programs, unable to formulate next steps. Like some liberals who continued to fight for the right of labor to organize long after the Wagner Act had done its work, many progressives continued to fight against stationary desks in schools where movable desks were already in use. For some young people in the post-World War II generation, the ideas of the progressives became inert—in Whitehead's sense of "right thinking" which no longer moves to action. Dewey in the very last essay he published on education likened these progressive ideas gone stale to mustard plasters taken out of the medicine cabinet and applied externally as the need arose. Other young people of this same generation simply developed different preoccupations, different concerns, different rallying points. The old war cries, whatever their validity or lack of it, had a hollow sound; they no longer generated enthusiasm or impelled to action. Like any legacy from a prior generation, they were too easily and too carelessly spent; rarely, perhaps, were they invested lovingly in something new. This is a problem of generations, and we must deal realistically with it, like it or not.

As a fourth reason for the decline of the movement I would cite the more general post-World War II swing toward conservatism in political and social thought. This is readily comprehensible, since if progressive education was part of progressivism writ large, it should not be surprising if a reaction to it comes as a phase of conservatism writ large. We have seen during the past decade a decided reaction to many political ideas of the thirties; to many of the social ideas of the thirties; to many of the child-rearing ideas of the thirties. The reaction to many of the pedagogical ideas of the thirties has come along with them. As educators, I think we have been reluctant to accept these associations; many within our fold, I suspect, would like to be progressives in education and conservatives in everything else. The combination, of course, is not entirely impossible, though it may well be intellectually untenable. John Dewey addressed himself to the point on the flyleaf of *Characters and Events:*

> Let us admit the case of the conservative: if we once start thinking no one can guarantee what will be the outcome, except that many objects, ends and institutions will be surely doomed. Every thinker puts some portion of an apparently stable world in peril, and no one can wholly predict what will emerge in its place.

We have here, by the way, an incomparably clear statement of what for Dewey was progressive about good education; it gives the lie to much nonsense about his philosophy being anti-intellectual.

The final and perhaps the most important reason for the decline of the movement is that American society has simply gone beyond many proposals of the progressives. We live in a very different America from the one which gave birth to progressive education. The great immigrations are over, and a flow of recent publications by David Riesman, Will Herberg, and others is dramatically redefining the problem of what it means to be an American. Our industrial economy is entering upon an era marked by the harnessing of vast new sources of energy and the rapid extension of automatic control in production. This prodigious advance has rendered many of our notions of vocational education anachronistic; and it has thrust to the fore the school's traditional responsibility for transmitting and extending knowledge of every sort and variety. (You will recall that the Rockefeller Brothers Report on education last year indicated that it was *this* pressure rather than any Sputnik which had created the "crisis" situation in education.) Then, too, the rise of new educational media, the proliferation of social agencies under public sponsorship, and the rapid extension of industry-sponsored training programs—the "classrooms in the factories" that Harold Clark and Harold Sloan have labelled the real pedagogical revolution of our time—have shifted the balance of forces in education. Whereas the central thrust of the progressive movement was *centripetal*—it revolted against narrowness and formalism and sought to extend the function and services of the school—it seems to me that the central thrust of our own period is *centrifugal*—it is seeking to define more precisely the central responsibilities of the school, to delineate those things which must be done by the school because if the school doesn't do them, they won't get done.

My point here is merely to urge that what is progressive for one era is not necessarily progressive for another, a truism which reform movements must bear in mind when they become too wedded to specific programs. What makes *sense* to one generation may well be *nonsense* to the next.

Granted this, it seems to me that progressive education in the best sense may well be needed today as much as ever. John Dewey wrote in the Preface to *Schools of To-Morrow:*

> This is not a text book of education, nor yet an exposition of a new method of school teaching, aimed to show the weary teacher or the discontented parent how education should be carried on. We have tried to show what actually happens when schools start out to put into practice, each in its own way, some of the theories that have been pointed to as the soundest and best ever since Plato, to be then laid politely away as precious portions of our "intellectual heritage."

Granted we have gone beyond the reform programs of the last generation, there are still kindergartens that could learn much from Patty Smith Hill, slum schools that could take profitable lessons from Jane Addams, and colleges that still haven't realized that the natural curiosity of the young can be a magnificent propellent to learning. The Progressive Education Association is dead; and progressive education itself needs searching reappraisal. But I think we will find that some of the best of what the progressives tried to teach has yet to be applied in American schools.

AFTER PROGRESSIVE EDUCATION, WHAT?

The student has read excerpts in support of progressivism in education written in the 1930s by Dewey and Childs, criticisms of progressive education made by Bagley in the 1930s and by Rafferty in the 1960s, and a critical and objective appraisal by Cremin of what happened to progressive education. The student will now be presented with an analysis of our present educational needs utilizing in part the contributions of Dewey and his colleagues and relying in part on new directions and ideas to meet the emerging needs of our swiftly changing society. This excellent analysis is made by psychologist and educator Jerome Bruner. His main concern has been the nature of the educational and cognitive processes. He has served as a member of the President's Advisory Panel on Education and has authored several books and essays. His book The Process of Education *was hailed by reviewers as one of the most influential works on education in the 1960s.*

Jerome S. Bruner

Saturday Review *(June 17, 1961)*, *58–59, 76–78. Reprinted by permission of the author and the* Saturday Review.

In 1897, at the age of thirty-eight, John Dewey published a stirring and prophetic work entitled "My Pedagogic Creed." Much of his later writing on education is foreshadowed in this document.

Five articles of faith are set forth. The first defines the educational process: "All education proceeds by the participation of the individual in the social consciousness of the race. This process begins unconsciously almost at birth, and is continually shaping the individual's powers, saturating his consciousness, forming his habits, training his ideas, and arousing his feelings and emotions." A second article of faith embodies Dewey's concept of the school: "Education being a social process, the school is simply that form of community life in which all those agencies are concentrated that will be most effective in bringing the child to share in the inherited resources of the race, and to use his own powers for social ends. Education, therefore, is a process of living and not a preparation for future living." In a third credo Dewey speaks of the subject matter of education: "The social life of the child is the basis of concentration or correlation in all his training or growth. The social life gives the unconscious unity and the background of all his efforts and all his attainments. . . . The true center . . . is not science, nor literature, nor history, nor geography, but the child's own social activities." A view of educational method gives form to Dewey's fourth faith: "The law for presenting and treating material is the law implicit in the child's own nature." For Dewey, the law was that of action: "The active side precedes the passive in the development of the child-nature. I believe that consciousness is essentially motor or impulsive; that conscious states tend to project themselves in action." And finally, Dewey's fifth thesis: "Education is the fundamental method of social progress and reform."

One reads the document today with mixed feelings. Its optimism is classically American in its rejection of the tragic view of life. It defines truth in the pragmatic spirit: truth as the fruit of inquiry into the consequences of action. It expresses a firm faith not only in the individual's capacity to grow but in society's capacity to shape man in its own best image. The final lines of the creed are these: "Every teacher should realize the dignity of his calling; that he is a social servant set apart for the maintenance of proper social order and the securing of the right social growth. In this way the teacher always is the prophet of the true God and the usherer in of the true kingdom of heaven."

Yet the very wholesomeness—the optimism, the pragmatism, the acceptance of man's harmonious continuity with society—leaves one uneasy. For in the two-thirds of a century between 1897 and today, there has been not only a profound change in our conception of nature, but also of society and the world of social institutions. Perhaps more important, we have lived through a revolution in our understanding of the nature of man, his intelligence, his capabilities, his passions, and the forms of his growth.

Dewey's thinking reflected the changes, though he was limited by the premises of his philosophical position. But between Dewey's first premises and our day, there bristles a series of revolutionary doctrines and cataclysmic events that change the very character of the inquiry. Two world wars, the dark episode of Hitler and genocide, the Russian Revolution, the relativistic revolution in physics and psychology, the Age of Energy with its new technology, the sardonic reign of skeptical philosophy—all of these have forced a reappraisal of the underlying premises in terms of which we construct a philosophy of education.

Let us, then, re-examine the premises, being guided by what we know today of the world and of the nature of human nature. But there is matter that is liable to some misinterpretation in an enterprise such as this, and we do well to clear it up at the outset. One writes against the background of one's day. Dewey was writing with an eye to the sterility and rigidity of school instruction in the 1890s—its failure to appreciate particularly the nature of the child. His emphasis upon the importance of direct experience and social action was an implied critique of the empty formalism of education that did little to relate learning to the child's world of experience. Dewey did mighty service in inspiring a correction. But an excess of virtue is vice. We, in our day, are reconsidering education against the background of such an excess. Misunderstanding often converted Dewey's ideas into sentimental practice that he deplored: "Next to deadness and dullness, formalism and routine," he wrote in his Creed, "our education is threatened by no greater evil than sentimentalism." The sentimental cult of "the class project," of "life adjustment" courses, of fearfulness in exposing the child to the startling sweep of man and nature lest it violate the comfortable domain of his direct experience, the cloying concept of "readiness"—these are conceptions about children often divorced from experiment on the educational process, justified in the name of Dewey. His was a noble yet tender view in his time. But what of our times? In what form shall we speak our beliefs?

Education seeks to develop the power and sensibility of mind. The task of education is twofold. On the one hand, the educational process transmits to the individual some part of the accumulation of knowledge, style, and values that constitute the culture of a people. In doing so, it shapes the impulses, the consciousness, and the way of life of the individual. But education must also seek to develop the processes of intelligence so that the individual is capable of going beyond the cultural ways of his social world, able to innovate, in however modest a way, so that he can create an interior culture of his own. For whatever the art, the science, the literature, the history, and the geography of a culture, each man must be his own artist, his own scientist, his own historian, his own navigator. No person is master of the whole culture; indeed, this is almost a defining characteristic of that form of social memory that we speak of as culture. Each man lives a fragment of it. To be whole, he must create his own version of the world, using that part of his cultural heritage that he has made his own through education.

In our time, the requirements of technology press heavily upon the freedom of the individual to create images of the world that are satisfying in the deepest sense. Our era has also witnessed the rise of ideologies that subordinate the individual to the defined aims of a society, a form of subordination that is without compassion for idiosyncrasy and that respects only the instrumental contribution of the individual to the progress of the society. At the same time, and in spite of ideologies, man's understanding of himself and of his world—both the natural and social world—has deepened to a degree that warrants calling our age an intellectually golden one. The challenge of the times ahead is to employ our deeper understanding not only to the enrichment of society but to the enrichment of the individual.

It is true, as Dewey said many years ago, that all education proceeds by the participation of the individual in the social consciousness of the race, but it is a truth with a double edge. For all education, good and bad alike, is of that order. We know now to what degree, to take but one example, the very language one speaks conditions and shapes the style and structure of thought and experience. Indeed, there is reason to believe that thought processes themselves are internalizations of social intercourse, an inner colloquy patterned by early external dialogues. It is this that makes education possible. But education, by giving shape and expression to our experience can also be the principal instrument for setting limits on the enterprise of mind. The guarantee against limits is the sense of alternatives. Education must, then, be not only a transmission of culture but also a provider of alternative views of the world and a strengthener of the will to explore them.

After a half-century of startling progress in the psychological sciences, we know that mental health is only a minimum condition for the growth of mind. The tragedy of mental illness is that it so preoccupies the person with the need to fend off realities with which he cannot cope that it leaves him without either the nerve or the zest to learn. But mental health is a minimum condition. The powers of mind grow with their exercise. Adjustment is too modest an ideal, if it is an ideal at all. Competence in the use of one's powers for the development of individually defined and socially relevant excellence is much more to the point. After a half-century of Freud, we know that the freeing of instinct and inclination is not an end in itself but a way station along the road to competence. What is most prophetic for us about Freud in this second half of the century is not his battle against the fetters of rigid moralism, but his formula: "Where there was id, let there be ego."

Education must begin, as Dewey concluded his first article of belief, "with a psychological insight into the child's capacities, interests, and habits," but a point of departure is not an itinerary. It is equally a mistake to sacrifice the adult to the child as to sacrifice the child to the adult. It is sentimentalism to assume that the teaching of life can always be fitted to the child's interests, just as it is empty formalism to force the child to parrot the formulas of adult society. Interests can be created and stimulated. In this sphere it is not far from the truth to say that supply creates demand, that the challenge of what is available creates response. One seeks to equip the child with deeper, more gripping, and subtler ways of knowing the world and himself.

The school is entry into the life of the mind. It is, to be sure, life itself and not merely a preparation for living. But it is a special form of living, one carefully devised for making the most of those plastic years that characterize the development of *homo sapiens* and distinguish our species from all others. School should provide not simply a continuity with the broader community or with everyday experience. It is the special community where one experiences discovery by the use of intelligence, where one leaps into new and unimagined realms of experience, experience that is discontinuous with what went before, as when one first understands what a poem is or what beauty and power and simplicity inheres in the idea of the conservation-of-energy theorems—that nothing is lost, only converted, and that measure is universally applicable. If there is one continuity to be singled out, it is to convert the autistic sense of the omnipotence of thought of the young child into that realistic confidence in the use of thought that characterizes the effective man.

In insisting upon the continuity of the school with the community on the one side and the family on the other, John Dewey overlooked the special function of education as an opener of new perspectives. If the school were merely a transition zone from the intimacy of the family to the life of the community, it would be a way of life easily enough arranged. It is interesting to examine the educational systems of primitive societies. It is almost universal that there comes a point, usually at puberty, where there is a sharp change in the life of the boy, marked by a *rite de passage* that has as its effect the establishment of a sharp boundary between childhood ways and the ways of the adolescent.

It would be romantic nonsense to pattern our practices upon those found in preliterate socieites. I would only ask that we attend to one parallel: that education not confuse the child with the adult and recognize that the transition to adulthood involves an introduction to new realms of experience, the discovery and exploration of new mysteries, the gaining of new powers. This is the heady stuff of education and it is its own reward.

In the *shtetl* of Eastern Europe, the traditional Jewish ghetto, the wise scholar was a particularly important figure—the *talmud khokhem*. In his mien, his mode of conversation so rich in allusion, his form of poise, the wise man was the image not of a competent but, rather, of a beautiful person. Traditional Chinese society also had its image of the beautiful person, one who blended knowledge and sentiment and action in a beautiful way of life. The ideal of the gentleman served perhaps the same function in Europe of the seventeenth and eighteenth centuries. It is perhaps in this spirit that Alfred North Whitehead urged that education must involve an exposure to greatness if it is to make its mark. I would urge that the yeast of education is the idea of excellence, and the idea of excellence comprises as many forms as there are individuals, each of whom develops his own image of excellence. The school must have as one of its principal functions the nurturing of images of excellence.

A detached conception of idealized excellence is not enough. A doctrine of excellence, to be effective, must be translatable into the individual lives of those who enounter it. What is compelling about the *talmud khokhem,* the Chinese scholar-administrator, the eighteenth-century gentleman, is that they embody ways of life to which each can aspire in his own way and from which each can borrow in his own style. I believe, then, that the school must also contain men and women who, in their own way, seek and embody excellence. This does not mean that we shall have to staff our schools with men and women of great genius, but that the teacher must embody in his or her own approach to learning a pursuit of excellence. And, indeed, with the technical resources opened by television and the like, one can also present the student and his teacher with the working version of excellence in its highest sense. In the years ahead, we shall learn that the great scholar, scientist, or artist can speak as easily and honestly to the beginner as to the graduate student.

The issue of subject matter in education can only be resolved by reference to one's view of the nature of knowledge. Knowledge is a model we construct to give meaning and structure to regularities in experience. The organizing ideas of any body of knowledge are inventions for rendering experience economical and connected. We invent concepts such as force in physics, the bond in chemistry, motives in psychology, style in literature, as means to the end of comprehension. The history of culture is the history of the development of greater organizing ideas, ideas that inevitably stem from deeper values and points of view about man and nature. The power of great organizing concepts is not only that they permit us to understand and sometimes to predict or change the world in which we live; it lies also in the fact that ideas provide instruments for experience. Having grown up in a culture dominated now by the ideas of Newton with a conception of time flowing equably, we experience time moving with an inexorable and steady one-way arrow. Indeed, we know now, after a quarter of a century of research on perception, that experience is not had direct and neat, but filtered through the programed readiness of our senses. The program is constructed of our expectations and these are derived from our models or ideas about what exists and what follows what.

From this, two convictions follow. The first is that the structure of knowledge—its connectedness and the derivations that make one idea follow from another—is the proper emphasis in education. For it is structure, the great conceptual inventions that bring order to the congeries of disconnected observation, that gives meaning to what we may learn, and makes possible the opening up of new realms of experience.

The second conviction is that the unity of knowledge is to be found within knowledge itself, if the knowledge is worth mastering. To attempt a justification of subject matter, as Dewey did, in terms of its relation to the child's social activities is to misunderstand what knowledge is and how it may be mastered. The significance of the concept of commutativity in mathematics does not derive from the social insight that two houses with fourteen people in each is not the same as fourteen houses with two people in each. Rather, it inheres in the power of the idea to generate a way of thinking about number that is lithe and beautiful and immensely generative—an idea at least as powerful as, say, the future conditional tense in formal grammar. Without the idea of commutativity, algebra would be impossible. If set theory—now often the introductory section in newer curricula in mathematics—had to be justified in terms of its relation to immediate experience and social life, it would not be worth teaching. Yet set theory lays a foundation for the understanding of order and number that could never be achieved with the social arithmetic of interest rates and bales of hay at so much per bale. Mathematics, like any other subject, must begin with experience, but progress toward abstraction requires precisely that there be a weaning away from the obviousness of superficial experience.

There is one consideration of economy that is paramount. One cannot "cover" any subject in full—not even in a lifetime, if coverage means visiting all the facts and events and morsels. Subject matter presented so as to emphasize its structure will perforce be of that generative kind that permits reconstruction of the details or, at very least, prepares a place where the details, when encountered, can be fitted.

What, then, of subject matter in the conventional sense? The answer to the question "What shall be taught?" turns out to be the answer one gets to the question "What is nontrivial?" If one can once answer the question "What is worth knowing about?" then it is not difficult to distinguish between what about it is worth teaching and learning and what is not. Surely, knowledge of the natural world, knowledge of the human condition, knowledge of the nature and dynamics of society, knowledge of the past so that one may use it in experiencing the present and aspiring to the future—all of these, it would seem reasonable to suppose, are essential to an educated man. To these must be added another—knowledge of the products of our artistic heritage that mark the history of our esthetic wonder and delight.

A problem immediately arises concerning the symbolism in terms of which knowledge is understood and talked about.

There is language in its natural sense and language in its mathematical sense. I cannot imagine an educated man a century from now who will not be somewhat bilingual in this special sense—concise and adept in a natural language and mathematics. For these are the tools essential to the unlocking of new experience and the gaining of new powers. As such, they must have a central place in any curriculum.

Finally, it is as true today as it was when Dewey wrote that one cannot foresee the world in which the child we educate will live. Informed powers of mind and a sense of potency about coping are then the only instruments we can give the child that will be invariant across the transformations of time and circumstance. The succession of studies that we give the child in the ideal school need not be fixed in any but one way: whatever is introduced, let it be pursued continuously enough to give the student a sense of the power of mind that comes from a deepening of understanding. It is this, rather than any form of coverage over time, that matters most.

The process and the goal of education are one and the same thing. The goal of education is disciplined understanding. That is the process as well.

Let us recognize first that the opposite of understanding is not ignorance or simply "not knowing." To understand something is, first, to give up some other way of conceiving of it. Between one way of conceiving and a better way, there often lies confusion. It is one of our biological inheritances that confusion produces emergency anxiety, and with anxiety there come the defensive measures—flight, fright, or freezing—that are antithetical to the free and zestful use of mind. The limiting fact of mental life in child and adult alike is that there is a limited capacity for processing information—our span, as it is called, can encompass six or seven unrelated items simultaneously. Go beyond that and there is overload, confusion, forgetting. The degree to which material to be learned is put into structures by the learner will determine whether he is working with gold or dross. For this reason, as well as for reasons already stated, it is essential that before being exposed to a wide range of material on a topic, the child first have a general idea of how and where things fit. It is often the case that the development of the general idea comes from a first round of experience with concrete embodiments of an idea that are close to the child's life. The cycle of learning begins, then, with the particular and immediate, moves toward abstraction, and comes to a temporary goal when the abstraction can then be used in grasping new particulars in the deeper way that abstraction permits.

Insofar as possible, a method of instruction should have the objective of leading the child to discover for himself. Telling children and then testing them on what they have been told inevitably has the effect of producing bench-bound learners whose motivation for learning is likely to be extrinsic to the task at hand—pleasing the teacher, getting into college, artificially maintaining self-esteem. The virtues of encouraging discovery are of two kinds. In the first place, the child will make what he learns his own, will fit his discovery into the interior world of culture that he creates for himself. Equally important, discovery and the sense of confidence it provides are the proper rewards for learning. They are rewards that, moreover, strengthen the very process that is at the heart of education—disciplined inquiry.

The child must be encouraged to get the full benefit from what he learns. This is not to say that he should be required to put it to immediate use in his daily life, though so much the better if he has the happy opportunity to do so. Rather, it is a way of honoring the connectedness of knowledge. Two facts and a relation joining them are and should be an invitation to generalize, to extrapolate, to make a tentative intuitive leap, indeed even to build a tentative theory. The leap from mere learning to using what one has learned in thinking is an essential step in the use of mind. Indeed, plausible guessing, the use of the heuristic hunch, the best employment of necessarily insufficient evidence—these are activities in which the child needs practice and guidance. They are among the great antidotes to passivity.

Most important of all, the educational process must be free of intellectual dishonesty and those forms of cheating that explain without providing understanding. I have expressed the conviction elsewhere than any subject can be taught to anybody at any age in some form that is honest. It is not honest to present a fifth-grade social studies class with an image of Christopher Columbus as a typical American teen-ager musing after school with his brother, Bart, about what lies across the seas—even if the image set forth does happen to mesh with the child's immediate sense of social experience. A lie is still a lie—even if it sounds like familiar truth. Nor is it honest to present a sixth-grade science class with a garbled but concrete picture of the atom that is, in its way, as sweeteningly false as the suburban image of Columbus given them the year before. A dishonest image can only discourage the self-generating intellectual inquiry out of which real understanding grows.

I believe that education is the fundamental method of social change. Even revolutions are no better than the ideas they embody and the invented means for their application.

Change is swifter in our times than ever before in human history and news of it is almost instantaneous. If we are to be serious in the belief that school must be life itself and not merely preparation for life, then school must reflect the changes through which we are living.

The first implication of this belief is that means must be found to feed back into our schools the ever deepening insights that are developed on the frontiers of knowledge. This is an obvious point in science and mathematics, and continuing efforts are now being instituted to assure that new, more powerful, and often simpler ways of understanding find their way back into the classrooms of our primary and secondary schools. But it is equally important to have this constant refreshment in fields other than the sciences—where the frontiers of knowledge are not always the universities and the research laboratories but political and social life, the arts, literary endeavor, and the rapidly changing business and industrial community. Everywhere there is change and with change, we are learning.

I see the need for a new type of institution, a new conception in curriculum. What we have not had and what we are beginning to recognize as needed is something that is perhaps best called an "institute for curriculum studies"—not one of them, but many. Let it be the place where scholars, scientists, men of affairs, artists, come together with talented teachers constantly to revise and refresh our curricula. It is an activity that transcends the limits of any of our particular university faculties—be they faculties of education, of arts and science, of medicine or engineering. We have been negligent in coming to a sense of the quickening change of life in our time and its implications for the educational process. We have not shared with our teachers the benefits of new discovery, new insight, new artistic triumph. Not only have we operated with the notion of the self-contained classroom, but also with the idea of the self-contained school—and even the self-contained educational system.

Let me consider again what I said about the images of excellence and the role of constant curricular refreshment in helping produce those images. The Nobel laureate or the Ambassador to the United Nations, the brilliant cellist or the perceptive playwright, the historian making use of the past, or the sociologist seeking a pattern in the present—these are men who, like the student, are seeking understanding and mastery of new problems. They represent excellence at the frontiers of endeavor. If a sense of progress and change toward greater excellence is to illuminate our schools, there must be a constant flowing back of their wisdom and effort to enliven and inform teacher and student alike. There is not a difference in kind between the man at the frontier and the young student at his own frontier, each attempting to understand.

How put the matter in summary? Perhaps it is best to parallel John Dewey's "Credo": That education is not only the transmission of culture, but that it also gives shape to the power and sensibility of mind so that each person may learn how to inquire for himself and build an interior culture of his own. That the school is entry into the life of mind, with all this implies about confidence in the use of mind to push to the limit and test the implications of what each has come to know. That the subject matter of education is knowledge about the world and its connectedness, knowledge that has a structure and a history that permits us to find order and predictability in experience and delight in surprise. That the method of education is the method involved in any understanding—a disciplined and responsible effort to know on one's own and to convert what one has understood into an ordered representation of the world that respects the particular but recognizes the intellectual indispensability of the abstract. That the school continues to be the principal instrument of social progress in an era of swift change and that, as such, it find means of constantly refreshing and altering its instruction by feeding back the new insights of our times into its curriculum. All of these things depend in the end upon cultivating and giving expression to the forms of excellence that emerge in our varied society. Any aims less ambitious than these are surely unworthy of the challenges we face.

REFERENCES

1. Bruner, J. S. *The Process of Education*. New York: Random House, 1963.
2. J. J. Goodnow, and G. A. Austin. *A Study of Thinking*. New York: John Wiley & Sons, 1956.
3. Dewey, John. *My Pedagogic Creed*. New York: E. L. Kellogg and Company, 1897.

SELECTED REFERENCES

CHAPTER 1

BUTTS, R. FREEMAN. *A Cultural History of Western Education.* New York: McGraw-Hill, 1955.

BUTTS, R. FREEMAN AND LAWRENCE A. CREMIN. *A History of Education in American Culture.* New York: Holt, Rinehart and Winston, 1953.

COLE, LUELLA W. *A History of Education: Socrates to Montessori.* New York: Holt, Rinehart and Winston, 1950.

CUBBERLEY, E. P. *Public Education in the United States.* Boston: Houghton Mifflin Company, 1934.

GOOD, HARRY S. *A History of American Education.* New York: Crowell-Collier and Macmillan, 1960.

MEYER, ADOLPHE E. *An Educational History of the American People.* New York: McGraw-Hill, 1957.

MULHERN, JAMES. *A History of Education: A Social Interpretation.* 2d ed.; New York: The Ronald Press Company, 1959.

POWER, EDWARD J. *Main Currents in the History of Education.* New York: McGraw-Hill, 1962.

THUT, ISSAK N. *The Story of Education: Philosophical and Historical Foundations.* New York: McGraw-Hill, 1957.

CHAPTER 2

BROOKOVER, WILBER, AND DAVID GOTTLIEB. *A Sociology of Education.* New York: American Book Company, 1964.

CLARK, BURTON. *Educating the Expert Society.* San Francisco, Calif.: Chandler Publishing Company, 1962.

COLEMAN, JAMES S. *The Adolescent Society.* New York: Crowell-Collier and Macmillan, 1961.

DAVIS, ALLISON. *Social Class Influence upon Learning.* Cambridge, Mass.: Harvard University Press, 1951.

GINZBERG, ELI, ET AL. *The Optimistic Tradition in American Youth.* New York: Columbia University Press, 1962.

461

GOVERNOR'S COMMISSION ON THE LOS ANGELES RIOTS. *Violence in the City: An End or a Beginning?* (December 2, 1965).

HALSEY, A. H., ET AL. (eds.). *Education, Economy and Society.* New York: Crowell-Collier and Macmillan, 1961.

HAVIGHURST, ROBERT. *Education in Metropolitan Areas.* Boston: Allyn and Bacon, 1966.

HAVIGHURST, ROBERT, AND BERNICE NEUGARTEN. *Society and Education.* 3d ed.; Boston: Allyn and Bacon, 1967.

HENRY, JULES. *Culture against Man.* New York: Random House, 1963.

HOLLINGSHEAD, AUGUST. *Elmtown's Youth.* New York: John Wiley & Sons, 1949.

LANDES, RUTH. *Culture in American Education: Anthropological Approaches to Minority and Dominant Groups in the Schools.* New York: John Wiley & Sons, 1965.

MEAD, MARGARET. *The School in American Culture.* Cambridge, Mass.: Harvard University Press, 1950.

NEA PROJECT ON INSTRUCTION. *Education in a Changing Society.* Washington, D.C.: National Education Association, 1964.

RIESSMAN, FRANK. *The Culturally Deprived Child.* New York: Harper & Row, Publishers, 1962.

Social Forces Influencing American Education. Sixtieth Yearbook of the National Society for the Study of Education, Part II. Chicago: University of Chicago Press, 1961.

SPINDLER, GEORGE D. (ed.). *Education and Culture: Anthropological Approaches.* New York: Holt, Rinehart and Winston, 1963.

SPINDLER, GEORGE D. *The Transmission of American Culture.* Cambridge, Mass.: Harvard University Press, 1959.

CHAPTER 3

ASHTON-WARNER, SYLVIA. *Teacher.* New York: Simon and Schuster, 1963.

BEREDAY, GEORGE. *Comparative Method in Education.* New York: Holt, Rinehart and Winston, 1964.

BEREDAY, GEORGE, ET AL. (eds.). *The Changing Soviet School.* Boston: Houghton Mifflin Company, 1960.

BONE, LOUIS W. *Secondary Education in the Guianas.* Chicago: Comparative Education Center, University of Chicago, 1962.

BOWEN, JAMES. *Soviet Education: Anton Makarenko and the Years of Experiment.* Madison, Wis.: University of Wisconsin Press, 1962.

CRAMER, JOHN AND GEORGE BROWNE. *Contemporary Education: A Comparative Study of National Systems.* New York: Harcourt, Brace & World, 1965.

GEZI, KALIL I. *The Acculturation of Middle Eastern Arab Students in Selected Colleges and Universities.* Washington, D.C.: American Friends of the Middle East, 1960.

HU, CHANG-TU. *Chinese Education Under Communism.* New York: Bureau of Publications, Teachers College, Columbia University, 1962.

KING, EDMUND J. (ed.). *Communist Education*. Indianapolis: The Bobbs-Merrill Company, 1963.

KING, EDMUND J. *Other Schools and Ours*. 3d ed.; New York: Holt, Rinehart and Winston, 1967.

MAKARENKO, ANTON S. *The Collective Family: A Handbook for Russian Parents*. Translated by Robert Daglish. New York: Doubleday & Company, 1967.

MATTHEWS, RODERIC D., AND MATTA AKRAWI. *Education in Arab Countries of the Near East*. Washington, D.C.: American Council on Education, 1949.

RICKOVER, HYMAN G. *Swiss Schools and Ours: Why Theirs Are Better*. Boston: Little, Brown & Company, 1962.

SPINDLER, GEORGE D., AND LOUISE SPINDLER (eds.). *Case Studies in Education and Culture* Series. New York: Holt, Rinehart and Winston.

THUT, ISSAK N. AND DON ADAMS. *Educational Patterns in Contemporary Societies*. New York: McGraw-Hill, 1964.

ULICH, ROBERT. *The Education of Nations*. Cambridge, Mass.: Harvard University Press, 1961.

UNESCO. *The Needs of Asia in Primary Education: A Plan for the Provision of Compulsory Primary Education in the Region*. Educational Studies and Documents, No. 41. New York: UNESCO, 1961.

U.S. DEPARTMENT OF HEALTH, EDUCATION, AND WELFARE. *Education for Freedom and World Understanding*. Washington, D.C.: Government Printing Office, 1962.

CHAPTER 4

CONANT, JAMES BRYANT. *The Education of American Teachers*. New York: McGraw-Hill, 1963.

EDUCATIONAL POLICIES COMMISSION. *The Contemporary Challenges to American Education*. Washington, D.C.: National Education Association, 1958.

EDUCATIONAL POLICIES COMMISSION. *Contemporary Issues in Elementary Education*. Washington, D.C.: National Education Association, 1960.

EHLERS, HENRY, AND GORDON LEE. *Crucial Issues in Education*. 3d ed.; New York: Holt, Rinehart and Winston, 1964.

GROSS, NEAL. *Who Runs Our Schools?* New York: John Wiley & Sons, 1958.

LIEBERMAN, MYRON. *The Future of Public Education*. Chicago: University of Chicago Press, 1960.

MELBY, ERNEST O. *American Education under Fire*. New York: Anti-Defamation League of B'Nai B'Rith, 1951.

PRESIDENT'S COMMISSION ON NATIONAL GOALS. *Goals for Americans*. Englewood Cliffs, N.J.: Prentice-Hall, 1960.

ROCKEFELLER BROTHERS FUND. *The Pursuit of Excellence*. Doubleday & Company, 1958.

SCOTT, C. WINFIELD, ET AL. *The Great Debate: Our Schools in Crisis.* Englewood Cliffs, N.J.: Prentice-Hall, 1959.

STINNETT, T. M., AND A. J. HUGGETT. *Professional Problems of Teachers.* 2d ed.; New York: Crowell-Collier and Macmillan, 1963.

THAYER, V. T. *The Role of the School in American Society.* 2d ed.; New York: Dodd, Mead & Company, 1966.

U.S. DEPARTMENT OF HEALTH, EDUCATION, AND WELFARE, OFFICE OF EDUCATION. *Contemporary Issues in American Education.* Washington, D.C.: Government Printing Office, 1965.

WHITEHEAD, ALFRED NORTH. *The Aims of Education.* New York: Crowell-Collier and Macmillan, 1957.

CHAPTER 5

BROWN, B. FRANK. *The Nongraded High School.* Englewood Cliffs, N.J.: Prentice-Hall, 1963.

BRUNER, JEROME S. *The Process of Education.* New York: Vintage Books, 1960.

Educational Television: The Next Ten Years. Stanford, Calif.: The Institute for Communication Research, 1962.

GAGE, N. L. (ed.). *Handbook of Research on Teaching.* Skokie, Ill.: Rand McNally & Company, 1963.

GETZELS, JACOB, AND PHILIP W. JACKSON, *Creativity and Intelligence.* New York: John Wiley & Sons, 1962.

GOODLAD, JOHN, AND ROBERT ANDERSON. *The Nongraded Elementary School.* New York: Harcourt, Brace & World, 1963.

Individualizing Instruction. Sixty-first Yearbook of the National Society for the Study of Education, Part I. Chicago: University of Chicago Press, 1962.

MILLER, RICHARD. *The Nongraded School: Analysis and Study.* New York: Harper & Row, Publishers, 1967.

NEA PROJECT ON INSTRUCTION. *Planning and Organizing for Teaching.* Washington, D.C.: National Education Association, 1963.

NEA PROJECT ON INSTRUCTION. *Schools for the Sixties.* New York: McGraw-Hill, 1963.

SHAPLIN, JUDSON T., AND HENRY F. OLDS, JR. (eds.). *Team Teaching.* Harper & Row, Publishers, 1964.

SMITH, WENDELL, AND JULIAN MOORE. *Programmed Learning: Theory and Research.* Princeton, N.J.: D. Van Nostrand Company, 1962.

STODDARD, ALEXANDER. *The Dual Progress Plan.* New York: Harper & Row, Publishers, 1961.

STODDARD, ALEXANDER. *Schools for Tomorrow: An Educator's Blueprint.* New York: Fund for the Advancement of Education, 1957.

STODDARD, GEORGE. *The Dual Progress Plan.* New York: Harper & Row, Publishers, 1961.

The Cost of a Schoolhouse. New York: Educational Facilities Laboratories, 1960.

Trow, William C. *Teacher and Technology.* New York: Appleton-Century-Crofts, 1963.

Trump, J. Lloyd. *Focus on Change: Guide to Better Schools.* Skokie, Ill.: Rand McNally & Company, 1961.

CHAPTER 6

Bagley, William C. *Education and Emergent Man.* Camden, N.J.: Thomas Nelson & Sons, 1934.

Bode, Boyd. *Progressive Education at the Crossroads.* New York: Newson, 1938.

Childs, John L. *American Pragmatism in Education.* New York: Holt, Rinehart and Winston, 1956.

Counts, George. *Dare the School Build a New Social Order?* New York: The John Day Company, 1932.

Dewey, John. *Democracy and Education.* New York: Crowell-Collier and Macmillan, 1916.

Dewey, John. *Experience and Education.* New York: Crowell-Collier and Macmillan, 1938.

Dewey, John. *My Pedagogic Creed.* New York: E. L. Kellogg and Company, 1897.

Dewey, John. *The School and Society.* 2d ed.; Chicago: University of Chicago Press, 1943.

Cremin, Lawrence A. *The Transformation of the School: Progressivism in American Education, 1876–1957.* New York: Vintage Books, 1964.

Hook, Sydney. *Education for Modern Man: A Non-Perspective.* New York: Alfred A. Knopf, 1963.

Hullfish, H. Gordon, and Philip Smith. *Reflective Thinking: The Method of Education.* New York: Dodd, Mead & Company, 1965.

Hutchins, Robert. *The Conflict in Education in a Democratic Society.* New York: Harper & Row, Publishers, 1953.

Kilpatrick, William. *Philosophy of Education.* New York: Crowell-Collier and Macmillan, 1951.

Maritain, Jacques. *Education at the Crossroads.* New Haven, Conn.: Yale University Press, 1943.

Rafferty, Max. *What They Are Doing to Your Children.* New York: New American Library, 1964.

INDEX

467